RECONFIGURING CITIZENSHIP
AND NATIONAL IDENTITY
IN THE NORTH AMERICAN
LITERARY IMAGINATION

SERIES IN
CITIZENSHIP STUDIES

· · · · · · · · · · ·

EDITORS

Marc W. Kruman
Richard Marback

RECONFIGURING CITIZENSHIP
and National Identity *in the* North American Literary Imagination

....

KATHY-ANN TAN

Wayne State University Press
Detroit

19 18 17 16 15   5 4 3 2 1

Library of Congress Control Number: 2015940583

ISBN 978-0-8143-4140-7 (cloth: alk. paper)
ISBN 978-0-8143-4141-4 (ebook)

An earlier version of chapter 11, "Exile, Migration, and the "Poetics of Relation":
Edwidge Danticat's *Brother, I'm Dying* and Dany Laferrière's *The Return*," was previ-
ously published as "Creating Dangerously": Writing, Exile and Diaspora in Edwidge
Danticat's and Dany Laferrière's Haitian Memoirs." In *American Lives*, edited by Alfred
Hornung (Hrg.). American Studies: A Monograph Series. Heidelberg: Universitätsver-
lag Winter, 2013. 249–61. Reprinted by permission of the author.

Designed and typeset by Bryce Schimanski
Composed in Adobe Caslon Pro

For my parents, Cecilia and William Tan,
and in memory of my grandmother Dolly Seet (deceased 2006) who,
not knowing her own birth date and having no passport
to record the information, celebrated her birthday instead
every first Saturday of the Lunar New Year.

CONTENTS

IV. DIASPORIC AND INDIGENOUS CITIZENS

ACKNOWLEDGMENTS

This book manuscript is a revised version of my habilitation thesis, the written component of a highly regarded, if increasingly debated, academic qualification extant in many parts of Europe including Germany, the country of my "arrival" and now—in a predictable case of life imitating art—my citizenship. Given the intellectually and mentally demanding nature of the habilitation process, I am thankful to have had the invaluable support of colleagues, friends, and peers who have aided me in the completion of this project.

My first thanks must go to Ingrid-Hotz Davies, whose rigorous, careful, and insightful reading of early drafts of this manuscript assured me that I was on the right track, while always pushing me to think harder in order to make each revision sharper, clearer, more accurate. For all the laughs over chicken saag and mango lassi, conversations about episodes of Miranda ("Such fun!"), and for empathetically recognizing my "Monk moments" when they inadvertently arose, a warmest thank-you.

Heartfelt thanks also to Bernd Engler, whose unequivocal support over the last twelve years at the University of Tuebingen has set a foremost example of how intellectual vigor and abiding generosity need not be mutually exclusive in the academic world. Sincere thanks also to my other readers—Barbara Buchenau, Stephanie Gropper, and Horst Tonn—for their astute comments and suggestions. Alfred Hornung deserves my thanks and gratitude for his generosity in reviewing my manuscript and providing recommendations for improvement. I also wish to thank my other blind peer reviewer, who was contacted by Wayne State University Press. Your incisive observations and helpful suggestions have been invaluable in the process of revising this manuscript and making it a better work of scholarship.

I am also grateful to colleagues and friends at the University of Maryland, College Park—especially Christina Walter, Keguro Macharia, Sangeeta Ray, and Bob Levine—for allowing me to present, as a visiting lecturer in the fall of 2010, what was then work in progress, and for responding so encouragingly with suggestions and constructive feedback. Warm thanks also to Kathryn Wildfong and Marc Kruman of Wayne State University Press for inviting me to be part of their new series on citizenship studies.

Last but not least, deepest thanks to Cecile Sandten, without whom this book would probably not have reached completion. For your continued interest in collaborating on various projects, your generosity, unfailing support, encouragement, insightful reading and comments, productive feedback, healthy distractions, and wonderful sense of humor, I am ever grateful.

RECONFIGURING CITIZENSHIP
AND NATIONAL IDENTITY
IN THE NORTH AMERICAN
LITERARY IMAGINATION

INTRODUCTION

· · · · · · · · · ·

Citizenship in Transit(ion): From Established Definitions to Alternative Paradigms

Jin-me Yoon's photograph of her mother, part of her work *A Group of Sixty-Seven* (see figure 1 in the color insert) is striking in several ways at once: a person of Asian descent, Korean, as we later learn, looks out from a painted background of snow-capped mountains and a mirrored lake. The subject of the photograph is looking directly into the camera. She is smiling slightly, a sparkle in her eyes, her composed, level gaze both affirming and demanding a sense of recognition and acknowledgment. Her bright red blouse, a marker of difference, contrasts starkly with the more subdued hues of blue and green in the scenery behind her, yet her occupying center frame, literally the center of the painting's "X" composition, positions her squarely within the mountainous landscape, thereby making her part of it.

This portrait photograph is one of 134 (two panels of 67 chromogenic prints each) by Korean-born Vancouver-based artist Jin-me Yoon, collectively titled *A Group of Sixty-Seven* (1996) (see color insert). The title of the artwork is a reference to the year 1967, which marked the one hundredth anniversary of Canadian Confederation as well as the year that anti-Chinese immigration restrictions in Canada were lifted and the Immigration Act was revised to allow migrants with a higher level of education or skilled workers to enter the country based on a point system. It was this change in immigration regulations that enabled Yoon's siblings and her mother to join her father, a student at that time, in Canada in 1968. Sharing similar stories, the sixty-seven subjects of Yoon's installation are from different generations of the Korean Canadian community who migrated to Vancouver after the revision of the Immigration Act. The title of the piece, *A Group of Sixty-Seven*, is also a reference to the Group of Seven artists in Canada, whose landscape paintings in the 1920s and early 1930s came to symbolize the earliest aesthetic expressions of a "genuine," "authentic," and distinctly Canadian national identity.[1] A seminal member of the Group of Seven artists was Lawren Harris, whose paintings in the 1920s were increasingly abstract depictions of landscapes in the Canadian north.

By positioning sixty-seven subjects of Korean descent, including her own mother, in front of Lawren Harris's painting *Maligne Lake, Jasper Park* (1924), an iconic representation of Canadian landscape,[2] Yoon engages two interrelated concerns. The first centers around the question of how national identity and place are closely interlinked, and critically addresses the issue of how archetypal images of Canadian identity and landscape have come to seem "natural" and representative. The second raises the topic of how bodies perceived as culturally foreign or "other" to this "authentic," unmarked (white, male, heterosexual) Canadianness unsettle, challenge, and reconfigure dominant perceptions and constructions of national identity.

Moreover, by inserting her subjects into the unpopulated, "pristine" landscape of one of the most famous Group of Seven paintings, Yoon critically counters the overt representation of Canada in the latter as *terra nullius* (a Latin expression meaning "land belonging to no one"—hence referring to territory that is not subject to any sovereign power). Such depictions of the Canadian wilderness are clearly problematic as they erase the presence of the First Nations who inhabited the land before the European (French and British) settlers colonized it.[3] Visually, therefore, the sixty-seven subjects of Yoon's piece challenge the "naturalness" of Lawren Harris's rugged, unspoiled Canadian wilderness, hence addressing the exclusions and marginalizations caused by the widespread acceptance of the Group of Seven paintings as the first major Canadian national art movement. Yoon's Korean Canadian subjects match the spectator's gaze, demanding that the viewer's attention be directed first and foremost at them and not the seemingly "natural" or scenic background view. Their shoulders continue the lines of the image's "X" compositional form, making them simultaneously part of, yet also distinct from, their surroundings. In other words, they simultaneously interrupt their environment while also positing a sense of continuity and oneness with it, and hence claiming a right to habitation and belonging.

Jin-me Yoon's *A Group of Sixty-Seven* thus aptly illustrates how visual markers and prevalent notions of national identity and, by extension, accepted definitions of citizenship, need to be revised in order to take into consideration what I term "alter-national"[4] and post-national configurations of identification and belonging. This claim is certainly not new, and had already been posited by scholars, mostly from the decolonial school of thought,[5] who critiqued national identity as an inherently discontinuous and contradictory construct even in the very moments of its (re)production. What these studies suggest is that the post-national, rather than being a phenomenon that comes after (as the prefix *post* suggests) the birth of a nation, is concomitant with its very birth pangs. That is, rather than a consequence of late twentieth- and early twenty-first-century globalizing processes that have "made the world a smaller place" and forced a reconsideration of the role and significance of the nation-state, the post-national imaginary is the concurrent result of efforts to define the national.

While the term *post-national* did not become common usage until recently, in the context of work by human rights activists and advocates of citizenship for migrants,[6] it has become common to speak of a "transnational imaginary" (Wilson and Dissanayake 1996; Saldívar 2006) that characterizes the ethnically and culturally diverse literatures from the United States and Canada. While the body of work on trans- and post-national identity and imaginaries[7] continues to expand considerably, most studies, however, seek to move *beyond* the nation as a conceptual frame of reference.[8] Few have argued for the enduring usefulness of the nation as a construct/category and attempted to reinscribe its parameters and imaginaries from *within* (Sassen 2002, 278). In this light, Jin-me Yoon's installation *A Group of Sixty-Seven* is striking because it does not seek to do away with, or transcend altogether, notions of national identity or the Canadian nation. Rather, her artwork interrogates the visual narratives embedded in iconic national sceneries and landscapes that constitute a certain model of national identity. In this way, Yoon's piece attests to the continuing centrality of the nation as a concept within a North American framework while concurrently exposing and critiquing its underpinning logic of homogeneity as well as its intersectional[9] exclusions, erasures, and elisions of difference. Yoon's photographs thus visually exemplify what Saskia Sassen has termed a "de-nationalized"—though

3

here I would rather use "alter-national"—sensibility in their critique and interrogation of the repository of iconic images and archetypal narratives of the nation (in this case, the national myth of Canadian wilderness)[10] that have come to form what Lauren Berlant terms the "National Symbolic."[11] Yoon's "revision" of Harris's painting, in particular its nationalistic sentiment of "natural," quintessential Canadian identity, represents an intervention into the composition of Canada's National Symbolic and a deconstruction of its historical assumptions and foundational myths. Yet Yoon's artwork *also* signifies a claim to, and a stake in, that identity: to alter the words of Langston Hughes's well-known poem, it claims that "I, Too, Sing Canada."

Taking Jin-me Yoon's *A Group of Sixty-Seven* as a fitting point of departure, this study seeks to uncover paradigms of "alter-national" and post-national identities as well as emergent modes of willful, precarious, queer, and diasporic subjectivities that call for a reorientation of dominant understandings of nationhood, citizenship, national identity, and national literature(s) in a North American context. For the sake of clarification, my use of the term *post-national* does not refer to a "citizen of the world" mentality that has become prevalent in a late-capitalist era of globalization in which the role of nation-states and the significance of national formations have become markedly different than during the height of nationalism in the period from the late nineteenth century to the end of the Second World War. Rather, in a manner analogous to my understanding of how the hyphen often employed in the term *post-colonial* denotes not a temporal marker of an era that began in the aftermath of colonialism but a mode of philosophical and political theory informed by the continued impact of colonialism on the present, I use *post-national* as an index of the continued influence and interference of the nation-state in alternative forms of collective identity in national spaces—forms that challenge, transgress, and surpass—but also continue to be influenced and impacted by—the geopolitical boundaries and cultural imaginaries of the nation. As indicated earlier, I am not suggesting doing away with the concept/construct of the nation entirely. Rather, I am interested in the persistence and continued relevance of ideas of the nation and national identity while at the same time suggesting that these two concepts have to be modified in order to account for "alter-national" and post-national paradigms of claims to belonging, claims that have been articulated, if silenced, simultaneously from the very beginnings of the nation.

The extent to which post-national imaginaries and identity formations have arisen in the United States and Canada, rather unsurprisingly, differs. This can be attributed to the disparate foundational myths of the two nations and their divergent historical trajectories, particularly in terms of their negation of their respective British settler colonial histories. While the larger picture is necessarily more complex, it can nevertheless perhaps be broadly argued that ideas of national consciousness and collective identity have not been ingrained so deeply in the Canadian imaginary as they have in the continental American one. That is, unlike the situation that the American colonists faced in the thirteen British colonies, which declared themselves sovereign and independent states in 1776, there was never a necessity dictated by political expediency for the earliest Canadian settlers to break ties with the British completely—much to the contrary, in fact.[12] Thus, as T. D. MacLulich's observation that "most assertions of the Canadian identity are still comparative rather than absolute" (1988, 13) suggests,[13] Canadians' sense of national self has historically been, and continues to be, understood as relational rather than unequivocal. Whereas Canadian identity has often been depicted as an "elusive" entity that resists definition (Cohen 2007), and the search thereof has itself been largely characterized by elements of satire,[14] irony, and self-introspection,[15] the persistence of a strong national and cultural imaginary in the United States—even by an *ex negativo* rejection of what it "means" to be "American"—attests to the continued centrality of the national imaginary in a U.S. context even, or perhaps especially, in historical moments of its crisis and potential transformation.

The differing metaphors that have found currency within the discourse of immigration in the two countries are also indicative of their respective attitudes with regard to nationhood and the assimilation of foreignness or "otherness" within the boundaries of the nation-state. While the ubiquitous "melting pot" (Zangwill 1909) metaphor of assimilation pervaded American popular culture and literature in the early twentieth century until its replacement in the 1960s with the perhaps equally unfortunate "salad bowl" comparison, the (granted, not unproblematic) "cultural mosaic" (Gibbon 1938; Hutcheon 2007) model of multiculturalism has remained entrenched in the Canadian popular imagination ever since its bicultural (francophone and anglophone) and Indigenous origins. In other words, multiculturalism has been integral to official discourses of Canadian identity since Confederation on July 1, 1867, which marked the beginnings of the Canadian nation. It was declared a defining characteristic of Canadian federalism in 1971 by former prime minister Pierre Trudeau's official policy of multiculturalism; the endorsement of the Canadian Multiculturalism Act in 1988; and section 27 of the Canadian Charter of Rights and Freedoms, which supports the "preservation and enhancement of the multicultural heritage of Canadians."[16]

Yet at the same time, "multiculturalism" has been a highly contested and controversial term, particularly within a Canadian context, as critics such as Barbara Godard have articulated: "[Multiculturalism is] a policy of liberal cultural pluralism, . . . [which] works to reproduce binary oppositions of white/color and fails to expose the power relationships of systematic racism that work to erase difference" (1994, 650). In preference, Godard advances the use of the terms *multilingual* and *multiracial* in her call for a consideration of Canadian literature as a transnational and comparative literature, in order to enact a paradigm shift in the ways in which national literatures are often territorialized according to the geopolitical boundaries of their nations. As she maintains, "Deterritorialization . . . is the condition of literatures in Canada" (646). Similarly, more recent work in the field of Canadian literary and cultural studies[17] has realigned the parameters of the critical debate by bringing the aspects of diaspora, indigeneity, transculturalism, and difference in Canadian literature into sharper relief. Such contemporary scholarship, several chapters in this present study included, seeks to bring about a critical reconsideration of how Canada and Canadian literature are situated in ongoing debates about transnational and diasporic identity, decolonization, and globalization. This is a timely reassessment because, as Kit Dobson (2006) has pointed out, literature has played a key role in the fostering of national identity in Canada since the Massey Report in 1951.[18] It is thus apt that literature should also play a key role in the reconfiguration of the nation(al) in the new millennium.

Indeed, the crucial relationship between nation and narration was evinced about a century earlier during the literary period known as the American Renaissance,[19] which marked the beginnings of a mature and distinctively "American" literature and culture. Predominantly white, Anglo-Saxon, Protestant, male writers of the American Renaissance such as Ralph Waldo Emerson, Henry David Thoreau, Walt Whitman, Nathaniel Hawthorne, and Herman Melville rose to prominence in this period and their works, such as Hawthorne's *The Scarlet Letter* (1850), Melville's *Moby-Dick* (1851), Thoreau's *Walden* (1854), and Whitman's *Song of Myself* (1855), have become the mainstay of canonical American literature. These writings expressed a conviction that American writers had to carve their own way in a departure from the styles, forms, and traditions of European literature in order to reflect and establish the foundations of a uniquely "American" cultural identity based on the national ideals of democracy and freedom. Accordingly, this period in the United States witnessed heated debates in the political, literary, and social realms on the concepts of citizenship, political membership, and national identity[20] as well as the question of to whom the rights associated with these concepts were/should be extended. In comparison, literature that emerged in the aftermath of Canadian Confederation in 1867 largely reflected not a national/federal outlook but an enduringly regional one. Despite the efforts of post-Confederation novels[21] to broach the issue of Canadian understandings of national identity, therefore, there were no explicit formulations or definitions of Canadian identity in literature. This is why, as late as 1972, eminent Canadian writer Margaret Atwood felt compelled to assert, although tongue-in-cheek, in *Survival: A Thematic Guide to Canadian Literature*, that "such a thing [Canadian literature] did indeed exist" (xviii).[22]

To come back to the Group of Seven artists, therefore, one could argue that it was not primarily in the genre of literature, but in painting, that the notion of a distinctive "Canadian" national identity first began to emerge in the 1920s. The highly influential landscape paintings of the Group of Seven, which reflected and propagated the spirit of Canadian nationalism, spurred several like-minded attempts in the genres of fiction and poetry. Yet the latter were not, unlike the works of the American Renaissance writers, urgent entreaties for the creation of a discrete national identity[23] but literary and aesthetic reflections of a national mentality that had emerged as a response to, and a means of surviving, the Canadian "wilderness" and its inhospitable landscape. A closer look at another painting by Lawren Harris, *North Shore, Lake Superior* (1926), and its ekphrastic counterpart published in the same year, A. J. M. Smith's poem "The Lonely Land: Group of Seven," will illustrate this claim.

Harris's painting depicts a big pine stump[24] in the middle of the canvas, with Lake Superior, the largest of the Great Lakes, in the background. The pine tree has clearly been destroyed by the forces of nature and has withered to a gnarled, grayish black stump. Yet the painting depicts not death or destruction but life and courage. The composition of the picture concentrates the viewer's gaze on the left surface of the stump, which is illuminated by the sun's rays—a gesture symbolizing hope. Similarly, the clear waters of Lake Superior, too, are illumined by the sun, signifying that the beauty of the national landscape will prevail despite the harshness of climate indicated by the dark clouds. Montreal-based writer Smith, influenced by Harris's work and other paintings by the Group of Seven, wrote "The Lonely Land: Group of Seven," which similarly expresses the notions of strength and perseverance in the face of extremities of weather and severe conditions in the wilderness—a sense of survival that in that period came to be regarded as intrinsic to the Canadian "national condition":[25]

> Cedar and jagged fir
> uplift sharp barbs
> against the gray
> and cloud-piled sky;
> [. . . .]
> This is a beauty
> of dissonance,
> this resonance
> of stony strand
> this smoky cry
> curled over a black pine
> like a broken
> and wind-battered branch
> when the wind
> bends the tops of the pines
> and curdles the sky
> from the north
>
> This is the beauty
> of strength
> broken by strength
> and still strong. (1978, 38–39)

Written three-quarters of a century after Susanna Moodie's *Roughing It in the Bush* (1852), one of the earliest narratives that reflected the disorienting experience of "roughing it" in Canada's backwoods, Smith's poem inverts the "gloomy picture" in Moodie's memoir of a typical Canadian "black, cold day;

no sun visible in the grey dark sky; a keen, cutting wind, and hard frost" (2007, 305) that awaited the "home-sick [British] emigrants during their first winter in Canada" (109). Instead, Smith's poem is an attempt to convey a sense of determination, perseverance, optimism, and even beauty in the face of hardship and conflict, qualities that were to form the basis of a distinctive Canadian national identity. Foretelling Margaret Atwood's central argument, survival remained a central part of that identity.

One more comparison will suffice to illustrate the difference in the processes of engendering national identity in the United States and Canada—the depiction of national landscapes in essayistic writing. The paintings of the Canadian Group of Seven and the poetry they inspired can fruitfully be compared to the works of the Hudson River School of painters and writers who emerged in the mid-nineteenth century in the United States. In his "Essay on American Scenery" (1836), Thomas Cole, widely regarded as the founder of the Hudson River School, writes of the "overflowing richness," the "vastness and importance" of "American Scenery," which "ought to be of surpassing interest" "to every American" because "it is his own land; its beauty, its magnificence, its sublimity—all are his," "his birthright" (1).[26] In the same vein as the ethos of American Renaissance writing, Cole distances himself from the European landscape painters of the seventeenth to nineteenth centuries, claiming the uniqueness and distinct quality of American scenery and wilderness: "Nature has shed over *this* land beauty and magnificence, and although the character of its scenery may differ from the old world's, yet inferiority must not therefore be inferred; for though American scenery is destitute of many of those circumstances that give value to the European, still it has features, and glorious ones, unknown to Europe" (7, original italics).

Anticipating charges of inferiority and subordination to the magnificent landscapes, historical castles and churches, and cultural heritage of Europe, Cole stresses that what America lacks in history, it makes up for in spirit—with "truly American character" (1836, 12). It is the latter that permeates the mountains, streams, rocks, rivers, meadows, skies, forests of "*this* [chosen] land," that accounts for its "beauty and magnificence" of which Europe remains unaware. In stark contrast to the description of Canada as a backward, barren, disorienting, and godforsaken wilderness in Moodie's *Roughing It in the Bush*, as a "land of waters" whose "dark prison of . . . boundless woods; / No rural charm poetic thought inspires" and whose agricultural landscapes "show cultivation unimproved by art" (2007, 109), Cole's poetic essay celebrates the American spirit of adventure, new beginnings, independence, and freedom.

It is this American spirit, this "quintessential" Americanness, that has pervaded popular culture and the public imagination, and become embodied in various national icons from the Marlboro Man to Uncle Sam. While it is not the aim of this present study to provide a detailed commentary on the different ideological frameworks of cultural (re)production in the United States and Canada, one might argue that one difference lies in Canada's lack of (perhaps because it never strived so hard to cultivate one) a unitary repository or archive of founding myths such as that of the United States. Rather, Canadian folklore can be divided into the subcategories of Indigenous (Algonquian, Iroquoian, Siouan, and others), French Canadian, and English Canadian founding myths. As Caroline Rosenthal summarizes, "Unlike the United States, Canada lacked founding myths and master narratives that could be applied *to the nation as a whole*" (2008, 291; my emphasis).[27] As a result, the national imaginary[28] has had a longer, and thus, at least potentially, more contested, trajectory in the United States than in Canada. It is this divergence in the developments of the American and Canadian national imaginaries since their earliest periods that has led to different understandings, manifestations, and definitions of the term *citizenship* in the two countries. Nevertheless, one point of similarity has emerged as a result of the geopolitical situation of both countries as liberal democracies in North America: the impact of heightened global mobility as well as transnational and transcontinental migration on conventional definitions and understandings of citizenship.

This study therefore sets out to critically investigate the various metaphors, configurations, parameters, and articulations of U.S. and Canadian citizenship that are enacted, renegotiated, and revised through the literary imagination. I have chosen this approach not merely as the logical default option of a literary and cultural studies scholar but also because literature clearly plays, and has always played, a central role in the fashioning and dissemination of dominant ideas that constitute the national imaginary—specifically, ideas of citizenship, nationhood, and belonging. In mapping the intersections between literature and citizenship, my project thus juxtaposes close readings of literary texts with a more interdisciplinary approach that draws on theories of citizenship, sovereignty, governmentality, justice, and recognition from the disciplines of political science, sociology, anthropology, ethics, and philosophy, but also acknowledges the critical interventions of queer theory as well as theories of precariousness, subalternity, exile, and diaspora from decolonial and postcolonial studies. Despite, or perhaps due to, the interdisciplinary nature of citizenship studies as a field, the intersections between literature and citizenship—more specifically, the ways in which literature concomitantly reflects but also (de)constructs discourses of citizenship and identity/belonging—have yet to be explored extensively.[29] In offering a literary and cultural studies approach to citizenship studies, this study seeks to build on some of the work that has addressed this juncture.

My central thesis is that prevailing notions of citizenship and national identity are, in periods of emergence and crisis, reimagined along transnational and post-national lines of social, political, cultural, sexual belonging. This reimagining is carried out *by* and *in* the literary texts themselves through the act of reading as well as through various forms and "acts of citizenship" (Isin and Nielsen 2008) that do not neatly fit into established frames of citizenship in Western liberal democracies. These acts propose and enable alternative understandings of nation, collectivity, and community that challenge dominant ideas of American and Canadian selfhood and national identity. They are performed by several types of bodies that fall outside of the normative legal definitions of citizenship—first, the willful or wayward citizen who is ambivalent about her or his own relationship and allegiances with her or his country and hence deemed "unpatriotic"; second, the precarious refugee or asylum seeker, the undocumented migrant, the stateless person, or the exile who is deemed an undesirable subject and hence ineligible for citizenship via naturalization; third, the queer body who demands the right to be read as equal but is constantly marked as deviant from the heteronormative reproductive logic of the nation; fourth, the long-term denizen or permanent resident who remains, intentionally or otherwise, an unnaturalized noncitizen of the host country; and finally, the Indigenous subject, whose notions of citizenship, belonging, community, and nationhood are closely bound to understandings of Native sovereignty and the right to decide who comprises the Indigenous nation. Collectively, these disparate subjects are often classified and perceived by the majority of society as ambivalent, a threat (as risky bodies instead of bodies at risk), willful, transgressive, deviant, different, and hence unacceptable. As a result, they are marginalized and often excluded from nationally sanctioned narratives of American and Canadian citizenship. They are, in other words, bodies that repeatedly have to (re)negotiate their very existences in the public spaces of the nation in which they have come to reside, compelled to challenge and overturn the ways in which they have been interpellated, identified, and read.

This study therefore traces the development of citizenship from established definitions to alternative models that include transnational, post-national, and diasporic modes of belonging, but also forms of willfulness, insurgency, transgression, precariousness, queer interventions, denizenship, and Indigenous citizenship that call for a reorientation of narratives of national assimilation and identification. It stems from an observation that, over the last decade, cross-disciplinary debates on the term *citizenship* in the fields of literary and cultural studies, sociology, political science, and anthropology have concurred that conventional definitions of citizenship are becoming ever more obsolete. As Engin Isin has observed, increasingly, critics are conceiving of citizenship less as a fixed or static legal entity and more as "a set of practices (cultural, symbolic and economic) and a bundle of rights and obligations (legal, political, and social) that define membership in a polity" (1999, 267). These new conceptualizations of citizenship enact a "constant re-imagining of transnational affiliations vis-à-vis dominant[ly] held notions of nationhood and selfhood" (Schlund-Vials 2006).[30]

I offer a word of explanation regarding my methodology and selection of primary texts that form the basis of my close reading and critical observations. This study adopts a synchronic approach in its analysis of how notions of citizenship and national identity have existed at different points in American and Canadian history in order to point out significant parallels and correspondences. To this end, I have avoided diachronically plotting out a linear trajectory of all the important historical moments in which definitions and understandings of citizenship have been questioned, challenged, and revised: numerous excellent studies in the social sciences, especially in the fields of history, law, political science, and sociology, have already copiously covered this ground.[31] In distinction, my contribution to existing debates on citizenship adopts a "case-study" methodology informed by a literary and cultural studies approach. It brings together, for the first time, a selection of canonical and lesser known U.S. and Canadian writings that call for a reconfiguration of ideas of nationhood, citizenship, and national identity in a North American context. Correspondingly, each section seeks to put into conversation literary works from different historical periods, geographical settings, and sociopolitical eras that offer multiple perspectives on a particular "type" of body or subject who does not fit neatly into conventional, nation-oriented definitions of citizenship, and who thus, in my opinion, paves the way for a consideration of "new" or alternative modes of post-national belonging and collective identification.

Part 1 focuses on the literary depiction of "willful" or "wayward" citizens whose acts of "civil disobedience" (see Thoreau 2013) renegotiate the parameters of citizenship, nationality, and national identification. The first chapter frames my discussion by establishing a historical perspective through the analysis of two polemic narratives written in a period of literary nationalism in American history commonly referred to as the American Renaissance. Through the use of irony and satire, Nathaniel Hawthorne's *The Scarlet Letter* (1850) disputed the political legitimacy of the American nation by casting a critical eye over its federal administrative system and mocking its national symbols while, through the use of invective, Walt Whitman's *Democratic Vistas* (1871) called for the birth of a new national literature that would establish the foundations of American democracy. These early texts thus already exemplified alternative ways of reimagining the nation that departed from the conventional political symbols and icons of the United States in the mid-nineteenth century. In so doing, Hawthorne and Whitman were perhaps themselves the "willful" citizens of their time. In chapter 2, I turn my attention to the playfully political "citizen-in-process" in Canadian writer Gail Scott's *Heroine* (1987), a complex fictional metanarrative that broaches the topic of Quebecois nationalism and separatism in the aftermath of the October Crisis in 1980 in Montreal. Scott's novel is an acute commentary and reminder of the bilingual foundations of Canada, which together continue to undermine and complicate attempts at defining an "authentic" unitary Canadian national identity. Finally, chapter 3 takes up the trope of "willful" or "wayward" citizenship in Philip Roth's American trilogy as embodied in the fictional characters of a rebellious teenage daughter who turns her back on the American Dream (in *American Pastoral*, 1997), a Communist who is denounced for his "un-American" sympathies during the McCarthy era (in *I Married a Communist*, 1998), and a black classics professor who passes as a white Jew (in *The Human Stain*, 2000). Through the multiple perspectives of these characters as well as the use of metafictional elements in the novels, Roth compels us as readers to reexamine our conceptions of "Americanness" and rework our assumptions of what it is to "*be* American" and "*feel* American," hence foregrounding the affective components of national identification and citizenship. All three novels thus question, challenge, and reinscribe the dominant narratives of the nation, national identity, and collectivity in post–World War II America.

Part 2 of this study turns to the ways in which precarious bodies, because they are interpellated as threatening, undesirable, and unacceptable, are excluded from dominant discourses on citizenship and national belonging. Nevertheless, the existence of these precarious subjects—the undocumented migrant, the stateless person, the asylum seeker, the refugee, the displaced—in the margins of the nation also critiques and points out the failure of neoliberal models and narratives of citizenship. The literary narratives in this section all variously call attention to the limits of systems of "identity management" and securitization that regulate the boundaries of the nation-state. Chapter 4 centers on Lebanese American writer Etel Adnan's early critique of xenophobia and sectarian nationalism during the Lebanese Civil War in *Sitt Marie Rose* (1977) and a personal account of her exile from Beirut and move to the United States in the experimental prose text *In the Heart of the Heart of Another Country* (2005). Adnan's writings demonstrate an "ethics of narration" (Booth 1990; Nussbaum 2007), one akin to that which Judith Butler recently called for in order to create an alternative perception of political subjectivity that is attuned to conditions of vulnerability, injurability, and precariousness (2004, 3). Adnan's narratives demand a sense of accountability; they engender a politics of intervention that challenges traditional, and often exclusionary, notions of citizenship and national identity. Chapter 5 picks up on the notions of precarity and susceptibility as embodied by the figure of the displaced subject. It focuses on a landmark case of black marginalization in Atlantic Canadian history: the forced relocation in the 1960s of the residents of Africville, a predominantly black, underclass population that lived on the outskirts of Halifax, Nova Scotia, to inner-city council housing in the name of urban renewal. The visual, musical, and literary narratives that pay tribute to the Africville case illustrate a mode of regional identity, pride, and separatism that challenges notions of national identity and nation-based models of citizenship. Of these texts, I have chosen to examine George Elliott Clarke's *Whylah Falls* (1990), an intertextual and intermedial fictional counter-narrative inspired by the Africville evacuation and resettlement that writes against and deconstructs established notions of "home" and belonging within the boundaries of the nation. Chapter 6, the last in this section, rounds up my discussion of precarious citizenship by concentrating on the situation of undocumented migrants in the nation-state. Focusing on Amitava Kumar's multigeneric, conceptual collage work, *Passport Photos* (2000), I examine how the text is an attempt both to break the stereotypes and exclusionary logic that govern U.S. immigration discourse and to find a new poetics of diaspora and post-national citizenship. A satirical commentary on the national obsession with legal documentation and paperwork in U.S. immigration control, Kumar's book invites being read as "a forged passport," "an act of fabrication against the language of government agencies" (Kumar 2000, ix) that exposes the problematic logic of immigration regulations and laws governing American citizenship.

Part 3 of this study turns to a consideration of queer citizenship, or the rights to citizenship and political membership claimed by queer bodies. The first chapter focuses on Djuna Barnes's early modernist classic, *Nightwood* (1936), paying attention to the challenges that the queer American expatriate (often perceived as ex-patriot) living in Europe poses in terms of national (dis)identification. I explore how the topographies of the nation are disrupted by forms of sexual transgression and "dissident"/deviant sexualities that challenge the predominantly heterosexual reproductive logic of nation-based citizenship in America. The next chapter investigates how queer migrant bodies' claims to sexual citizenship challenge dominant processes of national identity formation and, accordingly, how queer diasporic narratives not only demand but also open up new forms of recognition and belonging through a textual strategy of queer affect. I base my observations on close readings of two novels by queer Caribbean Canadian writers: Dionne Brand's *In Another Place, Not Here* (1996) and Shani Mootoo's *Valmiki's Daughter* (2008). Finally, chapter 9 shifts the focus to AIDS narratives written by Sarah Schulman in the 1990s that revisit the physical, emotional, and political terrains of the AIDS epidemic in New York City in the 1980s. I read Schulman's novels *People in Trouble* (1990) and *Rat Bohemia* (1995) alongside the manifestos and press releases of Queer Nation, an LGBTQ activist organization formed in 1990 in New York City by members of ACT UP (AIDS Coalition to Unleash Power). I seek to unpack the latter's logic of queer nationality, its subversion of identity politics, and its espousal of class politics. I demonstrate how these fictional and political writings inspired by the AIDS pandemic at its height in the 1980s represented a powerful response to the Reagan administration's policy of silence on the AIDS health crisis.

Part 4 is an examination of how "new" and alternative forms of citizenship, such as denizenship, urban citizenship, diasporic citizenship, and Indigenous citizenship, continue to broaden the parameters and reconfigure the borderlines of nation-based forms of citizenship, identification, and collective belonging. Chapter 10 focuses on the contemporary cityscape or new metropolis as an ideal site for the emergence of "insurgent citizenship" (Holston 1998), understood as the assertion of socioeconomic, cultural, and political rights beyond the normative and legal frameworks of formal citizenship. My assertion here is that challenges to prevalent forms of citizenship and the emergence of new modes of subjectivity take place not only *in* but also *through* the construction and negotiation of narrative spaces. I draw my observations in this chapter from close readings of two recent novels, Dionne Brand's *What We All Long For* (2005) and Dinaw Mengestu's *The Beautiful Things That Heaven Bears* (2007). The next chapter in this section traces how a textual poetics of exile and forced migration is articulated in two Haitian works of literature: Edwidge Danticat's memoir *Brother, I'm Dying* (2007) and Dany Laferrière's autobiographical novel/work of autofiction, *The Return* (2009). My focus lies in how these writings embrace exile as, in keeping with Edward Said's observations in his essay "Reflections on Exile" (2001), both a physical and mental displacement, both a political condition and a frame of mind that offers critical ways of rethinking notions of home, nation, citizenship, and belonging in diasporic and migrant narratives. While Danticat refracts the lens of personal memory from *lòt bò dlo* ("the other side of the water" in Haitian Creole), Laferrière maintains a "poetics of relation" (Glissant 1997a) with the land of his origin that becomes the basis for his post-territorial understanding of national identity. Both strategies of writing differently illustrate how the realities of exile and displacement renegotiate existing models of national belonging and identification, generating new forms of substantive, or lived, citizenship.

The final chapter of this section looks closely at the phenomenon of Indigenous citizenship, in particular membership of the Cherokee Nation. It examines how notions of the nation, kinship, and community in Indigenous narratives differ from, challenge, expand, or simply reject modern ideas of nationalism posited by, for example, Benedict Anderson, who famously defined the nation as a socially constructed and mediated "imagined community" (1983). While critical studies on U.S. and Canadian national imaginaries abound, Indigenous/First Nations nationalisms have received less attention in academic scholarship. In other words, conventional studies of the national tend to remain within the paradigms of the modern nation-state and not the Indigenous nation. Chapter 12 thus explores different understandings of the nation that have been advanced by Indigenous scholars, writers, and activists such as Daniel Heath Justice, a citizen of the Cherokee Nation, who understand their political and cultural sovereignty as derived from the Creator. To what extent are definitions of Indigenous citizenship and nationhood that are voiced in Indigenous writing viable and existing ways of understanding community, collectivity, and nation? What are the repercussions of persistently finding value in the word *nation* (whether as a symbolic or literal entity) in an Indigenous context, despite the extensive deconstruction of national(ist) formations in the twentieth century? Finally, to complicate matters, what about the marginalization and exclusion of subjects who claim Cherokee citizenship but who are repeatedly rejected by the Cherokee Nation, for instance, in the ongoing Cherokee Freedmen versus Cherokee Nation controversy? I address these questions in my close readings of the novel *Abraham's Well* (2006) by Sharon Ewell Foster and the historical biography *Ties That Bind: The Story of an Afro-Cherokee Family in Slavery and Freedom* (2005) by Tiya Miles.

How do Indigenous, diasporic, migrant, exiled, queer, expatriate, precarious, separatist, "unpatriotic," and "willful" communities invoke, critique, and reconfigure notions of national identity and citizenship that have become established in dominant political and social discourses? These considerations lead us back to the concerns of place, nation, community, and kinship in Jin-me Yoon's *A Group of Sixty-Seven.* Figure 4 (see color insert), which is the corresponding piece to the one with which I began my introduction, depicts a "back" view of Jin-me Yoon's mother as she looks straight ahead at another archetypal depiction of Canadian landscape that is closely associated with the Group of Seven paintings. Interestingly, the painting, Emily Carr's[32] *Old Time Coast Village* (1929–30) was inspired by the Indigenous communities of the Pacific Northwest Coast.[33] One of Carr's mature works in which she explores the interrelated themes of place and identity, *Old Time Coast Village* is also one of a group of paintings that were a bridge to her late works in the 1930s. The latter portrayed raw landscapes in the Canadian wilderness, especially forests, through her increasingly theosophical perspective. In Jin-me Yoon's visual, it is not only the subject, Yoon's mother, who is looking into Carr's painting. By extension, the viewer is also made to behold this landscape painting by a "Canadian icon"[34] who, throughout her career, visually documented the sculptures and totems of the Indigenous peoples of the Pacific Northwest Coast, hence acknowledging, if also exoticizing, the history and heritage of the First Nations in Canada before it became a British settler colony. In Yoon's photograph, the four totem poles that are in the center of Carr's *Old Time Coast Village* are obscured by the body of Yoon's mother in a gesture not of elimination, I suggest, but of identification (between the Korean Canadian migrant and the Indigenous Canadian and their analogous histories of marginalization). By extension, Yoon's piece confronts *us* as viewers with the question of where and how *we* fit (or not, as the case may be) into the constructed narratives of history and culture that have shaped dominant nation-based understandings of identity and belonging. Her visual makes *us* part of the aesthetic and political gaze, and thus part of the collective project of unsettling, contesting, and reconfiguring prevailing constructions of citizenship and national identity in which this study, *Reconfiguring Citizenship and National Identity in the North American Literary Imagination*, too, seeks to partake.

PART 1

. . . .

Willful Citizens

I

NEGOTIATING AMERICANNESS AND RENARRATIVIZING THE "NATIONAL SYMBOLIC" IN THE AMERICAN RENAISSANCE

··········

Nathaniel Hawthorne's *The Scarlet Letter* and
Walt Whitman's *Democratic Vistas*

The American Civil War era (1861–65) witnessed a state of emergency in the United States that suspended civil liberties otherwise protected by the Bill of Rights in the U.S. Constitution. It also marked a watershed in American history with regard to notions of citizenship and national identity.[1] In the antebellum years, the issue of slavery that divided the Northern and Southern states reflected not only the interests of slave owners in preserving unequal power relations but also a more fundamental concern about definitions of U.S. citizenship and who had the right to claim it. In the aftermath of the Civil War and the ratification of the Fourteenth Amendment in 1868, which conferred the right of citizenship upon all African American men, U.S. citizenship continued to be a contested entity because not all black freedmen were immediately recognized as American citizens, especially in the Southern states. The Reconstruction Era (1865–77) that followed the Civil War was therefore a significant period in which heated debates on issues of citizenship and national identity persisted.[2]

The beginning of the Civil War marked the end of the "American Renaissance," a period in which the urge to produce a new and distinctly "American" national literature dominated the efforts of writers. It was an era in which many of the so-called American masterpieces were written and published, works that engaged with ideas of American democracy and national identity and were defined in distinction to British heritage and culture. As F. O. Matthiessen summarizes, "Emerson, Hawthorne, Thoreau, Whitman and Melville all wrote literature for democracy. . . . They felt it was incumbent upon their generation to give fulfillment to the potentials freed by the [American] Revolution, to provide a culture commensurate with America's political opportunity" (1941, vx). The intellectual atmosphere and philosophical climate might certainly have been conducive in the early and mid-1800s for literary and cultural enunciations of a distinct and unique American national identity, and such articulations may undoubtedly have flourished. Nevertheless, scholars have noted that this cultural self-articulation did not take place effortlessly. Rather, as Lauren Berlant convincingly argues in her study of citizenship and nationalism in America in the mid-nineteenth century, *The Anatomy of National Fantasy*, the American Renaissance emerged as a result of "widespread pressure to develop a set of symbolic national references whose possession would signify and realize the new political and social order" (1991, 29). Literary culture in the 1850s was therefore both a reflection of the demand for alternative forms of national identification that would replace existing emblems and symbols of patriotic proclamation and nationhood[3] and a considerable factor that contributed to that demand, especially in the run-up to a bloody civil war whose issues of slavery, regional economic differences,[4] and questions of sovereignty over the right of states to secession would bitterly divide the country.

Significantly, what emerged in the writings in the period of the American Renaissance was thus a sense that claims to a distinctively American national identity were not unanimous but often indeterminate and fractured. At the same time that writers in the mid-nineteenth century responded to the call for a uniquely American literature and the development of a collective national identity, therefore, they also expressed the difficulty of constructing a sense of collectivity precisely because of the escalating conflicts around the issues of slavery and secession that were dividing states and their citizens.

Many of the works from this period thus depicted, explicitly or implicitly, the crisis surrounding the concept of the American nation and the principles of federalism. They sought to intervene in dominant modes of cultural nationalism[5] by construing the nation in ways that departed from the federalist attitudes, as well as the patriarchal and filiopietistic logic, that governed the public and private realms of everyday life. These forms of interpolation reflect what I call, in an adaptation of the term by Edward Said, a "critical nationalist"[6] outlook on the part of American Renaissance writers. One prime literary example that undertook this project was Walt Whitman's poetry collection *Leaves of Grass* (1855). Whitman's magnum opus takes up Ralph Waldo Emerson's concerns in his essay "The Poet" (1844) that the United States needed to develop its own national literature and express its unique "home-grown" identity as well as its virtues and vices—a task that befell the nation's poets. Understandably, most Whitman scholars have focused their critical attention on *Leaves of Grass*, tracing its expansion and alterations over the course of its different versions. As a result, some of his later essayistic works, especially the long treatise *Democratic Vistas* (1871), have yet to be paid the extensive attention they deserve.

This chapter redresses this imbalance by analyzing Whitman's *Democratic Vistas* and placing it in conversation with another significant text from the mid-nineteenth century, Nathaniel Hawthorne's *The Scarlet Letter* (1850). I argue that both texts articulated a necessity, in the midst of increasing ambivalence toward the future unity of the American nation, to take stock of, redefine, and consolidate what it meant to be an American citizen and to contend what the defining traits of a national literature were. Due to the challenging nature of the task at hand—to imagine and put into practice a new idea of national literature that departed extensively from established modes of national identification that relied on popular icons of American culture, symbols that were themselves newly coined in emblematic gestures of independence from the British—these writings, I suggest, were *themselves* willful and transgressive. In their attempts to reinvigorate definitions of nationhood, citizenship, and national identity in an era of national crisis unprecedented since the Revolutionary War, these works were polemic, controversial, and uncompromising in their level of social critique, especially on spiritual and moral issues, and in their desire for far-reaching changes in the mindset of the American nation. With these agendas in mind, I will focus on these writings' renegotiation of notions of Americanness and their renarrativization of what Lauren Berlant terms the "National Symbolic"—"the order of discursive practices whose reign within a national space produces . . . the 'law' in which the accident of birth within a geographic/political boundary transforms individuals into subjects of a collectively-held history" (1991, 20).

In short, I will focus on how these writings reinscribe the notion of citizenship in a period of national crisis using two different modes. The first, as demonstrated by Hawthorne's *The Scarlet Letter*, is a mode of ironic skepticism that deconstructs the national symbols, icons, and political allegiances that American citizens, as national subjects, were expected to embrace as part of a larger national collectivity. The second, as evinced by Whitman's *Democratic Vistas*, is a more affirmative mode of faith in the efficacy of literature in cultivating a distinct and unique national identity, one premised on the tenets of American democracy and sovereignty—yet, the protracted insistence of Whitman's prose and his disparagement of the state of contemporary American literature hint at the considerable difficulty of this effort. In the following, I will juxtapose these two different models of literary critique and examine how they both seek to revise and invigorate the relationship between nation and narration. My methodological approach does not assume the nation an absolute or stable entity; rather, I understand it as being in a state of ongoing construction and reconfiguration in line with, and counter to, other social and political formations.

My analysis of *The Scarlet Letter* is, first and foremost, concerned with its introductory sketch of the Custom-House. This prologue is significant because it reflects how, in this period, the term *citizen* was an elastic concept whose definition was subject to a larger nationwide debate. Accordingly, the prologue represents Hawthorne's critical project of reinscribing conventional notions of citizenship, national identity, place, and belonging that he perceived as in a state of crisis in the antebellum years. Indeed, in that period and during the Civil War, the very notion of a federation of united states was gravely questioned. The Southern states argued that each state had the right to secede from the Union and that the U.S. Constitution was null and void if it did not, first and foremost, ensure the rights and sovereignty of individual states in the nation. At the time Hawthorne published *The Scarlet Letter* in 1850, therefore, disputes over the issue of slavery and increasing sectionalism—due to the different social structures, political beliefs, and economies of the Northern and Southern states—had escalated and reached their peak.[7]

This tension was, accordingly, reflected in *The Scarlet Letter*, which deconstructs the very notion of a cohesive national identity and expresses the limits to collective identification within the nation's boundaries. In the Custom-House introduction, the narrator, whose experiences most critics have agreed were partly inspired by Hawthorne's own involvements in the federal service, informs the reader of his dismissal after three years of working as chief executive officer of the Custom-House in Salem,[8] where his task was to regulate what commodities might enter, and which might leave, the country's borders. Expressing Hawthorne's ambivalence about his own dependency on and complicity with forms of national privilege,[9] the narrator's critical attitude to the officially sanctioned ideas of the nation is marked by a sense of estrangement and defamiliarization.

This is enacted chiefly by a deconstruction of the national symbols and icons of the United States in the prologue. The opening description of the frontal edifice of the Salem Custom-House in the year 1850, with its American flag "float[ing] or droop[ing], either in breeze or calm" (Hawthorne 1983, 36), sets the tone for Hawthorne's sustained critique of structures of national privilege and identification. The large American eagle that hovers over the entrance of the Custom-House with outspread wings is described, for instance, not as a resplendent national emblem but as an "unhappy fowl" with a "truculency of attitude" who "looks on vixenly" with "no great tenderness, even in her best of moods" (37). This grotesque parody and satiric representation of the national symbol of the United States (perhaps *the* central symbol in American iconography ever since its inception at the Continental Congress of 1782) deconstructs it as a recognizable emblem of national identification. The eagle's indifferent, malicious, and vindictive nature also conceivably alludes to how this national icon slickly glosses over local political struggles, such as that between the Whigs and Democrats in which Hawthorne himself was caught up in at the time of writing, which resulted in his own dismissal from the Salem Custom-House.

Anticipating Whitman's diatribe in *Democratic Vistas* against "the official services of America, national, state, and municipal" that are "saturated in corruption, bribery, falsehood, mal-administration," and greed for "pecuniary gain" (2010, 12), Hawthorne launches his satirical invective against the Custom-House officers in Salem, who are mostly Whigs.[10] These are described as "a row of venerable figures . . . oftentimes . . . asleep in their accustomed corners, with their chairs tilted back against the wall; awaking, however, once or twice in a forenoon, to bore one another with the several thousandth rep-etition of old sea-stories, and mouldy jokes, that had grown to be pass-words and countersigns among them" (1983, 38, 45–46). Hawthorne's satiric depic-tion of the Custom-House officers is clearly laced with a skepticism toward their abilities and work ethic. The "reality" of their laziness and the banality of their languorous afternoons, spent recalling anecdotes and old jokes, con-tradict the façade of propriety and decorum that the narrator's "stern and black-browed" Puritan ancestors erected as part of their "dreary and unpros-perous condition" (41). In those ancestors' eyes, the narrator deems himself a willful subject, a "worthless, if not positively disgraceful . . . degenerate fellow" (41–42).

In the Custom-House sketch, therefore, Hawthorne not only describes his ambivalent attitude toward being dismissed from his position as a "pub-lic functionary of the United States" via the narrator's conflicting emotions about being the head of "such a patriarchal body of veterans" (1983, 43), he also discloses his conflicting feelings for Salem, the town of his birth. He writes, "though invariably happiest elsewhere,"

> there is within me a feeling for old Salem, which, in lack of a better phrase, I must be content to call affection. The sentiment is probably assignable to the deep and aged roots which my family has struck into the soil. It is now nearly two centuries and a quarter since the original Briton, the earliest emigrant of my name, made his appearance in the wild and forest-bordered settlement, which has since become a city. And here his descendants have been born and died, and have mingled their earthy substance with the soil; until no small portion of it must necessarily be akin to the mortal frame wherewith, for a little while, I walk the streets. In part, therefore, the attachment which I speak of is the mere sensuous sympathy of dust for dust. (40)

In this passage, the narrator confesses the unbreakable tangible bonds he feels with Salem, the birthplace of his ancestors. Yet he describes the attach-ment he feels to the town as "indolent and unjoyous" (43). Moreover, he is quick to note that the Salem of his boyhood is no longer the Salem to which he returns when he takes up the job of Custom-House officer. The narrator casts a critical eye on the insularity of Salem, a small provincial town in the 1850s, and the cultural amnesia at the heart of its way of life. In so doing,

Hawthorne is breaking the filiopietistic tradition of self-definition in New England. He is, effectively, seeking a different way of perceiving and constructing American history, culture, collective memory, and national identity—one that extends an understanding of the latter as less a fixed or static notion than a set of practices and relations shaped by interrelated historical, cultural, political, and ideological formations and tensions. Flouting tradition, the narrator of the Custom-House prologue also declares that he has little in common with his first ancestor, the "grave, bearded, sable-cloaked, and steeple-crowned progenitor" (40–41), a "legislator, judge, . . . bitter persecutor" with "all the Puritanic traits,"[11] who had more right of abode in Salem than he, since his own "name is seldom heard and face hardly known" (41).

Hawthorne ends his introduction to *The Scarlet Letter* by describing his dismissal from the Salem Custom-House as an act of decapitation and dryly refers to the novel he sets about to write as "the POSTHUMOUS PAPERS OF A DECAPITATED SURVEYOR" (1983, 73). Estranged from the town of his birth, and cynical about his dismissal due to his political convictions, Hawthorne concludes his sketch by emphatically writing, "I am a citizen of somewhere else" (74). This ambiguous statement can be read in at least two ways—as a declaration of nonbelonging ("I am *not* a citizen of here"),[12] or as an avowal that stakes a claim about belonging "*anywhere else but here.*" Both interpretations shed light on Hawthorne's self-imposed role as author-in-exile, which allows him to envision a version of American national identity in 1850 that breaks from its Puritan, New England roots. Nevertheless, the phrase "I am a citizen of somewhere else" also expresses the tension that Hawthorne faced between his personal and political convictions, between his perception of himself as a willful, "disgraceful" citizen who rejected the filiopietistic logic of New England aristocracy, and his self-reproach at being part of this very federal system that his personal beliefs rejected due to his employment as a civil servant.

Hawthorne's prologue to *The Scarlet Letter* thus represents a critical response to the project of nation-building and the reproduction of dominant forms of national identity in the United States in the mid-nineteenth century.[13] The narrator's darkly comic depiction of himself as a headless victim of the "guillotine" of federal party politics can be read as Hawthorne's recognition that the concept of American citizenship in the 1850s did not allow the desires of the private individual and the shared practices of the political/social collective to exist concurrently because they were regarded as intrinsically incompatible and diametrically opposite. American national identity was in a state of crisis, and the pressures exerted by individual states represented a tangible threat to the federal system. Hawthorne's response to this crisis is "to return to the body, to subjectivity, to material experience, and to everyday life to reconfigure what it means to be an American citizen. He does this in part by critiquing the claims of official nationalist discourse, but mainly by writing a new kind of history, a 'genealogy' of national identity, from 1640 [the seventeenth-century Puritan setting of the novel] to 1850" (Berlant 1991, 16). Critiquing the abstract and prescriptive nature of American citizenship[14] as represented in its national symbols, icons, spaces, and narratives, Hawthorne thus sought to reinvigorate forms of citizenship that centered on the substantive, lived experiences of the gendered national subject in order to propose new affective and corporeal sites of national identification. *The Scarlet Letter* reflects the sociopolitical sentiment of the period in which it was written, a period in which the symbolic order of the nation was frequently under threat by local allegiances and cronyism at the level of state politics.

The novel can thus also be read as a counter to the dominance of the male national subject in the public sphere that both constituted and reflected the patriarchal structures and power relations in mid-nineteenth-century American society. The tale of Hester Prynne's willful refusal to be shamed by her adultery constitutes Hawthorne's authorial gesture at an alternative form of female political agency that countered that of the male citizen in seventeenth-century Puritan Boston. Critics have also argued that the fictional character of Hester Prynne and her tale of adultery were Hawthorne's means of defying the social judgments bestowed upon him and his family, particularly on the maternal side.[15] By portraying how a mother and daughter, condemned in the eyes of the harsh, God-fearing Puritan community in seventeenth-century Boston, rise above their "womanly frailty" and defy patriarchal values, these critics contend, Hawthorne was vicariously redressing what he felt was his own social ostracism.

While this expression of personal grievance might certainly be true, I want to suggest that *The Scarlet Letter* also emerged out of a more fundamental and deep-seated need to forge, through literature, a national identity that the author felt was slipping out of his imaginative grasp. The narrator's repeated references to decapitation and death at the guillotine in the Custom-House introductory sketch are highly significant. He describes himself not only as a "politically dead man" (1983, 70) but, more specifically, as a decapitated Democrat of the United States who, like a victim of the French Revolution, dies in the fight for democracy and the inalienable rights of the citizen (*Déclaration des droits de l'homme et du citoyen*). The narrator also refers to himself as Washington Irving's Headless Horseman, the ghostly specter of a Hessian soldier who, while fighting on the side of the British in the American Revolutionary War, has his head severed by an American cannonball.[16] Both the decapitated French revolutionary and the Headless Horseman are victims of violence in the name of national sovereignty. Crucially, however, in "The Custom-House," the narrator is not merely a "hapless" victim caught in political skirmishes between the Whigs and Democrats. Rather, he also expresses an ambivalence with regard to what Lauren Berlant terms "national sentimentality" (1991, 2)—the form of sentimentality generated by the collapsing of the personal and political spheres in the United States into an affective space of public intimacy—an ambivalence compounded by discomfort with his own involvement in the workings of the federal office.

It is perhaps this incongruity that Hawthorne felt with respect to his simultaneous complicity with and opposition to the federal system that resulted in his creation of the fictional character of Hester Prynne, who becomes the embodiment of the willful citizen. It is Hester who must take Hawthorne's place at the scaffold in the marketplace, the apparatus of social discipline and symbolic site of collective identity. As the novel progresses, Hester's rehabilitation and reabsorption into society as a skilled seamstress is deemed by the patriarchal figures of Puritan law as her transition from willful to law-abiding, God-fearing, "good" citizen. Yet Hester remains stubbornly outside of the community: "In all her intercourse with society, . . . there was nothing that made her feel as if she belonged to it" (1983, 108). The scarlet letter A that sits on Hester's bosom thus not only functions as a marker of sin and shame but clearly distinguishes her from the rest of the townsfolk and the customary decorum of Puritan ways:

> On the breast of her gown, in fine red cloth, surrounded with an elaborate embroidery and fantastic flourishes of gold thread, appeared the letter A. It was so artistically done, and with so much fertility and gorgeous luxuriance of fancy, that it had all the effect of a last and fitting decoration to the apparel which she wore, and

which was of a splendor in accordance with the taste of the age, but greatly beyond what was allowed by the sumptuary regulations of the colony. (80)

By wearing the letter A on her breast, Hester is fulfilling the legal requirements of punishment meted out to her for her act of adultery by the Puritan courts of law. However, the A is also a symbol of defiance on two counts. First, it is a material signifier of Hester's flaunting of the stigma thrust upon her as an adulteress and hence a visible mark of her shamelessness, which defied Puritan codes of propriety and decorum. Second, it violates the regulations of the Massachusetts Bay Colony, which did not allow inhabitants from lower-class hierarchies to indulge in extravagant dress. The letter A with its gold embroidery thus becomes a symbol of continued transgression because Hester is metaphorically aligning herself with the same privileged magistrate class that constitutes the juridical body of law, those who are allowed such fineries of clothing.

Hester's "rehabilitation" from wayward to obedient and law-abiding citizen might therefore rather be read as Hawthorne's critical commentary on the materialism and hypocrisy that characterized the lifestyles of the Puritan magistrates:

> By degrees, nor very slowly, her handiwork became what would now be termed the fashion. . . . Vanity, it may be, chose to mortify itself, by putting on, for ceremonials of pomp and state, the garments that had been wrought by her sinful hands. Her needle-work was seen on the ruff of the Governor; military men wore it on their scarfs, and the minister on his band; it decked the baby's little cap; it was shut up, to be mildewed and moulder away, in the coffins of the dead. But it is not recorded that, in a single instance, her skill was called in aid to embroider the white veil which was to cover the pure blushes of a bride. The exception indicated the ever relentless vigor with which society frowned upon her sin. (1983, 107)

The revelation that the bridal veil, due to reasons of chastity and the symbolic transference of sin from the maker to the wearer, is the one "exception" that Hester's handiwork is not allowed to grace clearly depicts the duplicity of the Puritan magistrates and ministers, who have no qualms about using her needlework to grace their ceremonial and military garments.

Hawthorne's novel can hence be read as a critique of Puritan hypocrisy and superstition as well as the "relentless vigor" of its patriarchal law and customs. Furthermore, it is also a critical assessment of its masculine civil order, which is set in direct opposition to maternal/natural law, the law that binds and protects the bond between a mother (Hester) and her child (Pearl). In this respect, it articulates a counter–National Symbolic, one that is characterized by estrangement, defamiliarization, and skepticism in relation to established forms, symbols, narratives, and icons of national identity. In declaring himself to be "a citizen of somewhere else," the narrator of "The Custom-House" introductory sketch acknowledges the limitations of nationalism—and the hegemonic, sanctioned forms it embodies—while remaining open to "alter-national" forms of identity. Ultimately, therefore, I read Hawthorne's *The Scarlet Letter* as more than a satiric diatribe against Puritan bigotry or a tale of one woman's courage to stand against the dominant patriarchal forces that regulated women's bodies and their sexualities in that period, although these aspects are clearly present in the novel. More crucially, I read the tale as Hawthorne's experiment with citizenship in a period when the nation itself was perceived to be in a state of crisis, when the symbolic significance of the nation, like its mascot the American eagle, was perched threateningly on the verge of anachronism or banality, and when national identity was fractured along the lines of national, local, personal, juridical, political, and gender identifications.

What is significant about this experiment is its medium—that of the literary text. Writing in a time in America when literary culture was central in generating a set of national symbols and dominant narratives that would support federal structures, Hawthorne did just the opposite: he called into question the desirability of national intimacy and the efficacy of filiopietistic forms of juridical and legislative rule. In doing so, he *himself* effectively became a willful subject, a wayward citizen whose renegotiating of national identity and renarrativizing of the National Symbolic challenged the political legitimacy of the nation-state, even as he also sought to come to terms with his own involvement in the federal apparatus as chief executive officer of the Custom-House in Salem.

Hawthorne thus endeavored to reclaim and reinscribe the notions of citizenship and national identity, which he perceived to be in a state of crisis in the United States in the mid-nineteenth century. He did this not by reinforcing the federal system or arguing for the Union cause, but by a mode of defamiliarization, estrangement, and skepticism that shifted the locus of the nation away from abstract symbols and icons onto the corporeal body and its affects. *The Scarlet Letter* draws attention to the ways in which affect shapes processes of national identity formation and reinscribes the abstract quality of national symbols, icons, rituals, and narratives. It demonstrates how "the nation itself [is] a site of affective investment and emotional identification" (Berlant 2008, xi). The prologue to Hawthorne's *The Scarlet Letter* thus functions as the site of inscription of a critical nationalist politics/poetics, one that, in keeping with the ethos of the American Renaissance movement, seeks to renarrativize the National Symbolic and lay the grounds for new emergent forms of national identity based not on anachronistic structures of patriarchal patronage but on the cultural semiotics of a nascent American democracy. The scarlet letter A marks Hester Prynne as a willful citizen not only because she has committed the crime of adultery but because she represents the challenge of a female maternal law that defies and violates the male hegemonic order. Nevertheless, Hawthorne's attempt to reinscribe the basic tenets of nationhood is flagged by struggle and contradiction, by a feeling of complicity that he is part of the state apparatus he critiques, and by the irony that he is disenfranchised by this very system when the political tables turn on him.

At the time that Walt Whitman wrote his long tract *Democratic Vistas*, he, too, was working as a government clerk, albeit in Washington, DC. As Ed Folsom notes in his introduction to the facsimile edition of the original text, Whitman wrote his meditation on democracy's future in America "from the perspective of someone buried deep in the government bureaucracy . . . tediously copying the documents that kept the government running" (2010, xxxi–xxxii). The similarities to Hawthorne's involvement with the federal apparatus are striking, Ed Folsom argues, not least because Whitman had "placed himself in one of the most volatile centers of American political life, as the attorney general's office became the enforcement agency for the new civil rights amendments to the Constitution, outlawing slavery and granting equal protection and suffrage to the freed slaves" (xxxii). Despite the resemblance in their professional employments and their critical agendas of positing alter-national forms of citizenship and belonging in the American political/social order, Whitman adopts a very different mode of narrative critique in his writing than Hawthorne. In contrast to the mode of irony and skepticism with which Hawthorne deconstructs national symbols and narratives, as well as the ambivalence expressed in *The Scarlet Letter* with regard to matters of national privilege, Whitman's *Democratic Vistas* adopts a mode of affirmation that fervently expresses his faith in "a new theory of literary composition" (2010, 76) that would consolidate America's unique and exceptional national character. In this long treatise written in the aftermath of the Civil War, Whitman calls for the birth of a new American "national literature" that would "become the justification and reliance . . . of American democracy" (6). Whitman's essay stresses a need to depart from what he perceives as a "hollowness" in mainstream literature that merely "cop[ied] and reflect[ed] existing surfaces," pandering to the "taste" of the majority, which delighted in "cheap" modes of satire, mockery, and persiflage in verse that was written to "amuse, pass away time, celebrate the beautiful, the refined, the past, or exhibit technical, rhythmic, or grammatical dexterity" (14–15). In its stead, Whitman foresees "a poetry that is bold, modern and all-surrounding" (58), one whose vision is bent in the direction of the future and not the past.

Whitman's envisaging of a new form of hybridized national literature that merges individualism with forms of collective identification and patriotism provides the foundations for his philosophy of American democracy, encapsulated in Abraham Lincoln's famous phrase "the government of the people, by the people, for the people," which Whitman cites in his essay. Specifically, Whitman addresses the need for "a class of native authors, literatures, far different, far higher in grade than any yet known, sacerdotal, modern, fit to cope with our occasions, lands, permeating the whole mass of American mentality, taste, belief, breathing into it a new breath of life, giving it decision, affecting politics far more than the popular superficial suffrage." Whitman foresees this class of authors and literatures as the foundation, the base layer, of political and cultural life in America, as providing "a religious and moral character beneath the political and productive and intellectual bases of the States." Such a foundation, Whitman stresses, is absolutely necessary, for a nation's own distinctive literature is worth more to it than expansion of its territory by land acquisition:[17] "[T]he central point in any nation, and that whence it is itself really sway'd the most, and whence it sways others, is its national literature, especially its archetypal poems. Above all previous lands, a great original literature is surely to become the justification and reliance, (in some respects the sole reliance,) of American democracy" (2010, 6). In fact, Whitman even goes further to emphasize that a solidly democratic, national literature would "give more compaction and more moral identity . . . to these States, than all its Constitutions, legislative and judicial ties" (9).

Published six years after the end of the Civil War, Whitman's essay does not, however, reflect the author's optimism for the future. Rather, he admits his fear that the foundations of the newly unified American nation still possess "conflicting and irreconcilable interiors and the lack of a common skeleton." Nevertheless, with characteristic erudition and intellectual foresight, Whitman proposes that nothing would better solidify the nation's backbone and crystallize its national identity, thus bringing about the "genuine union" of Northern and Southern states, than a new national literature. As he advances,

> [N]othing is plainer than the need, a long period to come, of a fusion of the States into the only reliable identity, the moral and artistic one. . . . The true nationality of the States, the genuine union, when we come to a mortal crisis, is . . . neither the written law, nor . . . self-interest, or common pecuniary or material objects—but the fervid and tremendous IDEA, melting everything else with resistless heat, and solving all lesser and definite distinctions in vast, indefinite, spiritual, emotional power.

Claiming that "self-interest, or common pecuniary or material objects" merely reflect the "hollowness at [the] heart" (2010, 10) of the American condition, Whitman argues that there is a similar tendency toward a "scornful superciliousness" (11) in literature. Appealing to his readers to reject such forms of badinage, mockery, jest, and satire, Whitman entreats them to take on the project of reinventing national literature much more earnestly.

In his introduction to *Nation and Narration*, Homi Bhabha writes of the nation as a historical idea "whose cultural compulsion lies in [its] impossible unity . . . as a symbolic force." The nation's "coming-into-being," he argues, involves its ambivalent entering into a "system of cultural signification." The idea of the nation as a "continuous narrative of national progress" (1990, 1), such as depicted in nationalist discourses, is thus, in Bhabha's view, highly inaccurate. Rather, the idea is one that develops in bursts, in fits and starts, with gaps, discontinuities, and struggle. Bhabha's theories on narrating the nation reiterate just over a century later Whitman's critical observations. The latter's polemic insistence on the importance of a unique national literature that would consolidate and propagate the nation's symbolic and cultural signification indicates a concomitant acknowledgment that the American nation was in a state of fractious disunity at a federal level. Already positing an understanding of the nation as an "ambivalent figure" and underscoring "its conceptual indeterminacy, its wavering between vocabularies" (Bhabha 1990, 2), Whitman's response to the crisis in notions of nationhood, citizenship, and forms of collective identity in the Reconstruction Era is to propose alternative ways of reimagining the nation that departed from its dominant political narratives.

Yet it must also be stressed that Whitman did not seek to do away with the notion of the American nation altogether. Rather, his essay reaffirmed its centrality and importance as a concept, suggesting only an alteration of its existing forms of narrative and textual strategies. Whitman's conviction that literature was the main instrument that would effect a change in American citizens' notions of nationhood and collective identification is illustrated in the following passage, wherein he clearly encourages a "homegrown" American verse that did not merely stem from or look back toward Europe:

> What has fill'd, and fills to-day our intellect, our fancy, furnishing the standards therein, is yet foreign. The great poems, Shakespeare included, are poisonous to the idea of the pride and dignity of the common people, the life-blood of democracy. The models of our literature, as we get it from other lands . . . touch'd by the national test, or tried by the standards of democratic personality . . . wither to ashes. . . . Almost everything that has been written, sung, or stated, of old . . . needs to be re-written, re-sung, re-stated, in terms consistent with the institution of these States, and to come in range and obedient uniformity with them. (2010, 32, 77)

Whitman is adamant that national literature should not be overly influenced by Shakespeare or other "foreign" writers. Rather, American literature must emerge organically from American soil. It must be "vitalized by national, original archetypes" (50) and exemplify "a native expression-spirit" (56). "America demands a poetry," Whitman declares, that "must bend its vision toward the future, more than the past" (59). As he proclaims in the climax of his long treatise, America must bring forth its own national literature that will express its individuality of character, its "non-subordinated soul" (60). By indirectly referring to Emerson and his notion of the "oversoul" (expressed in the latter's essay of the same name from 1841), Whitman clearly indicates that *Democratic Vistas* is also a response to and a revoicing of Emerson's call, in his essay "The Poet" (1844), for a domestic national literature and the rebirth of the American poet to write about the nation's pressing issues. In Whitman's eyes, a nation is not merely represented and reflected by its literature: a homegrown national literature predicated upon the tenets of political democracy in the New World, as opposed to the parliamentary monarchy of Old World Europe, would shore up the American nation's steadfastness of character.

Whitman's bemoaning of the state of contemporary American literature and his entreaty for a new national literature that would both support and enunciate the basic principles of American democracy can be read as a rearticulation, some two decades later, of Hawthorne's fear of a "headless" national fiction that he expressed in the decapitation passages in the prologue to *The Scarlet Letter*. In this respect, both Whitman and Hawthorne conveyed an ambivalent relationship to forms of national sentimentality, national identification, and collective identity. Through literary acts of "civil disobedience" that questioned existing forms of citizenship and national identity, these two writers sought to engender alter-national forms of identification and belonging in the American nation: Hawthorne by proposing a female maternal citizenship centered on the individual (and not the state) body and its affects, and Whitman by calling for the birth of a distinctly American literature that would reinvigorate and disseminate ideas of democracy and nationhood among a still largely divided American nation. A juxtaposition of the two different models of critique adopted by Whitman and Hawthorne illustrates the mixture of affirmation and deconstruction, faith and skepticism that more broadly characterized the cultural and political climate in the United States during the American Renaissance and Reconstruction eras. This climate of ambivalence and duality provided fertile ground for debates on citizenship, national identity, and collective identification, particularly in and through the genre of literature.

PLAYFULLY POLITICAL

· · · · · · · · · ·

The Female Citizen-in-Process in Gail Scott's *Heroine*

In contrast to the ways in which dominant understandings of citizenship and national identity were debated, contested, and unsettled in the writings of Hawthorne and Whitman, my focus in this chapter is on a playful mode of resistance that culminates in a refusal of citizenship altogether. This mode of resistance is situated in the juncture between the political and the textual. It is located both *within* the text and *through* the act of writing—specifically, in the creation of what Montreal writer Gail Scott calls a "new female subject-in-process" (1989 11). Interestingly, this female subject-in-process rejects not only androcentric, heteronormative forms of citizenship[1] but also second-wave feminist ideologies of female empowerment and selfhood (originating in the women's liberation movement in the United States).[2] This deliberate occupying of a space of in-betweenness and liminality that evades categorization signifies a playfully ambivalent and subversive mode of critique that opposes any static or fixed concept of citizenship and national identity. It also challenges the reader to rethink and rework the culturally endowed and gender-biased modes through which national ideologies have been understood and reproduced. I will base the arguments above on a close reading of Scott's experimental novel, *Heroine* (1987).

The female anglophone protagonist of *Heroine*, variously named Gail Scott, Gail, and G.S., occupies a space of subversive play that is enacted not only on the level of content but, first and foremost, on those of form and language. The novel abounds with examples of linguistic play (puns, euphemisms, and the like), ironic wit, dryly humorous observations, allusion, slippage, and metafictional self-referentiality that set the tone of its satirical critique of "variously patriarchal, consumerist, Marxist-revolutionary and even feminist ideologies." As Meredith Quartermain aptly summarizes, these "[i]deologies are shown to be as fictional as novels when it comes to the real, living bodies they act upon. The work of fiction is to undo assumptions about its limits, formalities, and frontiers with opposing terms such as fact or reality" (2012, 115). "Reality," in Scott's novel, is set in the temporal framework of a continuous present, a "running self-reflexive commentary about now" (Scott 1989, 82) that undermines conventional linear structures of plot with a beginning, middle, and end. In the frame story, the protagonist and narrator, G.S., is lying in a bathtub in her room at the Waikiki Tourist Rooms in Montreal, Quebec, which she is renting in order to perform "an experiment of living in the present" (1987, 14). The novel takes place within the time frame of one day, with the narrator masturbating and thinking about her novel, a work of fictional autobiography, that she wants to write and feels she should be writing, whose conceptual protagonist is the eponymous "heroine."[3] It is October 1980, and the protagonist/narrator is listening to a program on the radio commemorating the tenth anniversary of the October Crisis in Montreal.[4] Through the news reportage, the past seeps in to inform a continuous present, and G.S.'s memories of the politically turbulent 1970s merge with the impending bleakness of the 1980s (under a Conservative government and a no vote on the Quebec Referendum that proposed secession from Canada).

Indeed, Gail Scott's "autobiografiction"—a term coined by Erin Wunker to denote "fiction that self-consciously draws the reader's attention to the possibility that it is, perhaps, autobiographical" (2007, 149)—rejects the idea of selfhood as unitary or singular in favor of subjectivity as process and plural. The female citizen-subject is therefore one "in the process of becoming" (Scott 1987, 22), yet Scott playfully undermines even this very process of becoming itself, deferring the point of completion. In Scott's autobiografictional novel, the narrative swirls in circular fashion, repeating and folding back upon itself, eschewing linear progression and indefinitely postponing the act of fulfillment and climax.

The circular structure of the narrative and the repetitions and retellings of the narrator's tale in the form of flashbacks signify a fracturing and subversion of the structures of "masculine" linear narration. As Camille Norton argues, "When a narrator discards the authority implicit in her position, she places herself in a theoretical relation to 'story,' to the idea of what a story is. As a result, she actively revises what 'story' means, and for women writers this revision of genre is a political act. . . . Scott struggles with the conventions of genre to make another kind of story—to construct a conceptual frame through which the heroine becomes intelligible" (2002, 26–27). Traditionally, "stories" that objectify women and depict female desire are typically characterized by what Rachel DuPlessis describes as their "plots of seduction, courtship, the energies of quest deflected into sexual downfall, the choice of a marriage partner, the melodramas of beginning, middle, and end, the trajectories of sexual arousal and release" (1985, 151). The narrator of Scott's *Heroine*, however, "doesn't submit to the tradition of either victim or bride-to-be." Subverting the main thrust of the male Bildungsroman, *Heroine* does not "develop character through plot and closure" (Markotic 2002, 38). Instead, the narrative—which can be described as what Virginia Woolf called an exercise in "mind thinking" (1953, 140)—languorously engages in the establishment of a pleasurable female "self-in-process," playfully arching toward not resolution but the continuation and infinite prolongation of the desirous process of becoming. As Nicole Markotic aptly summarizes, the narrator "doesn't desire completion; she doesn't desire ending. She desires desire, and its lack of imposed borders" (2002, 40).

Accordingly, *Heroine* eschews linear modes of fictional composition; through its repeated flashbacks, the work "flattens linear time, by folding and expanding time," stretching the moment into a continuous feminine present that challenges the linear progression of the "conventional patriarchal novel structure" (Quartermain 2012, 117). The intransigence of the attitudes of the "New Man," a concept of the model citizen in Communist ideology who would be selfless, erudite, and passionate about spreading the socialist revolution, are further ridiculed in a passage wherein the narrator recalls her ex-lover Jon saying with conviction, "[T]he human race has but two choices, barbarism or Marxist revolution." Jon is a parody of the "New Man," and the narrator's response to his reductive if impassioned statement, in which he sincerely believes there are only two alternatives in life, is to "laug[h] out loud, nearly hooting" (Scott 1987, 40). G.S.'s playful but also willful and subversive laughter characterizes her response to the androcentric revolutionary ideologies that sought change in the sociopolitical climate of the 1970s and early 1980s in North America.

This playfulness and subversion on the levels of narrative strategy and form are also reflected in the shifting and multiperspectival frames of reference ("the scene shifts"; "[t]he lens sweeps down"; "the lens turns" [Scott 1987, 10, 24, 54]) and the metafictional strategy of the novel. As already mentioned, in the frame narrative, the protagonist ("G.S."[5]) is lying in a bathtub in her room at the Waikiki Tourist Rooms, trying to bring herself to orgasm while also planning her novel. The story of the heroine in G.S.'s novel closely resembles/mirrors her own story until, at the (tentative) close of the novel, on its very last page, the identities of both women have merged into a singular "She—" (183). The use of the female pronoun as the emphatic last word of Scott's experimental novel indicates that the work is less an autobiografictional text about her "heroine," the narrator G.S., than one about the process of writing that heroine into being. In an act of female appropriation, the last chapter of Scott's book is titled "Play It Again, S," whereby the "S" presumably stands for "She" and not "Sam," as in the title of the famous 1972 film starring Woody Allen.[6] As Mark Monmonier has observed, "In Scott's writing, lines are drawn over territorial bodies, political bodies, cultural bodies, gendered bodies. Not surprisingly, writing, like cartography, proves to be less a descriptive activity than an investigative/interpretive one" (1991, 1). Indeed, *Heroine*'s metafictional text not only calls attention to itself as an investigative narrative, it directs the reader's notice to this very process of calling attention. This is playfully enacted by the two minor characters of the novel, a "Black tourist" and a "grey woman," who interrupt the circular flow of the narrative. In a metafictional moment, the black tourist in G.S.'s novel asks two comrades, "You tell me: how would you treat me in a novel? Among other things, I bet at every mention you'd state my color" (1987, 78). As if to prove her own character wrong, or in a willful gesture of refusal to prove him right, from that point on in the novel, the unnamed black tourist is referred to by Gail Scott, the author, only as "a tourist." Throughout the novel, the process of writing is also commented on in metafictional interruptions on the level of the frame narrative. G.S. reminds herself to write with "[clarity]. The trick is to tell a story. Keeping things in the same time register" (31). At various points in the novel, she tells herself to "cut the melodrama . . . [and] the pessimism" (31, 34), not to be maudlin and, in a pun on the word *heroin(e)* as drug and female protagonist, to "pull myself together, to get a fix on the heroine of my novel" (61). At the end of the book, having made the heroine feel humiliated and hurt because she has just read a letter Jon's lover wrote to him, G.S. interrupts herself and thinks, "NO. I can't let her disintegrate like this" (170).

In this vein, the narrator G.S. struggles to ward off the urge toward pessimism and melancholia, two dispositions traditionally marked as "feminine,"[7] in her attempts to bring her novel to completion. Here, Scott satirically explodes the stereotypical masculinist diagnoses of the symptoms of female melancholia.[8] The narrator G.S. languishes in French feminist notions of depression and melancholia as posited, for example, by Julia Kristeva. In her seminal essay "On the Melancholic Imaginary,"[9] Kristeva defines female melancholia as "a sorrowful pleasure," a "lugubrious intoxication" (1987, 5).[10] Suffering, and the writing of suffering, therefore becomes, in Kristeva's terms, "an 'in excess,' a force, a sensual pleasure" (12). What Kristeva describes as the "sensuality of suffering's pleasure" (13) is relevant to the narrator's extended act of female (self-)pleasure in Scott's *Heroine*. Although the narrator is masturbating in a bathtub and trying to bring herself to orgasm, her attempts are, perhaps *pleasurably*, enabled rather than frustrated by the palpable absence of her ex-lover Jon. In the novel that G.S. plans on writing, the heroine, too, is torn between leaving and reconciling with her ex-lover. At the end of the novel that G.S. writes, the heroine gives in to her pain and visits Jon again, and they make love, which gives her pleasure at the same time as it fills her with pain. This episode alludes to post-structuralist theories of pleasure in relation to the subject, especially Lacan's theory of *jouissance* beyond Freud's pleasure principle. In his lecture "The Ethics of Psychoanalysis" (1959–60; see Lacan 1992), Lacan states that in transgressing the prohibitions imposed on the subject's enjoyment, in going beyond the threshold or limit of pleasure, there is no longer pleasure but pain. For Lacan, jouissance is also intimately associated with a fear of castration and with the death drive. By focusing on female (self)-pleasure and appropriating Lacan's theories of jouissance and pain, Scott's narrative thus reinscribes the masculinist logic of the pleasure principle.

The novel also complicates the distinction between *plasir* (pleasure) and *jouissance* (bliss) drawn by Roland Barthes in *The Pleasure of the Text* (1975). According to Barthes, the "readerly" text, which does not challenge the reader's subject position, leads to the experience of pleasure, while the "writerly" text, which fractures existing structures, transgresses literary codes, and allows the reader to transcend her or his subject position, offers the experience of bliss. In embodying the narrative features of both the "readerly" and "writerly" text through its metafictional structure and the use of a frame narrative, Gail Scott's *Heroine* complicates Barthes's binary division and suggests that every text is more accurately a combination of both. By extension, the novel can be interpreted as Scott's critique of the androcentric tradition of psychoanalytical thought as represented by Freud, Lacan, and Barthes. Instead, *Heroine* playfully reinscribes the concept of jouissance in feminist critical theory in the early 1970s, especially in the works of Hélène Cixous, Luce Irigaray, Monique Wittig, and Julia Kristeva, wherein female pleasure is regarded as the source of female empowerment. More specifically, the narrator chooses a mode of playful ambivalence, a pluralist in-betweenness amid pleasure and pain that foregrounds the process of writing the "willful" body, the unruly female subject. Lying in her "nice warm tub" (Scott 1987, 61), "feeling cozy" (106), the narrator chooses an autoerotic mode of being in the continuous present that prolongs fulfillment. She chooses, in Kristeva's terms, "a voluptuous suffering" (1987, 13); ironically, it is this suffering that drives the narrative forward (or onward in its circular pattern), thus avoiding stasis even as it indefinitely postpones completion.

The narrator of *Heroine* is therefore not an unambiguously autonomous (Irigaray 1985) female subject. G.S.'s obsessive thoughts about her ex-lover Jon drive her toward the "thick black line . . . of pain" (1987, 171–73) and prevent her from unequivocally embodying the role of female citizen and liberated "New Woman."[11] In fact, Scott's novel adopts a rather tongue-in-cheek attitude to the feminist, lesbian, and women's liberation movements of the 1970s that demanded equality with the male sex (culminating in the passing of the Equal Rights Act by the Canadian Parliament in 1972).[12] In this sense, the narrator of Scott's *Heroine* seeks to "avoids the dilemma . . . of trying to make it on patriarchal terms—by situating herself beyond history"; this, however, is not an easy task. Scott therefore poses the question of how the female writer can exist as a speaking subject *without* limiting herself to the position of 1970s and early 1980s second-wave feminism where, in a turn of phrase from Hamlet's "To be or not to be" speech, "to be" would mean to liberate oneself from the restraints of patriarchal structures, to "kick and scrape our way out of the margins of patriarchy (the kitchen, the wife of the traditional heterosexual couple)" (Scott 1989, 121), and "not to be" at all is clearly not an option. In other words, in *Heroine*, Scott addresses the conundrum of how to locate a "subject-in-the-feminine" in writing without defining the feminine as an ex negativo of the masculine. The goal, therefore, becomes to transcend gendered stereotypes altogether, to find another vocabulary that adequately describes the mode of female subjectivity characterized by its playful yet politically subversive stance. After all, as the narrator of *Heroine* says impishly, "even feminists have their needs" (1987, 37), and the latter should not be repressed by a new form of feminist "liberation" that encourages freedom from longing and want, for this would effectively reproduce the patriarchal repression of woman's desire.

As Scott thus maintains, the challenge is to write into being "a new kind of heroine":

> A new heroine who is not merely the feminine of hero (*a name given to men of superhuman strength, courage, ability, favored by the Gods*). Nor heroine as it was implied in the 70s wave of Anglo-American feminist criticism. That is the (female) hero as a logical extension of nineteenth-century bourgeois notions of enlightenment.... And by extension, also of Marxist ideology. . . . In the latter paradigm, the (female) hero must end up successful in their specific project, be it personal, professional or "revolutionary." For there can only be victors and the victims, the former the subjects of progressive novels, the latter censored. (1989, 123)

The task of the female writer, in Scott's terms, is therefore to write from "a space of *herself-defined*" (126), a space of plurality or, in Gayle Rubin's terms, a radical "sexual pluralism" (1993, 171) that resists strict categorization and rigid ideologies. Scott expounds, "As I see it, 'selfhood' for women is not being one. . . . It is not being an essential core or a singular definition; it is process and it is plural" (1989, 50). Accordingly, the narrator of *Heroine* wants to "live large" ("*Mon Héroine a envie de vivre grande*") and in the plural (time frames, spaces, identities), sensing that this "is where the transgression starts" (120). Indeed, Scott herself admits that, in her writing, she is often torn between "certain expectations of my feminist community and my desire to be excessive" (129). The "revolutionary" anticipation of a female (re)invention of herself in writing, is, therefore, less enticing than a mode of excess and noncontainment. Consequently, Scott's writing proposes a model of indefinite postponement, of incompletion, that resists closure or "the tendency to become" (130) in favor of a more radical "dangl[ing] dangerously on the edge of meaning" (131). As she writes, it is the transgressive leap through "the layers of patriarchal 'meaning'" (132) that "moves [the female writer] beyond cognizance towards excess, towards the danger zones" (133).

The protagonist and narrator of Scott's *Heroine*, therefore, resists the strictures of identity politics in the form of categorization as a heterosexual female lover, second-wave feminist, lesbian, or Marxist revolutionary. Her "resistance to drawing rigid boundaries around herself (she's herself, yet also somehow linked to other women—neither unary nor 'deconstructed') *makes her incomprehensible to the male modernist*" (Scott 1989, 125). She refuses to be understood, legible, comprehensible under the scrutiny of the gaze of the "New Man"; her plurality encompasses the typecasts of "'revolutionary' but also petty bourgeois, the imperfect feminist and the badly-loved woman" (82). Rejecting the principles that delineate how avant-garde feminists and Marxist revolutionaries "should" behave—no hysteria (Scott 1987, 19), no monogamy (17), no melodrama (31), no pessimism (34), no nostalgia (50), no exaggeration (102) and the need to "be more rational" (84)—the narrator of *Heroine* suggests that female subjectivity can be confined neither to 1970s masculinist "revolutionary" rhetoric nor to that of a second-wave feminist politics of liberation. She is less a feminist revolutionary than a radical pluralist[13] who willfully occupies a space of incompleteness and liminality but also of multiplicity and overlap.

Heroine can thus be fruitfully be read in conversation with Gayle Rubin's essay "Thinking Sex: Notes for a Radical Theory of the Politics of Sexuality," which was originally published three years before Scott's experimental novel. Rubin makes the point that "from the late 1940s until the early 1960s, erotic communities whose activities did not fit the postwar American dream drew intense persecution." These "willful" communities, which included homosexuals, were regarded as sexual "deviants" (1993, 145.). According to Rubin's model of "the sex hierarchy," which proposes an alternative paradigm, one that transcends the distinction drawn by the majority of society between "good sex" ("normal, natural, healthy and holy" sexual practices) and "bad sex" ("abnormal, unnatural, sick and sinful" practices), masturbation is an undecided "major area of contest" (154). As Rubin argues,

> Modern Western societies appraise sex acts according to a hierarchical system of sexual value. Marital, reproductive heterosexuals

are alone at the top [of the] erotic pyramid. Clamoring below are unmarried monogamous heterosexuals in couples, followed by most other heterosexuals. *Solitary sex floats ambiguously.* The powerful nineteenth-century stigma on masturbation lingers in less potent, modified forms, such as the idea that masturbation is an inferior substitute for partnered encounters. (151; my emphasis)

The narrator of Gail Scott's *Heroine*, G.S., who "floats ambiguously" in a bathtub, masturbating and thinking about the novel she wants to write, can thus be read as a willful protagonist. Her stubbornness and persistence in engaging in her solitary act of sexual pleasure responds, I would argue, to Rubin's call for "[a] radical theory of sex [that] must identify, describe, explain, and denounce erotic injustice and sexual oppression" (149). Rejecting the idea that "masturbation is an inferior substitute for partnered encounters," Scott depicts the orgasm not as a "little death" (the French term for "orgasm" being *la petite mort*) but as the culmination of a process of becoming.[14] Sexual arousal, in this instance, is a performative enactment, an act of what can be termed "sexual citizenship."[15]

The narrator G.S. thus refuses conventional, patriarchal, and heteronormative notions of citizenship as well as homogenous forms of national, political, and ideological identifications. In so doing, she is also enacting what Scott herself has termed "one of the writer's most important tasks: a constant, rigorous criticism of her nation's dominant culture" (1989, 30). The *private* space of the bathroom/bathtub, which substitutes the *public* spaces of the nation (historically equated as the dominant sphere of citizenship), becomes, in effect, a space of willful citizenship-in-process. Accordingly, the narrator is the dissident subject who rejects, in Gayle Rubin's terms, "good, normal, natural, blessed" sexuality and opts instead for "bad, abnormal, unnatural, damned" sexual behavior (1993, 154). In doing so, she challenges aspects of sexual behavior and expression that have been deemed unacceptable.

Scott's *Heroine* hence voices the abject in writing, exploding taboos and stereotypes of the female subject in history. At the same time that she chides herself for being "hysterical," for "hysteria is not suitable in a revolutionary woman" (1987, 19), the heroine also satirically mocks the common diagnosis of female hysteria (by male physicians) common in the nineteenth century and its various depictions in medical discourse and literature.[16] The term can be traced back to ancient Greece, where female hysteria was thought to be caused by a "wandering uterus" (hence the term's etymology, as the Greek word for uterus is ὑστέρα, or *hystera*) or by a blockage of vaginal fluids resulting from a lack of sexual intercourse (it was thus also referred to as the "widow's disease"). The symptoms of female hysteria apparently ranged from nervousness and irritability to nausea, dizziness, and shortness of breath. Significantly, the common "treatment" for female hysteria was either manual stimulation by hydrotherapy (stimulating the vagina with a jet of water), or the use of electric-powered vibrators/dildos, first patented in 1870, so that women could reach the state of "hysterical paroxysm" (orgasm).[17] The female narrator of Scott's *Heroine*, who is in the bathtub letting the stream of water massage her "widow's beak" (126), her "small point" (36), for her own sexual gratification, thus cheekily critiques and inverts patriarchal and misogynist attitudes toward female hysteria patients in the nineteenth century who had "a tendency to cause trouble" (Maines 1999, 23). As the narrator lies "with her legs up," "treatment" becomes a pleasurable activity ("Oh faucet your warm stream is linked to my smiling face" [Scott 1987, 16]) for her.

The narrator of Scott's *Heroine* is therefore an autoerotic "female subject-in-process," "not the 'self' as a (feminist or otherwise) predetermined figure, but a complex tissue of texts, experience, evolving in the very act of writing" (Scott 1989, 11). For Scott, the process of writing becomes a political undertaking that necessitates "deconstructing traditional fictions about women" (62). *Heroine* can thus be read as an example of what Nicole Brossard termed "fiction-theory" (1977),[18] or a form of self-conscious feminist counter-discourse that emerged in Quebec in the late 1970s in opposition to the patriarchal, androcentric culture of fiction writing. As Gail Scott delineates, "fiction-theory" is characterized by a reflexive technique of "doubling-back over the texture of the text," "break[ing] continuity (the continuity of patriarchal mythologies) into fragments in order to question syntax/content." It is this "habit of stopping to reflect on the process within the text itself" (1989, 62) that characterizes *Heroine*'s cyclical pattern of narrative flow and interruption, repetition and fragmentation, as illustrated in the following example from the text:

> Clarity. The trick is to tell a story. Keeping things in the same time register. . . .
> Oh Mama why'd you put this hole in me?

> Stop. This is the city, 1980. . . . Cut the melodrama, two lesbians
> told me back in 77. . . .
> Oh my big mouth. My hungry mouth. Mother why did you
> make this hole in me? . . .
> No. cut the pessimism. (1987, 31–34)

The "holes" or gaps in the text leave spaces into which the reader can read her own (racial, cultural, linguistic, and so on) difference, hence challenging assumptions of sameness and uniformity that characterize patterns of dominance in society (Scott 1989, 53). The text of *Heroine* abandons conventional linear narrative and plot, playing with the "grammatical units of time represented by the sentence" (80) in order to create a form of "cyclical ascension and descent" that clearly contrasts with "the dominant pattern of linear rise to climax" (124).

Scott's long essay "Paragraphs Blowing on a Line," which comprises twenty-eight diary entries written in the same time period she was working on *Heroine*, provides an intertextual account of the process of the latter's composition. In "Entry 4," the author notes that there is "still not the semblance of a narrative, only the craziest images. . . . A bell in my head says Produce, produce. But I can't just sit down and write a novel about X. It all happens in the process of writing" (1989, 80–81) In "Entry 9," Scott reiterates that *Heroine* was conceived as "exploration, not prescriptive writing" (86). As a result, the narrative *itself* wrestles out of the author's grasp; it is willful, unwieldy, resistant, transgressive, discordant, and full of slippages. It "exclude[s] a straightforward resolution of the story" (87), foregoing "closure (firm conclusions)" for "spaces, questions," and "other possible representations [that] leave themselves open for reader intervention" (102). Evading any overarching structure or predetermined form, the text refuses to be "trapped in the preconceived notions ascribed to words by ideology" (89). As Scott writes in "Entry 17," "I shall clearly, willfully, have to invent this narrator as I go along" (95).

The references to shifting frames of reference, the lens through which the black male tourist surveys the city of Quebec, "sweeping down" (Scott 1987, 24), zooming in, and panning out, help to move along the "story" of the novel, the "line of narrative" that is "woven intertextually, encompassing elements of a community, past and present," "reconstructing the historically absent female subject" (Scott 1989, 75). In Scott's *Heroine*, therefore, the limits of conventional form are exposed, rejected, and transcended/transgressed in favor of a "pluralist language of spectacle." Scott expresses a certain "bored[om] with narrative" and a penchant for "inventing a new kind of play," (133), one that, as in Virginia Woolf's diary entry from 1927, foregrounds "Woman": "*Woman thinks . . . / He does. / Organ plays. / She writes*" (Woolf 1953, 103, cited in Scott 1987, 133).

Indeed, allusions to Virginia Woolf's envisioning of a grammar of "She" recur throughout Scott's *Heroine*. In contrast with the first word of the novel, "Sir" (Scott 1987, 9), which "signifies the power of patriarchy, and the inherited imbalance of who addresses whom" (Markotic 2002, 38), the last word of the book is simply, "She—" (Scott 1987, 183), with a dash of incompletion, of open-endedness, referring to the female subject still in the process of becoming.[19] This is an allusion to Woolf's significant phrase "I want 'She'" from a diary entry written in 1927. "But who is she?" Woolf writes. "I am very anxious that she should have no name. I don't want a Lavinia or a Penelope: I want 'She'" (1953, 140). Woolf's "I want 'She'" (as opposed to "I want 'her'") abolishes and rewrites the conventional rules of English grammar and syntax. As Christina Froula argues, "to want 'She' is to want woman as *subject* not *object*" (2005, 200; my emphasis). Rejecting female characters who have suffered at the hands of canonical male writers, such as "Virgil's Lavinia, a pawn in Aeneas's empire-building, Shakespeare's violated Lavinia, writing her story in sand in bloody stumps, or Homer's Penelope, stuck at home during life's adventure" (Froula 2005, 200), Woolf envisions a "She" who becomes both the private "I" and the impersonal pronoun "one," who writes, as Froula has aptly put it, "as a woman who has forgotten that she [as] a woman *might write*" (201).

Similarly, the heroine/narrator of Gail Scott's *Heroine* is an "unmarked" woman because she refuses to be labeled or pigeonholed, because she insists on "being always in a process of becoming," "refusing to see things as binary opposites like 'good—bad,' even 'masculine—feminine' as much as she refuses closed endings, fixed meanings." In Scott's own words, *Heroine* proposes a "new narrative" that aligns itself with "the ambivalence and excess of carnival." Referencing Mikhail Bakhtin's notion of the carnivalesque,[20] Scott's playfully political novel *Heroine* resounds with "the laughter that in the same breath assures transgression." It is a laughter that subverts and liberates through humor, burlesque, chaos, and sacrilege, upending hierarchies in a "world upside down" (Scott 1989, 134) and suspending, for one moment, the dominant codes and rules of society. This playfully ambivalent and politically subversive mode of critique that Bakhtin locates in the genre of the novel is espoused in the experimental, metafictional text of *Heroine*.[21] This mode of playful rebellion is less aligned with Cixous's laugh of the Medusa (who is, after all, a Gorgon or dreadful female figure subsequently beheaded by the male hero Perseus) than with the impish, mischievous, deliberately ambiguous grin of the Cheshire cat in Lewis Carroll's *Alice's Adventures in Wonderland*. The novel proffers less a Cixousian sense of female liberation through writing[22] than a critique of masculinist authority and hegemonic structures in society. The polyphonic quality of Scott's novel—as rendered by the voices and thoughts of minor characters such as the gray woman, the black tourist, Marie, and the Quebecois feminists—de-privilege any authoritative voice on matters of citizenship and (national, gendered, sexual) identity. The narrative has come full circle to the French-inflected accent of the Quebecois guard who tells the black tourist in the very first section of the novel that he can "on-ly put ca-na-dian monee in that machine" and that it is "an infraction" to put "foreign objects nor foreign monee in that macheen." By the provisional end of the novel, the narrator G.S. is no longer "a c . . ." (1987, 9) (an objectified, vulgar "cunt") but the female subjective personal pronoun "She—." In this respect, Scott deconstructs the culturally endowed and gender-biased modes through which national identification and sentiment have been constructed and proliferated.

In fact, the novel questions the very notion of national identification. In a sequence that recalls the author's own anglophone background, the narrator of *Heroine* expresses a lack of affinity with the Quebecois nationalists, Marxist revolutionaries, and francophone feminists even though she attends the demonstrations and meetings organized by them. Part of this has to do with the fact that the other francophone feminists and lesbians do not see her as one of them because she was raised in an Anglo-Protestant family. As Scott explains,

> In the late 70s, the idea that we might rupture patriarchal fictions by letting what we heard/sensed of our female bodies spill over into a new kind of writing seemed dazzlingly subversive. *Yet, as I read Cixous and other new French feminists, I felt a strangeness: a feeling my relationship to my body might be different than theirs. I began to think about how one's body is not only gendered, but is also linguistic, cultural, economic.* So the question for me became, what of the relationship

between writing and the rhythms, pulsions, memories of my Protestant body . . . mediated by an English-language inscription in-the-
feminine? (1989, 16; my emphasis)

As an English-Canadian/Anglo-Protestant writer in Quebec, Scott is highly
aware of "standing outside not only the other but also the image of self projected by the other" (1989, 16). Calling attention to the revolt in language and
form that characterized Quebecois women's writing in the 1970s,[23] Scott points
out the necessity of considering the different histories of progressive struggle in (anglophone) Canada and (francophone) Quebec. Hearing the call for
"female-sexed texts" (38) and an "écriture feminine"[24] by French feminists such
as Luce Irigaray and Hélène Cixous, Scott nevertheless notes the ambiguity of
this literary term for the anglophone Protestant Canadian women writer. As
she writes, "[M]aybe the call does not suit our English-Canadian needs. We
have to find our *own* solutions—and debunk our *own* myths" (39).[25]

Scott also expands on the differences she perceives between Quebecois
and anglophone Canadian definitions of and associations with the term *écriture féminine*:

In Québec, for example, *l'écriture féminist* (feminist writing) has
generally been rejected in favor of *l'écriture au féminin* (writing in-
the-feminine), because *l'écriture féminist* is felt to point towards a
content-oriented (and often narrowly political) interpretation of
text. While, in English, the term "feminist writing" is preferred to
"writing in-the-feminine," because, in our language "writing in-the-
feminine" fails to invoke the assertive experimental notes of female-
gendered writing that the French *l'écriture au féminin* implies.

Indeed, in response to the question posed in her women's writing group,
"*Qu'est-ce qui est incontournable dans le feminism quand on écrit?*"[26] (What of
one's feminist consciousness is essential/necessary in writing?) Scott's answer
is a "transgress[ing]" of the "limits of vision through the *play* of language"
(Scott 1989, 116). Likewise, the narrator of *Heroine* playfully avoids adopting a "narrow" or distinct identity politics by remaining in the realms of
experimentation and transgression, in the process of becoming. She oscillates
between Anglo-Protestant Canadian and Franco-Catholic Quebecois dispositions, refusing to be pinned down and acknowledging the concurrence

and mutual influence of both perspectives in debates surrounding national identity and separatism that had their origins in the period of sociopolitical change in the 1960s in Quebec (commonly referred to as the "Quiet Revolution") in the run-up to the October Crisis of 1970.

The marked divergence between (Franco-Catholic) Quebecois and (Anglo-Protestant) Canadian perceptions of the October Crisis are, according to Scott, "part of two ongoing different narratives in what is officially a common history" (1989, 45). This is depicted in an episode in *Heroine* wherein the narrator remembers how the Parti Québécois won the Quebec General Election on November 15, 1976. G.S. recalls, "A comrade looks at me, LA SEULE ANGLAISE, and says, almost worried: 'Well now how do you feel?'" (1987, 89–90). As a response, the narrator feels forced to raise her glass and shout, "*Vive le Québec libre*" (90) to demonstrate her support for the Parti Québécois and its cause, namely, the advocacy of national sovereignty for the province of Quebec that would entail its secession from Canada and its establishment as a sovereign state. *Heroine* therefore centrally "raise[s] the issue of how the English heroine (of a novel) might look against the background of contemporary Québec" (89). As Scott writes,

> She [the narrator of *Heroine*] also, somewhat perversely, perceives her body as absence inasmuch as it speaks a minority language in the Québec context (albeit the traditional language of the bosses). It is limited, outside of where things are really at. Everything happens in French. And my narrator prefers that the meaning be in another language. For she has consciously chosen her minority situation—which is very different than being colonized, when meaning happens in the other language and it's out of your power to do anything about it. (1989, 96–97)

Like the narrator, the author Gail Scott "has consciously chosen her minority situation" as an anglophone woman writer living in Montreal and writing predominantly in English. Yet she admits that her political sensibilities have inevitably been influenced and "colored by the politics and struggles of *les Québécois(es)*" (46). Indeed, Scott has described *Heroine* and her other Montreal novels as her attempts to transcribe the musicality of the mix of languages she encounters in the city onto the written page, to capture in writing the two very disparate social and political cultures in which she is immersed.

Heroine therefore maps out the complex and, at times, highly ambivalent relationship between self and nation, between forms of narration and the construction of national identity/identification from the perspective of a subject who has chosen her minority status in a bicultural and bilingual province. As Anthony Appiah and Amy Gutmann contend, "[T]he identity of the nation is tied up with the stories of individuals . . . [that] help to fashion a national narrative" (1996, 9). Self and nation are therefore intertwined through a process that Bina Toledo Freiwald terms "mutual mirroring" (2002, 17), which she describes as follows: "Nation offers the self (through the process of interpellation) an identity as a subject-of-the-nation, while individual subjects' autobiographical acts can (be made to) serve as both a model and a medium for the construction of the collective subject-nation" (18). By calling the unitary "self"/"citizen" into question and substituting it with a "self-in-process"/"citizen-in-process," the narrative of *Heroine* interrupts the process of identification between "self" and nation. Via its cyclical narrative structure, its repetitions, its mirrorings, and its merging of past and present temporalities, as well as its interspersion of French sentences that remain deliberately untranslated into English, the novel undermines "the idea of the nation as a continuous narrative of national progress" (Bhabha 1990, 1) and articulates the ambivalence of the concept of nation, especially in a Canadian context. In doing so, Scott's text adopts a discursive approach to the nation, whereby it is conceptualized and constituted in the process of its articulation rather than assumed as a given entity. In this respect, the text of *Heroine* can be regarded as an example of "ambivalent narration" that, according to Homi Bhabha, "holds culture at its most productive position, as a force for 'subordinating, fracturing, diffusing, reproducing'" (1990, 3, citing Edward Said). Such ambivalence is playful but also a deliberate intervention; it is a literary strategy that forces its readers to consider the "transgressive boundaries and 'interruptive' interiorit[ies]" (Bhabha 1990, 5) of the nation as a construct. In Scott's novel, Quebec and, by implication, Canada, becomes contested cultural territory, "eternally marked by [internal] cultural difference and the heterogeneous histories of contending peoples" (299).

Scott's *Heroine* therefore depicts how notions of identity and belonging become particularly fraught in the context of a political discourse driven by the dominant trope of the nation. The experimental novel comments on the political situation in Quebec, wherein cultural and linguistic differences and affiliations create not only social and economic tension but also contact spaces[27] of disjuncture, conflict, inequality, exclusion, multiplicity, and ambiguity. This is represented by the deliberate lapses and repetitions in the narrative that frustrate the text's linear progression or development. The shifts in perspectives, angles, viewpoints, and levels of narration create a discontinuity that playfully disrupts the binaries of public/exteriority versus private/interiority. The "intrusion" of intertextual references, including snippets of song lyrics, poems, newspaper headlines, and political slogans, also interrupts the flow of the narrative and delays its conclusion. Playfully political, the narrative of *Heroine* reinscribes the city's public and private spaces, transgressing the physical and mental boundaries that segregate its communities. The novel demonstrates that these spaces in Montreal—and, by extension, the Canadian nation—cannot simply be glossed over or encapsulated by strict political ideologies or prevailing categories of difference. Slippery when wet, the autoerotic female subject-in-process of Gail Scott's *Heroine* willfully resists and contests masculinist dominant ideas of citizenship and national identity, metafictionally questioning, contesting, and interrogating the ways in which prevailing national ideologies and homogenous "stories"/narratives of nation have been reproduced and disseminated in "multicultural" Canada.

3

WILLFULNESS AND
THE WAYWARD CITIZEN

· · · · · · · · · ·

Philip Roth's American Trilogy (*American Pastoral*,
I Married a Communist, and *The Human Stain*)

This chapter turns to the figure of the "willful" citizen-subject, who was perceived by the government as a threat to the political legitimacy and sovereignty of the American nation in the second half of the twentieth century. In particular, I will focus on how this "wayward" citizen-subject occupies a position of political resistance from which to affectively reimagine culturally endowed modes of national identification, hence contesting her or his exclusion from nation-centric discourses of collective identity and citizenship. My critical analysis will be based on a close reading of Philip Roth's American trilogy (*American Pastoral*, 1997; *I Married a Communist*, 1998; and *The Human Stain*, 2000), which attempts to reinscribe the dominant narratives of the nation, national identity, and collective identification in the post–World War II era, when the notion of "Americanness" was in crisis and undergoing transformation. All three novels thus variously question, challenge, and reconfigure traditional definitions of citizenship by exposing the discontinuous, fragmented, contradictory, and ambiguous elements of civil life in postwar America.

Willfulness as a Strategy: *American Pastoral* versus America Amok

At the heart of Philip Roth's novel *American Pastoral*, the protagonist, Seymour Levov, a third-generation American Jew from Newark, is accused by his brother of buying into an idealized national fantasy of America that does not exist. Jerry Levov's invective forms the core of the novel's critique of the "American pastoral":

> You wanted Miss America? Well, you've got her, with a vengeance—she's your daughter! You wanted to be a real American jock, a real American marine, a real American hotshot with a beautiful Gentile babe on your arm? You longed to belong like everybody else to the United States of America? Well, you do now, big boy, thanks to your daughter. The reality of this place is right up in your kisser now. With the help of your daughter you're as deep in the shit as a man can get, the real American crazy shit. America amok! America amuck! (Roth 1997, 277)

In Jerry Levov's bid to make his brother aware of what the "real" America is, he reminds him that Seymour's daughter Merry blew up the post office in Old Rimrock, New Jersey. The year is 1968, and Merry's bomb is an act of protest against America's involvement in Vietnam, a symbolic gesture of, in a nod to the radical leftist Weathermen[1] slogan, "bring[ing] the war home to America" (76). Rejecting what she perceives as her parents' bourgeois obsession with living as good, law-abiding citizens "in the American grain" (30) surrounded by "quaint Americana" (68), Merry Levov cuts her ties with her family and runs away from home. In doing so, she delivers a huge blow to her father, who is forced to question his "unconscious oneness with America" (20) and to reflect on his heretofore unscrutinized "liv[ing] in America the way he lived inside his own skin" (213). Merry's bomb represents an interjection into the smooth fabric of Middle American[2] existence, "disrupt[ing] the anticipated American future that was simply to have unrolled out of the solid American past" (85). As the "willful" female protagonist of *American Pastoral*, she becomes, as the narrator of the novel, Nathan Zuckerman, puts it, "the daughter who transports [Seymour Levov] out of the longed-for American pastoral and into . . . the Indigenous American berserk" (86).

American Pastoral is the first of a series of novels written by Philip Roth in the late 1990s and 2000 commonly referred to as his American trilogy.

The trilogy constitutes Roth's fictional study of three of the most significant decades in post-1945 U.S. history that pitted prewar American idealism and New Deal optimism against a postwar "America [run] amok." The periods are the McCarthy era of the 1950s, which witnessed the anti-Communist investigations of the House Un-American Activities Committee (HUAC) during the height of the Second Red Scare; the 1960s in the wake of Kennedy's assassination and during Lyndon B. Johnson's presidency, a period of social turmoil and political revolution, not least against America's involvement in Vietnam; and the 1990s, a decade of culture wars in which political correctness conflicted with the nation's obsession over the Monica Lewinsky affair that led to President Bill Clinton's impeachment.[3] At the center of the three novels lie protagonists who are regarded as willful because their political beliefs contest notions of "Americanness" and what it means to be an exemplary, law-abiding American citizen in post–World War II America amid Cold War paranoia and sociopolitical upheaval.

The fictional manifestations of "willful" citizenship in Roth's trilogy offer an alternative paradigm of citizenship to that proliferated by government rhetoric and public discourse in America that combined two models of citizenship—an "abstract," rational, prescriptive citizenship (the "good," law-abiding citizen) and an "affective" emotional citizenship (the "feeling" citizen whose emotions threaten insubordination).[4] The former model of abstract, prescriptive citizenship emerged out of pre–World War II models of American citizenship as gleaned from civic textbooks from the 1920s, including citizenship manuals and Boy Scout handbooks. Two brief examples will suffice here. The first is a passage from a citizenship handbook of 1928, *Conduct and Citizenship*, by Edwin C. Broome and Edwin W. Adams: "Remember: the same conduct which is necessary to a good member of your family or your work, is needed to become a good citizen of your local community, your state, your nation. *Good conduct and good citizenship are the same. The faithful performance of our daily tasks*, whether in the home, the school, or in any of the larger communities, *is a real test of our citizenship*" (quoted in McKnight-Trontz 2001, 87; my emphasis). The equation of good conduct and good citizenship in the public as well as private realms—of the home, the community, the state, and the nation—illustrates an abstract (and, one might add, impassive) approach to citizenship. According to civic textbooks from the 1920s to the 1960s,[5] therefore, it is respectable deportment, decent behavior, and "faithful performance of . . . daily tasks" that constitute the makings of a good citizen. The second example of abstract, prescriptive citizenship is taken from the seventh edition of the *Boy Scout Handbook*, used from 1965 to 1972:[6] "Today you are an American boy. Before long you will be an American man. It is important to America and to yourself that you become a citizen of fine character, physically strong, mentally awake, and morally straight" (Watson 1965, 11). Conceptualized as instructional manuals for the "training of citizenship through scouting," the *Boy Scout Handbooks* also contained prescriptive advice and instructions on how to serve one's "duty to one's country" (1). They therefore aimed to instill into Boy Scouts the virtues and qualities of a model American citizen.[7]

This mode of abstract, prescriptive American citizenship, which focuses on civic responsibilities rather than civil rights, espouses, to borrow a phrase from Lily Cho, "the fantasy of a passive, transparent, and readable national subject" (2009, 279), a fantasy of collective identification that is "realized and preserved by a politically legitimate nation-state" (Berlant 1991, 21). The clear-cut, black-and-white division between "good" (desirable) and "bad" (undesirable) citizens—as encapsulated in the 1932 maxim "Every good citizen in the community is a good influence. Every evil citizen is a bad influence" (quoted in McKnight-Trontz 2001, 6)—elides the complex ways in which notions of national belonging and identity are substantively practiced but also contested, subverted, and renegotiated on an everyday basis. This mode of abstract, prescriptive citizenship reduces, in other words, the complex processes of national identification to a unified, cohesive, "rational" concept delineated by the precepts of patriotism, unquestionable virtue, firm character, and strong mettle.

The second mode that comprised the dominant model of postwar American citizenship is that of "affective" citizenship, which acknowledges how national identification is driven by emotions and the role of affect. Although some scholarly work on this mode of citizenship has been done in the light of the "affective turn" (Clough and Halley 2007) in the 1990s, I argue that "affective citizenship" has a much longer history that is concurrent with, and not merely in opposition to, modes of "abstract citizenship" in the pre–World War II years.[8] While advocates of this model of affective citizenship have defined it as a more "transformative" (Mookherjee 2005, 31) and inclusive paradigm because it places at the fore a subject who feels[9] and whose multiple identifications along the lines of race, ethnicity, class, gender, and sexual orientation challenge the implicitly white, male, heterosexual, upper-middle-class qualities of the American citizen,[10] nationalist ideology clearly also turns on a politics of affect.

In their polemic but also ironic and deeply humorous scrutiny of American society from the 1940s to the 1990s, the novels in Philip Roth's American trilogy thus explore the productive tensions that arise from the concurrency of these two modes of "abstract" and "affective" citizenship. Through the stories of their "wayward" or "errant" protagonists, the novels suggest an alternative paradigm of "willful" citizenship that critiques the official symbols, icons, and narratives that pervade the public discourses and spaces of the American nation. This alternate model of citizenship also deconstructs the simple binary between the good, patriotic ("American") citizen and the disobedient, insubordinate ("un-American") citizen that was common in post-1945 American public discourse. In its critical examination of the articulation of American citizenship through discourses of justice, loyalty, and moral responsibility, Roth's American trilogy allegorically deconstructs the American nation and its predominant model of citizenship in the postwar era.

Roth's trilogy thus represents an interjection into dominant narratives of U.S. history and national ideology. This is enacted not only on the level of plot but also that of form, namely, through the use of a common metafictional device—a story about a writer composing a story. In all three novels, the narrator, Nathan Zuckerman, a white, Jewish writer (and Roth's alter ego), is called upon to listen to and document the protagonists' life stories. Via this framing device, Zuckerman relates the plots and characters through his perspective. In the first two installments of the trilogy, Zuckerman self-consciously disrupts his own storytelling process, reflecting on his inability to get the tale "right." He even confesses, in *American Pastoral*, that "the lonely writer . . . summons people out of words," but that often this process is "an astonishing farce of misperception" because "you never fail to get [these people and their stories] *wrong*" (1997, 35; my emphasis).[11]

This metafictional strategy foregrounds, as Derek Parker Royal has phrased it, the "fragmented, and highly contingent, nature of narrative production" (2007, 32). It also demonstrates a self-reflexivity about "how we [as writers but also as readers] structure our texts, how we construct our truths, and how we formulate our identities" (33), reminding us that "the world is our dream, our idea, . . . [and] our creation is false, or at least fictive" (Barth 1984, 75). By extension, Roth's metafictional technique in the American trilogy can be read as an articulation of the need for a self-reflexive critical examination of how discourses of citizenship and national identity are culturally coded and historically shaped—how they are written, so to speak, into being. Moreover, Roth's use of historical metafiction[12] puts forward the literary text as the medium in and through which the national symbolic is narrated. In this light, Roth's American trilogy builds upon the work of earlier, nineteenth-century literary writings by Nathaniel Hawthorne and Walt Whitman that were examined in chapter 1, works that reflected the American nation's attempt to redefine and reconstruct itself during the politically turbulent ante- and postbellum years.

One might therefore read Roth's *American Pastoral* as an exploration of the relationship between literature and politics, between notions of national identity and personal (class, gender, racial, ethnic, political, and religious) affiliations in an era of late capitalism in the United States.[13] The novel's protagonist, Seymour "Swede" Levov, lives an all-American existence as the teenage heartthrob and role model of the middle-class Jewish Weequahic community in Newark in the 1940s. The young Swede effortlessly embodies the notion of an "abstract" American citizenship that good fortune has bestowed upon him with his fair complexion, good looks, and athletic prowess—so much so, that even the Weequahic Jewish community "entered into a fantasy about itself" (1997, 3) with Swede Levov as their "household Apollo" (4), their "symbol of hope" (5). Indeed, ascribing the young Swede with the thoroughly "abstract" rather than the "affective" model of citizenship, Zuckerman refers to him as a "staid and stone-faced boy" (4) and recounts that "the love thrust upon the Swede seemed actually to *deprive* him of feeling" (5). With Miss New Jersey as his wife and his home the old stone house "he'd been dreaming about since he was sixteen" (189) the young Swede becomes the embodiment of the model American citizen in the immediate post–World War II era. He is the boy, as the narrator Nathan Zuckerman recalls, "we were all going to follow into America . . . an American not by sheer striving, . . . [but] by virtue of his isomorphism to the Wasp world—he does it the ordinary way, the natural way, the regular American-guy way" (89). In this passage, what seems a flattering depiction of the blond-haired, blue-eyed star athlete quickly depreciates into a harsh critique of the American Dream. More specifically, the ways of the "ordinary," "regular," quintessential American are exposed as those of a small group of privileged citizens, namely, middle-class white Anglo-Saxon Protestant males who are afforded the ease, the "naturalness" of performing their "Americanness."[14] So obsessed is the Swede with donning this mask of WASP

Americanness and completing his assimilation into the American myth that he adopts the legendary folk hero Johnny Appleseed as his own idol and role model: "Johnny Appleseed, that's the man for me. Wasn't a Jew, wasn't an Irish Catholic, wasn't a Protestant Christian—nope, Johnny Appleseed was *just a happy American*. Big. Ruddy. *Happy*. . . . The Swede had loved that story all his life" (316; my emphasis). The Swede's steadfast pursuit of his idealized American fantasy, the American pastoral, and his aspiration of "forthright evolving into a large, smooth, optimistic American" (207) manifest themselves in his identification with one of the foremost national legends. For the Swede, Johnny Appleseed, the real-life American pioneer agriculturist born as John Chapman (1774–1845), is the emissary of a happy, post-ethnic America free from racial and religious prejudice. To the Swede, Johnny Appleseed embodies the "all-American" values of loyalty and service to the country, honesty and integrity, charity, freedom, and the belief in American exceptionalism.[15] Thus, he is immortalized in grade school books as a national legend and has become a mainstay of American popular culture.[16]

Nevertheless, in a deconstruction of the underlying assumptions of the American Dream, Roth's *American Pastoral* asserts that the promise of success, prosperity, and recognition is not extended to everyone who strives for these goals. The aspirations of the fictional Swede and the real-life, or perhaps even larger-than-life, character of Johnny Appleseed epitomize the "vision of an American pastoral without history, violence, or complicity" (Tanenbaum 2004, 52) that "belie[s] the undercurrent of voices, black, colonized, and feminist, that would call the dream a lie" (Sigrist-Sutton 2010, 49). Nowhere is this more apparent than in the novel's portrayal of the political and countercultural revolutions of the 1960s.

In particular, *American Pastoral* fictionally depicts the true event of the 1967 Newark riots, wherein a large number of disenfranchised African Americans took to the streets in protest against an incident of police brutality.[17] The riots were the last in a series of events that responded to the decline of Newark's industries, a sharp increase in inner-city poverty, and the out-migration of the city's middle-class white population.[18] In Roth's novel, the Swede, who inherits his father's glove factory, Newark Maid, insists on staying on in the city during the riots and "h[angs] on in the face of industry-wide economic realities . . . for as long as he c[an]" (1997, 24). Throughout the postwar decades of political turmoil and social revolution from the 1940s to the 1960s, the Swede remains, in the narrator's view, someone who "devote[s] heart and soul to the illusion of stability," who "refuse[s] to register life's irrational element" (37). His life, as Nathan Zuckerman recollects decades later, "*had been the most simple and most ordinary and therefore just great, right in the American grain*" (31).

Remarkably, in contrast to his personification of an "abstract," impassive citizenship in his early years, as he grows older, the Swede's "aloofness" and his "seeming passivity" (1997, 37) fade away and are gradually replaced by a more affective form of citizenship characterized by an emotional embrace of all things he discerns "American": "[H]e loved America. Loved being an *American*. . . . All the pleasures of his younger years were American pleasures, all that success and happiness had been American. . . . The loneliness he would feel as a man without all his American feelings. . . . Yes, everything that gave meaning to his accomplishments had been American. Everything he loved was here" (206–13). Ironically, the Swede's unquestioning embrace of all things American conveys a naïveté, an innocence as well as ignorance, that renders him blind to his own complicity in the structure of national fantasy. The year is 1973, and the Swede's attempts to understand why his daughter Merry had planted the bomb in the post office in 1968 and his envisioning of her hate and shame for America paradoxically only reinforce his feelings of love and patriotism for his country. In this section of the novel, Nathan Zuckerman imagines what it meant to the Swede, and his daughter Merry, to be an American:

> For her, being an American was loathing America, but loving America was something he could not let go of . . . any more than he could let go of his decency. How could she "hate" this country when she had no *conception* of this country? How could a child of his be so blind as to revile the "rotten system" that had given her own family every opportunity to succeed? To revile her "capitalist" parents as though their wealth were the product of anything other than the unstinting industry of three generations. . . . He loved the America she hated and blamed for everything that was imperfect in life and wanted violently to overturn. (213)

The Swede's criticism of his daughter's ignorance ("she had no conception of this country") ironically belies his own obliviousness of the culturally endowed national narratives and structures of privilege in which he has become inextricably tangled and unequivocally internalized. His comfortable position does not afford him a mode of resistance or critique, of civil disobedience. Rather, it is his daughter Merry Levov who becomes the symbol of 1960s radicalism in the United States—she becomes involved with the Weathermen, a radical leftist group supporting black power and opposing the Vietnam War, whose strategy of violent bombings led to their designation as a terrorist group by the FBI.

As a willful and uncompromising voice of dissent, Merry Levov represents the voice of a counter-pastoral critique that, in the words of the Swede's brother, Jerry, "blasts away" the Swede's "façade" and "all [his] fucking *norms*" (1997, 275). Merry thus throws a spanner into the smooth workings of capitalism and middle-class bourgeois decorum in America. In her absolute rejection of Western neoliberal capitalism and U.S. national ideology, Merry Levov occupies the subject position of the abject "Other," becoming an embodiment of the subaltern subject. She suffers from a speech impediment, a stutter; she cannot speak, in a Spivakian sense, until she begins to make bombs: "That's when the stuttering first began to disappear. She never stuttered when she was with the dynamite" (259). In this way, Roth's novel provocatively suggests that violence and terrorism confer a form of agency and representation to those who are marginalized, disenfranchised, without a political voice. Nevertheless, Merry's act of "terrorism" is mitigated in Roth's novel through her conversion to Jainism and its philosophy of nonviolence. At the end of the novel, therefore, Merry's willfulness demands to be read as an manifestation of civil disobedience rather than "mindless" terrorism.

Nevertheless, it can also be argued that Merry, as a privileged daughter, cannot be a representative of the subaltern female subject, and that Roth's depiction of her is less as a radical, defiant female terrorist than as a "middle-class white girl, disoriented and lost in the voices of protest of her day, profoundly disconnected from social or cultural ties of any sort" (Sigrist-Sutton 2010, 65). In this reading of Roth's female protagonist, Merry's silence would be indicative not of the fact that she cannot speak but that she obstinately, willfully, defiantly *will not* speak in the climax of the novel's plot when the Swede finally finds her living a squalid existence in Newark as a Jain.[19] Merry is silent, hidden behind her veil, cut from the end of a stocking, not speaking when she is asked—commanded—by her father to speak the "truth":

"Now speak!" he commanded her.

But she wouldn't. He pried her mouth open, disregarding a guideline he had never before overstepped—the injunction against violence. . . . The father who could never use force on his child, for whom force was the embodiment of moral bankruptcy, pried open her mouth and with his fingers took hold of her tongue. . . .

"Speak!" he demanded. (1997, 265)

But, in a Bartleby-esque moment, Merry prefers not to. Like Cordelia, the youngest of King Lear's daughters in Shakespeare's tragedy, Merry will not speak. Her refusal to speak can be read as an act not only of willfulness but of agency. As Adrienne Rich (2003) has pointed out, silence can be interpreted as a form of empowerment rather than an indication of oppression.[20] In this light, Merry Levov's refusal to speak thus signals her refusal to buy into the all-American national ideology that her father, the Swede, demands she partake in. Merry's conversion to Jainism, an ascetic Indian religion characterized by abstinence from various sensual pleasures and an austere lifestyle that rejects material wealth, also represents an ultimate rejection of U.S. consumerist culture, Western capitalism, and the national fantasy of the American Dream. Merry tells her father, "I am done with craving and selfhood" (251), indicating her rejection of Western, post-Enlightenment individualism.

As the willful protagonist at the center of the first installment of Roth's American trilogy, Merry Levov thus epitomizes a rejection of post-Enlightenment individualism as well as the all-American values and tenets of a national fantasy that have been indoctrinated into her as a young child. Merry occupies a position located *outside* of the spaces of national identification and citizenship (as her reading of Fanon's text on Algerian women, *The Communist Manifesto*, and her conversion to Jainism indicate); her acts of resistance serve as interjections into the dominant discourse of national fantasy, as undertakings that undermine the political legitimacy of the American nation. As the willful citizen who effectively renounces her citizenship ("For her, being an American was loathing America"), Merry Levov also fictionally embodies a counter-politics to the wave of patriotism and American exceptionalism that surged through the United States in the 1940s as well as the politically conservative and conformist climate of the McCarthy era in the 1950s. It is this time period and its assimilationist narratives of national ideology as well as the key issue of "un-Americanness" that are taken up in the second novel of Roth's American trilogy, *I Married a Communist*.

In this novel, the narrator Nathan Zuckerman recalls the height of patriotism in the mid-1940s in the aftermath of World War II, when the entire American nation seemed to be swept away by "the reality of the myth of a national character to be partaken by all." Riding on the crest of this wave, Americans embraced a mode of "affective" citizenship with its "excited feelings of community that the war had aroused" (1998, 38). As Zuckerman reflects, "History had been scaled down and personalized, America had been scaled down and personalized: for me, that was the enchantment not only of Norman Corwin but of the times. You flood into history and history floods into you. You flood into America and America floods into you" (39). In Roth's use of antimetabole, a form of emphatic repetition ("You flood into America and America floods into you"), the emphatic and emotive registers of the excerpt vividly re-create the actual historic moment on May 8, 1945, when Norman Corwin's radio play, *On a Note of Triumph*, was broadcast to mark Allied victory in Europe and hence the end of World War II. Deemed the "most listened-to radio drama in U.S. history,"[21] Corwin's play captured the minds and hearts of an estimated 60 million listeners across America. Portions from the play are reproduced in Roth's novel, in sections wherein Zuckerman recalls the "stream of transforming, self-abandoning emotion" aroused in hearts of people who sat transfixed before their radios: "The power of that broadcast! There, amazingly, was *soul* coming out of a radio. The Spirit of the Common Man had inspired an immense mélange of populist adoration, an effusion of words bubbling straight up from the American heart into the American mouth, an hour-long homage to the paradoxical superiority of what Corwin insisted on identifying as absolutely ordinary American mankind: 'far-flung ordinary men, unspectacular but free'" (41).

The original emphasis on the word *soul* in the passage above, interestingly, recalls the culmination of Walt Whitman's *Democratic Vistas* wherein he declares that America's national literature must express the unique character, its "non-subordinated SOUL" (2010, 60). Norman Corwin's populist celebration of the "ordinary" American, what he calls the "little guy" and "common man"[22] in his radio play, is, however, critiqued by Roth because the "Ordinary Joe" or "Average Joe" is nonetheless an *American* Joe—a patriotic citizen in his outlook, his attitudes, and his emotions who identifies with the ideals of the national symbolic. The power of Norman Corwin's speech therefore lay, as Zuckerman recalls, in its ability to convince its listeners that they were "all, however small, a part of the revolution that confirmed the reality of the myth of a national character to be partaken of by all" (1998, 38). Zuckerman himself admits that, in the aftermath of Corwin's speech, he "didn't care to partake of the Jewish character" but of "the national character" because "nothing had seemed to come more naturally to my American-born parents, and nothing came more naturally to me" (39). It is this phrase, "national character," which is deconstructed in the novel's portrayal of the postwar decades, especially the McCarthy era of the 1950s.

I Married a Communist depicts how, in this period of the Second Red Scare, the American nation was swiftly and conveniently split into two camps—those whose allegiances were with America and hence who were deemed "American," and those who were perceived as "un-American" in their sympathies, largely because they were deemed Communist supporters. The latter were rooted out by the real-life sweep of unrelenting anti-Communist measures not only by Senator Joseph McCarthy but also by the House Un-American Activities Committee.[23] One of these measures was the compilation of "lists of names and accusations and charges. . . . Lists of anybody in America who has ever been disgruntled about anything or criticized anything or protested anything—or associated with anybody who has ever criticized or protested anything." These lists mark the names on them as "Communists or fronting for Communists or 'helping' Communists or contributing to Communist 'coffers,' or 'infiltrating' labor or government or education or Hollywood or the theater or radio and TV" (1998, 214). These words are spoken by Nathan Zuckerman's high school English teacher Murray Ringold. It is Murray who, in retrospect (it is the year 1977), summarizes McCarthyism as "the first postwar flowering of the American unthinking that is now everywhere" (284).

The eponymous protagonist of Roth's *I Married a Communist* is Murray's brother, Ira Ringold, nicknamed "Iron Rinn," a teenage ditchdigger and soldier turned radio star who becomes an Abraham Lincoln impersonator and hence a personification of the American nation's dedication to the principles of nationalism, equality, liberty, and democracy as detailed in Lincoln's famous Gettysburg Address of 1863. Ira Ringold's downfall occurs, however, when he is denounced as "un-American" because of his Communist affiliations. Indeed, Ira Ringold willfully rejects all his Middle American values— "Home. Marriage. Family. Mistresses. Adultery. All this bourgeois shit!"— and becomes "a Communist laborer dwelling alone in a room in East Chicago under a sixty-watt bulb" (1998, 281). In this manner, he becomes the embodiment of "popular-culture Communism" in the eyes of the American nation. "To the confused popular imagination," Zuckerman recalls, "Ira became the personification of Communism, the personalized Communist for the nation:

Iron Rinn was Everyman's Communist traitor" (282). Ironically, although the HUAC declared Communist sympathizers in the United States in the 1950s to be "un-American" in character, Roth points out that the Communist tracts were often couched in precisely the opposite terms. In the novel, for example, Zuckerman recalls the final pages of a Communist booklet he reads, titled *Who Owns America?*[24] "Not for one moment will we give rest to the usurpers, to the oligarchy which is bringing ruin to the nation. *Let no one question your patriotism, your loyalty to the nation.* Join the Communist Party. *As a Communist, you will be able to fulfill,* in the deepest sense of the word, *your responsibility as an American*" (my emphasis). Interestingly, therefore, Roth suggests that the emphasis on "national character" and the responsibilities of/ as an American citizen were embraced by both the Communist *and* the anti-Communist camps. Indeed, the rhetorical question "Is this America the kind of America you want to live in?" (237) that Nathan Zuckerman ponders after reading the pamphlet could effectively be asked by both factions. When the question is posed by the Communists, the anticipated answer would clearly be in favor of revolution against fascism and a strengthening of the labor unions. When it is posed by those seeking to eradicate Communism in the United States during the McCarthy era, however, the appropriate answer would involve shoring up the boundaries of the American nation in defense against the foreign threat of the Soviet Union, which incited Americans to perform "disloyal" and "subversive" activities against their own government. In this sense, therefore, *I Married a Communist* deconstructs the very concept of the American nation by complicating any unitary or absolute definition of "national character." Instead, the novel points to the ways in which this term was employed and appropriated by members of very divergent, even opposing, ideological and political groups.

Paradoxically, therefore, although Ira Ringold is regarded as a willful, dissenting, and wayward citizen with "un-American" sympathies and affiliations, his joining the Communist Party can actually be read as an act of reinscribing the discursive practices of the nation and hence one way, to recall the words of the Communist pamphlet *Who Owns America?*, of "fulfill[ing] his] responsibility as an American." Ira Ringold's retreat at the end of the novel to his rustic Walden-like shack in the countryside after being exposed as a "Machiavellian Communist" (1998, 245) in his wife Eva Frame's memoir, itself titled *I Married a Communist*, can thus be construed as a quintessentially American quest to get "back-to-nature/the wilderness" that, as

Nathan Zuckerman remarks, recalls "the earliest images—of independence and freedom" (72). Ira's pared-down existence in Zinc Town can be read as a reappropriation of Henry David Thoreau's two-year residence in a cabin close to Walden Pond, which he depicts as a period of self introspection and a quest of spiritual discovery in *Walden; or, Life in the Woods* (1854), a transcendentalist classic that has become one of the mainstays of the American literary canon. As Zuckerman knowingly reflects, Ira's retreat "has a history. It was Rousseau's. It was Thoreau's. The palliative of the primitive hut. The place where you are stripped back to essentials, to which you return . . . to decontaminate and absolve yourself of the striving" (1998, 72). The metaphors of decontamination, absolution, and a "back to basics" stripping down to the bare essentials in the passage above cast Ira's moving back to Zinc Town as a renunciation of the embellishments, aspirations, and values of Middle America. It depicts Ira's act as, to borrow a phrase from Thoreau's 1849 essay of the same name, one of civil disobedience that reinscribes dominant narratives of nationhood and national identity in an American context.

Ira's move to Zinc Town can thus be construed as an act of willful citizenship that seeks not to transcend the parameters of the nation but to reinscribe them from within its margins. By extension, Roth's *I Married A Communist* can be read as an attempt, in the genre of historical metafiction, to question, challenge, and reconfigure the discursive practices of the nation in postwar America. The novel critiques the labeling of American citizens who were members of the Communist Party as dissidents by the U.S. government and their stereotypical repressentation in popular narratives and literature.[25] The mode of obstinate and willful subjectivity embodied by Ira Ringold complicates the unequivocal binary of the good, patriotic citizen versus the insubordinate, "un-American" citizen that permeated the American popular imagination in the 1940s and 1950s.

The third novel of Roth's trilogy, *The Human Stain*, completes Roth's fictional exploration of willfulness as a mode of political intervention that challenges dominant narratives of the American nation. In this novel, the willful protagonist is a light-skinned African American who passes for a white Jew, a classics professor by the name of Coleman Silk who is Nathan Zuckerman's neighbor. To Zuckerman (and to the reader, as the novel adopts a first-person narration through Zuckerman's perspective), Coleman Silk is a mystery, an enigmatic subject who takes the American Dream and its frontier tradition to extremes, "throw[ing his] origins overboard" in the "pursuit of happiness."[26] He becomes a willful citizen-subject when he decides to "take the future into his own hands rather than to leave it to an unenlightened society to determine his fate" (2000, 120), thus embodying a position of will-ful self-(re)invention in postwar America. As a black man passing for a white Jew, Coleman Silk takes advantage of white privilege in America as a young adult in the 1940s up until 1965, which saw the end of the Jim Crow laws. His racial self-fashioning[27] and his conscious embodiment of white citizenship stem from his firsthand experiences of "what his father called the country's 'Negrophobia'" (103), when his blond girlfriend from Minnesota ends their relationship after she finds out that he is African American. Yet his reso-lute attempts to "shed" his ethnicity and his pursuit of a life that adheres to national discourses of "abstract" American citizenship (for instance, Cole-man joins the U.S. Navy as a white man) ultimately fall short. The irony is that he is forced to retire from his job as a classics professor when he uses the word "spooks," a derogatory slang term for black Americans, in class one day. Even though Silk insists he used the term in the sense of "ghosts," he is charged with racial prejudice.

Coleman's dismissal from the university because of his alleged use of po-litically incorrect, racist slang and the hysteria that builds itself around the episode constitute Roth's fictional depiction of the frenzied political climate of the 1990s in the United States, a decade of culture wars in which moral and political correctness conflicted with the American nation's obsession over "every last mortifying detail" (2000, 2) of President Bill Clinton's affair with Monica Lewinsky. The year 1998 was, as Zuckerman recalls,

> the summer of an enormous piety binge, a purity binge, when terror-ism—which had replaced communism as the prevailing threat to the country's security—was succeeded by cocksucking, and a virile, youth-ful middle-aged president and a brash, smitten twenty-one-year-old employee carrying on in the Oval Office like two teenage kids in a parking lot revived American's oldest communal passion. . . : the ecstasy of sanctimony. . . . It was the summer when—for the billionth time—the jumble, the mayhem, the mess proved itself more subtle than this one's ideology and that one's morality. It was the summer when a presi-dent's penis was on everyone's mind, and life, in all its shameless impu-rity, once again confounded America.

The humor in this passage is clearly laced with irony and sarcasm. Zuckerman, who, we recall, is Roth's alter ego, criticizes the way America is so easily enraptured by its national fantasy and its moral beliefs, to the extent that anything outside the boundaries of this system of virtue ("the jumble, the mayhem, the mess," "shameless impurity") makes society react swiftly by "blam[ing], deplor[ing], and punish[ing]" (2–3).

In *The Human Stain*, the twist in the story occurs at the end of the novel, when it is revealed that Coleman dies as a result of an automobile accident because, as his sister Ernestine tells Zuckerman, "the hospital that was nearest would not take colored, and he died by bleeding to death" (2000, 333). Unlike in the "traditional" passing narrative, however, such as Mark Twain's *The Tragedy of Pudd'nhead Wilson* (1894), Charles Chesnutt's short stories and novels, James Weldon Johnson's *Autobiography of an Ex-Colored Man* (1912), or Nella Larsen's *Passing* (1929), narratives that "dramatize the conflict between the performance of whiteness and the persistence of black consciousness that lies beneath" (Maslan 2005, 365), the revealing of Coleman Silk's "real identity" does not render him a more sympathetic or "readable" character to the reader. Even Nathan Zuckerman, who is entrusted to write Coleman's memoirs, thinks of him as an unfathomable character at the close of the novel. When he learns of Coleman's "secret." Zuckerman thinks in retrospect: "I couldn't imagine anything that could have made Coleman more of a mystery to me than this unmasking. Now that I knew everything, it was as though I knew nothing. . . . Was he merely being another American and, in the great frontier tradition, accepting the democratic invitation to throw your origins overboard if to do so contributes to the pursuit of happiness?" (2000, 333).

Even in his "unmasking" after his death, Coleman Silk stubbornly remains an unreadable character, an ambivalent, willful citizen. Coleman's impenetrability thus fictionally represents a contestation to the "sanctimonious" culture of morality and piety in the United States during the 1990s, when "the prevailing threat to the country's security" (2000, 2) is no longer Communism but the secrets of its citizens, even its president, who live "double" lives. Coleman Silk's identity is situated in historical discontinuity; it is shrouded in inscrutability rather than in legible and familiar markers of collective racial, ethnic, and cultural identification. In this regard, as Mark Maslan has pointed out, Roth's *The Human Stain* "participates in a larger debate concerning the historical foundations of collective identity" (2005,

366) in an American context. In the novel, the revelation of Bill Clinton's indiscretions, which become a national obsession in the public and private arenas of America's popular imagination, is clearly mirrored in Coleman Silk's much more low-key "unmasking." What emerges in the juxtaposition of the two is Roth's razor-sharp critique of America's national fantasy, as conveyed in the sense of "nausea" at the "smallness" of Middle American mindset and values in the stifling atmosphere of "speculation and theorizing and hyperbole" (2000, 3) that, at the level of the fictional narrative, are ultimately the cause of the scandal around Coleman Silk's unmasking, not his actual act of passing.

In its depiction of the social and political events spanning the 1940s to the 1990s in America, episodes that threatened to debunk national myths even amid renewed efforts to reinforce ideas of "Americanness" in the popular imagination, Philip Roth's American trilogy engages with the complex and conflicting impulses at work in the model of American citizenship in that period, which was characterized by two dominant modes—an "abstract" or prescriptive mode and an "affective" mode. The novels also go one step further in putting forward an alternative paradigm of "willful" citizenship that enables a mode of civil disobedience, resistance, and opposition that challenges nationally sanctioned and culturally endowed models of collective identity and belonging. Through the different stories of their willful and wayward fictional protagonists, set against the backdrop of real-life sociopolitical events, the novels compel a reconfiguration of established formations of national identity and a reworking of common assumptions of what it means to "be" and "feel" American. They foreground the multiple ways in which notions of national belonging, national identity, and citizenship are practiced, but also challenged and disrupted, in postwar America. In this regard, Philip Roth's American trilogy can be read as a critique of the homogenous structures in American society that reinforce the dominant narratives that underpin the political legitimacy of the nation, narratives that conceal and contain the discontinuous, incongruous, ambiguous, and even paradoxical nature of civil life within the discursive logic of national fantasy.

PART II
....

Precarious Citizens

4

PRECARIOUSNESS AND
THE ETHICS OF NARRATION

· · · · · · · · · ·

Etel Adnan's *In the Heart of the Heart*
of Another Country and *Sitt Marie Rose*

Having explored how willful subjects challenge the ways in which dominant national ideologies have been reproduced and circulated in national
narratives, thus demanding a reconfiguration of the established parameters of citizenship and national identity, this section turns to the ways in
which precarious bodies in a North American context—in the form of the
undocumented migrant, the stateless person, the asylum seeker, the refugee,
the exile, the displaced or coercively relocated subject—gesture toward the
limits of conventional models of nation-based citizenship and encourage a
different, more inclusive paradigm of political membership, social belonging, and economic participation. One such alternative paradigm is conceived
by Judith Butler in *Precarious Life: The Powers of Mourning and Violence*
(2004). In this study, she calls for an alternative critical perspective through
which to reflect on political life in a post-9/11 world: not one embedded in
a rhetoric of war, retribution, or "justice,"[1] but rather one centered around
the notions of injurability, vulnerability, and precariousness. As she argues,
"To be injured means that one has the chance to reflect upon injury, to find

out the mechanisms of its distribution, to find out who else suffers from permeable borders, unexpected violence, dispossession, and fear, and in what ways" (xii). According to Butler, therefore, the attacks on the World Trade Center on 9/11 are an occasion for self-reflection on our place as individuals within the larger framework of a global political community on which we are dependent but also to which we are bound out of a sense of "ethical responsibility" (xiii) and "accountability." This sense of interdependency foregrounds the condition of precariousness, which Butler deems not only characteristic of the lives of marginalized groups (undocumented migrants, refugees, racial and sexual minorities, detainees in Guántanamo, and so on) but also, more generally, as an intrinsic, universal human quality.[2] Indeed, she proposes that the understanding of a "common human vulnerability, one that emerges with life itself . . . [and] precedes the formation of 'I'" (16) can pave the way for a "non-violent ethics, one that is based upon an understanding of how easily human life is annulled" (xvii).

While I agree to a certain extent with Butler's theory of universal human vulnerability,[3] it is nevertheless the precariousness of those marginalized in Western societies as the "Other" (stateless persons, refugees, asylum seekers, undocumented migrants) or more particularly, the narrating of this condition of precariousness with which this current chapter is concerned. More specifically, I argue that the "naturalization"[4] in mass media of the injurability and vulnerability of the American public in the aftermath of 9/11, as well as a reinforcing and shoring up of ideas of the American nation, has been contested by depictions of the precariousness of the "Other" in diasporic narratives. This is enacted through an "ethics of narration,"[5] or what Wayne C. Booth defines as "an ethical criticism of narrative" and an "ethics of telling and listening" (1990, 7), that can be employed in a broader literary strategy of challenging dominant neoliberal discourses of the nation and hence in renegotiating established definitions of national identity and citizenship.

But let us return briefly to the aftermath of the attacks on the World Trade Center. When Butler noted that the condition of heightened vulnerability after 9/11 in the United States was met not with an increased effort to prevent the loss of more human lives but instead with a disproportionate amount of intensified aggression, "heightened nationalist discourse, [and] extended surveillance mechanisms" (2004, xi), she also observed that this resulted in an "unprecedented suspension of civil liberties for illegal immigrants and suspected terrorists" (3). In other words, the condition of heightened susceptibility in the aftermath of 9/11 led to an exploitation of the precariousness of the "Other," revealing the vulnerability of migrants, asylum seekers, exiles, and refugees to the will or decision of national governments. These lives, which were already precarious, were exposed to increased risk, insecurity, and even hazardous conditions of existence by the onset of stricter legislation and political measures.[6]

In an age of increasing securitization, therefore, especially in the aftermath of 9/11, the pervasive use of "identity management"[7] in the United States has led to heightened restrictive practices of citizenship that exclude people deemed "foreigners," proliferating an "us" versus "them" mentality that is deeply reductive and problematic. Biometric passports, facial recognition, retinal scans, and digitized fingerprints are only some of the methods of authentication and identification that not only serve as "technologies of control" (Nyers 2003, 1069) but also as strategies of exclusion, detention, and deportation. As Emily Gilbert observes, "Touted as a key prong in the 'war on terror,' biometrics have become integral to national security programs, specifically with regard to the regulation of borders . . . the sorting of the population through biometrics reinforces notions of belonging, entitlement and authenticity" (2010, 226–27). Biometrics[8] is thus a means by which individuals are read, coded, identified, and targeted, "render[ing] bodies legible and eligible, codifying people in terms of who is a threat; . . . desirable or undesirable; . . . deserving or undeserving" (239). The danger of biometrics, however, as Gilbert points out, is the "troubling tendency of conflating potentially *risky subjects* and *subjects who are at risk*; to portray subjects whose lives are insecure and precarious as the source of insecurity" (239–40). In a U.S. context, it is this misperception and interpellation of precarious bodies as "risky subjects" instead of "subjects who are at risk" in the public imagination that excludes them from dominant discourses of citizenship and political membership. Precarious bodies are often read as the *source* of the precariousness, instability, and unpredictability that endanger the boundaries of the nation rather than the *result* of policies of securitization and homogenization that marginalize "undesirable" bodies within the spaces of the nation.

In the following, therefore, I examine three literary texts that depict how specific manifestations of the precarious subject—the refugee, the exile, the stateless person—are at risk in an era of global migration and forced mobility that forecloses her or his rights to a sense of national belonging, political membership and citizenship. I have chosen to focus on two texts by Lebanese American writer Etel Adnan, *Sitt Marie Rose: A Novel* (1977) and her experimental prose text *In the Heart of the Heart of Another Country* (2005) and to conclude with a few remarks on Palestinian American literary theorist and postcolonial critic Edward Said and Swiss documentary photographer Jean Mohr's visual and textual explorations of Palestinian identity in the face of dispossession and exile, *After the Last Sky* (1986). These works were selected for two reasons. First, they demonstrate that literary and visual narratives on bodies at risk and precarious subjects did not emerge only in the aftermath of 9/11 but had already been published in the 1970s and 1980s. Second, these writings all foreground the lives of Palestinians (and Palestinian sympathizers), whose precariousness is due to contested international recognition of the state of Palestine. In this case, the condition of precariousness and vulnerability is linked directly to the deprivation of a sense of collective identity and belonging that corresponds with the (lack of) acknowledgment of geopolitical boundaries. Therefore, even though 9/11 may have been a trigger for a greater sense of ethical responsibility with respect to the rights of precarious bodies, an analysis of earlier works depicting the lives of Lebanese and Palestinians in periods of civil and political strife provides a broader comparative framework and hence critical perspective for thinking about what Seyla Benhabib terms "the rights of Others" (2004).

Put differently, all three selected works variously enact a reinstating of "the rights of Others" via different modes of an "ethics of narration" attuned to the aforementioned conditions of vulnerability, injurability, and precariousness. They are examples of what Martha Nussbaum has referred to as "narratives that explore the cosmopolitan obligations ... that enhance our understanding of suffering wherever it occurs" (2007, 49).[9] Etel Adnan's highly personal accounts of exile from Beirut in *In the Heart of the Heart of Another Country* as well as her critique of patriarchal structures and gender roles during the Lebanese Civil War in *Sitt Marie Rose* are rendered in a vocabulary of pain, loss, betrayal, disorientation, displacement, and absence that, nevertheless, demand recognition and a sense of accountability on the part of the reader. By comparison, Edward Said and Jean Mohr contest the dominant, and largely uniform, media representations of Palestinian lives in Western mass media by reversing the public's gaze: "We too are looking, we too are scrutinizing, assessing, judging. We are more than someone's object" (1986, 166). Breaking and dispersing the dominant gaze of the West, Said and Mohr offer alternative multifaceted portraits of Palestinian identity and daily life amid the experiences of displacement and exile. In a wider sense, therefore, Etel Adnan and Edward Said illustrate in their works that the notion of precariousness can be harnessed in a broader politics of intervention that challenges established lines of race, ethnicity, gender, and class that define "traditional," and often exclusionary, notions of citizenship and national belonging.

WAR, PLACE, AND THE BODY OF THE EXILE

Etel Adnan's semiautobiographical work *In the Heart of the Heart of Another Country* is a rewriting of and a response to William H. Gass's collection of stories *In the Heart of the Heart of the Country* (1968) about midwestern life in the United States. Adnan's collection comprises seven short pieces written from 1977 to 2004, five of which recall and mimic Gass's rhythmic repetitions of simple phrases in a series of paragraphs in his text. Here are two excerpts from the eponymous piece of Adnan's collection:

> PLACE
>   So I have sailed the seas and come . . .
>
>   to B . . .
> a city by the sea, in Lebanon. It is seventeen years later. My absence has been an exile from an exile.
>
> . . .
>
> PLACE
>   I left this place by running all the way to California. An exile, which lasted for years. I came back on a stretcher and felt here a stranger, exiled from my former exile. I am always away from something and somewhere. (2005, 1–4)

This inversion of a fairy-tale-like opening ("So I have sailed the seas . . .") is a response to the speaker of William H. Gass's story, who begins his tale with a "returning to B . . .". The quasi-mythical quality of the city of "B" in Gass's story is swiftly dissipated in Adnan's text by the speaker's experience of exile, of leaving the city of her birth and childhood ("Then I went away, *and the spell broke*" (4; my emphasis) and on returning to it again in the 1960s[10] in the run-up to the Lebanese Civil War (1975–90).[11]

Upon her return seventeen years later, the speaker's thoughts and observations no longer reflect her youthful love affair with the city but a sense of fatigue, disenchantment, and estrangement, a feeling of "exile from exile." Beirut has become an ungraspable, slippery, messy, and often-contradictory place—"the reality of Beirut was of a complexity defying definition" (2005, xi). This is compounded by the sense of alienation and vulnerability that the speaker feels upon once more inhabiting the country she had left as an exile, an émigré. "California was on my mind, working like a filtering device. My references belonged to two worlds, and were forcing me to shift gears, . . . to be mobile, edgy, and, most of all, *vulnerable*. I was used to a world now remote and, at the same time, getting used to a new one that was also my old world, and somewhere, deep inside, I was *alien to both*" (xii; my emphasis). The speaker's sense of alienation in both her country of origin and the country in which she has come to reside can be interpreted here as more than simply a mimetic representation of the conditions of precariousness and vulnerability that characterize the immigrant condition. Rather, I suggest, it can be read as Adnan's adoption of a politics of refusal to be at home in either, and hence both, countr(ies) and culture(s). It is this sense of being "alien to both" and a deliberate dwelling in the state of "vulnerab[ility]" and discomfort that become the central tenets of a poetics and politics of diasporic citizenship.

Adnan's meditations on vulnerability and injurability in *In the Heart of the Heart of Another Country* also constitute her critique of patriarchal Lebanese culture, which is executed along strictly gendered, ethnic, and religious lines, where "[e]very feminine act, even charitable and seemingly unpolitical ones, were regarded as a rebellion in this world where women had always played servile roles" (1977, 101). "Being a woman, I am invisible" (2005, 7), the speaker reflects, decrying a masculinist society where "[c]hildren are taught that little boys are superior to little girls. Yes. When Hassan beats Nedjma, Nedjma is beaten by her father for having been beaten, and this, ad infinitum" (8). The chain of violence enacted against women, the narrator declares, begins at birth and continues, inexhaustibly, into adulthood. The vulnerability and injurability of the female body is conveyed explicitly in a language of violation, abuse, barrenness, and loss: "Don't talk to me about my body. It has been battered, cut open; discs, nerves, and tissues have been removed. My belly, a zoological garden. My eyes, poor lighthouses, and my mind a rocky and barren garden, exactly like this place and the nonexistent house" (3). The speaker's belly has become a crude parody of a womb, housing not a human fetus but animals in a zoo. Her body has been cut open, and vital structures—discs, nerves, and tissues—have been surgically removed. Without these organs, her body becomes an empty receptacle, a dead vessel.[12]

It is not only the individual but also the collective inhabitants of Beirut who have been metaphorically and physically disemboweled and violated. In the section titled "POLITICS," for example, Beirut is personified as a moaning, grotesque, many-headed body, with torn muscles, blinded eyes, and cigarette-burned faces, whose vertebrae have been broken with an ax (2005, 14). Likewise, the second piece in Adnan's *In the Heart of the Heart of Another Country*, "Twenty-Five Years Later,"[13] is also a reflection on the speaker's childhood in Lebanon, her exile, and subsequent temporary return. She recalls her and her friends' somewhat naïve political attitude in Beirut in the early years of the civil war: "People were being assassinated as if they were flies and we went on dreaming, thinking that each defeat would lead to victory. Funeral lines were multiplying. We followed them. We thought that we had to go through the tunnel of death to start living again." "It was the same story everywhere, refugees waiting under their tents, political prisoners dying in hunger strikes" (30), the speaker recounts. The communal disembowelment and violation of the city and its inhabitants during the Lebanese Civil War takes on a more personal note during a gathering the narrator has with her Lebanese American friends in the United States: "Everyone digs into his memory to bring out what is most painful. John speaks of his mother's death. He received her in the mail, incinerated and put into a plastic box. 'I didn't know what to do with her,' he said, 'when she arrived that way in New York. I did not know any funeral rite. I had to invent one. I drew flowers on the little box that I did not dare open, and I put it in the garbage.'" Like the speaker, John is an expatriate living in America after having left Beirut, the "cruelest town in the world" (16). His personal confession about his helpless course of action upon receiving his mother's ashes starkly reflects the far-reaching extent to which the Lebanese Civil War and his experience of exile had left their mark on his sense of native traditions, customs, and rituals.

In her book *The Rights of Others*, political scientist and philosopher Seyla Benhabib argues for the entitlement of immigrants, refugees, and asylum seekers to social and political membership in a current global arena where state boundaries have become more porous, though by no means transparent or unconditionally open. Drawing on Hannah Arendt's treatise in *The Origins of Totalitarianism* (1951) on "the right to have rights," Benhabib observes that Arendt is "evoking a moral imperative" and invoking a "moral claim to membership and a certain form of treatment compatible with the claim to membership" (2004, 56). It is a claim of this nature that Etel Adnan's memoirs and writings, too, stake. They demand a sense of accountability and ethical responsibility, of political and social critique even, or perhaps especially, in conditions of exile, precariousness, and alienation. In this respect, Adnan's seven short pieces in *In the Heart of the Heart of Another Country* emphasize the importance of writing and artistic composition as a form of resistance and opposition, even if it documents how it feels to be "numb with apprehension," to be disillusioned by the ravages of war and "detached from [one's] environment, projected to an East of [one's] own mind, and alienated from [oneself]" (2005, xvi).

The last piece in Adnan's *In the Heart of the Heart of Another Country*, the prose poem "To Be in a Time of War," documents the poet's response to news coverage of the Iraq War in California, where she was living at the time of writing. The poem begins: "To say nothing, do nothing, mark time, to bend, to straighten up, to blame oneself, to stand, to go toward the window, to change one's mind in the process, to return to one's chair, to stand again" (2005, 99). The anaphoric repetition of the verb form "to—" throughout the entire poem paradoxically conveys a sense of paralysis and nonaction ("to say nothing, do nothing") in the guise of meaningless, routinized action ("to bend, to straighten up," "to stand," "to return to one's chair," "to stand again"). The speaker's sense of aimlessness and helplessness increases when she reads the front page of her newspaper, the printed type quickly dissolving in her mind's eye into the word "WAR": "[T]o look for the paper, take it out of its yellow bag, to read on the front-page WAR, to notice that WAR takes half a page, to feel a shiver down the spine, to tell that that's it, . . . to read that Baghdad is being bombed, to envision a rain of fire, to hear the noise, to be heartbroken, to stare at the trees, to go up slowly while reading, to come back to the front page, read WAR again, . . . to feel paralyzed, . . . to know helplessness" (101). The excerpt reflects a sense of disregard for the consequences of the Iraq War in Western mass media news coverage—not only regarding the loss of human lives, both of Iraqi civilians and U.S. soldiers, but also a sense of "cultural loss" in the "triumphant tone" (xvi) of such reporting. The narrative registers the speaker's oscillation from feeling "worn out" (103), a sense of "profound weariness" (107), and "a lead-like fatigue all the way down the body" (105) to being totally "disgusted" (103), "exasperated" (102), and "push[ing] aside fear" with "impatien[ce]" (115), "despis[ing]," "resis[ting]," "stand[ing] up," and "hat[ing] to death the authors of [war] crimes" (101–2).

At the same time that the poetic text depicts the speaker's sense of list-lessness, helplessness, frustration, and futility, therefore, it also stakes, via an "ethics of narration," a political and moral claim—the right of Iraq not to be invaded by U.S. troops in the guise of the effort to establish democracy in the country. The precariousness and vulnerability of the Iraqi citizens is described in their subjection to cruelty, torture, and humiliation—"To create terror, that's war. To wallow in cruelty, conquest. To burn. To kill. To torture. To humiliate: that's war, again and again" (2005, 103). The poem also polemically comments on the indifference of the majority of Americans to the brutality of the U.S. attack on Iraq—the speaker struggles "[t]o live with the knowledge that the Americans, the English, their allies, want the people of Iraq, the children, the men of Iraq, to be destroyed" (105). The "ethics of narration" in Adnan's prose poem is therefore one that addresses the long-term physical and mental effects of war, makes a strong claim for the right of Iraqi citizens to live in their towns and cities without being attacked by U.S. military forces and, finally, criticizes the United States for its warmongering attitude and the Western media for glorifying the Iraq War and proliferating a biased, one-sided outlook, in line with George W. Bush's rhetoric, that "the battle in Iraq is noble, it is necessary, and it is just."[14] In Adnan's poem, the speaker "buy[s] the New York Times and find[s] it disgusting" because of the "pictures glorifying war." She is "appalled by the number of civilian casual-ties" and "feel[s] ashamed of feeling so comfortable in the apartment." Look-ing out her window and "desir[ing] strongly to be in Baghdad, in defiance of the war," "taunting danger" (108), the speaker inhabits a mental disposition of diaspora, admitting that in "think[ing] of Beirut, dream[ing] of Palestine, miss[ing] Baghdad, [she is] reminded of the impossibility to be ever totally where one is" (110).

The disorienting effects of exile, exacerbated by being confronted with war in the Middle East, recall a sequence in the second piece in the collec-tion, "Twenty-Five Years Later": "I moved from city to city, travelled from person to person, and then *I tried to define myself through writing*, but that doesn't work, no, not at all, it *adds fiction to the fiction I became*, and from that place where I had a sense of my absolute importance I reached a fogged Olympus from which the gods and goddesses had long departed: I'm in *a disorienting wilderness*" (2005, 29–30; my emphasis). The speaker feels that the practice of writing only "adds fiction to the fiction" she has become. She has become "stranger to myself," and her attempts to define herself through her writing only frustrate her, making her "disorient[ed]," palpably feeling the lack of any stable, unified, authentic sense of self as a diasporic citizen-subject of Lebanon now permanently resident in California. Nevertheless, the nomad speaker who "moves from city to city" writes herself into being, even if that self is fiction(al), kaleidoscopic,[15] multidimensional. Increasingly, she finds herself writing from a conflation of "subject" and "object" positions because they have become "indistinguishable," "interchangeable" (32). Indeed, the speaker's precarious and transitory spatial existence extends to her experience of "felt time" and substantive (lived) citizenship. The speaker's (and, by extension, Adnan's own) meditation on time is also reflected in the titles of many of the pieces in *In the Heart of the Heart of Another Country*: "Twenty-Five Years Later," "Further On," "Present Time," "Time, Desire, and Fog," and "To Be in a Time of War." The seven pieces in the collection are also perhaps an indirect structural reference to the seven volumes of Marcel Proust's long multivolume novel, *In Search of Lost Time; or, Remembrance of Things Past* (*À la recherche du temps perdu*),[16] and its sustained exploration of the themes of involuntary and associative memory, which resonate in Adnan's writing.

TIME, MEMORY, AND THE ETHICS OF NARRATION

The themes of time and memory, place and displacement, war and violence in Etel Adnan's *In the Heart of the Heart of Another Country* are also references to an earlier work of hers on the Lebanese Civil War, *Sitt Marie Rose: A Novel*. Originally published in French in 1977 and translated into English in 1982, the book's setting is a segregated Beirut during the civil war,[17] divided by "a line running from north to south, with the essentially Moslem quarters to the west, and the Christian quarters to the east, while here and there, especially along the waterfront, there is a sort of no-mans-land of tourism and prostitution" (1977, 9–10). The strict spatial divide between the Christian eastern half, "more Westernized and efficient in war as in everything," and the Muslim western half, which "still retain[ed] the disorder of the Orient," is replicated in the structural division of Adnan's novel into two parts, titled "Time I" and "Time II." Together, they tell a fictionalized account of the real-life story of Adnan's friend Marie Rose Boulos, a Syrian immigrant living in Lebanon, director of a school for deaf-mute children in predominantly Christian East Beirut. Although she is Christian, Sitt Marie Rose crosses over into Muslim West Beirut in order to organize social aid services for the Palestinian refugees there. She is captured by right-wing Christian militia for her involvement with the PLO (Palestinian Liberation Organization), tortured, and executed in front of her students.

The first part of Adnan's novel, "Time I," is set before the civil war. An unnamed female narrator is asked by her friend Mounir (Sitt Marie's childhood sweetheart and leader of the Christian Phalangist militia) to write the script of his film that will document the lives of Syrian migrants in Lebanon. As "Time I" proceeds, violence gradually escalates in Beirut—"the whole country is responding without reserve to this call for violence" (1977, 13)—until civil war threatens to break out. "Time I" ends with the narrator telling Mounir that she is unable to write the film script for him because he wants to censor her political opinions. The second part of the novel, "Time II," is divided into three sections comprising seven chapters each. Each section recounts the death of Sitt Marie Rose from the different perspective of each of the seven characters involved, in the following order—Sitt Marie Rose's deaf and mute schoolchildren, Sitt Marie Rose herself, Mounir, Tony and Fouad (two friends of Mounir's), the peasant Friar Bouna Lias, and the unnamed narrator from "Time I." This fracturing of the action in "Time II" into seven different perspectives is metafictionally commented upon in the first part of the novel: "Action is fragmented into sections so that no one has an exact image of the whole process" (17). Each of the characters involved not only has her or his own perspective, these perspectives are mutually incongruent. This perhaps also represents Adnan's belief at the time of publication that there was no foreseeable political resolution to the civil war.[18]

Sitt Marie Rose depicts a Beirut divided not only along religious but also class and gender lines. The novel clearly critiques the patriarchal structures of the city and the gender roles assigned to women. Men don't want to be "bothered" (1977, 19) by women, think they "shouldn't even open [their] mouths," are "pig-headed" and "whores" (51). Women are thus caught in a "restrictive circle" beyond which rights such as higher education are out of reach. In chapter 2 of the second section, Sitt Marie Rose recalls her husband's reaction when she enrolls in the university, his sulking and resentment when she starts to lead a public life, attending "conferences, protests, social action, planning committees" (18) in support of various political causes. The speaker reflects the gendered roles women are expected to follow and the difficulty, even near impossibility, of leading a politically active life in the dominantly male public sphere in Beirut. In chapter 7 of "Time II," the unnamed narrator critiques the right-wing Christian militia men who execute Sitt Marie Rose: "Their women only exert indirect powers over them, powers that seem ineffective, or else are so strong that they, the men, can't recognize them as such. But a woman who stands up to them and looks them in the eye is a tree to be cut down, and they cut it down" (67).

Sitt Marie Rose is a cipher, an unreadable character, to the four men who murder her; they do not understand why she, as a Christian woman, would fight for the Muslim Palestinian cause and even take on a Palestinian refugee, a doctor and member of the PLO as her lover. Interestingly, the precarious "Other" in Adnan's novel is not only Sitt Marie Rose herself but also her male lover. Sitt Marie Rose

> thinks of that "other" whom she has just left, and who waits for her with her children in mortal apprehension. She had met him in the narrow streets of the Sabra camp the day she went to the U.N.W.R.R.A. [United Nations Relief and Works Agency for Palestine Refugees in the Near East] for the first time. . . . She saw how haggard these people were, and understood the nature of their new wandering. These were no longer nomads comforted by their tribe and their herd, but a people perpetually pursued . . . without a single square meter of certainty or security under their feet. They would have to forge a nation in the midst of total hostility.

Adnan's novel thus deconstructs notions of citizenship, nationality, and national identity by bringing the figure of the precarious "Other," the Palestinian refugee, into sharp relief against the right-wing Christian Phalangist militia, which regards Palestinians as foreigners in Lebanon who are as "out of place as a fox is in a wolf's den" (1977, 71). In the excerpt above, the notion of precariousness is directly linked to the fight for national sovereignty and autonomy of the state of Palestine, which has been occupied by Israel since the 1967 Arab-Israeli War. The Palestinian refugees' precarious existence "without a single square meter of certainty or security under their feet" literally reflects their disenfranchisement with regard to the rights of political identity and national status/statehood.[19] The historical facts that Adnan's novel alludes to are, indeed, significant. As a result of the 1948 Arab-Israeli War, 85 percent of Palestinians fled to the West Bank and Gaza Strip as well as to the neighboring countries of Lebanon, Jordan, and Syria. Scholars such as Michael Dumper have argued that the Palestinian refugee and displaced persons population, including undocumented persons, is the largest refugee and displaced persons population in the world (2006, 6). Dumper contends that the daily living conditions of these Palestinian refugees are precarious, especially in Lebanon where, unlike in Syria and Jordan, measures of political and economic integration as well as citizenship and legal residency status have not been extended to them.

Etel Adnan's *Sitt Marie Rose* thus reflects on two different forms of precariousness that are connected to notions of citizenship and nationhood. The first is depicted in the character of Sitt Marie Rose's lover, the Palestinian refugee, doctor, and supporter of the Palestinian Liberation Front who, when Sitt Marie Rose is captured and tortured, grieves for her by "discard[ing] all that he knew," "forg[eting] his name and age," and becoming "reduced to nothing but the consciousness of his own pain" (1977, 71). The second is rendered by the figure of Sitt Marie Rose herself, a Syrian-Lebanese female migrant who fights for the Palestinian cause and is hence regarded as a traitor, a transgressor, and a sympathizer with the enemy. The novel thus conveys the deeply conflicted historical trajectory of Lebanese identity politics. As an ambivalent and "undecipherable" character, an "unpatriotic" citizen who "leaves the normal order of things" and rejects the role that Lebanese society assigns to her, Sitt Marie Rose becomes a victim of the political body of the nation. As a "cell that contains the desire for liberty," she is "killed, digested and reabsorbed" (75) by the national body. In different ways, therefore, both Sitt Marie Rose and her lover are victims of the homogenous national, religious, and cultural identities that ideological narratives of the nation perpetuate. As a traitor and enemy, respectively, the two of them are regarded as risky bodies instead of bodies at risk that, therefore, must be contained and ultimately eliminated by the official state apparatus. Adnan's novel closes with the execution of Sitt Marie Rose in front of the deaf-mute children she teaches. The victimization of the precarious "Other" becomes complete in a macabre Dance of Death performed by the deaf-mutes, who move to "the rhythm of falling bombs their bodies receive from the trembling earth" (105). Sitt Marie Rose is, however, not alone in her death: "Second by second the inhabitants of this city that were her comrades fall" (104). Her comrades, members of the Palestinian Liberation Organization and Palestinian refugees whom she has helped by providing basic services such as shelter, food, and water, are thus also metaphorically eradicated by the state.

Sitt Marie Rose is punished and executed by members of the Christian militia because she is regarded as a traitor along the lines of religion, ethnicity, and gender ("She's a Christian and she went over the to Moslem camp. She's Lebanese and she went over to the Palestinian camp." Such black-and-white ("That's how it is. We must suppress them" [1977, 36]) regulations along strict, regimental lines ("I am absolute order. I am absolute power. I am absolute efficiency" [37]) demonstrate how precarization, or sustained methods of making the other's existence precarious, can be used as a specific instrument of national governance. This is a concept that political scientist Isabell Lorey terms "governmental precarization," which she defines as "modes of governing since the emergence of industrial-capitalist conditions . . . [that] cannot be separated in occidental modern societies from bourgeois self-determination. Governmental precarization means . . . a destabilization of ways of living and hence of bodies" (2011). In Etel Adnan's *Sitt Marie Rose*, the reader recalls that the members of the Christian militia, who deem it necessary to eradicate the Palestinian Muslims, hold strong allegiances with the West. The character of Mounir, for example, who becomes the leader of the Christian militia gang referred to as the Chababs, identifies with Frederick Barbarossa, the German Holy Roman emperor, because, rather banally, "he [Mounir] was himself slightly red-haired." In chapter 2 of the second section, Sitt Marie Rose recalls Mounir's schooling by French Jesuit priests "who oriented them [the students] toward Paris and the quarrels of the French kings" (1977, 47). Mounir and his other male classmates are described as "dream[ing] of a Christianity with helmets and boots, riding its horses into the clash of arms, spearing Moslem foot-soldiers like so many St. Georges with so many dragons." Sitt Marie Rose comments, recalling a conversation about the religious Crusades as reenacted by the French priests that motivated the boys to reject their own Lebanese cultural heritage:

> I remember telling him that, dressed up like a Crusader and marching in that procession, he must have been the most ridiculous thing in the world. He laughed and his laughter still sounds in my years: "You're just a girl. You don't know what it's like to be a twelve-year-old boy." I remember replying, "You come from here. You're not a foreigner. You don't come from France or England. You could never

be a Crusader." "Are you sure?" he asked with a sadness that misted
his eyes, "Then what am I going to become?" (48)

The exchange above illustrates Mounir's naïve misplaced sense of belonging
to Western culture and heritage, with which he is indoctrinated in school.
Significantly, it is a mere twelve-year-old Sitt Marie Rose who first shatters
his boyish dreams by pointing out that he is not a European but Lebanese,
deconstructing the dreams of affiliation that he and his other male classmates had with the West. Moreover, the novel critiques the double standards of the older Mounir and his peers in the Christian militia who, on the
one hand, are effectively influenced by "modern," Western neoliberal foreign
policies and, on the other, reinforce very traditional gender binaries/roles and
endorse patriarchal Lebanese structures of government. Mounir's conviction
that the French are superior to the Lebanese, who are, in turn, in a higher
hierarchical position to the Syrians and Palestinians, renders him, too, in a
precariously subjugated situation, one to which he ironically remains blind.
His situation is a fictional representation of the condition of others like him
who are subject to "precarization . . . as a neoliberal instrument of governance" (Lorey 2010).

Above, I have traced how an "ethics of narration" (Booth 1990; Nussbaum
2007) is employed in the poetic memoirs and experimental prose writings of
Lebanese American writer and artist Etel Adnan. It is this "ethics of narration" that drives the author's larger critique of the patriarchal and hierarchical
structures, xenophobia and, paradoxically, alignment with Western neoliberal
structures of government that influenced the daily lives of people in Lebanon
during the civil war. In Adnan's *In the Heart of the Heart of Another Country*
and *Sitt Marie Rose*, the precariousness of the "Other" (the people of Iraq, the
figure of the exile, the Palestinian refugee, the Christian woman who crosses
ethnic, religious, and gendered lines of division) is portrayed in a language
of disorientation, loss, death, pain, and violence. Yet the affective quality of
the narrative also demands a sense of moral accountability and empathy on
the part of the reader, who is made to bear witness, just as Sitt Marie Rose's
deaf-mute schoolchildren are made to behold her horrific execution. This
mode of witness and visual documentation is captured aptly by Palestinian
American literary theorist Edward Said and Swiss documentary photographer Jean Mohr's collaborative textual and photographic exploration of

Palestinian identity in the light of forced migration, dispossession, and exile, *After the Last Sky* (1986).[20]

VISUALIZING PRECARIOUSNESS: PALESTINIAN LIVES, EXILE, COMMUNITY

In his introduction to *After the Last Sky*, Edward Said makes some key observations about the representation of Palestinian experiences of suffering, exile, and displacement:

> There is no doubt that we do in fact form a community, if at heart a community built on suffering and exile. How though, to convey it? *The thing about our exile is that much of it is invisible.* . . . We are at once too recently formed and *too variously experienced to be a population of articulate exiles with a completely systematic vision.* . . . The whole point of this book is to engage this difficulty, to deny the habitually simple, even harmful representations of Palestinians, and to replace them with something more capable of capturing *the complex reality of that experience.* (1986, 5–6; my emphasis)

The close to two hundred pages of photographs and text that follow this introduction are an attempt to render visible and make tangible the complex nature of Palestinian lives. The "interplay of text and photos, the mixture of genres, modes, styles—do not tell a consecutive story" (1986, 6), Said writes; nor do they construct a "clear and simple narrative." Rather, the result is an "unconventional, hybrid, and fragmentary . . . alternative mode of expression" (5) that challenges dominant representations of Palestinians in mass media and popular fiction. Interestingly, in a comment similar to that of the speaker in Etel Adnan's prose poem "Twenty-Five Years Later" in *In the Heart of the Heart of Another Country*, who professes the interchangeability of subject and object positions, Edward Said, too, writes of a "double vision" that informs his textual project: "As I wrote, I found myself switching pronouns, from 'we' to 'you' to 'they,' to designate Palestinians. As abrupt as these shifts are, I feel they reproduce the way 'we' experience ourselves" (6). Such "multifaceted vision," he claims, is essential to any attempt to represent Palestinian lives.

The major themes of exile and displacement, fragmentation and a dispersed national identity—but also a sense of playful irony and introspection—echo and reverberate throughout the four chapters of the book, titled

"States," "Interiors," "Emergence," "Past and Future." "States" begins with a photograph taken by Jean Mohr at the Baddawi refugee camp in Tripoli, Lebanon (see figure 5 in the color insert). Said's textual commentary on the photograph runs as follows:

> Caught in a meager, anonymous space outside a drab Arab city, out-side a refugee camp, outside the crushing time of one disaster after another, a wedding party stands, *surprised, sad, slightly uncomfortable.* . . . Cutting across the wedding party's path here is the ever-present Mercedes, emblazoned with its extra mark of authenticity, the proud *D* for *Deutschland.* . . . [B]ecause Palestinians have no state of their own to shield them, the Mercedes, its provenance and destination obscure, seems like an intruder, a delegate of the forces that both dislocate and hem them in. . . . *The paradox of mobility and insecurity. Wherever we Palestinians are, we are not in our Palestine, which no longer exists.* (1986, 11; my emphasis)

My own interpretation of Mohr's photograph takes up where Said's leaves off: the Palestinian wedding party and the subjects' sense of slight discomfort and awkwardness at posing stiffly in front of the white, European, male photographer (Jean Mohr) is captured in the slightly artificial smile on the face of the woman standing next to the bride, holding the ceremonial *djembé* drum, her right hand, fingers extended on the drum's surface, in a gesture of faux play. The composition of the photograph also neatly replicates the gender divide in Palestinian society—the two men stand to the left of the bridegroom, and the two women stand to the right of the bride. The Mercedes juts rather incongruously into the bottom left of the picture, appearing overproportionally large, with its marker of nationality (D for Deutschland) out of place against the backdrop of the Baddawi camp in Tripoli which, one of the largest refugee camps for stateless Palestinians who fled in the 1948 Arab-Israeli War, is reduced to a "non-place" (Augé 1995).[21] The Baddawi refugee camp looms large in the background of the photograph, the gray cement walls and steel beams of its concrete shelters protruding unceremoniously. The wedding party is caught, even on this ceremonious occasion, in a no-man's-land, in a liminal space of unbelonging as "Palestinians . . . not in our Palestine, which no longer exists."

Like Etel Adnan's novel *Sitt Marie Rose,* therefore, Edward Said and Jean

Mohr's *After the Last Sky*, too, contains a critique of Palestinian society as divided along strict lines of national identification, gender, class, and religion. In chapter 2, "Interiors," Said writes how the phrase *min al-dakhil*, or "from the interior," has a special significance to the Palestinian ear because it has two meanings—first, it refers to "regions of the interior of Israel, to territories and people still Palestinian despite the interdictions of the Israeli presence" (1986, 51) and second, it is roughly equivalent to the phrase "to be privy to," and thus to be an "insider" to certain code phrases. The chapter "Interiors," therefore, is an extended meditation on the ways in which processes of inclusion and exclusion continue to haunt the displaced Palestinian subject—be it the secular, middle-class, intellectual exile living in the United States (such as Said himself) or the stateless Palestinian refugee living in abject poverty without proper health care in the Shatila camp in Lebanon. Finally, the phrase *min al-dakhil* also plays on the idea that Palestine is, above all, a state of interiority or a state of mind. In this respect, the text and photographs in this chapter offer the reader snapshot portraits, visual representations, of the interior lives of Palestinian exiles. Said ends the chapter with a long section on Palestinian women who, in his opinion, have been the most excluded, marginalized, and disenfranchised, even by "the effusively male character of Palestinian nationalism" (79):

> I recognize in all this a fundamental problem—the crucial absence of women. With few exceptions, women seem to have played little more than the role of hyphen, connective, transition, mere incident. . . . I can see women everywhere in Palestinian life, and I see how they exist between the syrupy sentimentalism of roles we ascribe to them (mothers, virgins, martyrs) and the annoyance, even dislike, that their unassimilated strength provokes in our warily politicized, automatic manhood. (77)

Any representation of Palestinian exile, Said thus asserts, must take into account the stories and experiences of Palestinian women. Chapter 2 ends with a description of the filmic narratives of two women who live as subjects of Israel, as depicted in Palestinian director Michel Khleifi's film, *The Fertile Memory*—Farah Hatoum, an elderly widow who remained in Nazareth after the Arab-Israeli War of 1948 and "refuses to sell land that she owns but that in fact has been 'repossessed' by Israelis," and Sahar Khalifé, a young novelist, teacher, and political activist who describes herself as a militant.

We have returned to Sitt Marie Rose's story, the exceptional story of one woman's resistance to her condition of precariousness and her experiences of dispossession. Like the deaf-mute schoolchildren made to witness Sitt Marie Rose's execution, we, too, as readers of Edward Said's and Jean Mohr's collective project on Palestinian lives, *After the Last Sky*, are made aware of our gaze. The closing paragraph of the book is reminiscent of Judith Butler's call for a nonviolent ethics based upon an understanding of human vulnerability and injurability, for political reflection and deliberation attuned to the various forms and manifestations of precariousness and precarization that characterize neoliberal societies in the Western and non-Western world. "I would like to think," Said concludes, "that we are not just the people seen or looked at in these photographs: We are also looking at our observers. We Palestinians sometimes forget that . . . *we too are looking, we too are scrutinizing, assessing, judging*. We are more than someone's object" (1986, 166; my emphasis).

"Who's looking at you now?" the last photograph in Said and Mohr's book (1986) seems to ask the reader rather cheekily. The photograph, captioned "After Jerusalem, 1979. The photographer photographed," captures two young children gazing up at the photographer. The expression on the face of the child on the right is mischievous, playful, daring, while the child on the left peers up at the photographer, looking through a handheld camera. Countering the high-angle shot of the photograph, which usually makes the figure or object of the image seem vulnerable or defenseless, the bold gestures of the children reflect the photographer's/viewer's gaze back upon themselves, triggering a moment of self-awareness and questioning "objective" modes of visual representation. The proliferation of typical images and stock photographs of Palestinian lives in the Western media—from pictures of women and the elderly in overcrowded refugee camps to news reports on protesters against Israeli occupation in the Gaza Strip and special features on Palestinian child soldiers—has resulted in a normalization of the (Palestinian) "Other's" condition of precariousness. These predominantly negative, dominant media representations of Palestinians[22] have led to a misconstruing of them as the source of risk, as risky subjects instead of subjects at risk. Etel Adnan's *In the Heart of the Heart of Another Country* and *Sitt Marie Rose* and Edward Said's *After the Last Sky* collectively oppose dominant representations of Palestinian lives as well as prevailing depictions of the political situation in the Middle East by reversing the

Orientalizing gaze that, one might note, has experienced a backlash and become all the more powerful in the wake of 9/11. Affective and unsettling, these works stake a moral claim for the rights of "Others" to avail themselves of political, social, and cultural membership. They also demand a sense of ethical responsibility and accountability on the part of the reader, engendering a politics of intervention that, as Martha Nussbaum (2007) has argued, challenges traditional, and often exclusionary, notions of citizenship and moral reasoning. The figures at the center of these fictional and semifictional narratives are characters who are precarious and excluded from the spaces of the nation; yet, at the same time, they are the ones who are transgressive, who dare to go against the grain of "the normal order of things" (Adnan 1977, 73) and reverse the dominant gaze, even when faced with the threats of persecution and death. By challenging conventional representations of the Israeli-Palestinian conflict and issues of segregation, national identity, and sovereignty in Lebanon and the Middle East as well as, more broadly, predominant depictions of political migrants, refugees, exiles, and diasporic subjects in Western mass media, the works of Etel Adnan and Edward Said demonstrate how the narrative imagination can foster a sense of post-national, cosmopolitan civic empathy through an "ethics of narration."

5

NARRATIVES OF UNHOMING, DISPLACEMENT, AND RELOCATION

· · · · · · · · · ·

George Elliott Clarke's *Whylah Falls* and the
Africadian Community in Nova Scotia

This chapter turns to an examination of precarious citizenship within a Canadian context. Specifically, it focuses on the poetics/politics of regionalism, as opposed to federalism, in the coastal territories of Atlantic Canada: the three Maritime Provinces of Nova Scotia, New Brunswick, Prince Edward Island, and the province of Newfoundland and Labrador.[1] Since the 1990s, this region has been the backdrop of a simultaneous narrative of crisis and transformation as reflected in, on the one hand, the decline of the independent fishing industry,[2] lower government subsidies, out-migration, an aging population, and uncertainty about the region's place in the Canadian nation, and, on the other, a regionalist revitalization of cultural vitality and regional identity in the last decade.[3] Accordingly, notions of citizenship and national identity have been debated, contested, and reworked in Atlantic Canada as part of attempts at "regional redefinition" (Wyile 2011, 2), of endeavors to articulate "the shared imagining of what constitutes the region" (Slumkoski 2011, 11).[4] This effort to convey a shared sense of regional(ist) rather than national identity and place is, however, and perhaps not unexpectedly, fraught with internal ruptures and differences. Critics have pointed out, for example, that the entry of Newfoundland into Canadian Confederation in 1949, and hence its union with the Maritime Provinces to form the geographical entity of Atlantic Canada, was met with ambivalence by both Newfoundlanders and the residents of the Maritimes.[5]

This chapter focuses on a landmark case in black Atlantic Canadian history that illustrates a particular form of regionalism, challenging the notion of a Canadian national identity while exploring the contested nature of spaces of "home" and "nation." The Africville relocation, as it has come to be known, was the forceful eviction and extinction of the Africville community, a predominantly black, underclass population that lived on the southern shore of Bedford Basin in the outskirts of Halifax, Nova Scotia, by the Halifax City Council between 1964 and 1970 in the name of "urban renewal." It was the culmination of years of systemic marginalization and exclusion of the Africville community, and their removal to inner-city council housing that, in many instances, only aggravated their precarious situations in terms of employment and social welfare. The Africville relocation and the legal charges that were pressed against the city council in its wake are significant because they destabilize notions of nation-based citizenship, identity, and belonging while also making claims for the inclusion of ethnic minorities and disadvantaged groups in regional(ist) politics.[6] The Africville removal has now been depicted in several works of fiction, music, and art that largely adopt a regionalist perspective, focusing on the "local color,"[7] customs, and cultural setting of the community of Africville.[8] They are also characterized by a strong sense of nostalgia for a lost community at the same time that they aim to voice sociopolitical critique against governmental policies that marginalized and disenfranchised the residents of Africville. The poetics of counter-hegemony in these works thus coexists with a nostalgic longing for lost community, kinship, and religious and cultural identity that is bound to a regional(ist) sense of place. What emerges is an underlying sense of mourning for the demise of a way of life in Africville that, despite its slumlike living conditions, was nevertheless home to its residents.

What follows is a critical reading of one exemplary fictional narrative of displacement and relocation based on the Africville evictions, George Elliott Clarke's *Whylah Falls* (1990). By way of Michel Foucault's concept of "counter-memory" (1977),[9] I argue that Clarke's narrative of "unhoming" and exile places itself in a larger archive of "counter-history" (see Foucault 2003, 79) in the repository of black Canadian history. Clarke's fictional poetic narrative also challenges official versions, documentations, and reports of the Africville resettlement by the Halifax City Council. I will examine also how Clarke's text itself becomes the site of resistance and struggle via what Homi Bhabha terms "textual strategies," "subtexts," and "figurative stratagems" (1990, 2), metaphorically enacting a reclaiming of the land taken away from Africville residents by the government of Nova Scotia. As a literary intervention that critiques existing and exclusionary nation-based models of Canadian citizenship, identity, and belonging, *Whylah Falls* forms part of a larger body of emerging work in Atlantic Canada that articulates a regional(ist) poetics of emergent subjectivity.[10]

Evidently, this is a poetics that is inextricably intertwined with the politics of home, which itself should be understood not only as a physical, spatial, and geographical location but as a cultural, socioeconomic, and ideological construct. In the Maritime Provinces of Canada, ideas of home and nation have been shaped by the legacies of British and French settler colonialism. This is particularly the case in Halifax, the capital of Nova Scotia, which was populated by American slaves after the American Revolutionary War (1775–83), Jamaican Maroons in 1796,[11] and black Loyalists to the British crown following the War of 1812. The residents of Africville, largely descendants of these populations,[12] were persistently marginalized by the government of Nova Scotia in the late nineteenth and twentieth centuries. Deteriorating living conditions led to the widespread perception of Africville as an eyesore and a black slum/ghetto, although there was a small minority of white residents living there.

In 1962, the Halifax City Council adopted the Stephenson Report of 1957 that proposed the relocation of Africville's residents to Halifax innercity council housing. The city council also passed the Rose Report of 1964, which promised better education, employment assistance, and job training for the Africville community (but did not specify intermediate-level goals or how these programs were to be carried out successfully).[13] The evacuation and resettlement of Africville's residents was carried out largely between 1964 and 1967 according to the liberal-welfare model of relocation that assured better housing and living standards in the name of "urban renewal." Not surprisingly, Africville relocatees did not receive the benefits promised them, and found themselves increasingly struggling with the higher costs of living in Halifax city. Many of them had to rely on social welfare.[14] On February 24,

2010, an official apology was made by Halifax mayor Peter Kelly, together with a $4.5 million compensation deal. However, the latter did not assuage two centuries of persistent socioeconomic discrimination and exclusion of an underclass black Canadian community.

HOME AND AWAY: A(R)CADIA VERSUS AFRICVILLE

The marginalization of black Nova Scotians can be traced back to the mid-eighteenth century, when the province was first inhabited by the slaves of British and French settlers as well as a minority of black freedmen.[15] In 1713, the British had conquered mainland Nova Scotia, which the vanquished French had called (continental) Acadia, after Arcadia,[16] the idyllic vision of pastoral beauty and unspoiled wilderness since Greek antiquity (see Virgil's *Eclogues*).

Encompassing the Maritime Provinces of New Brunswick, Nova Scotia (including Cape Breton Island), and Prince Edward Island as well as part of eastern Quebec and Maine, Acadia was one of five colonies of New France from 1604 to 1713. The region was highly contested territory, fought over by the British and French settlers in no fewer than six wars from 1688 (King William's War) to 1763 (the French and Indian War that was part of the Seven Years' War between the colonies of British America and New France). Acadia was also a contested space for other communities who lived and settled in the area, including the Indigenous Mi'kmaq First Nations and the black Loyalists who settled in the region in the aftermath of the American Revolutionary War. It is the latter group of black Loyalists who were the ancestors of the inhabitants of Africville, a small community of around four hundred residents located on the northern end of the Halifax peninsula on the southern shores of the Bedford Basin, relatively isolated from the rest of the city. Over the course of the nineteenth and twentieth centuries, Africville became home to Rockhead Prison (1853), the city's night waste disposal pits (1858), an infectious disease hospital (1870s), a trachoma hospital (1905), an open city dump and incinerator (early 1950s), and a slaughterhouse. Deteriorating living conditions, including lack of safe, clean drinking water, finally led to a proposal by the Halifax City Council to evacuate and resettle the Africville community in the city center housing projects of Mulgrave Park and Uniacke Square in the 1960s.

The entire resettlement project reflected the liberal-welfare model of relocation and was carried out with a "genuine concern" for the "deplorable" conditions in which Africville residents lived. As Clairmont and

Magill detail, there were broadly four models of relocation:[17] the development model (which seeks to eliminate economic or social "liabilities" to the state),[18] the liberal-welfare model, the political model (a revised version of the liberal-welfare model that emerged in the late 1970s that recognizes the conflict of interest between relocatees/evacuees and the city), and the traditional model (grassroots-, neighborhood-, and community-level initiatives of social change). The liberal-welfare model of relocation, according to which the Africville resettlement was carried out, emerged in the mid-1940s as a response to the "war on poverty," the increasing pressure "from below," and a broadening of the definition of "urban renewal" (Clairmont and Magill 1999, 7). This model was accompanied by a host of social welfare programs supplemental to housing policies meant to attack urban poverty and purporting to benefit the relocatees primarily. In fact, many relocation officials genuinely regarded themselves as the tenants' advocates. The liberal-welfare rhetoric shaped many post–World War II relocation projects nationwide in Canada and the United States.

As a landmark case in black Canadian history, the story of Africville has been recorded in the genres of print and visual media. The thirty-five-minute documentary film *Remember Africville*, directed by Shelagh Mackenzie and released by the National Film Board of Canada in 1991, was an attempt to chronicle the life and death of this predominantly black, underclass, Baptist community as well as to recount the controversial expulsion of Africville residents from their homes without proper recompense (those who did not possess title deeds to their homes were not remunerated) and redress the discrimination that they experienced. In the documentary, the former residents of Africville notably articulate a sense of community, kinship, and belonging—even a proud, separatist, regionalist identity ("a people by ourselves," as Joseph Skinner, one past resident, puts it) that remains even though their land and the homes built on them have been taken away from them. Skinner expresses the sense of freedom in living outside an environment of racial prejudice that, for him, the inner city of Halifax represented. The slogan "Africville should go back to the people," championed by Wanda Lewis, a former Africville resident, conveys the sense of belonging and possession the residents felt even though the rest of the city of Halifax perceived their home as a "social problem," an eyesore, a slum. One could argue that the Africville ex-residents' accounts are shot through with a sense of nostalgia and mourning that romanticizes community life despite dismal hygiene conditions, poor infrastructure, and meager resources. Despite the documentary's clearly laudable objective to visually document the story of Africville with archival footage and, presumably, its status as a gesture of reparation on the part of the National Film Board of Canada, the political edge of Mackenzie's film, in particular its critique of liberal-welfare attempts to eradicate urban poverty, is perhaps blunted by the sentimentalized[19] and rather homogenous accounts of Africville by its former residents.

In comparison, George Elliot Clarke's *Whylah Falls*, a fictional narrative inspired by the Africville evacuation and resettlement, offers a different depiction of this episode in black Atlantic Canadian history. Although Clarke's verse novel, too, tells a rather romanticized tale of Africville as the land of milk and honey (2000, 79)—as framed through the stories of love, desire, betrayal, jealousy, and violence in the community—it stresses that black Canadian identity needs to be recognized within the framework, and not merely within the margins, of the Canadian nation. Through the use of blues ballad and song, archival photographs, newspaper clippings, recipes, and intertextual literary references, Clarke's poetic text *itself* becomes an intermedial site of contestation that challenges nation-based notions of citizenship, identity, and belonging, critiquing the forces of exclusion and marginalization that are still present in Canadian society today.

WHYLAH FALLS, AFRICADIA, AND NEW MYTHS

Whylah Falls is a verse novel set in eight "acts"[20] that depicts the cultural geography of a region the author terms "Africadia"—a neologism that combines "Africa" and "Acadia." The novel was first published in 1990; the tenth anniversary edition features an extended introduction wherein Clarke details the influences on his narrative: the lyric(al), myth and history, music and traditions:

> *Whylah Falls* was born in the blues, the philosophy of the cry. . . . You have to structure the book like an orchestra, a cordance of brass, woodwind, string, percussion, and other instruments. . . . Consider the book as a symphony in which each poem is a passage, sometimes harmonious, sometimes cacophonous. *Hence, the narrative emerges from the lyrical—sometimes in counterpoint, at other times in harmony, now merging, now diverging, but always enjoying the liberty of concord and discord.* (2000, xi; my emphasis)

Clarke's conception of how the poems in the book should work together in counterpoint—in congruence yet also in dissonance—can be read alongside a critical observation he makes about Africadian (and, more broadly, black Canadian) identity. In the introduction to his anthology, *Eyeing the North Star* (1997), Clarke contends, "The variegate composition of the African-Canadian community frustrates trans-ethnic, trans-linguistic communication. (Hence, no truly 'national school' of African-Canadian literature has been created, nor will we ever see one)" (xviii). Clarke argues that the "fragile coalition" of African Canadian identities and their "variegate composition"[21] frustrate any attempt to speak of a collective African Canadian identity or experience. Accordingly, he contends that even within specific regional geographies, such as Atlantic Canada, it is difficult to speak of a homogenous black Maritime identity in the singular.

This is exemplified by the communities of people who lived in Africville. Although most visual and textual representations of the Africville relocation depict the community as a largely homogenous one, closer inspection has revealed that Africville was home to a more heterogeneous group of people. As the authors of the *Africville Relocation Report*, an independent study published in 1971, Donald Clairmont and Dennis Magill have argued, Africville was home to effectively four groups of residents: the "marginals/transients," who included a white underclass minority without "kinship ties or land/housing claims in the community," and "a handful of racially mixed families"; the "mainliners," who "had regular employment and property claims" and were thus, "comparatively speaking, the socio-economic elite"; the "oldliners," who had "kinship ties in Africville dating back to the 1840s"; and the "residuals," black residents without "ancestral ties in Africville," who did not possess legal land claims and some of whom were squatters (1999, 53). The coexistence of these four groups led to social differentiation within Africville that was related to residential location—the westernmost homes, which were of the poorest quality and housed mostly marginals/transients, were referred to as "around the bend"; the main settlement, which was divided by train tracks into "basinside" and "the hill," had the highest-quality housing and was populated by the mainliners and oldliners; while the southeastern corner of Africville, which was commonly referred to as "Big Town," housed mostly "residuals" who were bootleggers and squatters and often regarded by the majority of the Africville community as "cast-offs" who "gave everybody else a bad name" (Clairmont and Magill 1999, 53–56).

As Clairmont and Magill also point out, this internal distinction and division between the four major social groups in Africville was important as there was "significant variation by group in terms of orientation to community, attitude towards relocation, relocation negotiation style, and post-relocation adjustment" (1999, 56). Statistics revealed, for example, that it was the financially better-off mainliners who were most willing to move, and the oldliners, the marginal/transients, and residuals who were least willing to be relocated to council housing in the Halifax city center. Idealization of "old Africville" was particularly prevalent among elderly oldliners involved in the Baptist church who demonstrated a strong sense of pride and community. It is chiefly this mode of remembrance, which mourns the loss of a close-knit, self-sufficient, and fiercely independent group of black residents, that has become the adopted style of documentary reportages and commissioned works on the Africville relocation. What might initially seem a small homogenous community of Africadians, therefore, turns out to be a much more diverse and socially differentiated group of residents who do not uniformly exhibit or embrace a "collective consciousness," or a sense of unbroken continuity or heritage tied to the land of their ancestors. Interestingly, this undermines, or at least complicates, the very idea of "home" as a homogenous, uncontested place of origin and communal identity, the location of one's "roots" as well as cultural heritage, as the documentary by Sheilagh Mackenzie, *Remember Africville*, conveys.

George Elliott Clarke's caution against "essentialist nostalgia" and "talk of a 'collective consciousness'" (1997, xix) can thus be understood in relation to his critical observations concerning the heterogeneity of Africadian identity. It is this sense of plurality, Clarke argues, that distinguishes African Canadian identity from that of African Americans, as the latter "[project] an identity, steeped in a visceral history, that is only fitfully available in Canada" (xviii). By extrapolation, Clarke claims, there is no single unifying sovereign nation-state of Canada but a multiplicity of Canada*s*. Clarke's assertions recall Homi Bhabha's famous argument in *Nation and Narration* that, despite the "the attempt by nationalist discourses persistently to produce the idea of the nation as a continuous narrative of national progress," nations are much more "ambivalent" and "liminal" entities, replete with "transgressive boundaries" and "'interruptive' interiorit[ies]." Similarly, national myths are always situated in a competing discourse that renders them incomplete. "Despite the certainty with which historians speak of the 'origins' of the nation," Bhabha argues, its "cultural temporality . . . inscribes a much more transitional social reality" (1990, 1).

In this respect, one could read the multigeneric sections of poems, letters, song lyrics, and photographs in *Whylah Falls* as a metaphorical fragmentation of the dominant myths of the nation, even as it is the writer's task to "accumulate," "sift," and "alter" (2000, xvii) oral and written histories in order to create new myths for the next generations. Significantly, these new myths are not entirely disconnected from old myths of the nation but challenge and reinscribe, them *from within.* They constitute, to borrow a term from African American writer Toni Morrison, "rememories" (1987, 33)—physical entities (including the narrative spaces of the text) that trigger hurtful memories from the past but that continue to be significant in the present. As a writing strategy, rememories enable the poet/author to reinscribe histories of segregation, exclusion, and dispossession. *Whylah Falls* is therefore not only an attempt to represent but also to redress this landmark case in Canadian history whereby a dominantly black, socioeconomically disenfranchised community in Nova Scotia was evicted and displaced against its will and without proper recompense.

Morrison's notion of "rememory" references an earlier concept by Michel Foucault—that of "counter-memory." In his lecture on January 28, 1976, at the Collège de France, part of his series of lectures collected in the volume *"Society Must Be Defended,"*[22] Foucault used the terms *counter-memory* and *counter-history* to refer to popular memory, narratives, and accounts that exist in contradistinction to official and hence "authoritative" versions of a historical period and its political formations. "The history of some," he reminded his audience, "is not the history of others" (2003, 69–70). A counter-history thus provides a counter-perspective that resists and undoes established historical continuities, uncovering the disunities, gaps, and silences that have been elided (70), the heterogeneity that has been made uniform, in official narratives of the nation. As José Medina summarizes, "[C]ounter-histories . . . are centered around those experiences and memories that have not been heard and integrated in official histories. . . . [C]ounter-histories . . . are possible because there are people who remember against the grain, people whose memories do not fit the historical narratives available" (2011, 12). It is these memories, actual and imagined, of "what was omitted" (Clarke 2000, xxv) from official historical narratives that fill the pages of George Elliot Clarke's *Whylah Falls*, rendering it a counter-history in which those who have been excluded from the spaces of the (white, middle-class) Canadian nation are given voice. This is enacted by the text via two modes—one, an employment of the black vernacular and traditions of blues, jazz, and song (John Coltrane, Miles Davis, Billy Holiday, Bessie Smith,[23] and others) to convey "the liberatory phenomenon of African-American song disrupting standard literary discourse" (xxii) and two, a "writing back"[24] to the traditional corpus of Anglo-American literature and literary criticism. This "writing back" can be regarded as a form of "counter-storytelling," to borrow a term from critical race theory, which denotes the usage of narrative and storytelling to elucidate, challenge, and counteract experiences of racial prejudice and oppression.[25] This mode of writing back or counter-storytelling foregrounds the text itself as the site of resistance; in this instance, against the disenfranchisement of a mainly black community[26] within a region that itself has been marginalized and stereotyped by the rest of the Canadian nation. In this respect, *Whylah Falls* enacts a "revisionin[g] of" and "inventive engagement with" the past, one that "resist[s] the vision of the Maritimes as 'a place that didn't count any more'" (Wyile 2011, 232).

Whylah Falls can thus be read as an attempt to position the histories of black Atlantic Canadian literatures and regional cultural identities against the predominantly "white," Eurocentric literary theory and criticism that continue to shape ideas of "high" literature and literariness in anglophone cultures. Through the use of mimicry (Bhabha 1991),[27] the poems and fragments in the book refer to canonical works such as Sir Philip Sidney's "A Defense of Poesy" (written in 1579 and published in 1595), T. S. Eliot's "Tradition and the Individual Talent" (1921), William Empson's "Seven Types of Ambiguity" (1930), and Wimsatt and Beardsley's "The Intentional Fallacy" (originally published in 1945)—all these titles are incorporated as headings in different sections of Clarke's introduction to the tenth anniversary edition of the text. Collectively, they illustrate Clarke's ambiguous adoption and appropriation of these canonical literary texts. For instance, in the section titled "The Intentional Fallacy," Clarke refers to the eponymous term coined by Wimsatt and Beardsley to mean "a confusion between the poem and its origins . . . that ends in biography and relativism" (1954, 21). For Wimsatt and Beardsley, two literary critics who espoused the formalist movement of New Criticism in the mid-twentieth century, it was important to separate the text and its author (a position that T. S. Eliot had already outlined two decades earlier in his insistence on the extinction of personality in the essay

"Tradition and the Individual Talent"). In contrast, Clarke asserts the impossibility of extinguishing biographical details entirely and specifically stresses the necessity of preserving the details of a lost past, the oral and written narratives of a minority and marginalized regional community that have been eradicated in official historical accounts of the region. In an inversion of Wimsatt and Beardsley's insistence on the irrelevance of the author's intention or the "intended meaning" of a literary work, therefore, Clarke playfully yet defiantly emphasizes his authorial intention in his introduction. He plans to "improvise a myth" (2000, xi) that will resurrect a lost era in Halifax, Nova Scotia. By situating *Whylah Falls* squarely at a tangent to the works of the Anglo-American literary canon, Clark challenges their undisputed authority, substituting this institutionalized body of work with Africadian myths that "demand a different consciousness, a different landscape of the mind" (xvii).

Newspaper clippings, recipes, the names of flowers, popular songs, stories and yarns, cloths, scents, font and typeface—all these find their way into Clarke's research for *Whylah Falls*. For him, the process of writing becomes "an act of layering, of adding and subtracting certain timbres, tones, and tints" (2000, xvii) The multilayered nature of the text is accompanied by its polyglossic allusion to various literary "antecedents" that shaped the writing of the book. Clarke names his influences in two stanzas titled simply, "The Anxiety of Influence"—a clear reference to literary critic Harold Bloom's seminal work, *The Anxiety of Influence: A Theory of Poetry* (1973):

> Shakespeare Herrick Milton Wordsworth
> The King James Bible Hopkins Yeats
> Pound Eliot Thomas Heaney
> Rimbaud Baudelaire Rilke Blake
>
> Basho Li Po Mao Ondaatje
> Toomer Césaire Hayden Walcott
> Acorn Lorca Ginsberg Marquez
> Baraka Dylan Bly and Dove. (2000, xiv)

In illustrating the artificiality of the division of his influences into two groups of writers roughly distinguished, with a few exceptions, as white writers and writers of color, Clarke demonstrates that the lines of racial difference and categorization that separate the second group from the first are superficial.

Both groups of writers, and Clarke himself, depict the universal themes of love and unrequited romance, longing and rejection in their writings, in different ways. In *Whylah Falls*, moreover, the forces of desire and longing are driven by a powerful social critique of eviction, involuntary exile, socio-economic exclusion, class struggle,[28] and racial prejudice in twentieth-century Canadian society that underlie even governmental policies of "urban renewal" and relocation.

Clarke's verse novel is therefore at once a work of fictional documentation and social-economic critique, a tale of violence and sensual desire, a lament and love song, a work of memory and counter-history, and a sensuous narrative strummed and sung to the rhythms of blues, jazz, and gospel. The fictional protagonist, Xavier Zachary, a biracial (Mandinka-Mi'kmaq) poet and suitor of his beloved Shelley Clemence, leaves Whylah Falls because of socioeconomic exclusion, disempowerment, and class struggle, only to write letters home filled with longing—not only a longing for Shelley but a longing to return home and end his "wintry exile" ("Look Homeward, Exile," 2000, xxxi). Indeed, Xavier's love for Whylah Falls and his courtship of Shelley are often described concomitantly and thus intertwined—as illustrated in the lines

> I climb to Whylah Falls because I thirst,
> Hunger, for you, Shelley, and shake to touch
> Your house that slides down Mount Eulah to fog (17)

Xavier's experience of exile comes to an end when he returns to Whylah Falls and to Shelley. Nevertheless, it is not quite the homecoming to a life of bliss and bountiful pleasures that Xavier has anticipated, for Whylah Falls has become tainted with the racially motivated murder of Othello, Shelley's brother. A tragic character, Othello is shot in cold blood by a white man who suspects Othello is sleeping with his wife. When the jury acquit Othello's murderer, the community of Whylah Falls is plunged into confusion and grief. In the episode titled "The Argument" in the section "The Martyrdom of Othello Clemence," the text itself visually documents, much as in a newspaper article, Othello's murder. A black-and-white photograph, reminiscent of documentary photographs of lynchings in the United States, depicts his dead body in an overgrown field of grass and weeds, still clothed in a light shirt and trousers. In the passage on the facing page that describes the murder, the action is slowed down, then sped up; time and visual perception are fractured, splintered into fragments: "When he is shot, the mortal moment must be filmed from above and below, from behind and in front, from left and from right, in slow motion, normal speed, and fast, in close-up, and from a telescopic distance. The completeness of history must be depicted. Clemence must be photographed amid a chaos of primary colours which, at the split second he is shot, bleed to black-and-white" (2000, 101).

Othello's love for music is articulated by his strumming on a "dobro-chrome, steel-bodied guitar" (2000, 105). His "artistry" with the instrument (his "waterfall-hands cascade across the springs, leave, behind the glistening notes, a dark, inarticulate silence" (106) complements his rough, dark voice as he sings the blues ("Hurry Down, Sunshine," "Black Water Blues," and so on). When Othello is murdered, his guitar is "splintered upon a rock, freeing the twenty-four pale butterflies trapped behind the strings" (101). Although his life is ended prematurely, therefore, his cry, and the wail of the blues, a musical form that originated in African American spirituals and work songs that articulated victory and perseverance in the face of adversity, will continue to be heard. Accordingly, the fifth section of *Whylah Falls*, titled "The Martyrdom of Othello Clemence," mourns Othello's death, recounts his funeral wake (116) and reproduces his "Eulogy" (117).

Othello's death is followed by a sixth section, "The Gospel of Reverend F. R. Langford," in which the reverend, reading Othello's obituary in the newspaper, thinks to himself:

> Poor immigrant! If only, if only, if only, this land were not rosedust where the first fathers sleep, he would be mayor or county warden or even premier now. . . . He stares at the grey photograph of Othello Clemence in the obituary section and remembers his own one-third African, one-third Mi'kmaq, and one-third English inheritance, the reasons for his copper skin, straight-black hair, cinnamon eyes, and wide mouth. Reverend Franklin Roosevelt Langford . . . believes everyone is an alien, a refugee, *un émigré*. Everyone emigrates to the world from his or her mother. Heaven is everyone's true home. ("The Argument," 2000, 133)

Reverend Langford "considers Whylah Falls to be the New Eden, the lost colony of the Cotton Belt"[29] (134), although the irony is that he, too, like

Adam, eats of the forbidden fruit by indulging in alcohol and carnal pleasures. In a poem that he writes, "To the Government of Nova Scotia," he
calls Whylah Falls "granite country," a "home of hard rock and harder water"
that even wild geese abandon in their journeys to their "thatched colonies of
refuge." With no earthly possessions but "muscle, wine, and wind" and in an
allusion to the motif of flight in African American myth and folksongs,[30] the
Reverend Langford "lusts for wings" (149) to take him heavenward. Ironically, his longing comes to fruition in the form of a "miracle" (152), an act of
sexual consummation with Liana, the woman with whom he falls in love. The
section ends with a poem, "Close to Home," that he sings with "the emotion
of song" in "the philosophy of the *cry*" (xi). The poem begins with the lines

> Black train cry, black train wail;
> It don't matter,
> I'm close to home.
> Highway howl in rain and gale;
> It don't matter,
> I'm close to home (156)

Like Xavier Zachary and Othello Clemence, Reverend Langford, too, cries
out his "plain manifesto" in the "vernacular" (57). Like the other denizens and
residents of Whylah Falls, he struggles to call the village home, but declin-
ing social and economic conditions gradually makes him practice what he
preaches—that "home" exists not on this earth, in this lifetime, but in the
next, beyond the "pearly gates" of heaven (156).

Collectively, the poems, photographs, and fragments in George Elliott
Clarke's *Whylah Falls* piece together a rich visual and narrative tapestry that
chronicles, in an allusion to the Africville relocation, the fictional history of a
largely black and underprivileged community in Nova Scotia. This is a history
shaped by tangible forces of racial prejudice, socioeconomic exclusion, municipal negligence, and social injustice but also by romantic idealizations of young
love, fervent ardor, integrity, hope, and beauty. As a multilayered and intertextual cycle of poems, moreover, Clarke's text also metafictionally calls attention to its own materiality and constructedness, foregrounding, as opposed to
extinguishing, the biographical details of the fictional black community whose
members write their stories of desire, love, loss, racial discrimination, socioeconomic marginalization, and class struggle into being. By extension, therefore,

Whylah Falls proposes an understanding of prevailing notions of nation and home, identity and belonging as constructs/paradigms that have to be continually negotiated and reinvented, just as it is the task of the poet to accumulate, sift, alter, and transform the stories, accounts, and "facts" of a community into new alter-national myths (2000, xviii–xix). As counter-histories, these new myths are embedded in emergent regional(ist) literary fiction that challenges the homogeneity of dominant national narratives. As Clarke asserts, "[T]here [is] no other way to tell the truth save to disguise it as a story" (xxviii).

In Atlantic Canada, an expanse "undergoing profound economic and cultural change, even crisis," but where there has also concurrently been a "growing preoccupation with history," heritage and tradition,[31] it is these stories of unhoming, displacement, and relocation as experienced by marginalized communities that form a repository of regional(ist) resistance to dominant narratives of the Canadian nation and national identity that have omitted and elided these very local histories. As Herb Wyile encapsulates, "[A]ny consideration of the history of Atlantic Canada must be attentive to the structures of power within which the political, economic, and social achievements of the region took shape: the larger context of colonialism, the history of slavery, and the dynamics of global capital" (2011, 233). In this light, George Elliott Clarke's *Whylah Falls* can be read as a counter-hegemonic, intersectional work of contestation and lament that calls attention to the structures of power and lines of exclusion that have formed and shaped the region. The text itself becomes the site of struggle and the demand for reparation, metaphorically reclaiming the homes and the land that were taken away from the residents of Africville. The latter's experiences of deracination, uprooting, and displacement are reflected in a multilayered, musical, and polyglossic fictional narrative that reflects a sense of nostalgia but that also articulates a sociopolitical critique of housing policies as well as government programs of "urban renewal." Enunciating a resolutely Africadian poetics and politics of regional(ist) and alter-national identity, *Whylah Falls* thus makes a strong claim for the inclusion and involvement of ethnic minorities and marginalized groups in regional policy making, challenging dominant notions of Canadian citizenship, national identity, and belonging in the contested spaces of home and the nation. In this way, the text functions as an indirect yet effective form of political and social activism by fostering an alter-national model of collective identification that centers around notions of injurability, vulnerability, and precariousness.

6

CITIZENSHIP UNHINGED

· · · · · · · · · ·

Securitization, Identity Management, and the
Migrant in Amitava Kumar's *Passport Photos*

Prevalent perceptions of undocumented or "illegal" migrants, refugees, asy-lum seekers,[1] stateless persons, exiles, and displaced subjects in dominant discourses on migration often misread them as *risky* subjects instead of sub-jects *at risk*. These precarious bodies are often misidentified in the public imagination as the *source* of the threat and instability that compromise the boundaries of the nation rather than the result of systematic processes of exclusion and marginalization due to political decisions made at national and international levels, and of complex bureaucratic procedures and lengthy processing times of applications for refugee or asylum status.

In 2013, the UN Refugee Agency (UNHCR) reported that the number of refugees, asylum seekers, and internally displaced people worldwide had, for the first time in the post–World War II era, exceeded 50 million people.[2] Giorgio Agamben's entreaty in his essay "We Refugees" (1995) to take the figure of the refugee, the "only imaginable figure of the people in our day,"[3] as the trigger for conceptualizing a new philosophical mode of "perceiving the forms and limits of a political community" in the twentieth (and twenty-first) century has therefore become all the more pressing.[4] Agamben's essay, which was a response to Hannah Arendt's article of the same title that she published in the small Jewish periodical the *Menorah Journal* in 1943, takes up the condition of refugeeism as "the paradigm of a new historical consciousness," the starting point of a necessary "reconstruct[tion] of political philosophy" (114). Delineating the difference between "bare life" (*zoe*) and "political life" (*bios*), Agamben argues that the figure of the refugee "throws into crisis the original fiction of sovereignty" (115) because it uncovers the fiction that birth immediately leads to the concept of nation or, in other words, that birth is the very foundation of the nation-state's sovereignty (etymologically, the Latin word *natio* means "birth" or "origin"). Agamben's call to make the figure of the refugee the center of an alter-national model of historical and political consciousness and collective identification recalls Judith Butler's entreaty for a new theory of political reflection and deliberation based on vulnerability and injurability.

The rising number of refugees, asylum seekers, displaced, and stateless persons in the twenty-first century is also a reflection of the need to rethink the theory of "hard" borders, understood as concrete, fortified boundaries, including wire-fenced borders, walled borders, militarized borders, and checkpoints, put up to keep "illegal" intruders out of the country. Increasingly, therefore, the theory of "hard" borders has been substituted by a new concept of "soft" open and regulated borders, such as those at work within the European Union, that "rethink notions of sovereignty and democracy in the 21st century" (Mustov 2008, 1) and that effectively decouple "the linkage between membership in a particular national community and the rights and responsibilities typically associated with citizenship." As some critics have argued, a theory of "soft" borders envisions "democratic practices of social cooperation exercised through multiple and overlapping polities by individuals and groups with complex and fluid identities" (3).[5] Nevertheless, as the phenomenon of "Fortress Europe" has demonstrated, such a paradigm shift from hard border to soft border theory has nevertheless not yet adequately redressed the situations of precarious refugees, asylum seekers, and undocumented migrants who are still excluded from the rights of citizenship.

This state of exclusion from the rights of citizenship is explored by Hannah Arendt in *The Origins of Totalitarianism* (1951). In the chapter "The Decline of the Nation-State and the End of the Rights of Man," Arendt argues that the figure of the stateless refugee (in this instance, the Jewish person of Eastern European origin) embodies the most serious critique of the concept of human rights, as delineated by the French Revolution's

Declaration of the Rights of Man (*Declaration des droits de l'homme et du citoyen*) in 1789. Arendt points out that the Rights of Man, "supposedly inalienable, proved to be unenforceable . . . whenever people appeared who were no longer citizens of any sovereign state" (1973, 293). This was the case, Arendt argues, with Jewish people who had to endure the loss of their jobs, their homes, their communities, their nationalities—and hence their status as citizens in their countries. This loss of legal status, or what Arendt terms "the deprivation of legality" (295), constituted a deprivation of the basic *right to have rights*. As Arendt summarizes, "Something much more fundamental than freedom and justice, which are rights of citizens, is at stake when belonging to the community into which one is born is no longer a matter of course and not belonging no longer a matter of choice" (296). The interruption of the continuity of what should be a given—in this instance, the understanding that a person born in a particular country has the right to continue living in that country without undue persecution—constitutes a dehumanization of the figure of the refugee.

Although Arendt was writing about Jewish people who were expelled from Europe during World War II, modern-day measures of control and regulation endorsed by refugee host countries in the West due to a perceived global "refugee crisis" demand closer scrutiny. Such modern forms of "identity management" (Muller 2004) and national securitization have, within a U.S. context, contributed to the dominant culture of fear and a rhetoric of "otherness," an "us" versus "them" mentality in the national imagination. This has generated what Margaret R. Somers terms "the contractualization of citizenship" (2008, 2), which "effectively collapses the boundaries that protect the public sphere and civil society from market penetration, [hence] distort[ing] the meaning of citizenship from that of shared fate among equals to that of conditional privilege" (2–3). Clearly, the subjecting of citizenship to the market forces of supply and demand, and to the constraints of exigency, is problematic.

In this chapter, I will perform a close reading of a literary text that challenges dominant practices of securitization and border control in U.S. migration law by placing the South Asian diasporic body—variously the Nonresident Indian (NRI) or the H-1B visa[6] worker, the undocumented migrant, the refugee, and the asylum seeker—at the center of its narrative and by deconstructing the stereotypical assumptions, generalizations, and categorizations that plague the immigrant experience. *Passport Photos* (2000), by New York–based Indian writer Amitava Kumar, is a multigenre work of literary fiction, theory, poetry, popular journalism, cultural criticism, and photography organized in the structure of a passport that constitutes at once "a report on the immigrant condition" and a "search for a new poetics and politics of diasporic protest" (x). Through the use of irony, satire, mimicry, political invective, hybridity, and ambivalence, *Passport Photos* contests the theories of "hard" and "soft" borders in the form of national measures of identity management and securitization that have led to the regulation of the flow of human bodies that are marked as disqualified, dissident, or risky across national borders. Kumar's book thus represents a postcolonial counter-discourse, an act of "writing back" (Ashcroft, Griffiths, and Tiffin 1989); it constitutes the migrant's critical intervention into national discourses of identity management and securitization that dominate laws on immigration and naturalization in the United States. In particular, it explores the sites of resistance and slippage where "the information does not fit on the dotted line," where "the category, as with the question of nationality, splits," where "the rich ambiguities of a personal or cultural history . . . resist a plain reply or . . . demand a complex though unequivocal response" (xi).

DISQUALIFIED BODIES, SECURITIZATION, AND "IDENTITY MANAGEMENT"

The cover visual of Amitava Kumar's *Passport Photos* is a photograph depicting a woman of Indian or Pakistani origin posing for the camera, holding a toy model of the Statue of Liberty in her right hand in such a way that the photographer (Kumar himself) is able to capture both the model and the real Statue of Liberty behind the woman. The woman and the miniature tourist souvenir she is holding are captured in sharp relief, whereas the Statue of Liberty in the background on Liberty Island is blurred in comparison. In the larger inset of the photograph reproduced in the bottom half of the back cover, it is the miniature tourist souvenir that is enlarged, not the real Statue of Liberty. As one of the most prominent American icons, the Statue of Liberty is a colossal national symbol of the American ideals of freedom from oppression, friendship between nations, liberty,[7] democracy, equality, and justice. Together with Emma Lazarus's poem "The New Colossus," which was engraved on a bronze tablet and mounted inside the pedestal of the statue in 1903, the "Mother of Exiles," or Lady Liberty, as she is colloquially known, represents the United States as a nation of migrants, a land of opportunity for those seeking better lives.

The discrepancy between the American Dream and its "reality" is perhaps one of the most common of tropes in twentieth-century migrant literature. What the cover of Kumar's *Passport Photos* depicts, however, which is also conveyed in the woman's slightly tired, neutral facial expression as she poses for the snapshot, is the diminution of the Statue of Liberty to a cheap, mass-produced and mass-marketed commodity, a tacky tourist souvenir (probably made in China) that diminishes the original statue's grand scale as well as what it represents. The book cover also represents an ironic inversion of the lines "Give me your tired, your poor, / Your huddled masses yearning to breathe free" that the Statue of Liberty metaphorically "speaks" to the immigrants who encounter it as the first American landmark they set their eyes on. The cheap, tacky, pocket-sized Statue of Liberty souvenir thus symbolizes the marketing and contractualization of U.S. citizenship; the latter, and its accompanying American Dream, can be bought and sold, exported within the workings of a neoliberal market economy.

One last detail about the visual depicted on the book's cover is striking—there is a square with a thin white border drawn roughly over the woman's face, much like the kind that a digital camera's face-recognition software automatically positions over faces in portrait photographs. This gestures toward the central project of Kumar's book. *Passport Photos* was published in 2000, before the events of 9/11; yet it anticipates the heightened national security measures that event prompted, including processes of identity management and biometric authentication as well as a more restrictive tightening of U.S. immigrant law and policies.[8]

Parodying the information documented about an individual in a U.S. passport, *Passport Photos* is divided into nine chapters titled "Language," "Photograph," "Name," "Place of Birth," "Date of Birth," "Profession," "Nationality," "Sex," and "Identifying Marks." Each of these titles provides a thematic "trigger" for Kumar's critical reflections in that particular chapter, which center around how each one of these terms reflects existing power structures that, for the migrant, are a remnant of colonial histories and a reminder of neo-imperial practices in the present day. The first chapter, "Language," begins with the following passage:

> My passport provides no information about my language. It simply presumes I have one. If the immigration officer asks me a question—his voice, if he's speaking English, deliberately slow, and

louder than usual—I do not, of course, expect him to be terribly concerned about the nature of language and its entanglement with the very roots of my being. And yet it is in language that all immigrants are defined and in which we all struggle for an identity. That is how I understand the postcolonial writer's declaration about the use of a language like English that came to us from the colonizer. (2000, 17)

Centrally, the chapter is a deliberation on how the word *passport* has different functions in different linguistic cultures. "For those who live in affluent countries," Kumar observes, "the passport is of use for international travel in connection with business or vacations." "In poorer nations of the world," he continues, noting the disparity, "its necessity is tied to the need for finding employment, mainly in the West" (2000, 20). The opening chapter of *Passport Photos* thus conveys the duality of the passport: it is a document that provides its bearer with access and entitlement yet at the same time represents the hegemonic structures of exclusion that marginalize precarious subjects. As Kumar encapsulates, "[If], on the one hand, the meanings of words like passport and visa are tied to dreams and fantasies, they are also, on the other, inextricably woven into the fabric of power and social prejudice" (21).

The first chapter of *Passport Photos* also cites various examples from other postcolonial writings that "return us to language as the terrain on which difference is constructed or resisted" (2000, 23). These include Sri Lankan Canadian Krisantha Sri Bhaggiyadatta's *Aay Wha' Kinda Indian Arr U?* (1997), a book of poems with a cassette featuring a forty-minute soundscape of epic poetry interwoven with South Asian and North American Indigenous music that satirically asks what it "means" to be a South Asian living on First Nations' land in Canada. Kumar's chapter quotes the following excerpt from Bhaggiyadatta's poem:

> am i the Indian wearing salwar or a sari, a turban or a pottu
> on the subway platform at 10 p.m. . . .
> am i the self-sacrificing monogamous Sita
> or am i the strong-willed and passionate
> revengeful polyandrous Draupadi . . .
> or am i the "we shoulda met earlier" Usha of Urvashi

> am i the Indian who must submit to virginity tests
>   from immigration's con/insultants?
> am i the sponsored Indian whose husband owns her
>   for ten years or else . . . (22–23)

These questions voice the different stereotypical categorizations of the female Indian migrant subject as seen through Western/Canadian eyes. These cultural stereotypes are reinforced by visual markers of difference such as the wearing of a salwar kameez, a sari, a turban or pottu, which makes the Indian migrant all the more conspicuous on the subway platform. The female speaker of Bhaggiyadatta's poem satirically challenges these stereotypes of "high" and "low" Hindu culture: the roles of courageous women from the Hindu Sanskrit epics, the *Ramayana* (that of the "self-sacrificing monogamous Sita"), and the *Mahābhārata* (the "strong-willed and passionate / revengeful and polyandrous Draupadi"), but also the vivacious character of Usha/Urvashi (played by Bollywood actress Smita Patil) in the film *Bhumika*, who tells her hunky costar Rajan, "We shoulda met earlier."

The opening chapter of *Passport Photos* thus draws on personal anecdotes[9] as well as quotes from works by migrant and postcolonial scholars, writers, and activists including Salman Rushdie, Upamanyu Chatterjee, Pankaj Mishra, Homi Bhabha, Guillermo Gómez-Peña, and Alfred Arteaga. Kumar also inserts his own photographs that depict how governmental policies on migration are accountable for discriminatory practices along lines of linguistic, cultural, and class differences. For instance, one of Kumar's photographs features a sign at the U.S.-Mexico border that depicts an immigrant family "illegally" crossing the border, presumably from Mexico into the United States. The sign reads "Caution" in English but "Prohibido" (not "Caución") in Spanish, hence concurrently targeting the two linguistic groups with two very different messages—Americans should be wary of "illegal" Mexican migrants trying to cross the border, and Mexicans should know that entering the United States "illegally" without proper documentation is prohibited. How can such processes of discrimination be reversed, Kumar asks, such that the English language become a tool of "creative appropriation" instead of "an instrument of cultural domination" (2000, 25)? Kumar also wryly comments on the hypocrisy surrounding second-language acquisition for native English speakers and the speaking of the non-English mother tongue for migrants in the United States—"[T]he class bias in North American society . . . promotes bilingualism in the upper class but frowns on it when it becomes an aspect of lower-class life" (32). Citing two lines from Chicano performance artist, poet, and activist Guillermo Gómez-Peña's performance poem "Border Brujo" from the series *Documented/ Undocumented*, "I speak in English therefore you listen / I speak in English therefore I hate you,"[10] Kumar addresses the significance of language in the political undertaking of decolonization as well as its role in constructions of diasporic identity. Taking up Gómez-Peña's critical inquiry of how the English language can be turned around, wielded by the formerly colonized in the country of the colonizer, Kumar explores how it can be transformed from a "racial weapon in immigration" (32) into a "weapon of protest" (25) that contests the lines of discrimination and exclusion that immigrants and noncitizens face within a North American context.

The second chapter in Kumar's book, titled "Photograph," is an extended mediation on the passport photograph that serves the purposes of state regulation and immigration control. When *Passport Photos* was published in 2000, the United States had yet to introduce biometric or e-passports,[11] whereby a chip in the passport would contain information such as the photograph and personal information of the passport holder. Nevertheless, Kumar's book ironically anticipates several of the security and antifraud measures that the United States would adopt in the aftermath of 9/11, including the issuing of "high-tech counterfeit-resistant 'green card[s]'" that use "holographs, embedded photographs, thumbprints, and a wealth of electronic data making it easier for employers and law enforcement officers to tell whether an immigrant is entitled to live and work in the United States" (2000, 39). These security measures are, Kumar writes, part of a larger system of governmentality that utilizes "a technology that turns aliens . . . into lawbreakers, if not also terrorists" (40).[12]

As Benjamin Muller has convincingly argued in his article on identity management, "[B]iometric technologies are employed to conceal and advance the heightened exclusionary and restrictive practices of contemporary securitized citizenship." Muller contends that the introduction of biometric technologies reflects a "continued obsession with the preservation and regulation/restriction of specific rights and entitlements" (2004, 279) that has dramatically altered existing notions of political agency and citizenship politics. This paradigm shift from a politics of citizenship to one of identity management, Muller claims, effectively shifts the emphasis from notions of agency and political membership to the issue of *authorization* and questions of who should (and should not) have access to the rights of citizenship, which becomes a contract and contractualized:

> Identity management vis-à-vis biometrics attempts to transform citizenship into a quest for verifying/authenticating "identity" for the purpose of access to rights, bodies, spaces, . . . thus (purportedly) stripping away the cultural and ethnic attributes of citizenship. By concealing such matters in the technological and scientific discourses of biometrics, the ethnic/racial characteristics of contemporary citizenship practice . . . are stripped away. Although knowledge of one's identity is critical, the question of "authorizing access," and thus, authenticating, becomes much greater in this epoch of "homeland security" and "domestic terrorists." (280)

The reduction of the citizen to a set of biometric data for the sake of ease in verifying and authenticating access to the rights and spaces of national citizenship reflects a larger stripping away, by practices of immigration and border control, of not only an individual's cultural and ethnic attributes but also the components of emotion and affect. As Lily Cho maintains in her essay "Citizenship, Diaspora and the Bonds of Affect: The Passport Photograph," the foreclosure of emotion in a biometrical passport photograph, where the subject, according to the U.S. Department of State's guidelines for passport photos, must have "a neutral facial expression and both eyes open,"[13] "expose[s] a citizen-subject caught and composed for identification purposes" (2009, 276). This "neutrality" of expression in the case of the diasporic subject's passport photograph is significant, Cho asserts, because "[t]he diasporic subject's difference challenges the homogenizing stipulations of national citizenship and illuminates *the contradictions of citizenship*. These are *contradictions that turn on feeling*. Citizenship is both bonded by affect and, in the instance of its visual manifestation through the passport photograph, hindered by it. The injunction against emotion in passport photos projects a fantasy of a passive, transparent, and readable national subject" (279; my emphasis).

It is this fantasy of the "passive, transparent, and readable national subject" that is shattered in the second chapter of Amitava Kumar's *Passport Photos*. Deconstructing the "passivity" and "legibility" of the biometric passport photograph, Kumar foregrounds the representation of the racialized subject, which opens up a space of contradiction, overidentification, misrecognition, and interpellation. He writes, "[E]specially in a postcolonial context, an image will have to be seen as surrounded by other images, other words, and always, other worlds." The protocols of the passport photograph, its insistence on a "neutral" expression, is thus also a means of homogenization, of stripping the citizen-subject of her or his "home" context upon entrance into a foreign country. Challenging this enforced homogeneity and neutralization, Kumar calls for a reading of the immigrant's passport photograph as part of a larger system of "personal, political, economic, dramatic, everyday and historic"[14] components that "interrupt the authoritative discourse" (2000, 47) of securitization by the state and its classification, categorization, and disqualification of migrant bodies.

The subsequent chapters of *Passport Photos*, titled "Name," Place of Birth," and "Date of Birth," continue the author's search for a new poetics and politics of diaspora by deconstructing the triangulation between name, origin/place of birth, and identity: "In a very clear sense, the place of birth is a site, of memory, desire, what you will. It also becomes a site always under construction, seeking scrutiny and revision. . . . But there are also other questions, because there's always an elsewhere. That elsewhere recalls what has not been named and is, sometimes, unnamable." In order to illustrate the concept that "home" (place of birth) need not necessarily be the site of cultural or ancestral origin, which is, instead, deferred to an unnamable and unknown "elsewhere," Kumar uses the example of the descendants of Indian indentured laborers born in Trinidad. These Indo-Trinidadians perceive "in a particular vision of India their origin, their place of birth" (2000, 99), Kumar argues, yet this India is effectively an "imaginary homeland" (Rushdie 1991) constructed in the diasporic imagination. In other words, Kumar contends, although most Indo-Trinidadians identify as Indian and work to preserve "good Indian values," India is unfamiliar territory to them, being, in most cases, a land they have never set foot on.[15] In this sense, one cannot assume a direct relationship between one's place of birth and one's cultural identity.

Kumar cites another example of the complex relationship between the notions of "origin" and "identity" in the chapter "Date of Birth," namely, the artificial creation of the two distinct and separate nations of India and Pakistan in the historical event of Partition in 1947, which marked the end of British rule on the Indian subcontinent. As Kumar points out, Partition was not unequivocally a cause for celebration, nor did it represent the immediate

end of colonialism on the Indian subcontinent or the formation of two discrete national identities overnight. Rather, the enforced geographical division of the provinces of Punjab and Bengal led to the creation of ethnic and
religious minority groups and large-scale displacement as well as death, rape,
riots, and looting. Some 1 million people were killed and 10 to 15 million were
forced to leave their homes as refugees. As Yasmin Khan has pointed out, as
one of the first events of decolonization in the twentieth century, Partition
was also one of the bloodiest (2007, 6). In line with Khan and other scholars
who argue for a more expansive critical assessment of Partition that does not
fetishize or monumentalize it as a "singular, painful event," therefore, Kumar
argues for "a different process of remembering" (2000, 115), one that under-
stands Partition as the culmination of a longer historical and sociopolitical
trajectory of Indian nationalism and ideological divides as well as religious
and communal conflicts on the subcontinent. Acknowledging that Partition
played a key role in the requisite creation of Indian and Pakistani national
identities that were carved out diametrically, in definition *against* each other
(Khan 2007, 9), Kumar contends that the "problem" of the postcolonial
citizen is "not so much being unable to choose between two homelands,"
between two nation-states, as "being expected to choose *only one*" (2000, 117;
my emphasis). As Khan puts it, "[I]ndividuals were caught between the pull
of two opposing nationalisms and had their citizenship settled or fixed as
Indian or Pakistani" (2007, 10).

Those who sought to overcome or transcend this binary opposition by
migrating to the West, especially to the United Kingdom and the United
States, in the second half of the twentieth century are classified by the Indian
government under the acronym NRI, or "Non-Resident Indian."[16] NRIs,
who are permanently settled and residing outside India (excluding Pakistan
and Bangladesh) for the purposes of education, employment, or because of
family ties, have been eligible for Overseas Citizenship of India (OCI) since
2005.[17] OCI card holders do not, however, acquire the benefits of dual citizenship because of restrictions in India that include exclusion from the right
to vote, from holding constitutional or legislative positions in the Indian
government, from employment in the government of India, and from acquir-
ing agricultural or plantation properties in India. OCI card holders also do
not obtain an Indian passport.

Kumar's *Passport Photos* was published before the introduction of the
Overseas Citizenship of India scheme, and hence the book does not address

the widespread criticism that has been leveled at this system.[18] It does, however, criticize the designation of the NRI as "a nominational type that was invented by the government of India to lure the capital of affluent Indians living abroad, mostly in the U.S. and the U.K." (2000, 131). Kumar notes that NRIs are subject to different income taxation laws than resident Indians, and are also conferred tax privileges and given cheaper, refundable airline tickets when they are on a visit "home" (2000, 117). Accordingly, the sixth chapter in *Passport Photos*, titled "Profession," contains a poem by Kumar titled "N.R.I.," wherein the speaker, himself a nonresident Indian in the United States, struggles with the definition of the term. The poem clearly takes to task and critiques the development of a class of privileged Indian elites abroad, which has led to an increasing discrepancy between the lives of two categories of NRIs: on the one hand, "those Indian women who linger / outside the toilets in Heathrow airport / with their brushes and brooms" (132) and, on the other, those "watching Hindi film-videos / in their bedrooms in London and Washington D.C. / their beds afloat in a sea of Scotch" (133). NRIs who fall into the first group, Kumar contends, are "stigmatized even while—or rather, *because*—[they] serve, through [their] labor, the ends of progress and the preservation of the status quo for the affluent mainstream" (137). It is this group of NRIs whose precarious employment renders them disenfranchised migrants in the host country.

Kumar expresses his solidarity with these immigrants in a long poem that he sets in the American embassy of Calcutta and dedicates to the U.S. Immigration and Naturalization Service (INS). The speaker is an Indian man being interviewed by the INS official because he has submitted a H-1B work visa application. The poem contains various tongue-in-cheek responses to the questions asked by the immigration officer during the interview.

> "Do you intend to overthrow
> the government of the United States
> by force or fraud?"
> An old man who wants to visit
> a son in New Jersey
> wants me to help him
> with this question on the form.
> A friend tells me later of someone
> Who believing it was an either/or question

Tried to play it safe and opted
For the overthrow of the government
By fraud. (2000, 146)

This ironic humor deepens into a more serious critique and denunciation, in the second section of the poem, of the procedures of identity management and securitization to which the intending migrant is subject. Kumar clearly expresses his censure of the system in the sequence he relates wherein the visa applicant is asked the question, "Did you, the first time you went there, intend to come back?" The speaker's reply to the question is "Wait a minute . . . did you get a visa when you first went to the moon? Fuck the moon, / tell me about Vietnam. Just how precise / were your plans there, you asshole?" (147). The speaker's outrage at the arrogance and stereotypical assumptions of the presumably white U.S. official in the American embassy in this episode anticipates Kumar's own critique, in the next chapter of *Passport Photos*, of the tendency in the West to espouse simplistic and generalized categorizations of South Asian and Middle Eastern countries as misogynist and home to "repressive" cultures.

In the chapter titled "Sex," therefore, Kumar criticizes "the U.S. media's complete and arrogant separation of India from the West as a place where women are mistreated." "Among a host of other things," he writes, "what I find appalling is the repression of the complicity between oppressive, dominant forces in India and the U.S. Let's ask, for example, how U.S. multinationals like General Electric, with their marketing of ultrasound devices, profited from the heinous social practices in India. But the pious head-shaking by the CBS commentator ignores such complexities" (2000, 190). Kumar's thus criticizes American commercial broadcast networks such as CBS's reproduction of "neo-Orientalist Western imaginaries" (192–93) because they effectively mass-market cultural and ethnic differences as a commodity. It is not, however, only the U.S. media that is accountable for such actions but also, occasionally, expatriate Indian artists, too. Kumar notes, for instance, the extensive perpetuation of exoticized cultural stereotypes in the North American public imagination, critiquing Indian Canadian film director Mira Nair's otherwise bold and daring film *Fire*[19] for its "complicity with a neo-Orientalist paradigm of a woman on fire" and its problematic reproducing of a "monumentalized, mythical past" that is rendered in the film's opening framing shot of the Taj Mahal. In his critical assessment of the film's indiscriminating mimetic representation of "the India familiar to the Western media-watching eye" (193), Kumar proposes an alternative perspective that challenges such cultural stereotypes. Engaging the question of viewership, he suggests reading the film through the gaze of an Indian audience, an audience that will not fall into the "trap" of consuming difference in an act tantamount to voyeurism. This shift in perspective, Kumar argues, opens up "a more enabling discussion of the way the film helps us think through the issues of cultural production freed from narrower identity politics" (194).

It is this attempt to sidestep "the limits and pitfalls of easy sympathy" (2000, 193) engendered by a narrow identity politics that motivates Kumar's reflections in the last chapter of *Passport Photos*, titled "Identifying Marks." In particular, Kumar seeks to break two cultural stereotypes that flourish in the American popular imagination: first, that of the hardworking, thrifty Indian migrant on an H-1B visa and, second, as the Western gaze travels East, the figure of the veiled Muslim woman. In response to the *Washington Post*'s headline proclaiming that "Indians outnumber other applicants for H-1B visas," Kumar, who himself initially traveled to the United States on this visa, reminds the reader that workers on H-1B visas are paid lower wages less than their American counterparts and often have to accept precarious conditions of employment. Writing of the "economy of transience and dislocation" and the precarious "conditions of earning, mobility and return" (200) in which the H-1B migrant is entrenched, this final chapter of *Passport Photos* challenges the stereotypical depictions of South Asian migrants in the United State as the diligent, self-sacrificing, and disciplined "model minority" (Petersen 1966).[20] Seeking instead to trace "the identifying marks of Indians in the white imaginary" back to historical perceptions of "Indianness" (2000, 198), Kumar recalls the exclusion of South Asian migrants in the United States for more than half of the twentieth century,[21] one premised on the discriminatory racialization of these groups as "non-white" (197).[22]

In Kumar's opinion, it is the same principle of the West's overriding inability to deal with difference, and hence its exclusion of the "Other," that presides over the controversy over the figure of the veiled Muslim woman, or what is often referred to in Anglo-American contexts as the "headscarf debate." In Canada, a regulation requires Muslim women who observe the custom of wearing the burqa and niqab to remove them before taking the oath of citizenship. According to a rule from 2011, citizenship judges "need to be able to ensure individuals are actually reciting the oath."[23] There is no similar niqab or burqa ban in the United States because this would be deemed unconstitutional according to the First Amendment, which protects the right to freedom of religion and freedom of expression. Nevertheless, the irony is that the dominant perspective in the West is that the burqa and niqab are themselves the very symbols of masculine oppression and thus a denial of the woman's freedom of expression. In an attempt to cast the debate in a different light, Kumar asks, "What would it mean . . . to view the veil as a sign of unstable [rather than fixed] identity—and, by implication, the *feminine* as engaged in the struggle, a gendered struggle, within the postcolonial context but also between the East and the West?" Maintaining that prevailing Western perceptions of the veil as a symbol of patriarchal oppression effectively oversimplify the complexity of the issue, Kumar cites feminist writer Samira Haj's position in the debate: "the emphasis on Islam and tradition as the source of women's oppression results in a reductive, ahistorical view of women" (2000, 206). In a similar vein, Kumar suggests that instead of viewing the burqa as "a fixed mark of identification" (207), it can be regarded as "a field of meaning marked by varieties of conflict [where] gendered protest overlaps with other struggles" (207–8). "The veil," Kumar advances, "invites discussion as a sign, and hence its status as being open to contrary readings and caught in a struggle over history" (208).[24] Centrally, Kumar aligns himself with filmmaker, feminist, and postcolonial theorist Trinh T. Minh-ha's critical position on the issue: "If the act of unveiling has a liberating potential, so does the act of veiling. It all depends on the context in which such act is carried out, or more precisely, on how and where women see dominance . . . when they decide to keep or put on the veil they once took off they might do so to re-appropriate their space or to claim a new difference in defiance of genderless, hegemonic, centered standardization" (209, quoting Minh-ha 1988).

Similarly, *Passport Photos* encourages the reader to reflect on migrant acts as "transformative performances across a range of social sites" (2000, 225), as political interjections and interventions that disrupt, fracture, and call into crisis established definitions and understandings of citizenship, national identity, community, and belonging. The book is an attempt to engage with the complex reality of the migrant experience, of diasporic lives that are "shaped in the spaces between the pure appeals of home and adopted nation" (228) as well as an argument for "the possibilities of diasporic culture . . . that resist national wills and narrowly nationalist identities" (229).

It is this last call that constructs the alternative frame of reference posited by Kumar's book, one that demands not only a postcolonial but also a post-*national* reconfiguration of existing cultural narratives based on conventional understandings of the nation. These alternate paradigms demand both a destabilization of national frameworks and a critical reflection on the historical and contemporary processes of exclusion that reinforce "hard" and "soft" borders of citizenship and migration control. In this respect, Kumar's *Passport Photos* takes up Seyla Benhabib's call to, on the one hand, scrutinize the "practices and institutions regulating access to and exit from political membership" and their "rituals of entry, access, belonging and privilege" while, on the other, also considering how new forms of "disaggregated or unbundled" (2004, 1) citizenship[25] can decouple the ties between citizenship and nationality. It is these new forms of disaggregated citizenship that constitute new modalities of membership in an era of globalizing processes and mass migration, reflecting how identities are increasingly "shift[ing] and fractur[ing]" as "the relation of national identity to religious, gender, class, and ethnic identities blurs and re-forms" (Kerber 2009, 108).

By placing the various incarnations of the Indian migrant—the different classes of NRI, the diasporic person of Indian origin (PIO), the undocumented migrant, the refugee, and the asylum seeker—at the center of its multigeneric narrative, Amitava Kumar's *Passport Photos* thus proposes an alternative critical framework for political life that centers around interdependence, instability, and precariousness. The book acknowledges the importance of an "ethics of narration" that emphasizes accountability and is attuned to the conditions of precariousness, injurability, and vulnerability that migrants face. Centrally, the book raises the crucial question of how "those outside the nation—especially the members of a racialized diaspora—go about rewriting the nation" (2000, 161) or how the spaces of the nation are refashioned and reinscribed by migrant subjectivity. As the central figure in an age of postcolonial diaspora, Kumar argues, the immigrant demands a revision of established neoliberal Western understandings of nation, national identity, and citizenship. It is also high time, Kumar asserts, to challenge stereotypical racialized conceptions of migrants.

As a cross-generic literary work that deconstructs the structure and contents of the official passport, Amitava Kumar's *Passport Photos* documents the *un*official "experience of immigration—its pain as well as its silences and contradictions," narrating the "quotidian lives and struggles that animate such existences" (2000, 166). Recalling the following words by Edward Said from *After the Last Sky*, Amitava Kumar's *Passport Photos*, too, embraces unconventional, hybrid, fragmentary forms of essayistic and discursive expression as part of a larger politics and poetics of diaspora: "Since the main features of our present existence are dispossession, dispersion, and yet also a kind of power incommensurate with our stateless exile, I believe that essentially unconventional, hybrid, and fragmentary forms of expression should be used to represent us" (Said 1986, 6). By combining fictional prose and poetry, personal anecdotes, theory, postcolonial critique, photographs, newspaper commentaries, and citations from the works of other literary and cultural critics, Kumar calls into question the authorities of the passport as a legal document and of "official" discourses and sanctions on immigration. To this end, *Passport Photos* represents not only a form of postcolonial activism in the genre of literature but also a diasporic articulation of the "fragmentary ways [in which] the nation is being reinvented" (168). Ultimately, Kumar's composite analysis of the condition of diasporic existence and the physical and mental concepts of home/homeland not only captures the indeterminacies, ambiguities, and contradictions that prevail in the spaces of the nation, it also deconstructs nation-based paradigms of political membership and belonging by critiquing the various forms of social exclusion, categorization, authentication, neutralization, and homogenization to which the nonnational migrant is subjected. By placing this figure of the migrant at the center, Kumar's narrative foregrounds the dynamic tensions produced by those who collectively resist and question (and thus call for a rethinking of) processes of assimilation to conventional practices of U.S. citizenship. These acts of contestation not only counter the ways in which modes of exclusion, marginalization, identification, securitization, and control have come to dominate the discursive framing, management, and allocation of spaces within the nation; they also suggest new forms of alter-national identities and processes of becoming that are embodied by an affective, racialized politics of diaspora. It is this poetics and politics of diasporic protest that calls into question the very structures of legalization, legitimization, and normalization that undergird contemporary registers of political membership and citizenship in the United States.

PART III

· · · · · · · · · · · · · · · · · · · ·

Queer Citizens

7

SEXUAL CITIZENSHIP AND THE TRANSGRESSIVE BODY

· · · · · · · · · ·

Djuna Barnes's *Nightwood*

Having explored the alter- and post-national forms of subjectivity and belonging espoused by forms of willful citizenship and precarious subjectivities in the first two parts of my study, this section turns to the figure of the queer citizen whose sexual "transgressions" counter the heteronormative logic of the nation-state. In particular, it examines the concept of sexual citizenship, a theory and practice of recognizing the gendered and sexual components of citizenship that emerged in the 1990s as an alternative to conventional understandings of citizenship and national identity. A concept first introduced by David Evans in his seminal work, *Sexual Citizenship: The Material Construction of Sexualities* (1993), Evans's theory of sexual citizenship adopted a rights-based approach, defining it as the entitlement of sexual minorities to economic, formal, civil, political, and social rights. Since the publication of Evans's study, as Diane Richardson (2000) has noted, and in the context of social movements like gay liberation, feminism, and queer activism, a new body of work on sexuality and citizenship has emerged. Interestingly, however, not all critics adopt an unambiguous outlook on sexual citizenship. More recent scholarship has even critiqued the adoption of a rights-based approach to sexual citizenship as it "forecloses or denies aspects of sexuality written off as 'unacceptable,'" proffering a "modality of sexual citizenship that is privatized, de-radicalized, de-eroticized and confined in all senses of the word: kept in place, policed, limited" (Bell and Binnie 2000, 3).

It is at this juncture that I wish to enter the debate on sexual citizenship by examining how acts of sexual transgression constitute not only sources of private pleasure but also collective political acts of resistance. This chapter thus focuses on various forms of sexual transgression and their renegotiations of the dominant theory and practice of national citizenship. David Bell's essay, "Pleasure and Danger: the Paradoxical Spaces of Sexual Citizenship" is a useful point of departure, as my focus will be on acts of transgression in spaces "where a citizenship constituted through the citizen's sexuality . . . can be played out, and also *where it cannot*" (1995, 139; my emphasis). My aim is to explore the (physical, geographical, textual) sites of exclusion, conflict, and struggle where forms of "dissident"/deviant sexuality that disrupt the topographies of the nation are enacted and performed. In so doing, I will evaluate how "spaces of sexual citizenship challenge the transparent and hegemonic geography of citizenship" (150). Expanding on Bell's analysis of different forms of sexual citizenship and the spaces in which queer bodies operate, I will offer three new corporeal "sites" of sexual transgression for consideration: the expatriate lesbian body, the bestial and blasphemous body, and the transvestite and androgynous body. Subsequently, I will turn to a critical reading of Djuna Barnes's *Nightwood* in order to illustrate how these three "sites" of transgression constitute forms of queer citizenship that challenge structures of homogeneity, regulation, and constraint that govern the concept and the practice of citizenship in the American nation. Finally, I will argue that transgression is not only an important but also an integral component of sexual citizenship, one essential to a basic recognition that "different forms of sexual identity mark claims to citizenship status differently" (Bell and Binnie 2000, 33).

EXPATRIATION AND THE AMERICAN NATION
IN DJUNA BARNES'S *NIGHTWOOD*

Djuna Barnes's *Nightwood* (1936) remains her most well-known work for a variety of reasons—its experimental form, its overabundance of imagery and symbolism, its linguistic excess,[1] its bleak depiction of a love triangle between three women (Robin Vote and her two lovers, Nora Flood and

Jenny Petherbridge), its representation of bohemian Paris in the 1930s, and a most unforgettable fictional character, the cross-dressing quack physician, Dr. "Matthew-Mighty-grain-of-salt-Dante-O'Connor" (Barnes 2006, 87). In his 1949 introduction to Barnes's novel, T. S. Eliot praised it for its "great achievement of . . . style," "beauty of phrasing," and "brilliance of wit and characterization" (2006, xxii), and Jeannette Winterson called it a "nano-text," a work that functions in "homeopathic dilutions" to achieve its full effect over a longer course of time, comparing the experience of reading the novel to "drinking wine with a pearl dissolving in the glass" (2006, ix). Unsurprisingly, Barnes's novel has been read through feminist perspectives as a work of "Sapphic modernism" (Benstock 1994),[2] in which the sexual transgressions and social disobedience of its protagonists challenge the repressive nature of patriarchal structures in everyday life. Accordingly, *Nightwood* has been interpreted as a female modernist writer's response to masculine hegemony, as a sensitive exploration of how "history is constructed, who gets written in and who gets written out" (Smith 1999, 197). Critics have valued the novel for its engagement with questions of the "Other"[3] and the representation of difference, noting how all its characters are "exiles of one kind or another" (Winterson 2006, xi).

Few studies to date, however, have engaged with the subjects of the expatriate body and the American nation in *Nightwood*. More specifically, critics who discuss the expatriate experience in the novel usually do so in relation to Barnes's own biography, reading the novel as a roman à clef that depicts the feelings of alienation and estrangement experienced by the author, who herself was one among a group of disillusioned American expatriate writers in modernist Europe commonly referred to as the "Lost Generation."[4] Such studies overlook the fact that the mythic personality of Barnes the expatriate writer was, to a large extent, as Shari Benstock posits, "the creation of a male culture" that "found her beauty and caustic wit the occasion for commentary" (1986, 231).[5] Moving away from such modes of interpretation, my analysis of Barnes's *Nightwood* will shift the focus away from Barnes the American expatriate writer to the depiction of the expatriate lesbian experience and the representation of the American nation in her writing.

"Everyone in *Nightwood* is homeless, afloat between expatriate Paris and Berlin and a dreamlike America," claims Carroll Smith-Rosenberg, ensuing that not one of the novel's protagonists "can claim a certain identity, few a clear gender. Their existence denies the inevitability of all structure and categories. They are liminal" (1985, 290). This emphasis on liminality, marginality, suspension, and a homeless "floating" casts a rather bleak view on the expatriate experience and, more particularly, the expatriate body. Several critics have adopted this view of the novel, declaring, as Ahmed Nimeiri does, that *Nightwood* expresses "an original though dark and desperate vision" of the "experience of America" (1993, 100). In Nimeiri's reading of the novel, "American expatriation is not a pilgrimage to a new life away from America but an experience that ends in a retreat and entrapment into a life more sinister than that which has initially prompted the American to leave his country. . . . The structure of *Nightwood* conveys strongly the sense of the inevitable return of the American to America" (101–4). Nimeiri's reading, which communicates a problematic tendency to read "expatriates" as "ex-patriots" is, however, misleading because it oversimplifies the complexity of the expatriate experience depicted in Barnes's novel, which is lived not only physically but mentally, emotionally, and affectively. Rather than apprehending Barnes's *Nightwood* as an "express[ion of] the failure of American expatriation" (104), I propose an alternative interpretation that reads the novel's portrayal of the expatriate body and the world(s) she or he inhabits as sites of transgression that seek to broaden the constraining definitions of the American nation, and reinscribe or reimagine its national myths.[6]

Nowhere is this more clearly illustrated in the novel than in the characters of Robin Vote (an expatriate whose Americanness makes her an object of desire in the eyes of her husband, "Baron" Felix)[7] and her lover Nora Flood, who works in publicity for the circus. It is Nora's seeming embodiment of a corporeal form of American nationality or, to recall Lauren Berlant's terms, "an anatomy of national fantasy" (1991) that makes her enticingly attractive and captivates those in her presence:

> She was known instantly as a Westerner. Looking at her, foreigners remembered stories they had heard of covered wagons; animals going down to drink. . . . At these incredible meetings one felt that early American history was being re-enacted. The Drummer Boy, Fort Sumter, Lincoln, Booth, all somehow came to mind; Whigs and Tories were in the air; bunting and its stripes and stars, the swarm increasing slowly and accurately on the hive of blue; Boston tea tragedies, carbines, and the sound of a boy's wild calling; Puritan feet, long upright in the grave, striking the earth again, walking up

and out of their custom; the calk of prayers thrust in the heart. And in the midst of this, Nora. (Barnes 2006, 56)

Nora Flood therefore recalls the frontier myth in American history, the tale of the legendary West anchored so firmly in the American popular imagination, which romanticized the relationship between civilization and the wilderness. As Frederick Jackson Turner advanced in his groundbreaking 1893 essay *The Significance of the Frontier in American History*, in what is now commonly referred to as his "frontier thesis," American democracy emerged hand in hand with the westward expansion of the American frontier. "Steadily the frontier of settlement advanced," Turner declares, "and carried with it individualism, democracy, and nationalism" (2011, 22). While Turner's "frontier thesis" undoubtedly remains at the forefront of studies of the American West, scholars have more recently criticized it for omitting the role of women and racialized subjects in western expansion.[8]

Upon closer reading, therefore, the character of Nora Flood personifies not so much the American frontier myth as it does a feminist counter-narrative to this masculinist myth of the American West and its domestication of the feminized wilderness.[9] Barnes's insertion of her willful female protagonist, Nora Flood, an early stereotype of the masculine lesbian or "butch" white American woman, "in[to] the midst" of it all can thus be interpreted as a refusal to be marginalized by the androcentric nature of modernist literary criticism.[10] Through the character of Nora Flood, formulaic and romanticized conceptions of the American nation and its national myth are revised, reinscribed, altered, or simply rendered obsolete. In this respect, Barnes's characterization of Nora Flood anticipates Jean-François Lyotard's observations half a century later in an age of postindustrialism that "the grand narrative of American history has lost its credibility, regardless of what mode of unification it uses, regardless of whether it is a speculative narrative or a narrative of emancipation" (1984, 37).[11] Indeed, the American expatriate's physical journey *east*ward to Paris and the capitals of Europe, instead of westward, as in the frontier myth, symbolizes an inversion of the "Westward Ho"[12] movement of the American frontier over the years of U.S. expansionism. The expatriate's journey eastward to Europe during the early decades of the twentieth century can thus be interpreted as a metaphorical rejection of doctrines of American exceptionalism, the nation's history of westward expansion, and Frederick Jackson Turner's frontier thesis on the origins of American democracy and nationality.

What has often been read as Djuna Barnes's depiction of the expatriate's feelings of alienation, estrangement, insularity, loss,[13] and being an "outsider" as an American on the streets of Paris can thus be interpreted, instead, as a rewriting of the metanarratives of American myth and history. Moreover, writing from a position of remove, and not from within the boundaries of the American nation, might offer critical distance and a certain amount of freedom from censorship.[14] *Nightwood*, with its references to bestiality, blasphemy, transvestitism, incest, and homosexuality, would certainly have been banned in the United States had it not first been published in London and strongly supported by T. S. Eliot, who also wrote the introduction to Barnes's novel. Yet it is in these very acts of transgression and the spaces in which they are performed that Barnes locates the political. The characters in *Nightwood* evade easy categorization and exceed their shifting signifiers. They are expatriate and self-exiled denizens of a nightworld characterized by circus spectacle, theatricality, performance, and masking; their articulations of sexual citizenship demand a rethinking of the social codes and moral institutions (of state, church, family, and society at large) that regulate gender and sexuality in the American nation, while simultaneously enacting a reinscription of dominant national myths and ideologies.

FROM CITIZENSHIP TO BESTIALITY: THE TRANSGRESSIVE/"PERVERSE" BODY IN ACTION

The expatriate body is thus the first of three new "sites" of transgression that engender alter-national notions of sexual citizenship and belonging, which in turn challenge the national ideologies that circumscribe conventional ideas of U.S. citizenship. A second "site" of transgression is that of the "freakish," "perverse," or nonnormative body. In *Nightwood*, "freakishness" or "perversity" manifests itself in the bestial and blasphemous body of Robin Vote, who is "transgressive" because she enacts a "violation of accepted or imposed boundaries, especially those of social acceptability."[15] Critical opinion of the depiction of this female protagonist in the novel remains divided. While some deem Robin an "odd and paradoxical" character with "an empty center" (Smith 1999, 199), others declare her to be "the novel's sovereign power, shaping the destinies of those around her, the dummy that makes the ventriloquists speak, though a cause absent even from herself," a character "so perverse as to be unforgettable" (Cole 2006, 406).

Robin Vote's "perversion" is often attributed to her animalistic qualities, her bestiality, and her blasphemy; critics often refer to the episode at the end of the novel with Robin and Nora's dog in the chapel as "evidence." This definition of the term *perversion* as "sexual behavior or preference that is different from the norm, specifically that which is considered to be unacceptable or socially threatening" should be taken into consideration together with its earlier etymological definition, "the action of turning aside from what is true or right; the diversion of something from its original and proper course, state, or meaning; corruption, distortion."[16] Something (an intention, justice, the law of nature) can be "perverted," therefore, when its course is altered, when it is instable, not fixed, ambivalent. In this respect, the character of Robin Vote is indeed a "perverse" body, surrounded by characters in her life (Baron Felix, Nora Flood, and Jenny Petherbridge) who project their fantasies onto her in order to fulfill their own desires. As Elisabeth Bronfen notes, Barnes "delineates how, by . . . treating the central character Robin as an emblem, the other characters are guilty of trying to fix an ambivalent body into a stable figure, albeit a reduction necessary for their erotic and narrative desires" (1988, 170).

In agreement with Bronfen's line of reasoning, I argue that, in her satiric parody of the "beastly" homosexual, Djuna Barnes has created a "transgressive" figure in the character of Robin Vote who, in straddling the nature-culture divide in Western culture, remains deliberately elusive and ambivalent, occupying a liminal position that rejects fixed sexual and gender roles.[17] Through the character of Robin, Barnes also critiques the exclusion of nonnormative bodies who are labeled as "perverse" or "freakish" according to prevailing moral codes of social conduct. Robin's excess, her animalism, bestiality, and blasphemy, might render her a "freak" in the eyes of the social majority but, as Niall Richardson importantly asserts in his study *Transgressive Bodies*, the classification of bodies as "freakish" or "perverse" by/in popular cultural representations reflects an endeavor to tame and contain the threat posed by such bodies, or else to "sensationalize or eroticize [their] potential" (2010, 16). In *Nightwood*, Nora Flood feels drawn to Robin Vote's primeval animalism. Yet Robin refuses to be pinned down or tamed by Nora's affections; she refuses a constellation that would only replicate the heterosexual male gaze and its construction of the female adulteress/temptress. The physical affair between the two women, therefore, can be interpreted as a deconstruction of gender roles and a consummation of female desire that counters and reverses the masculinist gaze of "modernist primitivism" (Rubin 1984)[18] as exemplified, for instance, in the artworks of Paul Gauguin, Pablo Picasso, and Henri Rousseau that hypersexualize and objectify the female body.

Robin Vote's animalistic qualities and her "primitivism" are referred to several times throughout the novel. The reader first encounters her in the second chapter of the novel, "La Somnambule." Robin has fainted in her room in a nondescript and mediocre "middle-class hostelr[y]" (2006, 37), and Dr. Matthew O'Connor has been summoned to revive her. The Baron Felix, who has been drinking with O'Connor, accompanies him on his night call. When they arrive, the sight that greets them recalls a painting, a tapestry, a "a 'picture' forever arranged" (41): "On a bed, surrounded by a confusion of potted plants, exotic palms and cut flowers, fairly over-sung by the notes of unseen birds, which seemed to have been forgotten—half flung off from the support of cushions . . . lay the young woman" (38). This scene, often referred to as the "jungle passage" in *Nightwood*, in which Robin is literally framed by the open doorway as a painting is framed, can be interpreted as a satiric appropriation of Henri Rousseau's jungle paintings,[19] especially his last and arguably most famous painting, *The Dream* (1910).

Recalling the primitivism of Paul Gauguin's Tahiti paintings, the jungle in Rousseau's painting is highly exoticized, yet tamed.[20] The painting's composition is neatly ordered and well constructed; the lush foliage, colorful flora, and vibrant fauna look arranged, carefully laid into place. It is not a realistic representation but a culturally informed perception of nature—to use Barnes's own phrase from the novel, a "populariz[ation of] the wilderness." There is an excess of symbolism in Rousseau's painting—the creation myth, the temptation and taming of the snake, the naturalization, objectification, and hypersexualization of the female body. Rousseau's painting clearly illustrates fantasies about racial and sexual difference. The dark-skinned native snake charmer stands in the background, almost blending in with his surroundings, whereas it is the young white woman, reclining naked on a divan in the bottom left of the painting, her body painted in light and flesh-colored tones, who is foregrounded. In a mimicry of Adam's pose in Michelangelo's famous Sistine Chapel fresco, *The Creation of Adam*, the woman's hand, casually draped on the back of the divan, is extended not to the snake charmer but to the animals, the wide-eyed lions and the snake, that are under her spell. Similarly, in *Nightwood*, the Baron Felix and the reader fall under Robin Vote's spell, so startlingly fantastical is Barnes's description of her, with her "porous," "plant-like" flesh and her "phosphorous glow" (2006, 38).

Like Rousseau's reclining woman, Robin is framed by her junglelike surroundings. Unlike Rousseau's masculinist naturalization of women in his paintings, however, Robin Vote does not stay within the confines of her "frame." She lies on her bed, "heavy and disheveled," her legs, in men's "white flannel trousers," "spread as in a dance, the thick-lacquered pumps looking too lively for the arrested step." Unlike the woman in Rousseau's *The Dream*, Robin is not naked but fully clothed; yet even her clothing cannot mask the scent of her body:

> The perfume that her body exhaled was of the quality of that earth-flesh, fungi, which smells of captured dampness and yet is so dry, overcast with the odor of oil of amber, which is an inner malady of the sea, making her seem as if she had invaded a sleep incautious and entire. Her flesh was the texture of plant life, and beneath it one sensed a frame, broad, porous and sleep-worn, as if sleep were a decay fishing her beneath the visible surface. About her head there was an effulgence as of phosphorous glowing about the circumference of a body of water—as if her life lay through her in ungainly luminous deteriorations—the troubling structure of the born somnambule, who lives in two worlds—meet of child and desperado. (2006, 38.)

Robin is described as a mystical creature, a liminal character who inhabits, indeed, "invades," the worlds of animal, plant, oceanic, and human life, biological classifications that have emerged as a result of the nature-culture divide in Western anthropology.[21] Significantly, she is not confined to any one of these worlds but inhabits them all at once—and none at all. As Jules Sturm argues, Robin's "ambiguity refers back to the very oppositions between man and woman, human and animal, homo- and heterosexual by citing each of them simultaneously" (2007, 262) and ultimately renders them as obsolete and critically unproductive binaries. When Dr. Matthew O'Connor rouses Robin from her fainting spell by splashing water onto her face, she comes to, emerging from "some deep-shocked realm" (2006, 39) like "a woman who is beast turning human" (41). Occupying a position of transition and in-betweeness, "poised between day and night, character and myth, identity and its negation, [she] signals a numinous possibility too terrible to tame"

(Cole 2006, 397). Robin Vote's animalism has also been read as a form of monstrosity. Sturm, for instance, points out that the "real threat" of the monster is "its disruption of fixed meaning," which stems from the "multiplicity of interpretations [it] elicit[s]." Not only does Robin's "disobedient" and sexually "deviant" body inflame her lovers with its disruptive and excessive needs (or with the promise of fulfilling their projected desires), it also refuses to be tied down to one lover, preferring polyamory with both sexes. In this respect, Sturm argues, the character of Robin, in her refusal to be limited to a (gendered) home space and sexuality, "opens up the narrative to a range of affective possibilities" (2007, 266).

Robin's fictional embodiment of transgression as a form of empowerment thus lies not only in her flouting of social conventions and sexual norms but also in her flaunting of a life of excess[22] and decadence as an aristocratic pose that would have been deemed "un-American," inappropriate, and out of place in the 1930s. Written in 1932 and 1933, in the aftermath of the stock market crash of 1929 and at the height of the Great Depression of the 1930s,[23] *Nightwood* does not directly depict the economic hardships of the period. Nevertheless, the novel captures the decline of the exuberant and decadent flapper lifestyle in the Paris of the 1930s, a Paris on the cusp of change, suspended between past and future. After World War I, Paris had become a destination for American tourists and bohemians who were enticed by France's comparatively lax social regulations—the nonexistence of the prohibition of alcohol and the widespread existence of state-controlled legal brothels (*maisons de tolerance*)—as well as its intellectual and cultural climate. The stock market crash, however, and the early years of the Great Depression meant that only American social elites were rich enough to afford to live in Paris, and many expatriate writers and intellectuals, including Barnes herself in 1930, returned to the United States. The artistic, cultural, and intellectual vigor of a flourishing bohemian population on the Left Bank degenerated into a mindset of social escapism[24] and political anxiety. As Harvey Levenstein encapsulates in his in-depth study of American expatriation in Paris in the 1930s, "The Paris of the Jazz Age, which since the end of World War I had been a magnet for hundreds of thousands of American tourists, was no more" (2010, 4).

The character of Robin thus inhabits the night world of Paris as a manifestation of the past—not the immediate past of the Jazz Age but that of a further removed past, the cultural trope of decadent European aristocrats and libertines, which she embodies so thoroughly that those in her presence palpably feel its influence. She becomes "a trope for memory, myth, remembrance" (Smith 1999, 202), a "container for the repressed, instinctual, or pre-rational impulses of the other characters" (Carlston 1998, 71). Further on in the "jungle" passage, Robin is described as follows: "Such a woman is the infected carrier of the past: before her the structure of our jaws ache—we feel that we could eat her, she who is eaten death returning, for only then do we put our face close to the blood on the lips of our forefathers" (2006, 41). Robin's animalistic and bestial nature is here stressed, as it is several times throughout the novel, in a vocabulary of infection, consumption, ache, disease, death, and decay.[25] Standing by her bedside and watching her come to, the Baron Felix is engulfed with a cannibalistic urge to eat her. This rather grotesque impulse articulates a form of necro-nationalism, or a nationalism associated with death. Felix's urge signifies more than sexual longing—it conveys a deep-rooted desire to consume the nation by ingesting it bodily, as doing so would grant access to that nation's history and national identity. For the fraudulent Baron Felix, marrying an American is a means for him to gain access to a national identity wherein, in contrast to the restrictions of European aristocracy, which is inherited and not acquired, the trope of the "self-made man"[26] has been deeply rooted. As the Baron Felix crudely phrases it, "[W]ith an American anything can be done" (42).[27]

Nevertheless, not *everything* can be done. The past that Felix longs for cannot be retrieved and the future, in the form of Felix and Robin's sickly child, Guido, offers little comfort and no redemption. Ironically, Felix's desire to gain access to national heritage, identity, and an aristocratic past through the act of marriage fails precisely because he confuses a European tradition of "aristocracy, nobility, royalty" (2006, 11) with its opposite, the American cultural ideal/myth of the self-made man. His unquestioning belief in the efficacy of the nation and its national past, compounded by his myopic conviction that male heirs "would recognize and honor [this] past," leaves Robin unmoved. When she becomes pregnant, she "prepare[s] herself for her child with . . . a stubborn cataleptic calm" and, "[s]trangely aware of some lost land in herself, she took to going out; wandering the countryside; to train travel, to other cities, alone and engrossed" (49). Robin's rejection of motherhood, her refusal to be reduced to a female womb and receptacle for Felix's offspring—another "perversion" of the female "maternal instinct" in the eyes of dominant society—foreshadows the dissolution of their marriage. When she leaves him after saying that she never wanted a child in the first place, she disappears for three or four months, to resurface with Nora Flood.

Arguably, it is Nora who brings out the animal in Robin. In the oft-cited resolution of the novel, the short chapter titled "The Possessed," Robin, now back in America, feels the need to see Nora once more. She terrifies Jenny with her distractedness, her restlessness, her walking "the open country, pulling at the flowers, speaking in a low voice to the animals." True to the chapter's title, Robin is described as a possessed spirit who savagely attacks the fauna she encounters: "Those that she came near, she grasped, straining their fur back until their eyes were narrowed and their teeth bare, her own teeth showing as if her hand were upon her own neck." When Robin finally seeks out Nora by "heading up into [her] part of the country," her progress is described as like that of an animal—she "circle[s] closer and closer" (2006, 177), sleeping sometimes in the woods and sometimes in the derelict chapel on Nora's country estate. It is in this chapel that the climax of the novel takes place, where Robin and Nora are "reunited." Unfortunately, Nora accidentally runs into the doorjamb of the chapel, loses consciousness, and does not witness Robin going down on all fours in an eroticized struggle with Nora's dog:

> At the moment Nora's body struck the wood, Robin began going down, down, her hair swinging, her arms out. The dog stood rearing back, his forelegs slanting, his paws trembling under the trembling of his rump, . . . whining and waiting. And down she went until her head swung against his, on all fours now, dragging her knees. The veins stood out in her neck, under her ears, swelled in her arms, and wide and throbbing, rose up on her hands as she moved forward. (179)

Critics have variously interpreted this final scene, one of the most cryptic passages in the novel, which ends with Robin and the dog lying in physical, mental, and sexual exhaustion, the dog's head "flat along her knees" (180). Christine Coffman, for instance, reads this final scene as a reversal of the earlier description of Robin as a "beast turning human," an instance of a "human turning beast, the site onto which the primitivism at the heart of the symbolic is displaced" (2006, 135).

While critics' analyses of this final scene in *Nightwood* have diverged,[28] most concur that the setting of the dilapidated chapel is symbolic. Specifically, it has been thought to represent Barnes's "Sapphic modernist" contesting of the patriarchal moral institutions that regulate women's sexuality. As Coffman's puts it, "Robin's descent into animality tracks the unraveling of patriarchal religion and of the gendered and sexual regime upon which patriarchal society is founded. . . . Barnes unravels the Western symbolic in its own decaying chapel and opens up a space for its displacement" (2006, 135). In agreement with this interpretation, I read this final scene not as "the reenacting of the dynamics of a freak show performance that encourages questions but denies answers" or the culmination of a deliberately opaque, "indecipherab[le]" novel that "requires a refusal to understand" (Monahan 2008, 200) but, rather, Djuna Barnes's clear "participat[ion] in female modernism's larger interrogation of gender and the writing self under the male gaze" (Marcus 1991, 244). It is in the sexually transgressive nature of Robin's descent into bestiality and blasphemy that Barnes daringly locates the political. Recalling Niall Richardson's (2010) claim that popular cultural representations construct the "freak" or "nonnormative" body in order to tame, naturalize, and contain it, in this scene, Robin's transgressive body refuses to be contained as she howls, barks, laughs, grins, cries, and weeps. The final climactic scene of the novel is thus significant not only because its collapses the boundaries between human/animal, divine/human, nature/culture, and masculine/feminine that have been constructed in Western cultural discourse, but also in its embrace and assimilation of the "Other," the "nonnormative" body, as represented in the image of woman and dog lying side by side, touching, in mutual exhaustion and surrender.

SEXUAL AMBIGUITY AND THE PARISIAN NIGHT WORLD

Finally, a third new "site" of sexual transgression is located, I suggest, in the figures of the cross-dressing transvestite and the androgynous subject. In *Nightwood*, these two figures are conflated in the character of the Irish American quack doctor Matthew O'Connor, one of the denizens of the night worlds of Paris, Berlin, and the other capital cities of Europe. Like his fellow expatriates, Matthew O'Connor inhabits night worlds "of possibilities not limited by the linear logic of day, worlds which require a matching prose of flexibility and dreamlike openness that can convey ideas and sensations usually censored by rationality." It is these nocturnal spaces that the transgressive and freakish bodies—bodies who do not conform to the norm, whose stylistic and linguistic excess, as well as sexual ambiguity and androgyny, mark them as disobedient and unruly by mainstream society—inhabit in the novel. This is a counter-world of circus "freaks," sexual "deviants," and decadent expatriates whose occupying of this "other(ed)" space on a separate continent challenges the neat rhetoric of American "national life."[29] In *Nightwood*, therefore, the trope of the irrational, clandestine mirror-world of the night, where things are not what they seem and illusion merges with "reality," is used "as a means of questioning both personal and national identity and history" (Whitley 2000, 85), at one remove.

The central figure at the core of this night world of shadows and disguises is the transvestite and androgynous figure of "Dr. Matthew-Mighty-grain-of-salt-Dante-O'Connor" (Barnes 2006, 87). Leading a transgressive double life, he is a quack doctor, a self-professed gynecologist and physician by day and a cross-dresser who has sexual encounters with men by night. Matthew O'Connor is *Nightwood*'s most verbose character, and critics have singled out the fourth chapter of the novel, "Watchman, What of the Night?" as a paramount example of Djuna Barnes's linguistic dexterity and literary deftness.[30] In this oft-cited sequence, Nora Flood pays a visit to O'Connor at three in the morning because she wants to know the details of Robin's first encounter with Jenny Petherbridge. The sight that greets Nora's eyes makes her initially recoil in dismay: "In the narrow iron bed, with its heavy and dirty linen sheets, lay the doctor in a woman's flannel nightgown. The doctor's head . . . was framed in the golden semi-circle of a wig with long pendent curls that touched his shoulders. . . . He was heavily rouged and his lashes painted. It flashed into Nora's head: 'God, children know something they can't tell; they like Red Riding Hood and the wolf in bed!'" (85). Witnessing Matthew O'Connor in bed, dressed in drag and obviously expecting a gentleman caller, Nora inadvertently thinks of the wolf in the "Little Red Riding Hood" folktale who dresses in Grandmother's clothing in order to "eat" (a euphemism for oral sexual intercourse) Little Red Riding Hood. The association that Nora makes is not coincidental but reflects Barnes's "Sapphic modernist" reinterpretation of the children's fairytale,[31] which substitutes the allegorical rape of Red Riding Hood with the pleasures of consensual sex.[32]

"Playing the grandmother, bewigged and rouged," Shari Benstock observes, "Matthew O'Connor parodies women's language, steals her stories and her images in order to teach her about herself" (1986, 266). O'Connor's self-description as "a boy" who is simultaneously "the bearded lady"[33] and "last lady left in the world" (Barnes 2006, 107), his cross-dressing and love of makeup and women's perfume, make him both a transvestite and androgynous at the same time. The fictional character of Matthew O'Connor can thus be read as Barnes's playful assault on Freud's masculinist, andro-centric/phallocentric psychoanalytical theory. As Jane Marcus has noted, O'Connor's womb envy—he proclaims his desire for a "womb as big as the king's kettle" (97) so he can "toss up a child for [a good man] every nine months by the calendar" (98)—satirizes Freud's concept of penis envy. The latter's famous ancient totems and sacred objects that he collected in his rooms are also parodied in the rusty forceps, broken scalpel, perfume bottles, powder boxes, stockings, and women's underclothing strewn about unceremoniously in O'Connor's small and messy room (Marcus 1991, 244).

Matthew O'Connor's transgressive caricature of womanhood makes visible "the imitative structure of all gender, in that they dramatize the way 'normal' gender performances must be reiterated continually to sustain the projection of a unified gender identity" (Henstra 2000, 131). Problematizing the categories of masculine and feminine and ultimately rendering them meaningless beyond the contexts/confines of their social constructions, Matthew O'Connor simultaneously inhabits both, and hence neither singular one, of these states. A charlatan, garrulous drunk, and self-confessed "greatest liar this side of the moon" who loquaciously spouts anecdotes, hyperbolic comparisons, and witticisms, he nevertheless displays a sense of empathy and compassion, telling Nora, for instance, that he tells his "stories to people like you to take the mortal agony out of their guts" (Barnes 2006, 144). As T. S. Eliot comments, "[H]is monologues, brilliant and witty in themselves as they are, are not dictated by an indifference to other human beings, but on the contrary by a hypersensitive awareness of them" (2006, xix). In the chapter "Watchman, What of the Night?" for example, O'Connor is initially put out that it is Nora, and not the gentleman caller he has been expecting, who visits him at three o'clock in the morning. Nevertheless, he sees the state Nora is in, and responds to her wish to know the circumstances of Robin and Jenny's first encounter with a long treatise on the night in general, and Parisian nights in particular. Despite being protracted and rambling, Matthew O'Connor's discourse on the night acknowledges the "dark realities" of the human psyche and can be summarized by his maxim, "The Bible lies one way, but the night-gown the other" (Barnes 2006, 87).

In an inversion of the adage "Innocence is bliss," therefore, Matthew O'Connor obliquely tells Nora that mankind must confront what Catherine Whitley has termed "excremental history" (2000, 81), for it is the history of waste, of what is expelled out of the national body in its daily "functions," that determines the construction of national and personal identity. Whitley argues that, in a moment of authorial intrusion and critical commentary on American attitudes in the "Golden Twenties" (or the "Roaring Twenties"), when glittery façades often concealed grim realities of poverty and squalor, Barnes suggests that "a proper relationship to one's own excreta is analogous to a proper relationship to one's own personal and national history" (96). In the novel, Matthew O'Connor sketches out for Nora the difference between French and American attitudes to scatology: "The French are disheveled and wise; the American tries to approximate it with drink. It is his only clue to himself. He takes it when his soap has washed him too clean for identification. The Anglo-Saxon has made the literal error; using water, he has washed away his page" (Barnes 2006, 96). In fear of the dirt, the grime, the sordid mess and disarray of history ("Destiny and history are untidy; we fear memory of that disorder" [126]), and in an attempt to regulate, purify, and package U.S. history into a neat metanarrative, this passage seems to be saying, Americans wash themselves "too clean for identification," effectively erasing their identities and cutting themselves off from their own histories. By extension, the figure of the American expatriate can be understood as central to the process of bringing about a change in social and political attitudes. Rather than simply "fleeing" or abandoning the country and living at a geographical distance from their national history in a culturally different environment, American citizens can better appreciate, at one remove, the disorder and "messiness" of national history, its episodes of inclusion and exclusion, its marginalization of transgressive "Others," and take these issues to task accordingly.

Critics who argue that the character of Matthew O'Connor reveals a spiritual and emotional hollowness, that he offers "at best, an intellectualism unconnected to any meaningful experience and a verbalism that blunts the mind and dims the imagination" (Nimeiri 1993, 110), therefore, fail to grasp the more complex nature of the function of this character in the novel.[34] I argue that O'Connor represents a subversive, queer protagonist who enunciates a poetics and politics of alter-national citizenship. His sexual transgressions and his deconstruction (one might say "disemboweling") of the dominant discourses of nation and national identity via verbose rhetoric and camp performativity call these established concepts into question and substitute the neat historical metanarratives of American history with queer chronicles of the sexually anomalous "Other." As Carroll Smith-Rosenberg appositely summarizes, "Nightwood, while condemning conventional order, speaks eloquently of the experience of marginality and of deviance" (1985, 293).

As Matthew O'Connor says teasingly to Nora Flood, "I have a narrative but you will be put to it to find it" (Barnes 2006, 104). The text of *Nightwood* offers not a narrative but, as Jules Sturm posits, "a less restrictive place of reading, a place which emanates from a radical excess of meaning, . . . ultimately, a place for numerous productive ways of experiencing ambiguously-gendered bodies" (2007, 266). On the level of language, *Nightwood* is "a narrative of discontinuity" (Singer 1984, 66) and elaborate digression. Barnes constructs "sentences of multiple, discontinuous images which seem to digress from rather than to clarify a point" (Whitley 2000, 89), which gesture "beyond themselves to an unknown and unknowable referent," thus exploding "ideas of fixed identity, gender stereotypes, and linguistic referentiality" (90). Indeed, Matthew O'Connor's shape-shifting androgyny and transvestitism has led Carroll Smith-Rosenberg to read him as a "tragic trickster" figure in the novel who has "declared war against social convention" and, as a result, has to "live out the consequences of [his] actions," "sadly," "in defeat," and "in a mad night wood full of inversion and pain" (1985, 293).[35] Interpreting the "sorrowful" existence of Matthew O'Connor and the other "tragic tricksters" of *Nightwood* (Robin Vote, Nora Flood, and Jenny Petherbridge) as "a somber but not . . . inaccurate vision of the experience of the New Woman[36] . . . in the dark years of the 1930s," in particular, as an allusion to the expulsion of the New Woman from "the world of legitimacy and power" (294–95), Smith-Rosenberg argues that *Nightwood* conveys "the pain that accompanied public condemnation, social ostracism, and legal censorship" (295) in the 1930s. While this might be true to a certain extent,[37] Smith-Rosenberg's reading oversimplifies the complexity of the novel, which should not be read merely as a roman à clef or a direct representation of Barnes's own position in society.[38] Adopting a somewhat different perspective, I argue that *Nightwood* uses sexual ambivalence, androgyny, excess, decadence, linguistic verbosity, and a scatological approach to national history as tools of retaliation against the strictures of a prescriptive social order in the United States during the 1920s and 1930s. The latter included a politics of national efficiency and prohibition as well as cultural, gender, and sexual norms, despite the seeming emancipation of women through women's suffrage in the Jazz Age or the Golden Twenties.

My reading of *Nightwood* thus offers an alternative interpretation of how the novel challenges and subverts, rather than simply acquiesces to and depicts, the atmosphere of tension and unease in the America nation and in Europe in the 1920s and 1930s. The characters of Matthew O'Connor, Nora Flood, Robin Vote, and Jenny Petherbridge are less tragic tricksters than willful subjects and sexual denizens of the bohemian night worlds they inhabit. Accordingly, their nocturnal citizenship is enacted by acts of sexual transgression, dissidence, and deviance from the social norm, acts that reveal and contest the modes of restraint and governance that characterize the master narratives of American national history. In this respect, my reading departs from interpretations of *Nightwood* as "Barnes's bleak vision of the crisis of modernity" (Nabholz 2007, 269) or as a literary "allegory of a modernity ill at ease with itself" (Jervis 2008, 21). Barnes's novel is anything but ill at ease with itself; it does not shy away from depictions of the abject (which is situated, in Kristevian terms, outside of the symbolic order),[39] the uncanny, and the transgressive. Rather, it embraces these acts of abjection, deviance, and transgression—self-expatriation, sexual promiscuity, homosexuality, bestiality, blasphemy, sodomy, scatology, transvestitism, androgyny—and flaunts them flagrantly against the strictures of social, moral, and religious institutions. In *Nightwood*, transgression is thus conceived as an integral component of sexual citizenship that challenges the homogenizing forces of dominant national narratives.

8

QUEER MIGRATION AND CITIZENSHIP IN CARIBBEAN CANADIAN WRITING

· · · · · · · · · ·

Dionne Brand's *In Another Place, Not Here*
and Shani Mootoo's *Valmiki's Daughter*

This chapter continues my exploration of how queer sexuality disrupts and challenges prevailing constructions of normative, nation-based models of citizenship. Through the methodological lens of queer migration theory, I will examine how queer migrant bodies mark, and are marked in, their everyday spaces of interaction—the family, the community, the city, the nation—with other citizens within these spaces and, subsequently, how their claims to sexual citizenship challenge dominant processes of national identity formation. Central to my analysis of how these claims are articulated is a consideration of how queer diasporic narratives demand and open up alter- and postnational forms of recognition and belonging. More specifically, this chapter will assess how "new" affective ways of belonging that complicate and restructure existing heterosexual models of citizenship and national identity are imagined in the narrative spaces of the queer diasporic novel. I will focus on two Caribbean Canadian novels in particular—Dionne Brand's *In Another Place, Not Here* (1996) and Shani Mootoo's *Valmiki's Daughter* (2008).

QUEER MIGRATION THEORY AND THE DENATIONALIZING OF SEXUAL CITIZENSHIP

The emergence of queer migration scholarship in the 1990s was a response to an increasing awareness of the intersections between issues of migration and sexuality, in particular, how sexuality shapes dominant policies on issues of migration and diaspora.[1] Drawing on existing research in the fields of feminist scholarship, ethnic studies, and postcolonial theory, queer migration scholars such as Eithne Luibhéid and Martin F. Manalansan IV[2] have called for a rethinking of the dominant assumptions, theories, methods, and paradigms that structure sexuality and migration studies.[3] As Luibhéid summarizes in her contribution to a special issue, "Queer/Migration," of *GLQ: A Journal of Lesbian and Gay Studies*, there are two basic principles in queer migration studies, First, sexuality is understood as constructed within multiple and intersecting relations of power, including race, ethnicity, gender, class, citizenship status, and geopolitical location. Second, usage of the term *queer* acknowledges the diverse backgrounds and identities of subjects who do not fit neatly within a developmental narrative of LGBTQI identities nor the largely Eurocentric, neoliberal, progressive framework of these narratives.[4] Instead, queer migration scholarship "insists on recovering, theorizing, and valorizing histories and subjects that have been largely rendered invisible, unintelligible, and unspeakable in both queer and migration studies" (Luibhéid 2008, 171).

At the center of this project of recovery and reinscription lies a decentering of national(ist) frameworks and their official narratives. In their place, critics have emphasized the importance of various contact zones in transcultural and transnational spaces of interaction and the practicing of queer sexual citizenship in these spaces. Queer migration scholarship also critiques new forms of exclusion and marginalization that reproduce forms of nationhood and nation-based citizenship. In particular, it adopts a critical stance toward the perception of queer migrant bodies by the state as deviant and undesirable because they threaten to undermine dominant processes of national identity formation and reproduction that are enacted by "stable" institutionalized structures such as that of the conventional family. Because queer migrants are dominantly perceived as nonreproductive bodies or bodies who challenge the (heterosexual) reproductive logic of the nation, they are not regarded as at least potentially contributing to the nation's future. Accordingly, queer migration theory condemns the "racializing, (re)gendering and (de)nationalizing" (Luibhéid 2008, 174) of queer migrant bodies at immigration checkpoints, borders, and other points of entry into the nation-state. In the following, I will illustrate how two novels, one by Dionne Brand and the other by Shani Mootoo, respond to this forced "denationalizing" of queer migrant bodies by reconfiguring the spatiotemporal dimensions of nationhood and national identity, extending new forms of post- and trans-national belonging predicated upon a poetics/politics of queer diasporia. Crucial to these endeavors is a repositioning of the queer migrant body from an external threat to the "safe haven" of the nation and its "compulsory heterosexuality" (Adrienne Rich 2003)[5] to an integral part of the nation's social, political, and affective imaginaries.

This repositioning is enacted via what Engin Isin and Greg Nielsen have termed "acts of citizenship," or daily processes whereby subjects constitute themselves as citizens. Be they everyday "routines, rituals, customs, norms [or] habits" or "collective or individual deeds that rupture socio-historical patterns" (2008, 17, 2), "acts of citizenship" are complex procedures located somewhere between the realms of legal entitlement and lived experience. This emphasis on the acts, norms, practices, and identities that are performed—but also contested—on an everyday basis aptly illustrates the recent paradigm shift in citizenship studies from an understanding of citizenship as a static, legal concept to citizenship as a more complex and flexible process. As Isin and Nielsen encapsulate, "[C]itizenship is not only a legal status . . . it involves practices—social, political, cultural and symbolic." In other words, a citizen today should possess not merely legal status of belonging but also political and social recognition, access to economic resources, and the opportunity to partake in "ethical, cultural, sexual and social" (2) practices.

By foregrounding "acts of citizenship" that are performed on the level of narrative by their protagonists, Brand's and Mootoo's novels shift the focus away from abstract legal/political discourses of citizenship to the affective[6] and substantive ("lived") dimensions of citizenship. The texts reinscribe the spaces of home and nation, locating them as the sites of queer physical desire and emergent struggle. In so doing, these narratives challenge and rewrite the dominant discourses of nation building as well as prevailing representations of the "postcolonial condition" as dislocation, displacement, and loss in the works of an earlier generation of male Caribbean writers.

QUEERING THE NATION IN AFRO-TRINIDADIAN CANADIAN WRITING

Rewriting the dominant discourses of nation building and nationalism that emerged within a literary context of diverse post-independence Caribbean or West Indian writing by a generation of male authors such as Derek Walcott, Aimé Césaire, Kamau Brathwaite, V. S. Naipaul, George Lamming, and

Édouard Glissant is perhaps a daunting task. Nevertheless, the writings of Guay-aguayare-born Torontonian poet laureate (2009–12) and writer Dionne Brand have engaged in this project with considerable success, even earning the praise of Kamau Brathwaite himself as "our [the Caribbean's] first major exile female poet" (1985, 18).[7] Critical reception of Brand's work can be divided into early and later appraisals of her writings. Early literary criticism situated Brand's work within the longer tradition of West Indian writing, proclaiming her as a younger poet whose "literary inheritance" is "a legacy of Walcott, Brathwaite and oth-ers" (Chamberlain 1993, 269). Later reviews of her work, however, have come to focus more on the poetics of "statelessness" (Sanders 1989, 20) or "(dis)location," which "(dis)plac[es] or (dis)locat[es] the national narrative of subjectivity . . . into the diaspora of cross-cultural, -racial, -gender, -class, and -erotic identifica-tions" (Dickinson 1998, 114). These critics have applauded Brand's uncoupling of national identities from their strict geographical boundaries, her positing of identity as a fluid discursive construct, and her "investigat[ion of] the very possi-bilities of Black, female self-representation in Canadian cultural space" (Sturgess 2003, 53) in a poetic manifesto that recognizes that "no language is neutral."[8]

While these readings of Brand's work are perceptive, they are also, perhaps, too quick to hail the author as an ambassador of Canada's multiculturalism[9] and to applaud her writing as illustrative of the literary border crossing and diaspor-ic imagination that has brought about a reconfiguration and expansion of the boundaries of the Canadian nation.[10] Therefore, I suggest that a further differ-entiation must be made here—Brand's works seek to reconfigure not only the Canadian but also the *Caribbean* imaginary. In her first novel, *In Another Place, Not Here*, this is enacted by a textual strategy of queer affect that locates the queer body inside the spaces of the nation in an attempt to transform its social and cultural imaginaries, as well as its colonial past, from within. The title of Brand's novel is taken from her earlier volume of poems, *No Language Is Neutral* (1990):

> History will only hear you if you give birth to a
> woman who smoothes starched linen in the wardrobe
> drawer, trembles when she walks and who gives birth
> to another woman who cries near a river
> and vanishes and who gives birth to a woman who is a
> poet, and, even then. . . .
> *in another place not here*, a woman might touch
> something between beauty and nowhere (30–31; my emphasis)

The emphasis in the title of Brand's novel, I suggest, is on the word "here" (the Caribbean) and not "another place" (Canada).[11] Continuing the project of her volume *No Language Is Neutral*, Brand seeks to reconfigure the imaginative geographies of the Caribbean, the "here," to reconstruct it as a space of possibility where women will not merely be regarded as passive, trembling housewives and mothers, where they can express their sexual desires (for other women, too) without inhibition or discrimination. In this light, the abuse of one of the novel's two Afro-Trinidadian female protagonists, the sugarcane plantation worker Elizete, whose body represents the "black body forced open by centuries of slavery and sexual exploitation" (Bertacco 2009, 13), also constitutes a strong critique of the patriarchal attitudes and normative gender roles that are ingrained in the fabric of Caribbean life.

Raped nightly and beaten by her owner/husband, Isaiah, Elizete falls in love with Verlia, a political activist who comes back to the island (an unnamed island that closely resembles Grenada) from Toronto to incite the sugarcane workers to revolution. The novel is divided into two parts, told from the perspectives of the two women. The first part, titled "Elizete, Beckoned," is told from Elizete's perspective and charts her childhood, her meeting Verlia, their sexual relationship, Verlia's death, and Elizete's journey from the Caribbean to Canada thereafter in the hope of better understanding Verlia's previous life as a political activist in Toronto. The second part of the novel, titled "Verlia, Flying," is narrated from Verlia's perspective. It describes her travels from the Caribbean to Toronto at the age of seventeen and her return years later, fueled by political idealism and ideas of revolution. Notably, Verlia does not remain in Toronto but returns to the Caribbean to reinstate her political and sexual subjectivity within the spaces of the nation that previously excluded her. It is also significant that it is a lesbian relationship that allows her to do this, as Verlia finds redemption and shelter in Elizete, "a woman who knew how to look for rain, what to listen for in birds in the morning (Brand 1996, 202). Here, female sexuality and same-sex desire become the tools of expression and signification, voicing a poetics of queer diaspora that challenges existing heterosexual models of citizenship and national belonging.

This poetics of queer diaspora in Brand's novel is crucial because it seeks to reverse the disembodied metaphors of loss, violence, trauma, and erasure that have become encoded in narratives of the black Atlantic. Specifically, it reinscribes the central sites of slavery's historical and cultural imaginaries: the slave ship and the plantation. Acknowledging Paul Gilroy's well-known study of the experience of the Middle Passage in the emergence of black modernity in *The Black Atlantic: Modernity and Double Consciousness* (1993), Brand nevertheless challenges his omission of queer histories of the black Atlantic. *In Another Place, Not Here* tells the previously silenced stories of queer desire in the Caribbean by (re)locating the site of struggle, same-sex longing, and emergent lesbian subjectivity in the sugarcane plantation, the archetypal (heterosexual) site of the master-slave dialectic. Indeed, while Gilroy's insistence on "get[ing] beyond . . . national and nationalistic perspectives" (7) and his attunement to "structures of feeling, . . . communicating and remembering [the black Atlantic]" (3) are laudable, his analysis nonetheless makes short shrift of the same-sex relationships that were a part of this history.[12] Dionne Brand, on the other hand, reimagines and reembodies queer sexuality into the oceanic discourse of the Middle Passage and African diasporic identity.

Accordingly, the motif of water recurs throughout the novel, beginning with a passage narrated by Elizete wherein she lovingly describes Verlia. "That woman like a drink of cool water," Elizete thinks to herself, "like a shower of rain coming that could just wash me cool" (1996, 3–4).[13] Water gives sustenance and life, but it is also evidently the element most directly associated with the ordeal of the Middle Passage and the black Atlantic slave trade.[14] This is addressed in the novel's subplot in the story of Adela, the ancestor of the mean-spirited woman to whom Elizete was given away at birth, and who was forcefully brought over to the Caribbean from Africa as a slave. Adela's grief is transmuted into her refusal to learn the names of the plants and animals around her or even to name her own children; she insists that the Caribbean island to which she is forcefully relocated is "Nowhere."[15] As Elizete muses, "Adela was grieving bad for where she come from. And when she done calculate the heart of this place, that it could not yield to her grief, she decide that this place was not nowhere and is so she call it. Nowhere. She say nothing here have no name. . . . Adela call this place Nowhere and with that none of the things she look at she take note of or remember or pass on. She insist so much is nowhere she gone blind with not seeing" (19). "Nowhere" implies an absence, the antithesis of "Somewhere." Nevertheless, it is in a gesture of refusal and defiance that Adela consciously names the Caribbean island to which she is forcefully uprooted as a no place, a non-place.

This is significant as "Nowhere" subsequently becomes the trope of Afro-Caribbean diaspora that Brand develops in two ensuing works—the novel *At the Full and Change of the Moon* (1999) and her essayistic collection of prose writings, *A Map to the Door of No Return: Notes on Belonging* (2001).[16] The latter reconfigures the shifting territories of home, nation, and diaspora in the black Atlantic, Canada, and beyond. In it, Brand recalls how, as a young girl, she would pester her grandfather about the name of their ancestors. But her grandfather does not, or cannot bring himself to, remember, cannot "summon up the vision of a landscape or a people which would add up to a name"—a lack that he himself finds profoundly disturbing and disappointing. Recalling this incident, Brand considers how her early wish to know the name of her ancestors had metamorphosed into a deeper, more existential issue over time and opened up a palpable sense of loss and longing for a sense of origin:

> Having no name to call on was having no past; having no past pointed to the fissure between the past and the present. That fissure is represented in the Door of No Return: that place where our ancestors departed one world for another; the Old World for the New. The place where all names were forgotten and all beginnings recast. In some desolate sense it was the creation place of all Blacks in the New World Diaspora at the same time that it signified the end of traceable beginnings. (5)

This sense of loss and rupture—"a rupture in history, a rupture in the quality of being [that is also] a physical rupture, a rupture of geography" (Brand 2001, 5)—is depicted not as inherent in the experience of departing from one world for another but specifically as the brutal outcome of colonial forces of slavery and neo-imperialism. For the slave, there is no physical return to Africa, no repatriation save a spiritual homecoming in the moment of death—hence the image of the "Door of No Return." The painful experience of deracination and loss caused by being uprooted from Africa and forcefully relocated in the Caribbean, as well as the long journey of the Middle Passage, is imaginatively recounted by Elizete in an episode in the novel:

> All the way here, Adela, registering the stench of the ship, must have memorize the road to find she way out and the road was not only solid ground but water too, and so long it take, true is not time it take, is wrack and pull. So long she had time to balance the oceans and measure how much mouthful she would have to swallow to get

back but when she reach and find she-self locked in on all sides and not by nothing human, she drop, she call it Nowhere and begin to forget by forgetting the road. . . . But every different place they put her she take an opportunity to remember all the things that she was going to forget. (1996, 21)

Here, Brand refers to the tropes of memory and forgetting that recur in Afro-Caribbean literature. Adela's repeated act of invoking each instance of inhuman treatment in order to deliberately forget it, at every stage of the arduous crossing from Africa to the Caribbean, constitutes her own counter-discursive strategy of unforgetting (remembering) and unremembering (forgetting). Forcefully relocated and deprived of her connection to her past, Adela is left feeling bitter, filled with hatred and spite, "feeling something harder than stone and more evil than sense" (22). In contrast, in an attempt at "rememory,"[17] Elizete "watch[es] things and wonder[s] what Adela would call this is if it wasn't nowhere" (20–21). As part of a strategy of survival, Elizete reverses Adela's refusal to name the Caribbean island, thinking up names for the flora and fauna that surround her: "pull and throw push, make haste weed, jump up and kiss me flowers, waste of time plant . . . slippery throat peas, wet sea fern, idle whistle bird" (20, 23–24) and making herself "determined to love this [island] and never to leave" (25).

Elizete's imaginative naming of her surroundings illustrates her attempt to recover her past (by tracing it through Adela); nevertheless, she knows that this is futile, that there is no "original" self or "core" identity that can be retrieved. Like Brand's own quest for her ancestral history, Elizete's attempt in the novel to trace her origins does not achieve fruition; it leads her "nowhere." Perhaps, however, as Brand stresses, "the journey is the destination" (2001, 203). This can be read, I suggest, as the author's challenging of the broadly accepted viewpoint expressed in the writings of her Caribbean Canadian predecessors, such as the eminent Martinique-born writer Aimé Césaire, that Africa is the source of (Afro-)Caribbean identity.[18] For the Afro-Caribbean writer, Brand seems to be suggesting, tracing one's heritage and ancestry back to Africa is a much more complex and frustrating, if not entirely impossible, task. It is one that involves, to use a metaphor from *A Map to the Door of No Return*, "being a part, and sitting in the same room"[19] with history—a history of elision, forced migration, deracination, and haunting.

In *In Another Place, Not Here,* this is a past with which Elizete comes face-to-face when, in a trip that parallels her ancestor Adela's forced relocation from Africa to the Caribbean, Elizete leaves the Caribbean for Canada and arrives in Toronto as an undocumented migrant. Without a place to stay, she sleeps in a shopping mall, wandering about anonymously and eating scraps that people leave behind in the pizzeria and the Vietnamese restaurant. As one of the thousands of nameless and anonymous *sans-papiers* in the city, she lingers on the fringes of society, occupying its abject spaces: its back kitchens, toilets, and sidewalks off the beaten track: "Months and she still hadn't heard about Yonge Street because she hadn't looked that way, just stared at the hank of Canadian National and the factories beyond. Nobody told her about Yonge Street or Avenue Road or Yorkville. Nobody told her what wasn't necessary or possible or important for a woman from nowhere" (1996, 49). Yonge Street, the main street in Toronto where parades, including Gay Pride, street performances, and demonstrations are held, and Yorkville, a district well known as one of Canada's most exclusive shopping districts, are two areas in the city that remain unexplored by Elizete. The experience of being an undocumented migrant in the Canadian metropolis is a rude awakening for her, demystifying her imaginary constructions of "another place[s]" outside of the Caribbean, such as the fantasy she had had of flying away to Maracaibo, Venezuela, after plotting to kill her husband, Isaiah. In its stark depiction of the female undocumented migrant's experience in Toronto, which includes rape, prostitution, substandard accommodation, and working cleaning jobs in shifts, the novel broaches the difficult topic of citizenship as an exclusionary and highly selective process. Provocatively described in the novel as "Third World people going to the white man country," undocumented migrants from Africa and the Caribbean such as Elizete are forced to "lowe[r] themselves in their own estimation" because "nobody was interested in whether they felt mixed up or fucked up" (60). Their stories become "lies because nobody wanted to listen, nobody had the time" (61). In this "No Place" of multicultural, metropolitan, first world Toronto, an inverse parallel of Adela's "Nowhere," Elizete and the other undocumented female migrants with whom she shares her accommodation are robbed of their language, of their agency to speak,[20] and even deprived of their Caribbean "origins" ("that smell so compelling that it made you deny your origins ... you begin to speak with an accent to distinguish yourself, affect a tone with disdain in it, hold your behind in like the white girls in magazines" [60]). Toronto is depicted as a city that "resists knowing"; it is a place that, once again in a parallel to her ancestor Adela's experience, Elizete cannot map, size up, or name: "When she tried calling it something, the words would not come" (69) and she realizes that "her names would not do for this place" (70).

The novel's depiction of Elizete's existence as an undocumented migrant in the "No Place" of Toronto represents more than merely a parallel plot to the experiences of her ancestor Adela in the "Nowhere" of the Caribbean. Rather, Elizete's ordeal in the Canadian metropolis exposes the fantasy of the conventional migrant narrative, whereby each immigrant "travels smoothly from settlement to assimilation and then citizenship." In Toronto, Elizete becomes a fictional projection of the "undesirable" subject or "disqualified" body who threatens, destabilizes, and interrupts the "teleology of legal categorization, whereby the immigrant is first lawfully admitted as a permanent resident and then naturalizes to become a citizen" (Volpp 2005, 1595). The depiction of Elizete's exploitation as an undocumented female migrant in Toronto, a city whose public image boasts its self-professed multiethnic and multicultural ethos, illustrates Brand's critique of Canada's official policy of multiculturalism[21] by drawing attention to the underside of neoliberal capital and its transnational flows. More specifically, the narrative demands a reading of undocumented immigrants as not intrinsically "illegal" but defined as such by mechanisms of social control and political governance that draw up the lines of legitimacy in the first place. This is a viewpoint expressed in recent scholarship in queer migration theory that illustrates how "illegalization (like legalization), [too] is a *process*, not an essential quality attached to particular human bodies" and how illegality is "a status produced and imposed through shifting relations of power."[22] Clearly, such processes of regulation and hegemonic control are closely tied to notions of national security and national identification. It is for this reason that immigration control has misguidedly come to be regarded in the national imagination as "a reflection of, and mechanism for, national sovereignty" (Luibhéid 2008, 292).[23]

In Elizete and Verlia's rejection of restrictive identities, names, and categories, and in their nonassimilation into heteronormative Canadian society, the women's claims to sexual citizenship in *In Another Place, Not Here* are enunciated through a poetics of queer diaspora that complicates, challenges, and realigns dominant processes of national identity formation such as the "settlement, assimilation, and naturalization" model. In Sudbury, a city in Ontario that Verlia initially lives in with her uncle and aunt before moving to Toronto,

Verlia feels stifled. Verlia's aunt and uncle, who have adopted her, are described as Caribbean migrants desperate to "conform to some part of the puzzle" because they are "convinced that they will be rewarded with acceptance."

> Ordinariness. Man, woman, husband, wife, couple, parents, Black. They are counting on the first six words. They think that her addition will fill out some of the rest somehow . . . making them white in this white town. . . . It does not matter that in this white town, they will remain odd, they will never be noticed as fully there. They are imaginary. They have come as far north as they could imagine. And they have imagined themselves into the white town's imagining.

Rejecting her aunt and uncle's acquiescence to white superiority and their attempts to "blend in" (1996, 141) with the rest of white society, Verlia leaves Sudbury on a Greyhound bus bound for Toronto. There, she joins the black liberation movement in the struggle for decolonization, reads the works of Frantz Fanon about "the pitfalls of national consciousness" (sections from the chapter "Concerning Violence" from Fanon's *The Wretched of the Earth* [2004] are reproduced in Brand's novel), attends meetings of the Black Socialist Workers Party, sings revolutionary songs, "stud[ies] Che and learn[s] guerilla tactics from Mao" (160). She also starts a sexual relationship with a woman named Abena, with whom she lives out her desire not only for political revolution and social change but also for the intensity of sexual encounter with a woman's body ("the floor is wet with their sweat and oil and the slick of limbs and their shake and sudden, sudden sweet hastes" [187]). It is with Abena that Verlia "goes underground," making flyers, attending demonstrations, "strik[ing] blows against the racists and the imperialists" (189) until she decides she needs to return to the Caribbean to fight for the socialist cause.

In its fictional depiction of the invasion of Grenada (codenamed Operation Urgent Fury) on October 25, 1983,[24] the last section of the novel, which contains Verlia's diary entries when she returns to the Caribbean, strongly criticizes the U.S. policy of foreign intervention under the pretense of "keeping the peace" in situations of "civil unrest." The invasion was a historical event that Brand herself had experienced firsthand while working as an information officer for the Caribbean People's Development Agency in Grenada. In the novel, this historical episode simultaneously conveys anger, rebellion, and revolutionary hope but also disappointment, betrayal, transgression, and death. Verlia and her comrades, who resemble the hard-line Marxist and Communist supporters of the People's Revolutionary Army who overthrew the more moderate government of Maurice Bishop just days before the U.S. invasion, are caught in a hail of gunfire by U.S. Air Force aircraft. The episode, which closes the novel, describes Verlia's leap off the cliff as an act of defiance, a flying in the face of death. She goes down laughing, feeling weightless and deadly at the same time, on the way to "some other place already, less tortuous, less fleshy" (1996, 247), embracing, and becoming one with, the Caribbean Sea.

Verlia's ultimate act of transgression can profitably be read against what Achille Mbembe terms "necropolitics," which he defines as "contemporary forms of subjugation of life to the power of death [that] profoundly reconfigure the relations among resistance, sacrifice, and terror" (2003, 39). Mbembe argues that "the ultimate expression of sovereignty resides . . . in the power and the capacity to dictate who may live and who must die" (11). In a nod to Michel Foucault's assertion that "death is power's limit" (1990, 138), Mbembe asserts that "to exercise sovereignty is to exercise control over mortality and to define life as the deployment and manifestation of power" (2003, 12). Shifting emphasis, and hence the balance of power, from the condition of life to that of death, brings about, according to Mbembe, a blurring of "the lines between resistance and suicide, sacrifice and redemption, martyrdom and freedom" (40). In this respect, he proposes, death becomes a trans- or post-national form of sovereignty, a form of post-national "necro citizenship,"[25] that challenges traditional accounts of sovereignty that locate the latter within the boundaries of the nation-state or institutions ruled by the state.

In the concluding sequence of Brand's novel, Verlia's leap to her death in preference to being shot in the cemetery in a hail of gunfire is both an enactment of post-national necro citizenship and a reenactment of the historical deaths of the last remaining Carib natives who, in 1651, would rather jump to their deaths at Carib's Leap than be enslaved by the French colonizers.[26] In this regard, Brand pays tribute to the insurrections against slavery that occurred in various regions of the Caribbean.[27] At the same time, Verlia's leap can also be read as a reinscription of the spatial politics of diaspora—her queer migrant body is swallowed up by the Caribbean Sea, a body of water that is not, unlike land, marked and divided by fixed geopolitical borders. Verlia's queer migrant body and her act of suicide by drowning in the Caribbean Sea thus reinscribe dominant accounts of the black Atlantic by inserting her queer subjectivity into a narrative history from which she has been elided. In the moment of death, Verlia paradoxically reclaims citizenship as a queer subject and subverts the regulatory gaze of state nationalism that marks her as a deviant, nonprocreative, "counter-revolutionary"[28] body. At the end of the novel, therefore, Verlia has become the embodiment of a willful queer subject who, "having refused the heterosexual imperative of citizenship, . . . pose[s] a profound threat to the very survival of the nation" (Alexander 1994, 6). She physically becomes part of the archive of the black Atlantic, reinscribing its historical and cultural imaginaries with a politics of queer citizenship. In this respect, Brand's novel *In Another Place, Not Here* critiques and redresses different forms of exclusion and marginalization of the queer migrant body within the geopolitical and imagined spaces of the nation-state.

ARTICULATING QUEER DIASPORA IN INDO-TRINIDADIAN CANADIAN WRITING

The queer diasporic subject can reinscribe the nation's geopolitical spaces and cultural imaginaries in two ways: one, by situating her- or himself within the spaces of the nation and transfiguring it from within or two, by reappropriating the oceanic sites of the Caribbean diaspora as part of a larger archive of queer affect. It is this latter mode of queer subjectivity that Shani Mootoo's novel *Valmiki's Daughter* articulates, one that posits the Caribbean diaspora as the site of post-national diasporic citizenship. By depicting the stigma of homo- and bisexuality in contemporary upper-middle-class Indo-Trinidadian society, which is divided along the lines of race, class, and gender, Mootoo's novel also rejects the systematic containment, as well as the double "othering," of the queer body in the homogenous spaces of the nation, conceiving of sexual transgression as a form of queer resistance that destabilizes the neat binaries of home/nation, public/private, family/stranger, citizen/foreigner.

The male protagonist of Mootoo's novel is Valmiki Krishnu, an affluent Indo-Trinidadian doctor who leads a double life. On the one hand, he is a well-respected, responsible, upper-middle-class Indo-Trinidadian family man and highly esteemed medical practitioner; on the other, he has a lover, the working-class Afro-Trinidadian Saul, and he indulges in homosocial hunting trips with Saul and his friends. Valmiki's elder daughter, Viveka, ends up falling in love and having a sexual relationship with Anick, a white French woman married to Viveka's childhood friend Nayan Prakash. The

Krishnus and the Prakashes live in the affluent neighborhood of Luminada Heights in San Fernando, Trinidad, a district clearly set aside from
the rest of the city where only the more well-off locals and expatriates can
afford to reside. Living in this community implies keeping up pretenses in
the name of propriety, and Valmiki and Viveka are forced to conceal their
sexual orientations as a result. While the potentially transformative nature
of Valmiki's queer subjectivity is ultimately curbed by the heteronormative
framework of the Trinidadian nation and its sociocultural mores, Viveka
defiantly breaks out of the latter's boundaries, leaving Trinidad for Canada
at the close of the novel.

The novel's nonfictional setting of San Fernando, the second-largest city
in Trinidad, represents a departure from the imaginary cartographies that
provided the settings of earlier works by Mootoo, such as the town of Para-
dise in the country of Lantanacamara[29] in *Cereus Blooms at Night* (1996) or
the island of Guanagaspar in *He Drown She in the Sea* (2005). One may be in-
clined to interpret the choice of this nonfictional setting as the author's semiautobiographical revisiting of her childhood—Mootoo's own father, Romesh
Mootoo, was a medical doctor and the mayor of San Fernando—and as a
nostalgic drawing on the oral cultures of Caribbean storytelling and its aesthetic traditions. A closer look at how the city of San Fernando is described
in *Valmiki's Daughter*, however, reveals little nostalgia but rather an ironic
critique of the parochial and traditional family/community life in Trinidad,
with its moral codes and strictures. This is conveyed in a sequence from the
opening of the novel that uses second-person narration to describe the experience of standing at the Chancery Lane intersection in San Fernando:

> If you stand on one of the triangular traffic islands at the top of
> Chancery Lane just in front of the San Fernando General Hospital
> (where the southern arm of the lane becomes Broadway Avenue,
> and Harris Promenade, with its official and public buildings, and
> commemorative statues, shoots eastward), you would get the best,
> most all-encompassing views of the town. . . .
> Imagine you are a tourist let down from the sky, blindfolded,
> in the middle of a weekday, onto one of those traffic islands. Your
> senses would be bombarded at once. You would descend into a
> cacophony of sound, and a cacophony, yes, of smell. . . .

Despite the aural melee, what might well overwhelm you are this inter-section's odors. . . . A person might pass near enough for you to be assailed by his or her too-long unwashed body. . . . The stink of urine would, of course, be there, and surprisingly, that of human excrement, rising high on crests of wind and then thankfully subsiding. (2008, 7–9)

The above description of the cacophonous, traffic-congested streets of San Fernando and its pungent smells does not convey a nostalgic longing for a diasporic homeland. Rather, the chapter, titled "Your Journey, Part One," is a parody of a tourist-guide narrative that exoticizes the city—its sights, smells, dirt, and grime all being part of the "authentic" experience of a "third world" country. Mootoo's satirical appropriation of travel guides to San Fernando and Trinidad that are tailored to Western readers clearly critiques their Ori-entalist exoticization of the Caribbean, often characterized by a mixture of disgust and fascination as well as a quest for the most "authentic" experience the country has to offer. In the opening chapter of *Valmiki's Daughter*, the sights, sounds, and smells of San Fernando that are transposed onto the page do not depict Trinidad's cultural heritage, its musical traditions, or "mouth-watering," "exotic" cuisine (food being perhaps the most conventional marker of cultural difference). Instead, the descriptions of exhaust fumes stinging one's nose, the aroma of "over-used vegetable oils" used to fry split-pea frit-ters, the "nostril-piercing stench of incinerated medical wastes" (2008, 9), sweat, urine, and feces, oil-coated seaweed and dried-out barnacles are a rude sensory awakening. Although humorous, the description of "the entire town [being] drenched in an odor akin to that of a thousand pairs of off-shore oil workers' unwashed socks" (10) also makes the reader cringe.

The opening chapter is thus not a feast for the senses but an assault on them. Underlying this unflattering description of San Fernando is Mootoo's deeper critique of the segregation of the city's Indo-Trinidadian community along the lines of race, class, and caste. The stark juxtaposition of the "pee-sodden" Indian beggars lining the streets in the city center, with its dilapi-dated colonial buildings and the residential upper-middle-class neighbor-hood of Luminada Heights, with its "sea of green—the fronds of palm and coconut trees mixed with sampan, flamboyant, Pride of Barbados, mango trees—dotted with a confetti of colorful roofs" clearly demarcates the spatial borders separating privileged Indo-Trinidadians from their fellow Indo- and

Afro-Trinidadian working-class residents. Amusingly, it is the city's birds that do not "discriminate" along the lines of race, gender, or class: both the bronze statue of Queen Victoria and the statue of Mahatma Gandhi, depicting him "dhoti-clad and stepping briskly forward" (2008, 13), are equally "streaked in dried-white pigeon droppings" (19).

The novel's opening chapter thus establishes the lines that segregate the city of San Fernando, demarcations not only of wealth and privilege but also of social upbringing and decorum. The elevated location of the affluent Luminada Heights community, which affords spectacular views of the Gulf of Paria, is starkly contrasted to the shrubbery and streets of the inner city, haunt of the destitute and homeless. One of these is the minor character of Merle Bedi, Viveka's former classmate, who, disowned and thrown out of doors by her family because she is lesbian, must to turn to prostitution to survive. Shunned by the wealthy and respectable citizens because of her "questionable" morals, Merle is the only character in the novel who is openly marginalized because of her sexual identity. Once a talented piano player who played Beethoven and Debussy before her parents insisted that she was to study medicine, Merle has aged before her years, appearing "old and haggard," "thin, with the depleted meagerness of the alcoholic." She wears a "school shirt from not too long ago, . . . yellow and soiled," the men's trousers she wears are "several sizes too big for her" and "covered in dirt, dust, urine" (2008, 22), and she walks barefoot. Sleeping in the public spaces, promenades, and sidewalks of San Fernando's inner city, Merle Bedi is a precarious subject who has little or no means of reinscribing the urban spaces she inhabits as queer "spaces of insurgence" (Holston 1999b, 167). In comparison, it is the character of Viveka who situates herself in these spaces of rupture within the spaces of the home and nation.

Expressly going against her mother's wishes that she takes up a more "feminine" profession such as catering or flower arranging, "both of which, incidentally, could be done in the home" (2008, 101), Viveka reads English literature at university and aspires to be a literary critic. Her refusal to go through the motions and act with propriety as the only daughter of an upper-middle-class Indo-Trinidadian family is perceived as a transgression of social boundaries by her mother, who sees her own silent acquiescence to her husband's homosexual relationship with Saul as in keeping with her good upper-middle-class Indo-Trinidadian upbringing. As an English major at university, Viveka experiences "an elephantine thirst for Caribbean literature. The writings of Jamaica Kincaid, Dionne Brand, Jean Rhys, Derek Walcott, and Earl Lovelace provoked her to want to experience a Caribbean-ness, and a Trinidadian-ness more specifically, that was antithetical to her mother's tie to all things Indian and Hindu." This passage foreshadows Nayan's long speech in the novel that questions and contests the seeming homogeneity of Trinidadian national identity. Viveka develops a preference for the works of Afro-Trinidadian writers such as Kincaid, Rhys, Walcott, Lovelace, and even Dionne Brand; yet these are not canonical authors read within the context of an Indo-Trinidadian upbringing.[30] This causes some friction with her mother, Devika, who is not at all impressed with her daughter attending university. Rather, "in typical old-fashioned Indian manner," she finds Viveka "ambitious," "a quality that was not to be cultivated, and was not generally admired by people of Devika's generation" (99); a quality that is "manly" and hence not befitting a "good" Indo-Trinidadian girl.

At first glance, it seems that Viveka's refusal to act in a way befitting an obedient, upper-middle-class Indo-Trinidadian daughter is the trigger that causes the disharmony in the Krishnu household. In Mootoo's novel, however, the home space is already ruptured, "rent by colliding discourses around class, sexuality and ethnic identity" (Gopinath 2005, 15). The social and moral pretensions of the Krishnu household that are "shattered" by Valmiki's and Viveka's sexual transgressions on the level of the novel's plot constitute Mootoo's reconfiguration and reinscription of the homogenous and gendered spaces of home and nation as the sites of queer desire and pleasure on a metanarrative level. Thus, *Valmiki's Daughter* undermines the dominant metaphors of home and nation that are common motifs in diasporic Caribbean literature by exposing these concepts as social and cultural constructs. Valmiki's situation in the novel is a good case in point. Social convention dictates that, as the patriarch of the Indo-Trinidadian family, his role is that of a provider (of shelter, food, and other basic necessities) for his wife and family. Yet Valmiki cannot fulfill this role because he has "made a home" elsewhere—namely, under Saul Johnson's roof, in a house that Valmiki bought for his lover. He no longer sleeps with his wife, Devika, and does not know how to be a role model to his daughter, Viveka. Valmiki's role as a patriarch, a husband, and a "good" Indo-Trinidadian citizen is truncated by his "queerness," his same-sex desire. Put differently, his "queerness" threatens the heteronormative order of the Trinidadian nation and its moral institutions in which he has, as a respected doctor with an upper-middle-class, Brahmin, Indo-Trinidadian background, entrenched himself.

Such a reconfiguration of the spaces of home and nation in Mootoo's novel is significant because it "forcefully repudiates the elision of queer subjects from national and diasporic memory" (Gopinath 2005, 15). Mootoo also addresses the spaces of exclusion and segregation within the nation by acknowledging the imbrication of race/ethnicity and politics within a Trinidadian context. During the British colonial period, Afro- and Indo-Trinidadians were geographically separated, the former occupying the more urban region, and the latter the agricultural southern and central parts of the island.[31] Critics have argued that this imposed segregation steered the course of national(ist) politics and national identity in Trinidad.[32] This was contested terrain, especially during the reign of the People's National Movement (PNM) Party from 1955 to 1986, which led Trinidad and Tobago to independence in 1962. While the PNM declared itself to be a multiethnic and multicultural party, it swiftly came to be identified with the interests of Afro-Trinidadians, while the Indo-Trinidadians came to power in the opposition parties, in particular the United National Congress (UNC) and the Congress of the People (COP). Politics in the immediate aftermath of independence in Trinidad and Tobago was thus fraught with issues of national and cultural identity, and there were fierce debates about which ethnic group had contributed more significantly to building the nation. Indeed, the present-day widespread adoption of Afro-Trinidadian cultures and practices (what critics have termed the "three "Cs": callaloo, calypso, and carnival) as national symbols in Trinidad and Tobago[33] has led to considerable tension between the country's ethnic communities.[34] Although ethnic clashes are not common in daily life, discussions continue to center around the constructions of ethnic and cultural difference, national identity, and citizenship.

These concerns are expressed in Mootoo's novel through the character of Nayan Prakash, Anick's husband, who is depicted as a class-anxious, status-conscious Indo-Trinidadian who feels big only in his "small pond" (2008, 306). Nayan's insecurities with regard to the post-independence Trinidadian nation (and, more particularly, his place in it) render him a short-sighted caricature of a newly independent, ex-colonial/postcolonial subject who simply replicates and reinforces patterns of colonial subjugation and dominance. When he returns to Trinidad with Anick as his wife, Nayan says to Viveka (in a long speech that deserves quoting in full):

When I returned here I watched my friends and saw—I still see it— how they all think that because they are men—just because of that single fact—that they are special. Little do they know that among other men of the world, we are practically not visible. Not just in the white world, you know. Look, I have met men from African countries, from Kuwait, from India, and if only you could see how they treat us—or don't treat us, because in their eyes, too, we—the sugar-cane and cacao Indians, those of us from Trinidad, Guyana, Fiji—we don't exist. With the Indians from India we can bond over cricket, but other than that they—even they, who share our ancestors—dismiss us. As if *we are poor, poor, poor copies of an original that no longer exists. . . .* We have nothing of our own making—no style, no art or culture—to show for ourselves. So many years after leaving India, after losing the language, after *watering down the culture*, the religion, we're groping, still shy of becoming Trinidadian. Abroad, we exude no confidence in the way we move about. How can we? *We are not properly Indian, and don't know how to be Trinidadian.* We are nothing. . . . We gave up what was ours a long time ago and are trying too late to replace it with the same things. Too much has happened to us, we can't go back, but we don't know how to go ahead. . . . And the only place we can be big and confident is in the ponds we create for ourselves. (307–8; my emphasis)

Nayan's description of his experiences in Canada and France conveys the complex postcolonial condition of the Indo-Trinidadian citizen, a subject whose Indian and Trinidadian identities pull him in opposite directions while he is simultaneously confronted with Orientalist attitudes and prejudice. More particularly, Nayan's description of himself in the passage above renders him what Indo-Trinidadian writer V. S. Naipaul famously termed a "mimic man" in his novel of cultural displacement *The Mimic Men* (1967).[35] Like Naipaul's protagonist, Ralph Singh, Nayan Prakesh, too, is a "mimic man," a postcolonial subject suffering from a condition of shame, from a sense of dislocation and liminality, caught between an imitation/reflection of the colonizer's lifestyle and values on the one hand (though he knows he cannot fully assimilate into that culture) and, on the other, an inability to identify with the traditions, cultures, and religions of either the distant Indian subcontinent "homeland" or the newly independent (since August 31, 1962) Trinidadian nation. Nayan sees himself and all the other Indo-Trinidadian men around him as diluted, watered-down, simulacral[36] versions of an "original" Indian identity that no longer exists. His assertion that men like him "are not *properly* Indian" (my emphasis) yet "don't know how to be Trinidadian" indicates his firm belief in "authentic" forms of national identity. In this sense, Nayan remains blind to what Édouard Glissant has influentially termed the phenomenon of "creolization"[37] within the Caribbean, which emphasizes that no one ethnicity/culture dominates or has the right to hegemony over another.

Nayan does not dispute and counter the lines of discrimination that make men like him "invisible," that make them feel as if "[they] don't exist"; instead, he unwittingly reinforces, or mimics, them when he chauvinistically marries Anick as a trophy wife who will raise his status, his "worth" (2008, 309) in Trinidadian society because she is white. Yet, interestingly, Nayan departs from the urge to perceive of India as the origin and source of Indo-Trinidadian ethnic and cultural identity. Rather than trace his ancestry back through colonial histories of Indian indentured labor, Nayan distances himself from this "shameful" inheritance and chooses to create his own "small pond" where he can feel "big and confident" (306). The irony is that the name Chayu, which he chooses for the cacao estate he has inherited from his family, comically turns out to be a badly transliterated or "Indianized" version of the original French name of the estate, Le Ciel de Chaillou which, in turn, serves as a reminder and marker of the colonial legacy that Nayan refuses to acknowledge as part of Trinidadian history:

> A wax rubbing revealed the words *Le Ciel de Chaillou*. . . . The original French owners of the estate obviously knew the history of chocolate in France and had named it in honour of David Chaillou—"Chaillou's Heaven." It was a pleasant irony to Anick that she had ended up living in this particular estate, this particular house. The discovery of the name of the house was, to her mind, like unearthing an umbilical cord to France. It gave her a humorous sense of "right of presence." But the connection, and her talk of it in this manner, irritated Nayan. He had an ornate brass plaque made, on which was inscribed the single word *Chayu*. This is how the house had come to be known, with a name that sounded Indian enough, and so, according to Nayan, it would remain. (279)

Paradoxically, although Nayan bemoans his liminal identity as an Indo-Trinidadian, not "properly Indian" and not "Trinidadian" either, he settles for a name that "sounded Indian enough" for his cacao estate. This illustrates his utter refusal, when it comes to issues of ethnic and cultural identity at the heart of political and national discourses in Trinidad, to recognize the country's colonial past. His determination to rid his estate of any traces of this colonial history and his striving to establish a sense of security for himself in a world where "men like him [have fallen] off the radar" (308) ironically keep him shackled to the hegemonic structures of the nation's colonial legacy.

The foil to the character of Nayan, the postcolonial "mimic man," is Viveka, the queer postcolonial subject who reflects a more nuanced and complex understanding of the postcolonial "condition."[38] Centrally, Viveka reinscribes the postcolonial condition of shame that Nayan and the other "mimic men" have internalized as a form of, to recall Heather Love's terminology of affect, "feeling backward" (2007). Rejecting the intrinsic sense of shame that, according to Elspeth Probyn, is one of the strong affects that "radically disturbs different relations of proximity: to our selves, bodies, pasts" (2005, 156), Viveka adopts instead a strategy of queer resistance that counters what she deems the narrow self-absorption of the postcolonial condition that is represented in the literature of a first-generation of post-independence Trinidadian writers, for instance, in the works of V. S. Naipaul. In Naipaul's *The Mimic Men*, it is the protagonist Ralph Singh's sense of shame, when he fails as a politician in his country's post-independence nationalist government, that leads him to the self-realization that he can identify with neither the Hindu, Indian past he has idealized nor his present British surroundings in London. At the close of Naipaul's novel, therefore, shame leads to Singh's awareness that "home" is not the nation, an idealized past, or the seat of ex-colonial power to which he "writes back"; "home" is, instead, the act of writing itself. Although one might be tempted to read the end of Naipaul's novel as depicting Ralph Singh's transformation from "mimic man" to self-aware postcolonial diasporic subject, such an interpretation is problematic. This is because Naipaul's novel suggests that his protagonist's situation—displacement, dislocation, alienation, a sense of "incompleteness" (1967, 37) due to a life lived "in parenthesis" (51) as well as his Western-centric identification—is archetypal of the "postcolonial condition," which entrenches the postcolonial subject in a state of loss, lack, and rupture. This is why Ralph Singh is filled with a "deep, silent shame" when he thinks of his descent from an ancestry of "unimaginative, unenterprising, and oppressed" (83) people.[39]

Even though, therefore, V. S. Naipaul, like other writers of his generation from the Caribbean, attempted to indict colonialism by depicting its physical and psychological effects, it is the works of a younger generation of writers like Shani Mootoo that give a more differentiated and composite account of the (multiple) postcolonial condition(s) in the former colonies. At one point in *Valmiki's Daughter*, Viveka takes issue with Naipaul's (although the Trinidadian author is not named, it is presumably Naipaul) representations of post-independence Indo-Trinidadians: "He makes Indians out to be ugly, stupid, concerned only with their narrow knife-edged slice of life. He's criticizing his ancestors, but these are *my* ancestors too, and by implication he is criticizing me. And yes, I keep wanting to read on. He gets it right, but so what? Does he have to write it at all? I don't think he really hates us so much as he is gravely disappointed in what we have not become" (2008, 104–5). Considering that Shani Mootoo is actually Naipaul's granddaughter, this passage can be read as an authorial commentary on the ambivalent relationship that Mootoo has with Naipaul's work: it is both a strong influence on her own writing because of its accuracy, its precision, its "get[ting] it right" and also a body of masculine, canonical Indo-Trinidadian writing against which Mootoo positions herself as a queer, female Indo-Trinidadian writer living in Toronto.[40] In other words, the passage represents Mootoo's rejection of the "rhetoric of displacement and alienation," of "genetic uprootedness" (Nixon 1992, 21) and cultural dislocation, that underscores earlier West Indian narratives of Caribbean deracination.

Mootoo's novel thus seeks to reinscribe this dominant discourse of cultural dislocation by reframing the very notions of home and nation, gender and sexuality through the lens of a queer diasporic aesthetic, one that "refuses to subsume sexuality within a larger narrative of ethnic, class or national identity" (Gopinath 2005, 27). For the character of Viveka, her queer sexuality is not something she feels she can, or wants to, suppress. From an early age, Viveka's queerness does not render her an easy fit into conventional gender categories and social norms. Her sister Vashti describes Viveka as "mannish" in her appearance and mannerisms,[41] "kind of tough for a female [and] not like the other girls" because she doesn't "dress up or wear makeup [or] talk about boys" (2008, 89). Viveka imagines at times that she is an incarnation of Ardhanarishvara, the Hindu hermaphrodite deity composed of Shiva (right half) and his female companion, Parvarti (left half). As an adolescent, her first moments of sexual awakening are performed in the role of a blond-haired white boy named Vince, "short for 'invincible,'" who was "strong, powerful, peaceful, and could do anything and everything" (110). It is as Vince that Viveka experiences her first sexual encounter with Anick:

> She had felt, during the initial moments of their lovemaking, a sense of having taken on the form of a young man's body. Her body had become, albeit briefly, Vince's body, and in other moments, Anand's [Viveka's dead brother]. These two were suddenly young men; sturdy; muscled, handsome. As handsome as Anick was beautiful. It was strange how Vince and Anand had grown into such young men; this was the strongest sensation of that sort Viveka had ever had— of not being what she looked like, female. And yet, she knew now more than ever that her feelings and her way with Anick were hers and hers alone. Not a boy's. Not a man's. Whatever she was, these feelings were hers. . . . Perhaps she could be finished with Anand now. And with Vince. (322–23)

This first sexual encounter with Anick releases both Vince and Anand from Viveka's imagination and enables her to consummate her relationship with Anick as an Indo-Trinidadian woman loving a white French woman.

Yet Viveka's sexuality stubbornly refuses to be categorized or contained. In the weeks after their sexual encounter, Anick, not comprehending "the particulars of her own situation, the reality of Nayan, the Prakashs, of Viveka's own family, of their position in Trinidadian society" (2008, 357), pleads with Viveka to leave Trinidad for Canada, where "there were thriving communities of people like the two of them." Viveka, however, rejects Anick's plans, saying, "We'll never get far enough away. . . . Going away won't solve a thing for us" (335). Viveka's reaction signifies her refusal to be elided from the spaces of the nation or be regarded as unpatriotic because of her sexual orientation. She "kn[ows] who she [is]" and she "[will] not be diminished because of it" (360). Viveka does not want to become a second Merle Bedi, cast out because of her sexuality, excluded by her friends, family, and community. Valmiki, who has realized the nature of the "friendship" between the two women, tries to tell his daughter that Trinidad is "too small a place" for her, that "there is so much more waiting for [her] elsewhere," and that she should "take a deep breath, and leave this place behind" (354).

Valmiki's encouraging Viveka to leave the country and start life anew elsewhere is echoed in Anick's own pleading with her that they can "go away together" (2008, 357) once the child that she is carrying, Nayan's, is born. Viveka's shock at learning that Anick has continued sleeping with Nayan despite also having a sexual relationship with her turns into anger and resolve. She ends their relationship because she realizes that she cannot, will not, compromise: "She could not live clandestinely. She would not. Nor would she let her present sadness devour her. She had to train herself to remain above it, otherwise she would become like Merle. There simply had to be a place where she would fit in, and she would find that place" (359). "That place" is both physical and imaginary; it is, on the one hand, Toronto, a city home to much of the Caribbean diaspora and, on the other, the abstract space of a queer diasporic imaginary. At the novel's end, Viveka opts for a marriage of convenience with Trevor, a friend of the family's who lives and works in Canada, in order to leave San Fernando for Toronto, the place where she will begin her life anew. Viveka's partaking in the heteronormative institution of marriage at the end of the novel might come as a surprise; nevertheless, Viveka and Trevor's marriage is depicted as "a means to an end" (376). The epilogue of the novel, titled "24 Months," alludes to the two-year period that, in Viveka's opinion, their marriage will last (a more realistic estimate than Trevor's guess of five years). The epilogue can thus be read as a comment on the limits of the institution of marriage and a critique of its endurance as the dominant nationally sanctioned, social arrangement and legally recognized union between two people of the opposite sex. In the epilogue Viveka's decision to marry Trevor and leave Trinidad is also portrayed not as an act of expedient escape but one of courage: "You'd be surprised, Trevor. You'd be surprised at my courage right now" (395). It is this courage that enables Viveka to leave the "small island" of Trinidad without a "map of her future" (360), to enter into a contractual union with a man with whom sex is disappointing, mechanical, unfamiliar, and unsatisfying. In these last pages of the novel, therefore, Mootoo constructs a complex model of postcolonial queer desire that critiques the racial/ethnic, gender, class, and social hierarchies that regulate female desire while questioning the efficacy of heteronormative institutions such as marriage, the family and, ultimately, the nation.

By depicting how the queer migrant body renegotiates the spaces of home and nation, Dionne Brand's *In Another Place, Not Here* and Shani Mootoo's *Valmiki's Daughter* exemplify the works of a younger generation of queer Caribbean diasporic authors who contest literary representations of the postcolonial condition in the canonical writings of a previous generation of post-independence, mostly male Caribbean writers as one of dislocation, displacement, exile, alienation, placenessness, and liminality. The works of these younger writers articulate the claims of queer migrant bodies that refuse to be assimilated within heterocentric processes of national identity formation and reject the heteronormative institutions that regulate sexuality and desire within the boundaries of the nation. These claims form part of a larger poetics/politics of queer diaspora illustrating the complexities, even impossibility, of homogenous national identity formations. As Gayatri Gopinath argues, queer citizenship enacts a "complicated navigation of state regulatory practices and multiple national spaces . . . one that is often profoundly mobile, contingent, and evasive, and that demands a more nuanced theorization of the interplay of state and nation" (1995, 121). In the Caribbean, moreover, the multiple and distinctive histories of different ethnicities, cultures, religions, and the processes of "encounter, interference, clash, harmony and disharmony between [these] cultures" that Édouard Glissant defined as "creolization" (1997a, 33) have to be taken into account.

Whereas the writings of Dionne Brand focus on and seek to renegotiate Afro-Caribbean traditions and histories, those of Shani Mootoo turn a critical and contemplative eye on Indo-Trinidadian culture: its customs, social attitudes, and class-based and gendered politics. The narratives open up new forms of post-national and diasporic subjectivities that reconfigure existing heterosexual models of citizenship and national belonging. As examples of a flourishing body of new Caribbean Canadian writing that reinscribe the postcolonial conditions of fragmentation, loss, and nostalgic longing, departure and (non)return, the works of Dionne Brand and Shani Mootoo foreground queer female desire as a form of political and social intervention that counters the prevalent heteronormativity of national narratives. The novels are testimony to a new form of affective, diasporic citizenship whose intrinsic dissonances, in Lily Cho's words, enable "a mode for understanding the contradictions and possibilities of Canadian literature." In calling for a reorientation of Canadianness that includes, and not marginalizes, queer migrant identities, the works of Dionne Brand and Shani Mootoo articulate "the possibilities of a national culture which embraces historical and cultural displacements" (2007, 105). The novels' decentering of national(ist) frameworks and their official narratives is accompanied by an undermining of dominant processes of national identity formation and reproduction carried out by institutionalized structures such as that of marriage and the nuclear family. In this light, the novels challenge dominant perceptions of the queer migrant body as an undesirable threat to the heteronormative logic of national citizenship, positing queer migrant subjectivity as an integral and vital component of the nation's political, social, and affective imaginaries.

9

QUEER(ING THE) NATION
· · · · · · · · · ·
ACT UP and AIDS Activism in Sarah Schulman's
People in Trouble and *Rat Bohemia*

Continuing my exploration of how literary representations of queer subjectivities depict sexual transgression as a political act that challenges the
homogenizing and assimilationist discourses of the nation, this chapter will
focus on narratives of AIDS activism that "queered" the American nation
in the 1980s and forced the national public to confront its preconceptions
of homosexuality and the "lifestyles" of its nonconformist subjects. As Julia
Epstein contends, in dominant media coverage at the height of the AIDS
health crisis in the United States in the 1980s, the HIV-positive body was
represented as an infected body, a body "penetrated by . . . notions of conta-
gion, pollution, and threatening communicability" (1992, 293). Such dominant
media depictions of people with AIDS, Epstein maintains, can be termed
"narratives of containment," or narratives in which HIV-positive bodies were
portrayed as receptacles of the deadly virus and public health policy was
aimed at the "containment" of this illness.[1] Although such media narratives
of containment sought to limit the spread of HIV by targeting specific high-
risk groups such as homosexual males and ethnic minorities, they also paradoxically presupposed "the inevitability of contact with the Other" (307).[2]

This chapter explores how New York lesbian author, playwright, and activist Sarah Schulman's novels *People in Trouble* (1990) and *Rat Bohemia* (1995) invert the logic of such stigmatizing narratives of containment. Specifically, Schulman's writings oppose and challenge the institutional marginalization of HIV-positive people as well as the systemic processes of (economic, political, societal, sexual) control and regulation through which they are interpellated.[3] My argument is that the novels critique the "narratives of containment" and isolation, creating instead what Steven F. Kruger has termed "narratives of proximity," or "account[s] of growing familiarity with AIDS, people with AIDS, and the politics of the AIDS crisis" (1996, 259). In other words, Schulman's novels invert the banal, simplified, and offensive media representations of people with AIDS, challenging the images, associations, and stereotypes that were reinforced and perpetuated in the guise of "educating" and "informing" the American (and global) public about HIV.[4] They also reveal the complex relationship between AIDS and notions of national identity, collective identification, and citizenship in the United States during the height of the AIDS health crisis in the 1980s.

DIVIDED WE STAND: UNEQUAL CITIZENSHIP IN *PEOPLE IN TROUBLE*

Although *People in Trouble* has been described as Schulman's "most naturalistic work" (Andermahr 2011, 718), one written in a mode of "social realism,"[5] I argue that this is not entirely the case. Rather, I perceive the novel as more complexly adopting two different narrative modes that do not rely solely on a straightforward realist mode of narration. The first involves a direct critique of the level of misinformation, prejudice, and homophobia rampant in American society,[6] of the disenfranchisement of gay men and lesbians in the 1980s by the conservative Reagan administration, which pursued an official policy of silence on AIDS and, finally, of the neoliberal capitalist economies that fostered gentrification in parts of New York City such as the East Village, home to a large population of gay men and women.[7] The second narrative mode is that of satiric exaggeration, which is used to ridicule and oppose the culture of fear[8] that was prevalent in the United States in the 1980s, fueled largely by mainstream news and media coverage of the HIV/AIDS epidemic. This mode of parody and ridicule contains elements of the comic, which, as Christiansen and Hanson have compellingly argued in their study of different types of AIDS narratives, "humorously points out failings in the status quo and urges society to correct them through thoughtful action rather than tragic victimage" (1996, 161).

This narrative mode of satiric exaggeration functions as more than a corrective to the dominant depiction of people with AIDS as tragic victims of their own behavior: their promiscuity, their "aberrant" and "deviant" sexual practices, their drug habits.[9] As Steven F. Kruger has noted, it also "resists the impulse to construct the AIDS epidemic as one coherent narrative, moving from a moment of 'origin,' through a process of "spread,' to a definitive 'end'" (1996, 267). Indeed, Schulman's *People in Trouble* directly addresses the incoherence and incomprehension that characterized the 1980s at the height of the AIDS crisis. This is not a decade, the narrative seems to be declaring, in which anything "made sense": friends and lovers were dying at an alarming rate, regarded as second-class citizens without the right of access to medical care and treatment. In the midst of all this incoherence, the main modes of resistance that emerge are that of camp laughter, hyperbole, and satiric exaggeration—modes that are themselves uncontainable and akin to the grotesque, yet regenerative, Rabelaisian laughter of carnival which, as Stephen Greenblatt has argued, citing Mikhail Bakhtin, "turns the world topsy-turvy, challenges the dominant structures of authority, triumphs over fear and constraint, [and] breaks down what had seemed essential boundaries" (1990, 67).

Correspondingly, the queer characters in *People in Trouble* make indecorous, irreverent, and incongruous statements and jokes, revel in camp, and indulge in irony. The minor character of Jeffrey Rechtschaffen, a HIV-positive Jewish journalist whose "creative visualization approach combined with various medications . . . kept him alive for four years and three weeks when he was supposed to die in eighteen months," is described, for example, as a campy AIDS activist who "carried a teddy bear and went for daily massage," "did yoga and said 'I love you' to himself in the mirror every morning and night," and "wore a shirt that said I have AIDS—Hug Me" (1990, 73). In one sequence in the novel, Jeffrey describes the numerous closet cases who call the NYC AIDS hotline he works for: men who refuse to admit that they have sex with men, who are terrified that they are HIV-positive: "You have to give them every excuse in the world so they can tell you what they did without admitting to being gay. I think we should change the name of this country to the *United States of Denial.* This epidemic will never be taken care of properly until people can be honest about sex" (75; my emphasis). Unlike the men who call the hotline, Jeffrey is not in denial about his impending death. He even plans his own funeral, which is described as "just like Jeff, sentimental, deliberate and goofy," with a "rainbow gay liberation flag draped over his coffin and fresh strawberries and figs for everyone to eat." His sense of black humor and irony remain intact, even shortly before his death. When asked if he wants to submit an essay for an anthology of the works of journalists with AIDS, his response is: "No. . . . It wouldn't be fair. I mean, I'll be the only one in the whole book who is still alive and for the rest of my career I'll have to shake the stigma, you know, the AIDS thing" (93).

The characters with AIDS in *People in Trouble* are thus not portrayed as dreadful victims of their own "incorrigible" sexual practices, bodily drives, or lusts, as they are in the public imagination, but as lovers, family members, friends, mentors, and peers who do not die quietly but go down fighting. The two female protagonists of the novel, Molly, a lesbian ticket booth officer in an adult movie theater, and her lover Kate, a married artist, become increasingly involved in AIDS activism. The protests and demonstrations they join are depicted as part of a larger collective effort to fight against the widespread culture of fear and ignorance during the AIDS crisis as well as the misrepresentation and stereotypes that flourished in U.S. national media in that period.[10] The latter are what Schulman herself has described in her nonfiction book *The Gentrification of the Mind: Witness to a Lost Imagination* as a "dumb[ing] down," a "banaliz[ation]," and a "homogeniz[ation]" (2012a, 2) of the complex, diverse, fragmented, hybrid, and multiple nature of living with AIDS and the politics of the AIDS crisis. In this respect, *People in Trouble* is a "narrative of proximity" that contests and inverts techniques of "scarification" in dominant media coverage of AIDS as well as practices of "naturalization" through the repetition of stock images and glib stereotypes of people with AIDS. Schulman terms this form of homogenizing, this replacing of difference and radical alterity with sameness, as a process of "gentrification"; more specifically, a "gentrification of the mind, an internal replacement that alienated people from the concrete process of social and artistic change" (14).

In its sharp critique of mainstream media representation of AIDS in the 1980s in the United States, *People in Trouble* can thus be read as an example of what Schulman herself has termed "witness fiction" (1994, 195). Clearly, however, Schulman does not bear silent witness[11] to the marginalization and death of people with AIDS. Rather, *People in Trouble* employs an "ethics of narration" (Booth 1990; Nussbaum 2007) that fosters direct activism and intervention rather than passive observation. Funerals, which play a major part in the novel, become one of these sites of queer intervention, resistance, activism and, therefore, of the struggle for the right to citizenship.[12] For instance, Jeffrey's funeral becomes an occasion for Justice,—an underground organization of queer and AIDS activists which closely resembles the real-life activist organization ACT UP (AIDS Coalition to Unleash Power)—to meet and organize operations. At the funeral, Molly is asked by Bob, Jeffrey's friend and one of the Justice activists, to collect papers (it is revealed later in the novel that these are eviction notices served by landlords to their gay tenants) and bring them to a Justice meeting in Kate's building. Molly describes Bob as "the only person in the world who has come to me with something substantial to do in the face of all these funerals. I'm tired of feeling helpless in hospital rooms" (1990, 94), and she leaves the funeral charged with a renewed sense of faith in AIDS activism.

Molly's attitude to the AIDS health crisis contrasts sharply with that of Kate's husband's. Peter is a theatrical lighting designer who prides himself on being a liberal. Nevertheless, he disconcertedly feels as if he is being "slapped in the face by homosexuality practically every day" (1990, 31) with the onset of the AIDS crisis.[13] In order to occupy himself while Kate is openly having an affair with Molly, he goes out for dinner, takes walks, and goes bowling. The episode in which he instinctively ducks into a bowling alley is significant because it reflects his need for familiar surroundings (the bowling alleys of his youth in New Hampshire) in what he perceives as an increasingly unfamiliar world; it reflects his "nostalgia for a simpler life" (5), nostalgia for, more specifically, a pre-AIDS world.[14] When Peter observes a funeral one day from a coffee shop across the road from the church, his first thought is "Something is not right here," and then it dawns on him: "This is gay, he thought. This is a homosexual church." He quickly corrects himself, "realiz[ing] that it was not a homosexual church, but a Catholic one, filled with homosexuals" (31). Peter's almost comical fastidiousness at "getting it right" summarizes his attitude toward the AIDS crisis and homosexuality—trying to keep up a politically correct, nondiscriminating front while actually harboring deep-seated prejudices and heteronormative preconceptions pertaining to gender roles and sexuality.

After watching the funeral from a distance, Peter decides to go into the church because "he want[s] to be around gay people more," feeling "it would bring [Kate and him] closer together" (1990, 32). Unfortunately, he begins to feel threatened by the close proximity of homosexuality and people with AIDS and suffers a panic attack that causes him to quickly leave the church. Peter's initial detachment, his narcissistic ignorance, his silent observation of the funeral before he decides to enter the church as a "tourist . . . watching another culture" (33) contrast with Kate's experience of Jeffrey's funeral that she, too, witnesses from a distance, watching Molly as she attends. Kate realizes that there are two communities attending the funeral: one, formed in response to the AIDS epidemic, mourning the loss of a loved one, and the other composed of the parents and family of the deceased, maintaining distance from the first community because they are in denial about their relative's sexuality. It is the latter community that haunts Kate's thoughts: "There was a deprivation that accompanies this kind of ignorance. She couldn't get them out of her mind" (100). Later in the novel, Scott, one of the leaders of the Justice movement and James's lover and companion, dies and Kate attends his funeral, which takes place at the same church where she had previously observed Molly at Jeffrey's funeral. No longer a passive observer or silent witness, Kate, "too, [becomes] a mourner" (219).

Scott's funeral is the precursor to the final confrontation in the novel between property tycoon Ronald Horne (real-life mogul Donald Trump thinly disguised) and the Justice activists who, dressed in black T-shirts with pink triangles,[15] gatecrash the opening ceremony of the latest addition to Horne's colossal real-estate empire, the satirically named Taj McHorne, a new office and condominium complex that is part of Horne's larger plan to convert apartments left vacant by deceased AIDS patients into "luxury co-ops for intact nuclear families, which statistics show are the least likely to spread AIDS" (1990, 210). Ronald Horne's real-estate projects are central to Schulman's fictional depiction of the real-life gentrification of New York City in the 1980s. The increasing privatization of public spaces and land, racial and class stratification, evictions and forced relocations, the homogeneity of consumption: all these, Schulman contends, "undermin[ed] urbanity and recreat[ed] cities as centers of obedience instead of instigators of positive change" (2012a, 28).[16] It is at the Justice demonstration against the Taj McHorne in the novel's final symbolic confrontation between left-wing progressive activism and neoliberal capitalism that Kate sets her own art installation,[17] which had been specially commissioned for the inauguration event, on fire, thereby intentionally creating a scenario in which Ronald Horne becomes caught in its flames.

Kate's ultimate act of anarchy at the Justice demonstration against neocapitalism in New York City places her squarely in the community of the novel's eponymous "people in trouble," a citizenry that shares firsthand experience of the AIDS crisis, homophobia, and the exclusion of queer communities in the

American metropolis. In contrast to her husband Peter's stasis, his continued ignorance about AIDS, and his stereotypical views of masculinity, Kate's development as the novel progresses transforms her from a white, upper-middle-class, self-identified bisexual artist—a character aroused and thrilled by the "naughty" excitement of buying lacy bras for her lover Molly—to a queer activist who challenges official and mainstream media "narratives of containment" with her own fiery "gestures of proximity." Ironically, Kate's act of protest acquires her such renown that she begins "working extensively in burning installations and quickly got commissions from a number of Northern European countries to come start fires there" (1990, 225). In Amsterdam, for instance, she is contracted to work "on a blazing sculpture in honor of the people of Cambodia" (226).

This is perhaps a commentary, at the end of the novel, on the larger mechanics of collective resistance movements that have to, on the one hand, transcend individual experiences and sympathies and, on the other, navigate the workings of a self-regulating, neoliberal market economy and its strategies of control, even adopting its logic to undermine the system and "beat it at its own game." In the novel, the Justice activists start their own clandestine operation of manufacturing fake documents—birth certificates and passports for undocumented migrants with AIDS to "get Medicaid to pay for [their] anti-AIDS drugs . . . and get welfare if [they're] too sick to work" (1990, 116–17). This sequence no doubt alludes to Schulman's critique of the disenfranchisement of nondocumented migrants and their descendants[18] in terms of the lack of health care benefits, college education, and Social Security in the United States. Justice also embarks on a systematic and organized operation to collect credit card and calling card numbers so that people with AIDS can purchase the medication and treatment they need and make calls to their loved ones for free: "There was a whole caucus of waiters working in expensive restaurants who could save the carbons from processed charge card forms. There were lovers of the dead and dying and the dying themselves who hadn't gotten around to canceling their plastic. . . . And there was a battalion of travelers who volunteered to hang around pay phones in airports with open ears" (164). Criticizing the lack of affirmative action against AIDS in a laissez-faire economy (Schulman is alluding here to the deregulated, supply-side, trickle-down economic philosophy of Reaganomics), the Justice activists take matters into their own hands and turn the rationale of credit card purchasing to their own advantage.

Justice's collection of credit card information culminates in a massive "credit card day" spree: a free-for-all for the homeless, men in shelters, migrant groups, and the urban poor to buy as much food as they want from the big Pathmark supermarket, using the credit cards of AIDS patients in hospital who "send their love and authorization" (1990, 198). Here, Schulman is parodying the American daytime television program *Supermarket Sweep*, wherein contestants have one and a half minutes to dash through a supermarket, filling their carts with groceries that would amount to the highest total bill and hence highest score. In the narrative mode of comic and satiric exaggeration, the Justice activists first tell the crowd that "the following food is available for free: meat, fish, chicken, all protein, cheese, eggs, dairy, beans, flour, rice, fresh fruit, vegetables, good bread, real juice, nuts, peanut butter, spice, oils and other whole foods. Also vitamins" (197). In a humorous sequence, however, they quickly realize that the people wanted not only healthy food but also their share of junk food and "forgotten pleasures," like Fritos, diet Coke, Twinkies, frozen pizza, Spam, hot dogs, Cool Whip, peaches, and ice cream—"food that tastes so good in the mouth it makes a person feel human again" (198).

The "credit card day" spree might be an amusing episode in the novel, but it also constitutes a more serious commentary on the failure of the Reagan administration's economic policies to provide for its citizens—not only people with AIDS and members of the LGBTQI community but also those marginalized by neocapitalist economic policies, including the homeless and urban poor who have been priced out of their housing. Campaigning on the behalf of these eponymous "people in trouble," Justice is thus represented in the novel as an activist organization whose undertakings "mimic consumerism while opposing its capitalist foundations, insisting that money, credit, and (especially) food be available to all." Put differently, Justice's acts of intervention represent acts of queer citizenship that demand acknowledgment as well as political, social, and economic membership and participation for all members of society, regardless of class, ethnicity, race, gender, or sexual orientation. Tactically engaging in smart mobs[19] and other forms of political and social interventions, the Justice activists expose the complex network of forces, including "the church, government, capitalist enterprise, drug companies, the media" (Kruger 1996, 285), that marginalize and disenfranchise people with AIDS and other minority communities. Underscoring the impossibility of representing or recounting the AIDS epidemic in one coherent narrative, *People in Trouble*'s narrative of proximity fictionally portrays the controversies that surrounded the real-life ACT

UP advocates, their disparate methods of organized activism, and their polemic interventions during the AIDS health crisis in the 1980s in New York City.[20] Like ACT UP, the Justice AIDS activist group in Schulman's novel favors grassroots action and organized forms of political resistance that include "fold[ing], stuff[ing] and stamp[ing] sheets of newsprint [their AIDS newsletter] that might save some lives and would definitely increase the quality of others" (1990, 173) as well as confrontational public protests such as the sit-in demonstration in St. Patrick's Cathedral.[21]

To return to the two narrative modes that challenge the "narratives of containment" or mainstream media representations of people with AIDS, it is significant that political resistance is depicted in *People in Trouble* both as a direct critique of the disenfranchisement of LGBTQI individuals and marginalized communities and as an indirect form of queer activism that relies on campy performance, kitsch, and satiric exaggeration. One passage in the novel aptly illustrates the combination of both modes, direct and indirect, of critique/affirmative action. After an AIDS vigil, Molly is walking back to her car when she comes across James and Scott handing out leaflets:

> The older one [James] was black. He wore his hair in a large natural like Angela Davis used to do. . . . [H]e had effeminate floral print three-quarter pants like girls buy on Fourteenth Street. He had a gold loop and a ruby stud in one ear and a feather in the other. He was swish. He was an older black gay man who called other men "darling" and "girlfriend." On the center of each flower printed on his pants was the word *love*. . . .
> Molly . . . took a leaflet.
> DO YOU THINK IT'S RIGHT?
> That people are dying and the government does nothing? If you do not think that this is right then do something about it. . . .
> Molly walked home feeling open and vulnerable and then very angry with an energy that had nowhere to go. (1990, 47)

In this passage, James the Justice activist embodies the notion of camp as one manifestation of subversive gay laughter. As Paul Rudnick asserts, "[G]ay writers dra[w] on the repartee that is a form of gay soul, use camp, irony and epigram to, if not defeat the virus, at least scorn . . . [AIDS].

AIDS is not the end of gay life or gay laughter" (1993). Beyond its powers of subversion, however, camp can also be "reparative" (as opposed to "paranoid") when it is performed as a "communal," "queer-identified practice" (Sedgwick 2003, 127, 149). In *People in Trouble*, therefore, James personifies camp both as a subversive practice (via a performative exaggeration and parody of gender binaries) and as a reparative practice that challenges the American public to "do something about it." Molly's reaction to this challenge leaves her "feeling open and vulnerable and then very angry with an energy that had nowhere to go." In this way, *People in Trouble* "acknowledges anger as a response to grief, exploring its personal and public expression and what happens when grief is not generally acknowledged" (Andermahr 2011, 720).

The use of camp as a mode of queer resistance, political agency, inclusive citizenship, and social intervention is thus embodied by the character of James, who, not content with being "placated with a condition of free speech in a nation of no ideas," rouses the Justice activists to be "bigger" than "the machinery" and the "institutions that control information" (1990, 209). James's use of camp as a tool of queer ideology is contrasted in the novel to Kate's description of Peter as "such a girl":

> He was sweet from the first time they met. At that time he was a girl. His face was smooth, anyway, for a man, but Kate used to dress him up in girl's clothing. She'd put him in panties. They'd laugh and he'd prance around twisting his hips like a fag. She'd put her fingers on the lace and feel his dick underneath. He was not afraid to dress that way. He knew who he was. He was a girl.
>
> "Peter's such a girl," Kate would say to Molly every now and then.
>
> "What do you mean?"
>
> "He's a baby. He's passive. He whines and can't take care of himself. He never carries the heaviest thing." (23)

In comparison to James's wearing of "effeminate floral print three-quarter pants," Peter's cross-dressing in girl's underwear and his "pranc[ing] around . . . like a fag" are not examples of queer performativity. His "performance" is merely part of the foreplay before sex, a going along with Kate's arousal from seeing him in women's lacy underwear. Thus, Peter's cross-dressing is not a political act; it does not constitute an instance of queer performance in either the satiric exaggeration or reparative mode; it is not, in other words, an example of camp. Rather, it is the consequence of Kate's effeminizing and infantilizing of him, a deliberate rendering of the male/masculine subject helpless and dependent to her own advantage.[22]

Peter's inability to recognize the situation for what it is is reflected in his reaction to Kate's increasing penchant for dressing in drag. When Kate walks in from work one day in a man's suit and tie, Peter teases her, asking, "What's this? Is the Annie Hall look coming back?" (1990, 101). Blind to the motivations behind Kate's dressing in drag, Peter puts it down to a revival of the androgynous look sported by Diane Keaton in the cult American romantic comedy *Annie Hall*, directed by Woody Allen in 1977. Peter's lack of perceptiveness is accentuated in his follow-up thoughts, which once again reveal his conventional understandings of masculinity and femininity: "We still have sex. So what's the problem? Is Kate old enough for menopause?" (102). This is contrasted directly with Molly's perception of Kate's dressing in drag: "Kate was a man. Anyone in the street would have thought so. But she was a better man than most because she was so strikingly handsome in her black suit. She strode powerful and erect like a well-bred charming man. A male model perhaps. . . . She was the most handsome man on the street" (90). As the novel progresses, Kate's negotiations between male and female, straight and lesbian identities, render her a queer body, one that resists reading by those who reinforce the status quo such as her husband, Peter.[23]

The latter's narrow-mindedness is reflected in yet another episode in the novel wherein he unintentionally partakes in the Justice protest in St. Patrick's Cathedral (which, coincidentally, anticipated ACT UP's controversial real-life Stop the Church demonstration in the cathedral on December 10, 1989). Peter has merely stepped in for a brief rest. As forty members of Justice stand up, face the congregation, and speak of the hypocrisy of the Catholic Church, demanding affirmative care for people with AIDS, he realizes with a shock that

[t]hese are men with AIDS. . . . Forty of them. But that one doesn't look like he has it. He looks like he works out. The thin one has definitely got it. . . .

That black man, thought Peter. *I wonder if he's gay or if he got it from drugs*. . . . Peter noted that the man's voice and gestures were campy.

> They shouldn't have let him be the spokesman, Peter thought.
> They should have picked somebody more masculine, so people
> would be more sympathetic. (1990, 58)

Peter's thoughts reveal his inability to think outside of stereotypical perceptions of masculinity and femininity and beyond normative categories of gay and straight. As Kathy Rudy argues, "Queer politics are explicitly and intentionally designed to make 'straight' people feel extremely uncomfortable in order to make them think about how contingent the foundations of the repressive 'normal' world really are" (2001, 214). At the height of the AIDS health crisis, queer politics thus exposed and challenged the exclusion and metaphorical divesting of citizenship from LGBTQI bodies and people with AIDS, who were regarded as unnatural, misfits, or miscreants in the larger social and national imaginary.

Peter remains blind to his own narrow-mindedness and bigotry. His complacent objectification and categorization of people with AIDS reflect Schulman's larger critique of the simplistic and reductive representations of HIV and AIDS in U.S. mainstream media. The latter is depicted in the last section of the novel, which is a parody of the evening news in the aftermath of Ronald Horne's death:

ROLAND

> In the news tonight, Ronald Horne murdered in Forty-second
> Street melee. Congress approves new Contra aid plan. Mayor goes
> to bat for the peanut butter bagel and Masters and Johnson warn
> heterosexuals: new threat from AIDS.

SUSIE

> Thank you, Roland. Real-estate mogul Ronald Horne met a fiery
> death today when a freak accident occurred during a riot by AIDS
> victims. (1990, 224).

This news skit[24] clearly satirizes dominant representations of HIV and AIDS in American national media in the 1980s. Schulman is criticizing the latter for being indifferent and dismissive (Ronald Horne makes the headlines, but no mention is made of Justice), misleading and ignorant (the use of the term *melee* to describe Justice's political intervention as a confused skirmish),[25] facetious (juxtaposition to the story about the peanut butter bagel), and guilty of reinforcing the rhetoric of victimization (description of people with AIDS as "AIDS victims"). By referencing the Iran-Contra affair of 1986,[26] Schulman is also critiquing the Reagan government for carrying out contentious foreign policy while maintaining a domestic policy of silence and inaction on HIV/AIDS. The novel contrasts such governmental negligence with what Schulman describes as "the politics of accountability at the root of ACT UP's ethos" (2012a, 47). This politics of accountability, Schulman elaborates, is one that revolves around a strategy of making "pharmaceutical executives, politicians who have pledged to represent and serve the American people, religious leaders who claim moral authority—anyone who interfered with progress for people with AIDS . . . face a consequence for the pain they caused" through "courses of action that [are] doable and justifiable" (51).

By using a dual narrative strategy of direct critique and a more oblique playful, satirical and performative mode of commentary that uses camp, with its reparative and paranoid functions, as its central apparatus, *People in Trouble* critically intervenes into the dominant discourse on AIDS and the health crisis. The first narrative strategy of direct critique "attempts to record the patterns of social interaction and street encounters in a naturalistic mode, adopt[ing] an impressively broad social and political agenda, treating issues of homelessness, social deprivation, and cuts to welfare services that characterized Reagan and Bush's America" (Andermahr 2011, 719). The second mode, that of satirical excess, engages in more "non-accommodationist, anti-assimilationist, "in-your-face' techniques designed to draw attention to issues of sexuality and sexual preference in the public sphere" (Rudy 2001, 213). Via these two literary strategies, *People in Trouble* contests and rewrites the prevailing "narratives of containment" proliferated in American national discourse and mainstream media in the 1980s that isolated people with AIDS as victims of their own "deviant" sexual and drug-related practices. Schulman's novel also challenges the widespread perception of AIDS as a gay male disease that heterosexuals have to take extra precautions against. Last but not least, *People in Trouble* also foregrounds the central roles of narrative and representation in overturning the marginalization, oppression, and societal exclusion of American citizens with AIDS. The title of the novel does not, ultimately, refer only to people with AIDS—it includes all Americans, who would be in trouble if they were to persist in being citizens of the "United

States of Denial."[27] As a "witness narrative" or a novel of "witnessing," Schulman's *People in Trouble* is thus not solely a fictional documentation of HIV/AIDS activism, in particular the political actions of the real-life organization ACT UP. It is also a call for affirmative action and queer citizenship, both on the streets and in the sheets.

QUEER(ING THE) NATION: AIDS AS THE (UN-)AMERICAN EXPERIENCE

> And all along it has puzzled me that the AIDS experience is not recognized as an American experience, while for me it is *the* American experience. How can something be equally *the* and equally *not*? Because it belongs to people still considered, even postmortem, to be second-rate and special interest. It has not been integrated into the American identity of which it is a product. . . . No true, accurate, complex, deeply felt and accountable engagement with the AIDS crisis has become ingrained into the American self-perception. It puts those of us who do know what happened into the awkward position of trying to remember what we used to know in a world that officially knows none of it. (Schulman 2012a, 69)

The quote above by Sarah Schulman perceptively draws a direct relationship between the AIDS crisis and notions of citizenship and national identity in America in the 1980s. Specifically, Schulman acknowledges the processes by which some personal experiences are claimed, adopted, and legitimized by larger, officially sanctioned collective narratives of national identification while others are marginalized or excluded altogether. In the context of the AIDS crisis in the 1980s, as argued above, U.S. dominant official narratives utilized a discourse of victimization and deviance that rendered people with AIDS as "unnatural" bodies, as aberrant and insubordinate citizens who were the victims of their own depraved sexual preferences and drug habits. Put differently, because people with AIDS were not viewed in the public imagination as law-abiding, model American citizens—and mainstream media did their share to depict them as insurgent, disrespectful, belligerent, and militant activists—their stories were not recognized as part of the national narrative (and hence the "National Symbolic,"[28] to recall Lauren Berlant's term) of the 1980s. Instead, the AIDS crisis was overshadowed by media coverage of American foreign policy related to the Cold War (for instance, the U.S. invasion of Grenada and U.S. aid to Mujahideen soldiers against the Soviet proxy government in Afghanistan), the Arab-Israeli conflict, and the financing of the right-wing paramilitary group in Nicaragua (which came to light in November 1986 in the Iran-Contra affair) as well as by domestic issues of homelessness, hunger, and poverty in the recession of 1982, rising deficits, and the overvaluation of the U.S. dollar.[29]

The Reagan administration's refusal to acknowledge the AIDS crisis[30] and its lack of government funding for HIV/AIDS prevention and research[31] were significant because they illustrated the government's nonacceptance of people with AIDS as American citizens. In contrast to the singular forms of transgressive sexual citizenship embodied by solitary expatriate, bestial/blasphemous, and transvestite/androgynous bodies, people with AIDS and queer bodies involved in ACT UP and Queer Nation represent a collective form of threat to the "sanctity" of national narratives because of their communal forms of protest and activism against the backdrop of a nationwide health crisis. The formation of the direct-action organization Queer Nation in March 1990 in New York City by ACT UP activists can thus be understood as a provocative "alter-national" form of queer citizenship and social belonging.

Nevertheless, this "alter-national" form of collective citizenship is not a straightforward or unproblematic alternative. As Jeffrey Escoffier explicates in his critical study of Queer Nation, the term *queer*—as opposed to "lesbian, gay or bisexual," which were deemed "awkward, narrow, and perhaps compromised words"—was meant to be "confrontational, opposed to gay assimilationists and straight oppressors while inclusive of those who had been marginalized by anyone in power" (1998, 202). Nevertheless, Escoffier is quick to point out the inherent semantic paradox in the formulation "Queer Nation":

QUEER = DIFFERENCE

NATION = SAMENESS

This intrinsic contradiction in the term "Queer Nation" [32] thus counterintuitively posed the risk of marginalizing those whose difference(s) did not conform to the "collective difference" of the new nation. As Escoffier summarizes, "Queer Nationals are torn between affirming a new identity—'I am queer'—and rejecting restrictive identities—'I reject your categories,' between rejecting assimilation—'I don't need your approval, just get out of my face'—and wanting to be recognized by mainstream society—'We queers are gonna get in your face'" (203) These tensions between sameness and difference, individuality and collective identification were thus integral to the formation of Queer Nation.[33] Rather than dismissing Queer Nation as an activist organization that ultimately disbanded due to irresolvable conceptual conflicts, however, I propose that the importance of Queer Nation as a case study lies precisely in its failure as an experiment in "alter-national" collectivity. This proposition requires a critical understanding of failure, as Judith Halberstam has argued,[34] as a central component of queer histories and as a key constituent of a collective politics of resistance and subversion.

It can therefore be argued that Queer Nation's politics of cultural subversion (sit-ins, kiss-ins, taking to the streets, and so on) did not square with its understanding of the nation as a homogenous entity. Hence, its adoption of the ultimate national form that would "affirm sameness by defining a common identity on the fringes" (Escoffier 1998, 203) created a disjuncture between queerness as difference and the form in which "collective difference" was performed in a politics of resistance: namely, through the logic of identification, or sameness. To apply Donald Pease's observations in his essay on post-national identity formations to the specificities of Queer Nation, the latter's demise could perhaps be attributed to the fact that its members, who were "reproduced [in dominant media, culture, and hence the national imaginary] as subordinated objects and denied identification with the meta-national," failed to "expose national identity as an artifact rather than a tacit assumption, a purely social construction rather than a metal-social universal" (1994, 5) when they could/should have done so.

Put differently, Queer Nation's demise was due to its adoption of a normative definition of nationhood that turned on sameness and homogeneity, which evidently clashed with its much more radical assertion of difference and its call to direct, even militant, action in its manifesto, "History Is a Weapon," which was originally distributed by ACT UP during the 1990 New York Gay Pride. An excerpt from this manifesto, for example, declared, "Being queer means leading a different sort of life. It's not about the mainstream, profit-margins, patriotism, patriarchy or being assimilated. . . . It's about being on the margins, defining ourselves."[35] Although this formulation expresses Queer Nation's rejection of social normativity, the movement nevertheless embraced the idea of a "queer nationalism"[36] that did not challenge or deconstruct the logic of homogeneity in nation-based models of membership, belonging, and citizenship. The problem, therefore, was that Queer Nation was ultimately organized around an ambivalent identity politics that risked separatism at the same time that it accepted nation-based models of collective membership and participation. As one activist put it, "The next lesbian and gay movement should not be called 'Queer Nation.' The name is irretrievably connected to identity politics. First, ditch 'Nation.' It suggests separatist aspirations, the battle for our 'own' place. Separatism will not solve the problems of the vast majority of lesbians and gay men, who have to work and live outside the 'nation'" (Sears 1992). Without implying at all that direct political action in the form of social movements, protests, and demonstrations is less discerning or perceptive than literary texts that function as sociopolitical commentaries and literary interventions, I want to argue that Sarah Schulman's novel *Rat Bohemia* is significant because it tells the story of queer bodies and people with AIDS who are excluded by the spaces of the American nation, and it goes one step further in challenging the concept of the "nation" as an assumed given.

Partly inspired by Daniel Defoe's *A Journal of the Plague Year* (1722), *Rat Bohemia* revolves around the experiences of four queer characters—Rita Mae Weems, a Jewish rat exterminator from Queens who works for the NYC Department of Health's Pest Control Division, her best friend, Killer, an odd jobber who falls in love with Troy Ruby, an activist briefly involved with Queer Nation, and David, one of Rita friends, an upper-middle-class, Jewish, HIV-positive writer—as they struggle to survive not in London in the year of the Great Plague (1665) but in the Lower East End of New York City, a district dubbed Rat Bohemia by the characters, in the 1990s. The novel is divided into four parts, each narrated in the first person from the perspective of one of the protagonists, and an appendix. Collectively, the four main sections of the novel address how, in the continued AIDS crisis of the early 1990s in the United States, questions of national identity and sexuality remain deeply intertwined. In the passage that follows, Killer is listening to her lover Troy describe her own involvement in Queer Nation:

> So, that was my role in the growth of Queer Nation. . . . One minor character in a minor movement. *Queer* did get old very fast, nowadays only academics take it seriously. But *Nation* managed to live on in

many fond conversations. Transgender Nation, Alien Nation, Reincar Nation. And all along the line no one noticed how much that word echoed with the secret store of nostalgic desire for normalcy, normalcy, normalcy. Those apple pie, warm kitchens and American flags that are trapped somewhere back there between the hypothalamus and the frontal lobe. Someplace in the Central Drawer where *One Nation Under God, Indivisible, With Liberty and Justice For All* resonates eternally. And that is why *Nation* is ultimately such a comforting word. And that is how I became an American poet. (1995, 111–12)

Schulman's tongue-in-cheek humor ("Reincar Nation") does not diminish her razor-sharp critique directed against the persistence of the centrality of ideas of the nation (that "comforting word") in the American public imagination. The passage satirizes the national symbolic in its various manifestations,[37] relegating these collective practices and codes to their metaphorical place in a deep "Central Drawer" (akin to *das Schubladendenken* in German). In addition, Schulman criticizes the heightened "nostalgic desire for normalcy, normalcy, normalcy" in New York during the years of the AIDS crisis, a longing that is equated with the "comforts" of typically American "apple pie" in warm kitchens.

Subsequently, reappropriating the American canon of poetry, Troy comments drily: "[S]ee, Killer, see how American culture is born. From Bob Frost [the poet Robert Frost] to my lips. . . . Two hundred and eighteen years of collective unconsciousness. Next thing you can guess, some little fairy from Ames, Iowa, will be jumping up and down rhyming *Seven years ago* and *homo* without any idea of how that free association was made!" (1995, 111). Troy's allusion to the opening of Abraham Lincoln's famous Gettysburg Address on November 19, 1863, in the midst of the Civil War, "Four score and seven years ago our fathers brought forth on this continent a new nation, conceived in liberty and dedicated to the proposition that all men are created equal" (a reference to the American Declaration of Independence) is clearly ironic. All men are *not* created equal and, at the height of the AIDS health crisis in the 1980s and 1990s, it is these "unnatural" and marginalized bodies that are excluded from the official discursive spaces of the nation and hence disqualified from the rights of citizenship.

Rat Bohemia thus centers around the lives of protagonists who literally and metaphorically fall outside of the spaces of the American "nation."

These characters live on the margins of society among friends who are heroin addicts, hustlers, people with AIDS, and members of Queer Nation. At one point in the novel, Killer says to Rita that they are "bohemians," people "with different ideas" that emerged from a history of counterculture movements, "hippies, beatniks, New Age, punks or Communists" (1995, 29). Nevertheless, Killer makes the distinction between the inhabitants of Rat Bohemia, the Lower East Side of New York City in the 1990s when gentrification had already begun, and the Beat Generation of writers and bohemian artists who, despite their breaking of social taboos, their antiestablishment and anticapitalist stance, were entrenched in U.S. national culture in the 1950s and 1960s and largely responsible for the revival of American Renaissance writer and transcendentalist Henry David Thoreau's works. In fact, the Beat Generation's politics of protest and confrontation were especially inspired by Thoreau's 1849 essay "Resistance to Civil Government (Civil Disobedience)."[38] As Killer says to Rita, "In the fifties, the Beats, those guys were so all-American. They could sit around and ponder aesthetic questions but a cup of coffee cost a nickel. Nowadays, with the economy the way it is, you can't drop out or you'll be homeless. You gotta function to be a boho. You have to meet the system head-on at least once in a while. . . . Nowadays you have to pay a very high price to become a bohemian" (30) The passage addresses the commodification of identities within U.S. neocapitalist culture. As Lauren Berlant asserts, "[I]dentity is marked in national capitalism as a property. It is something you can purchase, or purchase a relation to" (1997, 17). In contrast, the protagonists of *Rat Bohemia* refuse not only to purchase their identities but also to compromise their queerness as a source of political agency. Rather, they persist in their fight for the right to nondiscriminatory citizenship, even in the face of a terminal illness.

In a central passage in the novel, David, who is struggling with the public and familial denial with which is he faced, tells Rita about the affect of shame with which people with AIDS are confronted at the terminal stage of their sickness: "When people get really sick they're embarrassed and so crawl into their apartments and die. They feel defeated and no one is there to help them get down the stairs. Only the drug addicts are out there on their canes. The formerly beautiful homos just lie in bed waiting for God's Love—We Deliver to bring a hot meal and then spend the rest of the evening throwing it up" (1995, 45) As Heather Love has argued, shame is one of the affects, along with "loss, melancholia, failure" (2007, 6), and other forms of "feeling backward," that have plagued gay histories and queer politics. Locating her project within the wider scholarly "turn to the negative in queer studies" (2) and its "emphasis on injury . . . and damage" instead of affirmation and pride, Love argues for the necessity of not only avowing "the legitimacy of gay and lesbian existence" but of critically engaging with the way dominated and marginalized groups may "take advantage of the reversibility of power" because, citing Michel Foucault, "discourse produces power 'but also undermines and exposes it'" (2–3). Countering and seeking to expand Wendy Brown's notion of "Left Melancholy" (2003),[39] which she describes as characterized centrally by a "crisis of political motivation" (Love 2007, 12), Love seeks to infuse the traditionally nonpolitical affects of shame and melancholy with a queer political agency. Acknowledging the seminal work of Eve Kosofsky Sedgwick, Lee Edelman, and Leo Bersani on queer negativity,[40] Love thus argues for sexual shame as the basis of "alternative models of politics" (13), models predicated on the experience of failure because "the politics of gay pride will only get us so far" (147). In *Rat Bohemia*, HIV-positive David's *shameless* flaunting of shame, his camp exaggeration, his rejection of charity, his remembering and talking about his friends who died of AIDS all illustrate his reappropriation of what the national imaginary has delineated as negative affects.[41] David's gestures also signal a refusal to give in to the "nostalgic desire for normalcy, normalcy, normalcy" (111) that characterizes the tendencies of national narratives to homogenous, "dumb down," or romanticize traumatic episodes in national history.

Heather Love's critical work on shame and "feeling backward" therefore provides a useful theoretical framework for an interpretive reading of *Rat Bohemia*. In particular, it sheds light on the novel's resistive strategies against the appropriation of AIDS discourse by religious narratives of conversion and redemption. The novel's characters refuse to recognize AIDS as "a transforming experience" and resist the "romanticiz[ation]" of AIDS-related deaths. In the passage below, for instance, Rita speaks out against the public discourse on AIDS that, to her, is becoming "more twisted by the minute":

> So many want to believe that there is some spiritual message at the core of this disaster—something we all can learn. . . . That makes it more redemptive. We all know the only good homosexual is a dead one but if we can prove that we're getting some kind of benefit out of our own destruction then maybe straight people will have a little

more pity. But facts are facts. There is nothing to be learned by star-
ing death in the face every day of your life. AIDS is just fucking sad.
It's a burden. There's nothing redeeming about it. (1995, 52)

Rejecting the "redemptive" modes of organized religion in dealing with the
AIDS crisis, Rita goes one step further in associating these modes with the
character of national ideology. Instead, she declares: "I love the Viet Cong,
because that's the kind of American I am. I'm UnAmerican" (53).

This, I suggest, is the conundrum at the heart of *Rat Bohemia*—that
AIDS is simultaneously regarded and claimed as, first, *the* American experience that the nation has to publicly acknowledge and take measures against
(by AIDS activists including Schulman herself, ACT UP, and Queer Nation),
second, the *un*-American experience (as evinced by the Reagan administration's official policy of silence on AIDS and the relegation of people with
AIDS and the LGBTQI community to the rank of second-class citizens),
and third, the un-*American* experience (as conveyed in media depictions of
AIDS in Africa or AIDS as an African disease).[42] Ultimately, therefore,
Schulman's novel proffers an alter-national poetics that challenges the discourse of victimization and deviancy, as well as strategies of normalization,
adopted by mainstream "narratives of containment" on HIV/AIDS in order
to eradicate this "unnatural" disease from the spaces of the "good," "clean,"
and "natural" American nation.

Wary of any form of nation-centric identity or collective identification,
Schulman also critically objects to "homonationalism," a term she takes up
from fellow queer scholar Jasbir Puar[43] that describes the phenomenon of how
gay people who have gained widespread social recognition and legal rights are
"accepted and realigned with patriotic or nationalist ideologies of their countries" and end up constructing the "Other" (for instance, Muslims of Arab,
South Asian, Turkish, or African origin) as "homophobic" and fanatically heterosexual, instead of identifying with them as fellow minorities (2012b, 103–4).
Rat Bohemia resists this pull toward homonationalism by foregrounding, as in
Schulman's earlier novel, *People in Trouble*, the disenfranchisement and marginalization of minority communities in New York City on the grounds of
their sexuality, gender, class, race, and ethnicity. In one sequence in *Rat Bohemia*, Rita compares Walt Whitman's depiction of Brooklyn in "Crossing
Brooklyn Ferry," from *Leaves of Grass*, to her own visual and affective experience of the most populous of New York City's five boroughs:

I was reading a book called *Leaves of Grass*. It was all about the way people felt during the last century when Brooklyn was its own city and you had to take a boat to get there. I guess those Brooklynites stood on deck and watched the green grass of their homeland waving long and luxurious in the sun. . . .

Today you need to take the D train to get there. It sails right over one of the most beautiful stretches that America has to offer, that highway between the two boroughs. . . . There's . . . Wall Street where all the rich people of the officially beautiful world sit. On the other side are the projects where the saddest and most dangerous beautiful people of the unofficial world exist despite crime statistics, poverty graphs and the neglect quotient. (1995, 47)

Schulman's depiction of Brooklyn's descent into decay, crime, poverty, and neglect, as captured by the description of the borough's deterioration from a "homeland" of "green grass" waving "long and luxurious in the sun" to a concrete jungle housing "the projects" of the "unofficial world," is striking. This demographic change, the passage above suggests, is due not to the influx of "undesirable" citizens but to the municipal neglect and socioeconomic disenfranchisement of communities that are reduced to "the saddest and most dangerous beautiful people of the unofficial world." Schulman's criticism of the divide in the American nation between these citizens and the rich citizens of the "officially beautiful world" forms part of her larger critique of nationhood and nation-based models of citizenship, in particular the stratification of society, and hence the contours of entitlement, along the lines of class, gender, sexual orientation, and ethnicity.

Sarah Schulman's novels *People in Trouble* and *Rat Bohemia* thus attest to the ways in which the HIV/AIDS epidemic in the United States in the 1980s and 1990s was both a national crisis and one that challenged and undermined prevalent ideas of the nation, citizenship, participation, and entitlement, even as the U.S. government sought to shore up the concept of the American nation in its foreign policy. Not only were national funds not granted to institutions such as the Centers for Disease Control and Prevention for AIDS research and prevention but people with AIDS were also misrepresented, stereotyped and, effectively, victimized in mainstream media campaigns and news reports. *People in Trouble* and *Rat Bohemia* thus portray the ways in which "personal homophobia becomes societal neglect" (Schulman 1998, 23) in the midst of the AIDS crisis. The novels seek to challenge and overturn stigmatizing national narratives of containment, substituting these with narratives of proximity. They reflect Schulman's commitment to her larger project of queer activism that seeks to question and challenge dominant heteronormative notions of citizenship, belonging, and national identification in the spaces of the American nation and its public imagination.

PART IV
....
Diasporic and Indigenous Citizens

10

NARRATING CONTESTED SPACES

· · · · · · · · · ·

Denizens and Resident Aliens of the (New) Metropolis
in Dionne Brand's *What We All Long For* and Dinaw Mengestu's
The Beautiful Things That Heaven Bears

> *What the industrialized states are faced with today is a* permanently resi-
> dent mass of noncitizens, *who neither can be nor want to be naturalized
> or repatriated. . . . For these noncitizen residents, T. Hammar created the
> neologism* 'denizens,' *which has the merit of showing that the concept* 'citizen'
> *is no longer adequate to describe the sociopolitical reality of modern states.*
>
> Agamben 1995, 134

Giorgio Agamben makes two critical observations in the quote above: first, that the concept of "citizenship" is no longer adequate in describing the sociopolitical reality of modern state formations and second, that the emergence of alternative concepts such as "denizenship"[1] reflects a need to think beyond the conventional frameworks of the nation. Taking Agamben's observations as a point of departure, in the following three chapters, I will examine how "new" forms of denizenship, urban citizenship, and diasporic citizenship—but also a much older concept of Indigenous citizenship—represent alternatives to and question the continued relevance of nation-based forms of citizenship, identification, and collective belonging. In so doing, I will deconstruct the common assumption of "fully fledged" citizenship as the most desired of statuses.

In agreement with the viewpoint of immigration and legal scholar Linda Bosniak, I argue that a "romanticized" view of citizenship often obscures the inherent ethical ambiguities of the concept. As Bosniak maintains, "The idea of citizenship is commonly invoked to convey a state of democratic belonging or inclusion, yet this inclusion is usually premised on a conception of community that is bounded and exclusive. . . . [T]he divided nature of citizenship . . . [raises] questions about who it is that rightfully constitutes the subjects of the citizenship that we champion. . . . Citizenship of, and for, exactly, whom?" (2006, 1). I want to use Bosniak's statements as a trigger for considering the ways in which the status of denizenship might offer an alternative form of belonging, and hence a different mode of emergent subjectivity, that reassesses the "benchmark" of formal citizenship. Rather than accepting the dominant point of view that denizens occupy a space of marginality in the nation-state, which relies on a center-periphery model, I want to shift the conceptual framework of identity to that of alter- and post-national modes of belonging[2] in a manner consistent with my approach in the previous sections of this study. I also want to suggest that, contrary to popular opinion, not all denizens are in a process of transition: from the status of foreign national to resident alien to citizen. Rather, some might regard the status of denizen as a permanent one; they might choose *not* to apply for citizenship of the host country and hence not to enter into the process of "naturalization."[3]

Expanding on recent scholarship that has focused on how the conditions of precariousness, disenfranchisement, and dispossession embodied by stateless, exiled, and undocumented individuals can be regarded not only as the outcome of neoliberalism but also as an indication of its failure,[4] this chapter examines what forms of resistance and opposition emerge in the contested spaces of the new metropolis[5] that denizens and resident aliens occupy. A similar development in recent urban theory has led to an increasing emphasis on the role of cities in modern understandings of citizenship (Holston 1999b). As scholarship on "cosmopolitan citizenship" (Soysal 1994; Linklater 1998) and "urban citizenship" (Holston and Appadurai 1999; Isin 1999, 2000; Bauböck 2003; Varsanyi 2006; Cunningham 2011) in the last two decades has demonstrated, a critical (re)assessment of the role and importance of cities in new conceptual formations of citizenship is well under way. As Engin Isin aptly describes it, "Global cities are spaces where the very meaning, content and extent of citizenship are being made and transformed" (2000, 6).

Put differently, in the present era of late modernity, there have been concerted efforts to reconsider the city as a "strategic arena for reformulations of citizenship" (Holston 1999a, vii) in order to uncover possible alternatives to nation-state-based notions of identity and belonging (Purcell 2003, 566). These alter-national forms of political subjectivity regard the city as a physical site of contestation and change in which its denizens continually constitute the meanings and practices of citizenship anew (Varsanyi 2006, 234–35) and demand forms of acknowledgment, membership, and participation as well as socioeconomic, cultural, and political rights beyond those commonly associated with national citizenship. In line with critics who regard citizenship as less a static, legal institution and more as a process (Varsanyi 2006; Isin and Nielsen 2008), therefore, I am interested in how this practice is constantly interrupted, questioned, and renegotiated by what James Holston terms "acts of insurgent citizenship" (1999b, 155–73) that challenge and alter the dominant, prescriptive codes via which urban spaces operate. These claims to the city, which include acts of civil disobedience that "empower, parody, derail, or subvert state agendas" (167), represent the diversity of substantive lived citizenship in practice.

Ethnic enclaves, migrant and queer neighborhoods, squatter settlements and slums, homeless shelters, gated communities, and gentrified areas in the city center (Holston 1999b, 167)—these are some of the "contact zones" of "coercion, radical inequality and intractable conflict" (Pratt 1992, 6) wherein denizens' demands for recognition are made and claims to belonging are staked. Mapping these contested spaces of insurgent citizenship in the city reveals a direct relationship with "the spatial conditions of dispossession and its implications for politics" (Butler and Athanasiou 2013, 70). As heterogeneous and palimpsestic sites,[6] cities and their insurgent spaces generate and witness emergent forms of subjectivity and belonging, even as these "assertion[s] of legitimacy" are challenged and renegotiated by new forms of urban segregation and exclusion.[7] The conflation and contraction of racial, religious, class, cultural, and gender identities in the spaces of the new metropolis produce and generate "new identities and practices that disturb established histories" (157), thereby creating new practices of urbanity. As Holston and Appadurai remark, "[W]ith their concentrations of the nonlocal, the strange, the mixed, and the public, cities engage most palpably the tumult of citizenship" (1999, 2). Especially in large cities, which are susceptible to sharp rises in socioeconomic inequality (as reflected in a higher incidence of economic eviction, mortgage foreclosures, homelessness, and poverty), "new notions of membership, solidarity, and alienage" emerge that "generate new morphologies of social category and class" (10).

Therefore, in the critical opinion of urban theorists, cities today are ideal sites for the emergence of new modes of subjectivity, recognition, belonging, and what Edward Soja terms "spatial justice"[8] for the assertion of new forms of socioeconomic, ethnocultural, and political rights outside the normative and legal framework of formal citizenship.[9] The urban thus becomes a crucial site "for articulating new transnational and diasporic identities" (Holston 1999b, 169), for dismantling the dichotomy of inside/outside prevalent in dominant discourse on citizenship and national belonging.[10] A municipal politics that acknowledges different forms of urban citizenship might thus present an alternative model to the limitations of national citizenship and alter the prevailing codes and practices by which public spaces—and hence spaces of collective identity, community, and belonging—in the new metropolis are configured.

URBAN CITIZENSHIP AND NARRATING
THE MULTICULTURAL CITY

As Rainer Bauböck envisions it, urban citizenship should be "a formal status of local citizenship that is based on residence and disconnected from nationality." It must be "freed from constraints imposed by national and state-centered conceptions of political community" in order to facilitate "multiple local citizenship and voting rights within and across national borders" (2003, 139). Arguing for a strengthening of city autonomy vis-à-vis the state, while mindful of the fact that cities cannot simply reverse their incorporation into nation-states, Bauböck maintains that "we should conceive of the city as a political space inside the territorial nation-state where multicultural and transnational identities can be more freely articulated than at the provincial or national level. New forms of urban citizenship might promote a cosmopolitan transformation of national conceptions of membership from below and from within" (142). Bauböck's envisioning of an alternative form of membership "from below," one whose main locus is the city, is akin to Bhabha's notion of "vernacular cosmopolitanism" (1991, xviii) or what Benita Parry (1991, 41) and Stuart Hall (2008, 346) have termed "cosmopolitanism from below." Such a form of membership from below, in Bauböck's estimation, is "one that would transform national identities and national ideologies," shift the balance of power away from nation-states, "hel[p] to overcome some of the exclusionary features of national citizenship" (2003, 157), and lay the foundations for cosmopolitan democracy.

Bauböck's envisaging of urban citizenship as a status of membership and belonging based on one's residence in the city is comparable to Monica Varsanyi's envisioning of urban citizenship whereby "a person would become a 'citizen' not by explicit consent of fellow citizens, but merely by presence and residence in a place." In her article "Interrogating 'Urban Citizenship' vis-à-vis Undocumented Migration," Varsanyi points out the increasing discrepancy between the legal status of *de jure* citizenship (membership in a nation-state) and "the growing *de facto* long-term residence of noncitizens" (2006, 229) that has arisen in the last few decades. Specifically, she focuses on the status of undocumented migrants, arguing, in line with legal scholar Linda Bosniak, that most critical scholarship on citizenship does not take into consideration the factor that not all migrants have "access to formal citizenship and thus are at the mercy of state power" (2006, 231).

I agree with Varsanyi's critique insofar as much critical work in the field of citizenship studies has, understandably, regarded undocumented or "clandestine" migrants as precarious, subaltern, systematically dispossessed subjects. Notwithstanding the obvious veracity of this depiction, few studies have actually taken the dispossession of these residents of the city seriously as a contestation of established notions of formal neoliberal citizenship.[11] Judith Butler is an exception. Her recent trilogy of works—*Precarious Life: The Powers of Mourning and Violence* (2004), *Frames of War: When Is Life Grievable?* (2009), and (with Athena Athanasiou) *Dispossession: The Performative in the Political* (2013)—is a collective meditation on the precarious and dispossessed subject's refusal to become disposable and thus a serious inquiry into how precariousness can foster an "'other-centered' ethics of recognition" (Butler and Athanasiou 2013, 68) and solidarity in the pursuit of global justice. Like Butler, I, too, am interested in how dispossession might be constituted as a form of political responsiveness that "gives rise to action and resistance," thus allowing one to "enter into forms of collectivity that oppose forms of dispossession that systematically jettison populations from modes of collective belonging and justice" (xi). One such site of dispossession and insurgency can be located in the phenomenon of urban gentrification, which has led to ethnic minorities and lower-income groups being gradually priced out, and thus displaced from, their historical neighborhoods. It is a prime example of new forms of segregation, exclusion, and fortification that make the city an interminably contested space, home to the widening gap "between the promises of formal citizenship and the realities of exclusion" (Varsanyi 2006, 235).

In the following, I will trace how the dynamics of dispossession, insurgency, and a "cosmopolitanism from below" are mapped out in two fictional narratives of the North American metropolis—one set in Toronto and the other in Washington, DC. In keeping with recent theories of space and spatiality,[12] I claim that challenges to prevailing forms of citizenship and the emergence of new modes of subjectivity take place not only *in* but also, more significantly, *through* the construction and negotiation of narrative spaces. I suggest two broad narrative modes via which the above is enacted. The first adopts a seemingly positive view of multiculturalism in the modern city, which is depicted as a palimpsestic urban nexus, reinscribed and reclaimed by its denizens via various acts of urban citizenship. The city's occupants include successive generations of immigrants who increasingly claim their "rights to the city,"[13] moving beyond the established boundaries of their ethnic enclaves. The ensuing "new spaces of citizenship" are a result of the "compaction and reterritorialization" of the city when new residents with diverse "histories, cultures, and demands . . . disrupt the normative and assumed categories of social life" (Holston 1999b, 168). In this narrative mode, the city's contested spaces are regarded as an inherent part of life in the colorful, bustling, pluralistic urban metropolis, part of what gives the city its indelible atmosphere and character. In comparison, the second mode of narration espouses a more critical outlook on multiculturalism and is attuned to the disenfranchisement, marginalization, and exclusion faced by ethnic minorities and other minority groups. This approach critiques Western neoliberal narratives of progress by depicting how racial prejudice, socioeconomic exclusion, political disempowerment, and cultural stereotypes keep the city's contested spaces unresolvedly "sites of insurgence." Ultimately, both modes of narrating contested spaces in fictions of the new metropolis attempt to articulate the claims made by marginalized and dispossessed groups, and to critique the new strategies of control, securitization, and exclusion that are characteristic in urban communities. Two novels will serve here to exemplify the two narrative modes I have outlined above: Dionne Brand's *What We All Long For* (2005) and Dinaw Mengestu's *The Beautiful Things That Heaven Bears* (2007). Both novels illustrate how the literary text not only maps out but also becomes the site of struggle, documenting the "processes that textualize and narrate the social" (Canclini 2001, 77).

MULTICULTURAL CITIZENSHIP IN THE CITY
ABOVE THE 43RD PARALLEL

"The political and social lexicon of space, city and architecture and of the distinctions between public and private has become obsolete," Roemer van Toorn argues, and it has to be rewritten in order to take into account the experience of "simultaneity, multiplicity . . . interaction, hybrid[ity and] ambivalence" (1999, 90). Using van Toorn's claims as a trigger for considering how this act of "rewriting" might be enacted, I argue that nowhere is the "political and social lexicon of space, city and architecture" more imaginatively rewritten than in literary narratives: more specifically, in the subgenre of urban fiction. In Dionne Brand's novel *What We All Long For*, the city of Toronto, with its diffuse urbanism,[14] the metropolitan sprawl that characterizes its "exopolis" (Soja 1992, 95), is depicted in all its squalidness and splendor. Toronto is one of the largest multicultural cities in the world, with almost half of its residents foreign born[15] the city's polyglossic and polyphonic rhythms are reflected in the different strands of plot that come together in Brand's novel. As the multigenerational and multiethnic Torontonian protagonists inhabit and traverse the geographies of the city, their identities are "historically constituted, imagined, and reinvented in ongoing processes of hybridization and transnationalization" (Canclini 2001, 77–78). In their everyday negotiations as denizens of the city, Brand's characters unsettle traditional ways of belonging, engendering alternative forms of urban membership that have been grouped together under the broader umbrella term of "cultural citizenship" (Rosaldo 1994; Delgado-Moreira 1997; Ong 1999; Turner 2001; Chidester 2002; Delanty 2002; Ommundsen et al. 2010), rejecting cultural assimilation in favor of cultural difference.[16]

With reference to the first mode of narrating contested urban spaces that I outlined earlier, even though Brand's intricate narrative seems at first glance to embrace a positive view of multicultural life in the city,[17] a closer reading reveals that the novel's four protagonists are less fictional ambassadors of Canada's official policy of multiculturalism than intercultural denizens of the city of Toronto who disrupt, challenge, and reconfigure the spatial, social, and cultural relations in the metropolis, creating "new spaces of citizenship" (Holston 1999b, 168). In *Strange Multiplicity: Constitutionalism in an Age of Diversity*, James Tully proposes an intercultural notion of citizenship whereby one's sense of belonging is always related not only to one's own culture but to other cultures as well. After all, Tully argues, no single culture exists in a vacuum; rather, cultures "exist in complex historical processes of interaction with other cultures," and hence they are "densely interdependent in their formation and identity" (1995, 11). Stressing inclusion and the acknowledgment of cultural differences, Tully argues for a "constitutional association which recognizes and accommodates cultural diversity . . . and provides the social basis for critical reflection on, and dissent from, one's own cultural institutions and traditions of interpretation." As he claims, "[T]he possibility of crossing from one culture to another is available and unavoidable, for each citizen is a member of more than one culture" (207).

This is illustrated in Brand's novel, which begins with a description of Toronto: "There are Italian neighborhoods and Vietnamese neighborhoods in this city; there are Chinese ones and Ukrainian ones and Pakistani ones and Korean ones and African ones. Name a region on the planet and there's someone from there, here. *All of them sit on Ojibway land, but hardly any of them know it or care because that genealogy is willfully untraceable except in the name of the city itself* (2005, 4; my emphasis).[18] The intersecting of cultures in this passage is twofold. Daily contact between different cultures in the metropolis clearly renders the experience of "crossing" cultures and switching languages a regular, everyday activity. Contact within cultures themselves is also a plural experience because, as Tully rightly points out, "cultures are not internally homogenous. They are continuously contested, imagined and reimagined, transformed and negotiated, both by their members and their interaction with others" (1995, 207).

Indeed, the case is particularly complex in Canada, which is not only a settler nation[19] where different ethnicities have come to reside but also a country with a considerable Indigenous (First Nations and Métis) population amounting to almost seven hundred thousand.[20] The erasure of Indigenous history and the marginalization of First Nations and Métis in Toronto are thus problematic and reflect, perhaps, the divide not so much between the "white" and "ethnically visible minority" populations in the city as that between the Native populations (those who were First Nations) and all those who settled or came after (the "Seconds"). In the above quotation from *What We All Long For*, Brand critiques this awkward omission and even deliberate eradication of First Nations' claims to the city not only in official discourses but also, by extension, in popular culture, literature, and the arts. She draws attention to the different theories of the origins of the name "Toronto" and its etymological meanings,[21] gesturing to the broader regard of the city by Indigenous populations, ironically, as a gathering place for many people, as a place of plenty.

Despite the proliferation of scholarship on Canada's multiculturalism, therefore, only more recently have critics also specifically engaged with Canada's Indigenous histories.[22] It is in this light that Will Kymlica contends that a shared identity may be difficult to develop in a "multination" or "polyethnic"[23] nation like Canada, where distinct cultural heritages (including First Nations and Métis) have been part of a society of "deep diversity" (1995, 189–91) from its earliest beginnings. One recalls Canada's former prime minister Pierre Trudeau's attempt to "lessen" that deep diversity by affirming a unifying Canadian constitutional identity in the Charter of Rights and Freedoms (enacted in 1982)—to the dismay of the ten provinces, which demanded recognition of cultural distinctiveness (in the case of Quebec)[24] and acknowledgment of cosovereignty (see Tully 1995, 11–12).[25] As this historical episode illustrates, there is no singular or homogenous native Canadian identity to begin with. Rather, "the experience of cultural difference is *internal* to a culture" (13).[26] Toronto is therefore an intercultural urban nexus where cultural identities and horizons are altered, hybridized, and entangled in/by its denizens who navigate, traverse, and inhabit the city.

In Brand's *What We All Long For*, the four second-generation Canadian protagonists, Tuyen, Carla, Jackie, and Oku, endeavor to articulate their urban citizenship via different means. As "intercultural citizens whose cultures crisscross, overlap and interact" (Tully 1995, 166), the four of them navigate the "overlapping territories" and "intertwined histories" (Said 1993, 1) of Toronto's public and private geographies, engaging in daily acts of refusal and practices of resistance that give rise to a "simultaneous reshaping of social and spatial relations in cities" (Graham and Marvin 2001, 138): "They'd never been able to join in what their parents called 'regular Canadian life.' The crucial piece, of course, was that they weren't the required race. Not that that guaranteed safe passage, and not that one couldn't twist oneself up into the requisite shape; act the brown-noser, act the fool; go on as if you didn't feel or sense the rejections, as if you couldn't feel the animus. They simply failed to see this as a possible way of being in the world" (Brand 2005, 47). For Tuyen, Carla, Jackie, and Oku, who feel "as if they inhabited two countries—their parents' and their own" (20), the "burden of hyphenation" (Mahtani 2006,

168) is one that influences their daily interactions with the city. Their refusal to fit into "regular Canadian life" constitutes an act of resistant citizenship that contests socially constructed notions of homogenous Canadian identity. Not simply hyphenated as Vietnamese-Canadian, Caribbean-Canadian, Africadian (black Nova Scotian) and Jamaican-Canadian, Tuyen, Carla, Jackie, and Oku demonstrate that "the act of claiming a Canadian identity . . . mean[s] the occupation of a distinctly contradictory space, where one can both embrace a sense of country and still unveil the exclusion of specific histories of oppression and resistance" (170).

This is illustrated in the way that Oku tries hard to avoid the cultural stereotype that dominant white, middle-class Canadians make of him. Brand's narrator relates, "That's why he cultivated the persona of the cool poet—so that he wouldn't have to get involved in the ordinary and brutal shit waiting for men like him in the city. They were in prison, although the bars were invisible" (2005, 166). Like Oku, Jackie, too, is only too familiar with the racial stereotyping of young black men in Canada. Tuyen's, Carla's, Jackie's, and Oku's acts of intervention in the multicultural metropolis—for instance, Tuyen's resymbolizing and artistic appropriation of Toronto's CN Tower, the world's tallest free-standing structure, as a *lubaio*, a Chinese signpost and sculptural bricolage to which she pins the city's longings, prayers, and wishes—constitute examples of Bhabha's "vernacular cosmopolitanism," or "a political process that works *towards* the shared goals of democratic rule, rather than simply acknowledging already constituted 'marginal' political entities or identities" (1991, xviii).[27] These acts of vernacular cosmopolitanism, these "everyday deeds of translating between cultures" (Bhabha 2000, 139), take place in the here and now, as the four protagonists struggle to live in the present and put their (and their parents') pasts, "the past that had never been their past" (Brand 2005, 47), behind them. As Michael Buma summarizes, "[C]itizenship and belonging give way to *becoming* in *What We All Long For*, and Brand's protagonists—like the city in which they live—are constantly being reinvented" (2009, 13; my emphasis).

This process of becoming is, nevertheless, one that is continually frustrated and contested. For Tuyen, the second-generation daughter of Vietnamese boat people who fled Saigon during the Vietnam War in the late 1970s, the acts of reinvention and cultural translation take place not only on the levels of gender, class, and sexuality (for example, she breaks the codes of propriety and decorum that her two older sisters, born in Vietnam, observe)

FIGURE 1. Jin-me Yoon, *A Group of Sixty-Seven*, 1996 (detail of artist's mother, front), 134 chromogenic prints. Collection of the Vancouver Art Gallery, Acquisition Fund, 1996. Courtesy of the artist and Catriona Jeffries Gallery.

FIGURE 2. Jin-me Yoon, *A Group of Sixty-Seven*, 1996 (detail, right panel), 134 chromogenic prints. Collection of the Vancouver Art Gallery, Acquisition Fund, 1996. Courtesy of the artist and Catriona Jeffries Gallery.

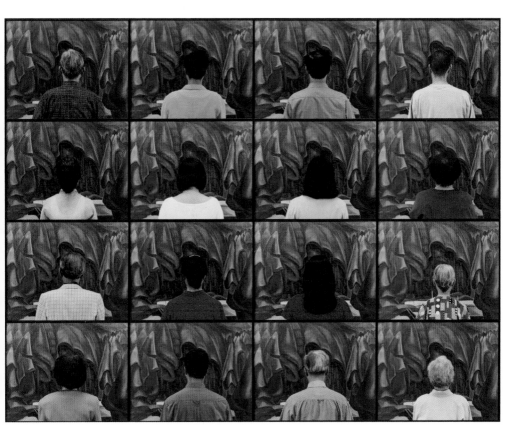

FIGURE 3. Jin-me Yoon, *A Group of Sixty-Seven*, 1996 (detail, left panel), 134 chromogenic prints. Collection of the Vancouver Art Gallery, Acquisition Fund, 1996. Courtesy of the artist and Catriona Jeffries Gallery.

FIGURE 4. Jin-me Yoon, *A Group of Sixty-Seven*, 1996 (detail of artist's mother, back), 134 chromogenic prints. Collection of the Vancouver Art Gallery, Acquisition Fund, 1996. Courtesy of the artist and Catriona Jeffries Gallery.

FIGURE 5. Jean Mohr, *Tripoli, Badawi* [sic] *Camp, May 1983*. Courtesy of the photographer.

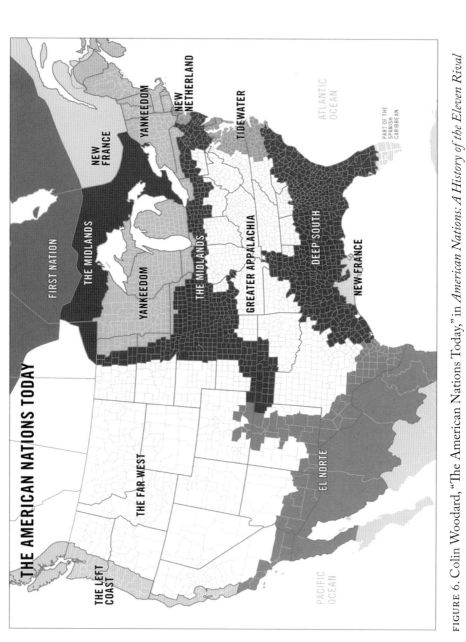

FIGURE 6. Colin Woodard, "The American Nations Today," in *American Nations: A History of the Eleven Rival Regional Cultures of North America* (2012). Courtesy of the author.

but on that of language. Born in Toronto, she is assigned the role of "interpreter," "annotator," and "paraphrast," "required to disentangle puzzlement; any idiom or gesture or word," and "counted on to translate" (2005, 67) for her parents. Tuyen realizes at one point, however, that "she had been unable to translate in all her years as her parents' interlocutor. She had not even been able to get the story fully spoken" (69). She recognizes that, like her brother Binh, who was also born in Toronto, "their culture was North American despite their parents' admittedly ambivalent efforts to enforce Vietnamese rules" (125).

Linguistic difference and the failure of cultural translation play a significant role in Carla's life, too. A biracial daughter of a white mother and black father, Carla resents Jamaican cooking and culture, balking at the smell of the dried cod, fresh thyme, and mangoes when her stepmother, Nadine, cooks Jamaican food for her father.

> Her [Carla's] ears registered discomfort at the sound of accented voices pausing in self-derision, in boastfulness, or in religious certainty. She hated this language that made herself unhear, unthink, and undream. She never actually learned it except to understand her father, Nadine, and their friends, and to translate it to her teachers and anyone official. She had been a translator herself, knowing a language the way a translator whose first tongue is another language knows it. She did not live in it. (2005, 131)

Just as she does not "live in" the Jamaican English of her father's generation, Carla refuses, too, to inhabit her surroundings in the "gay ghetto" of Toronto, where she lives in a high-ceilinged, loftlike apartment above a cheap clothing store. Although the neighborhood is in a young, "hip" area of the city, residence to "a few hip-hop poets, two girls who made jewelry and knitted hats, and an assortment of twenty-somethings who did various things like music and waitering" (23), she does not feel entirely at home. In comparison to Carla, who adopts a detached relationship with the city of Toronto, either observing it quietly out her window or speeding through its streets on her bicycle, her brother Jamal, who, being "troubled and black" (34) and "in the wrong place at the wrong time" (35), ends up in jail for carjacking, has a different perception of the city: "Jamal didn't see the city as she did. . . . she saw the city as a set of obstacles to be crossed and circled, avoided and let pass.

He saw it as something to get tangled in" (32). Admittedly, this is Carla's perspective of her younger brother's view of the city, and not his own. Nevertheless, Toronto is described here as a place in which lives are entangled, where they are "doubled, tripled, conjugated—women and men all trying to handle their own chain of events, trying to keep the story straight in their own heads," but in which "the lines of causality [are juggled], and before you know it, it's impossible to tell one thread from another" (5).

The metaphor of entanglement recalls Arjen Mulder's concept of "transurbanism," which he defines as "urbanism plus transformation" or "a theory of cities in transit" (2002, 7–8) that bears witness to a "continual transformation process of temporary coalitions, collisions, hybridizations and migrations" (8). Mulder's description of the city as "an unstable system, a living system which is in a state of continual decomposition, but which also continually reorganizes and rearranges itself, which expands and shrinks" (7) fittingly describes the fictional Toronto depicted in Brand's novel. Never remaining static, alive with its sounds and smells and perpetually in motion, the city of Toronto in *What We All Long For* becomes the repository of its citizens' longings, memories, and fortunes. The latter differ, naturally, from generation to generation and from individual to individual. Tuyen's parents, for example, who were Vietnamese refugees, had high hopes for starting a new life in Toronto, only to have their expectations dashed after six months in the Chi Ma Wan refugee camp in Hong Kong and losing their first-born son, Quy, on their journey. Tuyen's father, Tuan, and her mother, Cam, have to give up their professions as an engineer and a doctor respectively because Canada does not recognize their skills and qualifications. Resignedly, both of them finally open a restaurant, giving in to the cultural stereotype and "see[ing] themselves the way the city saw them: Vietnamese food," although "neither Cam nor Tuan cooked very well" (2005, 67).

Tuyen's parents' claims to the city are therefore truncated by forms of cultural stereotype, prejudice, and exclusion that are prevalent in neoliberal "multicultural" societies. In Brand's oblique critique of the overwhelming paperwork—certificates, forms, documents, and permits—that immigrants accumulate before being allowed to remain in the host country, a phenomenon only amplified by practices of securitization and identity management that have entered both the U.S. and the Canadian cultural imagination,[28] Tuyen's mother develops a "mad fear of being caught without proof, without papers of some kind attesting to identity or place." She "laminate[s] everything in sight when she discovered a shop, Vickram's, that did laminating," but especially "birth certificates, identity cards, immigration papers, and citizenship papers and cards" (1995, 63) Her fear of being caught sans papers, as an undocumented migrant without official forms of identity, reflects the notion that, as Minelle Mahtani has argued, "questions of national belonging still figure predominantly . . . within the particular context of the Canadian landscape." At the same time that the text articulates a politics of emergent intercultural and transnational subjectivity, positing an alternative version of urban, ethnocultural citizenship to that of Canada's official policy of multiculturalism,[29] therefore, it also becomes the site of struggle, of unfulfilled hopes and deferred reunions,[30] thus conveying new forms of exclusion, prejudice, and dispossession. The latter are a product of "overarching national constructions that long have been anchored through whiteness" (Mahtani 2006, 169) and reveal the Sisyphean task of reshaping and restructuring Canadian identity in the new millennium. Rather than undertaking this project of redefining Canadianness, however, Brand's novel seems to explode the concept of nationhood altogether. As Michael Buma has observed, "Brand appears less interested in re-orienting 'Canadianness' than in rendering it obsolete. . . . *What We All Long For* appears to foreclose entirely on the possibility of any homogenous national identity" (2009, 13).

As the protagonists of the novel pursue their journeys in search of what they all long for, they encounter various obstacles in (and in the form of) the city. Nowhere else is this clearer than in Jackie's story line in the novel: upon relocating in 1980 from their Africadian community in Halifax, Nova Scotia, to Alexandra Park, an urban housing estate in Toronto, her parents quickly realize that "after [the] city gets finished with you in the daytime, you don't know if you're coming or going" (2005, 95). The new metropolis of Toronto, therefore, is not a cosmopolitan haven and, by extension, Brand's *What We All Long For* is not, as it has been suggested, a prime example of "21st century CanLit" (Buma 2009, 13) that, in a marked turn away from earlier discursive tropes in Canadian literature such as the wilderness, nature, the garrison mentality, and survival,[31] mimetically depicts and embraces, the "realities" of multicultural life in contemporary Canadian, yet globalized, urban spaces. Rather, I argue that Brand's novel is a more nuanced and differentiated critique of Canada's official policy of multiculturalism;[32] it is an exploration of how cities are contested spaces that witness the emergence of new forms of denizenship and belonging that transcend the strictures of formal nation-based models of citizenship.

INSURGENT CITIZENSHIP AND NARRATIVES
OF GENTRIFICATION

Dinaw Mengestu's *The Beautiful Things That Heaven Bears*, too, explores the city as an urban site of insurgency, as a contested space where alter-national forms of identity and citizenship emerge. The novel depicts how gentrification and its results—heightened rates of foreclosure and economic eviction[33]—substitute multiplicity, difference, and diversity with sameness, and reconfigure the lines of racial/ethnic- and class-based divide in the city. In doing so, Mengestu's novel depicts the changing demographics of the historically African American neighborhoods of Logan Circle and U Street/Shaw in Washington, DC, from a neighborhood that was "predominantly poor, black, cheap, and sunk into a depression" (2007, 35) in the 1970s, to one with refurbished luxury houses and apartments three decades later. The protagonist of the novel, Sepha Stephanos, is an Ethiopian migrant who flees the Red Terror (1977–78) in order to begin a new life in the United States when he witnesses Communist soldiers beating his father to the point of death. Sepha runs a failing corner shop—a small store with "hideously green tiled floors," "bad fluorescent lighting," and "five tightly packed aisles" of "cheap processed foods" (27)—at the less affluent end of P Street in Logan Circle, an area in which he also lives, in a "cheap, sometimes cockroach-infested, apartment" (16). Referencing the use of Walter Benjamin's flâneur in recent theories of urban spectatorship to depict the condition of postmodern alienation in the metropolis,[34] Mengestu's protagonist walks and quietly observes the way gentrification and "urban renewal" have changed the demographics of his neighborhood.[35] Powerlessly sucked into the economic change that manifests itself around him, painfully aware that he is not part of the community of wealthy new inhabitants in the area, Sepha echoes the "passive and helpless observations of people stuck living on the sidelines." He muses, "The neighborhood's changing, things are changing, it's not like it used to be, I can't believe how much it's changed, who would have thought it could change so quickly, nothing is permanent, everything changes" (23).

As Julio Ramos observes, "[S]trolling is not simply a way of experiencing the city" objectively or passively but "a way of representing it, of looking at it, and recounting what is seen" (2001, 128). While strolling, Sepha weaves his perceptions together into a visual and experiential narrative of the city, intertwining the disjointed and multiple nature of urban life. It is through this narrative that he tries to understand how his urban surroundings are being transformed by processes of gentrification. Nevertheless, any attempt to narrate the city can result only in fragmentary shards, collage-like glimpses of its multiple and heterogeneous spaces of participation.

Without offering a more detailed analysis of Benjamin's flâneur, for limited space would only do injustice to the complexity of his theories of urban spectatorship, I would like to briefly consider one aspect of this theory—the flâneur's "suspended temporality." This is an obvious reference to Benjamin's other well-known character, the "angel of history," inspired by Paul Klee's painting *Angelus Novus*. The face of Benjamin's angel, who "is turned toward the past" even as the storm of progress "irresistibly propels him into the future to which his back is turned" (1992, 259–60), depicts his being caught in an impasse. Benjamin's flâneur, too, stands "at a crossroads between past and future, where the former is not his personal one but the convergence of diverse traditions that have formed the city and the latter is not fixed, but is open to active intervention to be shaped by those in the present" (Cunningham 2011, 37). Like the flâneur, Mengestu's protagonist Sepha Stephanos is also caught at a crossroads between past and future. As a denizen, or permanent resident, of Washington, DC, he embodies a form of resistant "cosmopolitanism from below." In comparison to the city's description as a "crossroads" (2005, 3) in Dionne Brand's *What We All Long For*, where one "can stand on a simple corner and get taken away in all directions" (154), in Mengestu's *The Beautiful Things That Heaven Bears*, it is the image of circles, more specifically, Logan Circle and Dupont Circle, from which paths (both metaphorical and literal) radiate like the spokes of a wheel (of life), that is foregrounded in the novel. For example, it is on a park bench in Logan Circle, at the foot of an impressive statue of Major General John A. Logan, and hence a personification of the American Civil War, that Mengestu's protagonist reflects on the last seventeen years of his life in the nation's capital, and his falling in love with an upper-middle-class white woman who buys and renovates the house next door to his.

Sepha is one of a few residents of color left in Logan Circle, a historic district located between the Dupont Circle and Shaw neighborhoods. During the Civil War, Logan Circle was the site of Camp Barker, a former barracks converted into a refugee camp for newly freed black slaves from nearby Virginia and Maryland (Blight 2007, 93). In the 1980s and 1990s, the district was notorious for drug use and prostitution, but by the early 2000s, gentrification and urban development had led to a "revamping" of the area's image and thus a sharp increase in property prices. Old buildings were torn down to make way for new luxury refurbished units that were attractive to a largely white, upper-middle-class clientele. This has resulted in a change in the district's demographics, with white residents making up 46 percent of its population and black residents a mere 32 percent, in comparison to a 50 percent black population in the entire capital in 2010. In their article in the *Washington Post*, "Number of Black D.C. Residents Plummets as Majority Status Slips Away," Carol Morello and Dan Keating single out the main cause of demographic change as "almost 15 years of gentrification that has transformed large swaths of Washington, especially downtown."[36]

Thus, while Dinaw Mengestu's novel has been praised, unsurprisingly, as a moving "tale of an Ethiopian immigrant's search for acceptance, peace, and identity,"[37] "thoughtfully portray[ing]" the "isolation and frustration of immigrant life" (Kulman 2008),[38] I argue that at the novel's core lies a much more incisive critique of gentrification and a recognition of the "shifting sociabilities and cultures . . . that transform the legal regimes of state and local community" (Holston and Appadurai 1999, 10) in the U Street/Shaw and Logan Circle areas of Washington, DC. By depicting how migrants and denizens in these enclaves are economically further disadvantaged, displaced, and evicted, and the mounting class tensions that result, Mengestu's novel portrays the flip side of neoliberal policies of "urban renewal" in the nation's capital. The denizens of the city partake in the "tumult of citizenship" (2) in order to articulate their claims to "spatial justice" (Soja 2010), subjectivity, and recognition.

Thus, one could argue that *The Beautiful Things That Heaven Bears* refuses to be read as a conventional immigrant's tale[39] or a Bildungsroman of one migrant's dream to make a new life for himself in America. Sepha's dispassionate and realistic demeanor undermines the archetypal narrative of the "American Dream" that remains deeply entrenched in the popular imagination of the nation and beyond. As Sepha confesses,

> Here, in Logan Circle, . . . I didn't have to be anything greater than I already was. I was poor, black, and wore the anonymity that came with that as a shield against all of the early ambitions of the immigrant, which had long since abandoned me, assuming they had ever really been mine to begin with. *As it was, I did not come to America to find a better life. I came here running and screaming with the ghosts of*

an old one firmly attached to my back. My goal since then has always been a simple one: to persist unnoticed through the days, to do no more harm. (2007, 41; my emphasis)

Sepha's vehement denial that he came to America to "find a better life" (a rather stereotypical phrase in conventional narratives of migration to the United States) and his description of fleeing political persecution demystifies the "American Dream" from the very outset, even before he lands on American soil. It is debunked as a fictional construct not only by Sepha but also by his Congolese friend, Joseph. In one episode, while walking home after a night out, past the Capitol and the Washington Monument, Sepha reflects, "[T]here is no mystery left in any of those buildings for us, and at times I wonder how there ever could have been" (46). He concludes, "After seventeen years here, I am certain of at least one thing: the liberal idea of America is at its best in advertising" (98). Likewise, his friend Joseph, who had "memorized the Gettysburg Address off the memorial's walls," stops going near it after "reality . . . settled in" and he realizes that migrants like himself are no longer, and never were, "the children of the revolution" (47). Even worse, instead of sending money home like the archetypal U.S. immigrant, Sepha admits at one point in the novel that his mother once sent him "a money order worth three hundred dollars more than all of the money I had ever sent" (41).

Destitute and on the point of having his store repossessed after months of being unable to make his rent payments, Sepha abandons it, simply walking away one day. The nonlinear narrative recounts this sequence in a series of episodes that are interspersed throughout the novel. In the first, which occurs about a third of the way into the novel, Sepha leaves the shop and cash register open and simply walks away from it, following a retired, white, middle-class tourist couple on their self-guided walking tour of DC westward, along the length of P Street, crossing Fourteenth to Eighteenth streets to arrive at Dupont Circle. The route is significant because it represents a compact lesson in American history: from the statue of Major General John A. Logan in Logan Circle commemorating his patriotism and leadership in the Union army during the American Civil War, past the corner of Sixteenth and P, from which the White House is visible and to the north of which is Striver's Section, a historical residential enclave of upper-middle-class African Americans including Frederick Douglass and his son, and finally arriving at Dupont Circle, a historic area for the gay community.

As Sepha walks from Logan Circle to Dupont, however, it is not the official historical narrative of American patriotism and civil rights he pieces together but an alternative narrative of gentrification that recalls the area as it was before the onset of newly built town houses, refurbished luxury units, and two-story organic grocery stores—in the days when it was still an underprivileged area notorious for its prostitution, drug use, cheap Chinese takeaways, dubious auto repair shops, rundown grocery stores selling "wilted vegetables and grade-D meat" (2007, 75), and the black-owned bookstore where "the black empowerment books gathered dust" (75–76). This version strongly contrasts with the "official" historical guidebook narrative that the tourist couple are digesting at their "slow, leisurely pace" (74), a version encapsulated in the act of the husband pointing to the White House and saying to this wife, "That is where *our* president lives" (77; my emphasis). The ease with which the white husband and wife, whom Sepha imagines are from the Midwest, claim their American heritage stands in sharp relief to Sepha's chosen self-exile, his rejection of assimilation and integration into a national narrative that discriminates against economically disadvantaged ethnic migrants like himself. Instead, he prefers to self-identify as a dispossessed and diasporic immigrant who is driven to abandon his foreclosed corner store: "I wonder if this is what it feels like to walk out on your wife and children. If this is what it feels like to leave a car on the side of the highway and never come back for it. What is the proper equation, the perfect simile or metaphor? I'm an immigrant. I should know this. I've done it before" (74). It is Sepha's uncle, Berhane Selassie, who has experienced this firsthand, having been forced in Addis Ababa to "disappear in the middle of the night without telling a single person" (97), leaving his house and all his possessions for the soldiers who arrive at his door two weeks later. Once enjoying a lifestyle with money and power in Ethiopia, even living "just outside of Addis on a sprawling ranch" (96) designed after Frank Lloyd Wright's Prairie house, Uncle Berhane is forced to leave during the Communist Revolution because his last name (Selassie)[40] "was once associated with the cabinet members and princes of the old empire" (116). In Washington, DC, Berhane works as a taxi driver during the day and as a parking attendant in the evenings. He lives in a one-room apartment, a far cry from his opulent house and lifestyle back in Addis Ababa, in the residential area of Silver Spring.

A microcosm of Ethiopia, the real-life suburb of Silver Spring in Maryland is home to a large population of Ethiopian migrants who, as it is fictionally described in Mengestu's novel, "moved there after the revolution and found to their surprise that they would never leave" (2007, 115). The apartment complex where Uncle Berhane lives is almost entirely occupied by Ethiopian refugees: "Within this building there is an entire world made up of old lives and relationships transported perfectly intact from Ethiopia. To call the building insular is to miss the point entirely. Living here is as close to living back home as one can get, which is precisely why I moved out after two years and precisely why my uncle has never left" (116).

When Sepha walks away from his soon-to-be repossessed store, he decides to visit Uncle Berhane in his apartment. Without his uncle's knowledge, he opens Berhane's shoebox of unsent letters addressed over the years to various presidents of the United States, informing them, with a new immigrant's naïveté and zeal, about the massacres going on in Ethiopia, entreating them to come to Ethiopia's aid because of "the deep friendship between the two countries." Uncle Berhane's earliest letters, such as the ones to President Carter, are "open, emotive, . . . free, . . . deeply personal, . . . a plea to be heard" (2007, 123). His tone becomes gradually more disillusioned, however, and the letters become shorter and "increasingly distant with time" (122) until they cease altogether. Here, the epistolary text itself becomes the site of insurgency and struggle, of frustrated hopes and expectations, recounting Sepha's father's execution and the torture of "anti-revolutionaries." Sepha realizes that he has returned to his uncle's apartment in search of one thing—"narrative." He surmises, "Perhaps that's the word that I'm looking for. Where is the grand narrative of my life? *The one I could spread out and read for signs and clues* as to what to expect next. It seems to have run out, if such a thing is possible. It's harder to admit that perhaps it had never been there at all" (147; my emphasis).

Sepha's description of the "grand narrative of my life" as one he can "spread out and read" like a map is a reference, I would suggest, to the fold-out map of Washington, DC, that the retired, well-to-do, white American tourists consult on their walking tour of the city. Unlike them, the only map in Sepha's possession is a fading one of the African continent on a wall in his corner shop, which he, Joseph, and Kenneth (his other close friend from Kenya) used as the board for a game they played. One of them would name a dictator, and the other two would have to guess the date of the coup and point to the relevant country on the map. The stark contrast between what the two maps represent—the map of Washington, DC, standing in for the

United States and its political ideals, the map of Africa signifying a chart of political atrocities in the form of dictatorships, coups, uprisings, and civil wars—not only conveys the different socioeconomic conditions of the two but also critiques the proliferation of national ideologies and fantasies in the American public imagination that are, in reality, accessible only by a privileged minority. The difference between the status of the retired American couple, who can leisurely consult a map and embark on a self-guided tour of Washington, DC, with "an assured, confident authority" (2007, 71), stopping to admire historical landmarks, and Sepha's own plight—a former refugee, now a Green Card holder after seventeen years in the United States, living in dismal conditions with a failing grocery store—crystallizes how out of place he is in an increasingly gentrified neighborhood in the American capital.

Despite trying to carve out a new life for himself, therefore, Sepha continually chides himself for trying to rise above his status, for having "forgotten who [he] was with his shabby apartment and run-down store," for having "tried to recast [himself] into the type of man who dined casually on porcelain plates and chatted easily about Emerson and Tocqueville while sitting on a plush leather couch in a grand house" (2007, 80). In an unexpected turn of events, however, Mengestu's novel ends with Sepha breaking out of his flâneur-like "suspended temporality." In a moment of decision, feeling that he has been "dangled . . . long enough" like "a man stuck between two worlds," Sepha chooses one world—the one where he is happy to claim his store, imperfect as it is, "entirely as [his] own" (228). At the end of the novel, therefore, Sepha rejects the role of the flâneur and embraces a form of denizenship in "the city that [he has] made his life and home" (173)—but on his own terms. For Sepha, abandoning his store is a necessary move in order for him to realize that he is "never going to return to Ethiopia again" (175) because all he has of that country are nostalgia and memory, and "what you're returning to can never be the same as what you left" (174).

Dionne Brand's *What We All Long For* and Dinaw Mengestu's *The Beautiful Things That Heaven Bears* depict the cities of Toronto and Washington, DC, as contested spaces, as the strategic locations of new and insurgent forms of social identities and emergent subjectivities that challenge and rework the dominant practices by which the public spaces of the nation are regulated and organized. Both novels demonstrate how literary narratives "encompass the dispersed meanings of a large city" (Canclini 2001, 80) and, conversely, how the city is represented, "narrated, described [and] explained" (81). In Brand's "multicultural" novel, the children of Toronto's first-generation Vietnamese, Jamaican, and African immigrants strive to claim the city as their own. In the contested spaces of the metropolis, the four second-generation protagonists struggle to escape the disappointment and resentment of their parents' experiences of migration to the city. Yet the novel is less a mimetic representation of Canadian multiculturalism than a critique of how it has become a central component of the nation's popular image. Instead, the narrative bears witness to the emergence of alter-national forms of urban citizenship, denizenship, and diasporic belonging. In comparison, Dinaw Mengestu's *The Beautiful Things That Heaven Bears* is an atypical immigrant's tale in which the Ethiopian protagonist Sepha Stephanos comes to terms with the realities of migration, class struggle, cultural prejudice and, most important, gentrification in a economically disadvantaged, historically black neighborhood of Washington, DC. For him and others like him, the city becomes the birthplace of emergent forms of "transnational and diasporic identities" (Holston 1999b, 169), "urban citizenship," denizenship, and vernacular "cosmopolitanism from below" that challenge and modify prevalent discourses and constellations of national citizenship. These new emergent subjectivities take place not only in but also through the construction of narrative spaces. In this way, the literary text *itself* becomes a tool of critique, challenging neoliberal strategies of exclusion and segregation, official policies of multiculturalism and economic gentrification, and nation-state models of citizenship.

11

EXILE, MIGRATION, AND THE "POETICS OF RELATION"

· · · · · · · · · ·

Edwidge Danticat's *Brother, I'm Dying*
and Dany Laferrière's *The Return*

Moving on from modes of emergent subjectivities in the urban spaces of the nation that challenge the efficacy of nation-based models of citizenship, this chapter traces how the works of Haitian-born writers Edwidge Danticat and Dany Laferrière embrace exile as both a physical displacement and a mental state of mind, as both a political and an affective condition that opens up new critical ways of rethinking notions of home, nation, citizenship, and belonging. Addressing the relationship between literature and exile, the works of Danticat and Laferrière contemplate the role of the author who writes from a position of diaspora, at one remove from her or his country of origin, which is the point of both departure and (imagined or actual) return. Echoing Edward Said's description of exile as both "a political condition and a critical concept" (Barbour 2007, 293), their writings articulate the immigrant artist's desire to "interpret and possibly remake his or her own world" through the medium of literature, in particular, the genre of life writing (Danticat 2010, 18). This gives rise to an intimate textual poetics and politics of exile that open up a space of creative belonging within the narrative itself.[1] In other words, the act of writing does not merely serve a descriptive[2] or mimetic purpose but also enacts a mode of cultural belonging, an act of creative citizenship.

In this vein, the articulation of a textual poetics of exile in the works of Danticat and Laferrière constitutes an act of defiant intervention, an act of, in Danticat's own words, "creating dangerously" (2010, 19) that challenges the politics of cultural forgetting and historical erasure that are deeply ingrained in Haiti's long and complex history, one that has encompassed long periods of U.S. occupation, political dictatorship by the Duvalier family, and United Nations military intervention.[3] In this chapter, I will therefore examine how these two writers' individual techniques of "creating dangerously," of bearing witness and recording personal histories of Haitian exile, offer different ways of critically understanding and conceptualizing notions of home and nation, citizenship and belonging that remain central to discourses of diaspora and migration. While Danticat uses the lens of personal memory and distance from the homeland to create works of diasporic intervention, Laferrière sustains a "poetics of relation" (Glissant 1997a) with the land of his birth, a textual strategy that suggests a post-territorial understanding of national identity.

At this point, it might be useful to recall Edward Said's reflections on exile, taken from his essay of the same name. Said writes, "Willfulness, exaggeration, overstatement: these are characteristic styles of being an exile, methods for compelling the world to accept your vision—which you make more unacceptable because you are in fact unwilling to have it accepted. It is yours, after all. Composure and serenity are the last things associated with the work of exiles" (2001, 145). In this passage, Said makes an observation on the difficult, almost paradoxical, task of the writer or artist in exile—a desire to create in her or his work a vision of the world that conveys the disjuncture and rupture of the experience, while at the same time conceding that "true exile is a condition of terminal loss" (137), a "fundamentally discontinuous state of being" (140), a feeling "out of place" that cannot be ameliorated or "transformed" in/by the literary text.[4] This exilic frame of mind is, however, not one of passivity; instead, it manifests itself in the literature of exile as a stubborn willfulness,[5] a defiant intransigence, a mode of hyperbole that allows the "unsettling force [of exile to] erupt anew" (149) on every page. It is this mode of insubordination that bears close resemblance to the "disobedient" act of the literary imagination that Edwidge Danticat terms "creating dangerously."

This expression first appears in her collection of essays of the same name, *Create Dangerously: The Immigrant Artist at Work*: "There are many possible interpretations of what it means to create dangerously, and Albert Camus, like the poet Osip Mandelstam, suggests that it is [the act of] creating as a revolt against silence, creating when both the creation, and the reception, the writing and the reading, are dangerous undertakings, disobedience to a directive" (2010, 11). For the exiled or diasporic Haitian author, writing dangerously from *lòt bò dlo* ("the other side of the water" in Haitian Creole) is thus a practice of social critique and political resistance against the country's history of military oppression, dictatorship, and the "enforcement of peace"[6] that have silenced dissident voices of opposition. To create dangerously therefore implies both to write in a way that will unsettle, make an impact, cause injury and to write knowing that writing *itself* is a risky business,[7] "a dangerous vocation," as Dany Laferrière describes it in his most recent autobiographical novel, *The Return: A Novel (L'énigme du retour)* (2011, 140).

EDWIDGE DANTICAT: WRITING DANGEROUSLY —MEMOIR AS DIASPORIC INTERVENTION

Having sketched out the rubrics of a poetics of "dangerous creation," I would like to move on to a closer examination of how it is manifest in Miami-based Edwidge Danticat's autobiographical and critical writings on exile, diaspora, departure, and return. Danticat's memoir, *Brother, I'm Dying* (2007) examines the cultural dislocation of exile from the points of view of her father and uncle, who left Haiti for New York and Miami respectively, speaking/writing on their behalf "because they can't" (26).[8] Piecing together their life stories from "official documents" and "the borrowed recollections of family members," Danticat makes "an attempt at cohesiveness," at re-creating a narrative she learns "out of sequence and in fragments" that "forc[e her] to look forward and back at the same time" (25). By adopting this method of historicizing by narrativization, and by giving a cohesive structure to the past in order to "make sense" of it,[9] Danticat's memoir illustrates that autobiographical writing is not merely descriptive and mimetic but always also an act of literary construction and composition. In Danticat's memoir, therefore, the act of retelling serves a function over and above that of documentation and witnessing—it serves as a means of intervention, of participation in the historical and political narratives of a country from which one has been expelled.[10]

Indeed, *Brother, I'm Dying* offers less a "documentary" account of Haiti's history of U.S. occupation (1915–34), Aristide's first and second presidencies (1991–96 and 2001–4) and exile (2004–11), and the Duvalier family dictatorship (1957–86) than an intimate portrayal of the lives of two brothers (Danticat's father and her uncle Joseph), their deaths in America (her father dies of pulmonary fibrosis and her uncle of acute pancreatitis in an asylum detention facility in Miami), and Edwidge's love for them both. Significant historical events are recounted not via factual narration but through the lens of private memory. For example, the end phase of the U.S. occupation of Haiti is framed through an event Danticat describes as "Uncle Joseph's most haunting childhood memory" (2007, 245)—his witnessing, in 1933, a group of young American soldiers playing football with the decapitated head of a Haitian man. Similarly, the coup d'état of February 2004, which resulted in President Jean-Bertrand Aristide's removal from office and his forced exile to the Central African Republic, at which time UN peacekeeping forces were stationed in Haiti, is not recounted directly in the narrative. Only the aftermath of the coup is related through description of a series of personal events in late October 2004 that eventually drive Uncle Joseph into exile—his church is burned down as a result of a confrontation between UN peacekeeping troops and civilians they mistake for gang members. It is thus through Uncle Joseph's recounting of this incident that Danticat broaches the controversial topic of UN "peacekeepers" taking innocent lives in attempts to restore "order" in Haiti.

These and other personal events, stories, recollections, and conversations are woven together to form the fabric of Danticat's intimate textual poetics of memory, exile, and "dangerous" telling in *Brother, I'm Dying*. Memories are passed on and kept alive from generation to generation despite the discontinuities of exile.[11] In *Create Dangerously*, she emphasizes the importance of memory for the exiled Haitian writer: "For the immigrant writer, far from home, memory becomes an even deeper abyss. . . . [W]hat happens when we cannot tell our own stories, when our memories have temporarily abandoned us? What is left is longing for something we are not even sure we ever had but are certain we will never experience again. . . . How does one write under these conditions?" (2010, 65). The central role of memory in life writing has been put forward by critics such as James Olney, who famously defined autobiography as "the life imitated or recounted" via "the faculty of memory . . . that captures or recaptures, constitutes or reconstitutes that life" (1980, 237). In a similar vein, Georges Gusdorf wrote positively about the ways in which memory allows "a certain remove" that enables the writer "to take into consideration the ins and outs" of past experiences when setting them down in an autobiographical work. By addressing the ambivalent nature of migrant memory—a repository of nostalgic longing, yet simultaneously an "abyss" of "mis-memory" and nonmemory—Danticat subverts such straightforward processes of memory and retrieval, of "recounting" and "reconstituting," that Olney and Gusdorf traditionally conceive as central to the project of life writing. *Brother, I'm Dying* also departs from Gusdorf's insistence that an autobiographical work should be "complete and coherent," that it should "recompose and reinterpret a life in its totality" (1980, 38). For Danticat, the act of retelling is a political one, not merely one that aims at a comprehensive depiction of events.

To come back to Danticat's question above, how indeed does the immigrant writer, "far from home," write under such conditions of unreliable and fallible memory? Danticat offers an answer in the penultimate essay of *Create Dangerously*, which takes the reader back to a public execution in Port-au-Prince, Haiti, on the afternoon of November 12, 1964. As this is the same scene with which the first essay in the collection begins, the reader is made once again to witness the deaths of Marcel Numa and Louis Drouin, two young Haitian exiles who, upon their return, were executed by François "Papa Doc" Duvalier for their guerilla efforts to topple his dictatorship. In this later essay, however, the perspective of the execution shifts to that of a young boy, Daniel Morel, who, after witnessing the execution, picks up the bloody spectacles that Drouin had been wearing. Danticat writes, "Perhaps if he had kept them, he might have cleaned the lenses and raised them to his face, to try to see the world the way it might have been reflected in a dead man's eyes" (2010, 137). As one critic has observed, "While Morel may not have peered through Drouin's glasses, an alternative perspective is drawn, one that transforms the official event-that-silences into a story of creation" (Duchanaud 2011).

It is this possibility of an alternative perspective of Haitian history, and thus a different narrative of the nation, that Danticat's writing offers—a perspective, one might argue, that requires peering through someone else's glasses and necessitates a certain amount of distance, of remove, of being in exile, perhaps, that challenges officially sanctioned narratives and chronicles of Haitian political history. More specifically, when voices of political dissent are silenced in Haiti and hence prevented from telling their stories, it is the task of the writer in exile to do so for them. In this respect, writers in exile continue to inhabit the ideological spaces of the native country metaphorically, even if they do not do so physically. They occupy, as Danticat terms it, a "floating homeland," which "joins all Haitians living outside of Haiti, in the *dyaspora*" (2010, 49). Thus, for Danticat, a physical departure from the geopolitical entity of Haiti does not preclude a continuation to reside in, to use a term by Edward Said once again, its "imaginative geographies."[12]

DANY LAFERRIÈRE: THE POETICS OF RELATION AND THE ENIGMA OF RETURN

As Montreal-based Dany Laferrière's writings, too, attest, writing from a position of remove can equip the author with a considerable "depth of field" of observation,[13] the likes of which Salman Rushdie describes in his essay "Imaginary Homelands": "If literature is in part the business of finding new angles at which to enter reality, then again our distance, our long geographical perspective, may provide us with such angles" (1991, 15). In Laferrière's recent autobiographical novel of prose poetry, *The Return* (2009), the narrator, who is also named Dany Laferrière and living in exile in Montreal, confesses

> What's for sure is that
> I wouldn't have written this way had I stayed behind.
> Maybe I wouldn't have written at all. (22)

Thus, exile, it seems, gives the writer a reason not only to write but to write the way he does—to "find new angles at which to enter reality" with a sense of urgency, with a lack of, to recall Edward Said's description, "composure and serenity." As the narrator of Dany Laferrière's *The Return* recalls, "As soon as I open my mouth, vowels and consonants pour out in a disorderly mess and I have stopped trying to control it. I discipline myself enough to try writing, but after a dozen lines I stop out of exhaustion" (12–13). When he is not fervidly writing, the narrator spends his time reading Aimé Césaire's *Notebook of a Return to the Native Land* in the bathtub. Upon hearing of his father's death, and in the days of preparation for his departure to Haiti that follow, it is through Césaire's long poem that Dany the narrator finds a moment of respite, of repose, of sleep, which he describes as "the only way / to return to the country / with [his] momentous news" (11).

It is through Césaire's *Notebook of a Return to the Native Land* that the narrator first metaphorically returns to Haiti after his father's death, even before he physically returns to the land of his birth. Maintaining what Édouard

Glissant terms a "poetics of relation"[14] to his native country, Dany Laferrière the narrator (and, by extension, Dany Laferrière the author) thus transforms the experiences of loss, separation, and departure that accompany exile into what Edward Said terms "an indefinitely postponed drama of return" (2001, 142). This sense of postponement, of time drawn out, is formally reflected in the structure of *The Return*, which is divided into two sections—the first, titled "Slow Preparations for Departure," spans a good fifty pages before it is followed by the second, titled simply, "A Return." In the first section, the narrator receives a telephone call in the middle of the night announcing that his father, who fled Haiti in the 1960s fearing persecution for his political activities, has died in New York. As he makes his preparations to journey back to Baradères, the Haitian village of his father's birth, to bring back his spirit, the narrator muses over the nature of exile and contemplates how one returns from exile. "Far from our country," he asks, "do we write to console ourselves?" expressing "doubts about the vocation of the writer in exile" (2011, 22).

The Return might thus be described as an extended meditation on the vocation of the writer in exile. As an exile narrative, it exists at a tangent to the narratives of the (Haitian and American) nation. The text suggests that a central part of the exiled writer's vocation involves engaging with a need, to quote Salman Rushdie once again, "to reclaim, to look back [upon]" a history, a place of origin, to (re)capture, "reflect," and depict that world with a sense of "imaginative truth" (1991, 10), while acknowledging the constraints of fallible memory and fragmented vision. Such work is creative, dangerous, and inherently political. It demands a perspective not only of detachment and distance that enables, to borrow a term from photography, a "deep perspective," but also one of openness and critical inquiry that hinges upon an understanding of the multiplicity of national histories and political discourses. To return to Edward Said, such a "plurality of vision" is one that enables "an awareness of simultaneous dimensions, an awareness that—to borrow a phrase from music—is *contrapuntal*" (2001, 148). For the writer or artist in exile, Said claims, life in the new environment is lived contrapuntally, or coexistently, simultaneously, against the memory of life in the old. It is this sense of contrapuntal awareness that the narrator of Dany Laferrière's *The Return* inhabits, one that does not fade away even after he has returned to Haiti. In fact, at one point, he reflects:

> suddenly I think of Montreal
> the way I would think

of Port-au-Prince when I was in Montreal.
We always think of what's missing. (2011, 119)

The narrator Dany's return is thus not "simply" a homecoming. For one thing, he stays in a hotel that he knows only tourists stay at, falls prey to bouts of diarrhea in the first week, feels like a "foreigner even in the city of my birth" (2011, 119), and is stared at by neighborhood children "as if I were a strange apparition" when he tries to speak to them in Haitian Creole. It is at this point that the narrator realizes that "speaking Creole is not enough / to become Haitian." Ironically, he realizes, "You can be Haitian only *outside* of Haiti" (147; my emphasis)—that is, when the language you speak and write becomes a marker of difference, when you are perceived as foreign and different, then the urge to tell your country's (hi)story becomes all the more strong.

To declare that one can be Haitian only outside of Haiti seems, at first, to be a counterintuitive claim to make. Put into the sociopolitical context of the Haitian diaspora, though, it begins to make sense that the geographical/territorial space of lòt bò dlo that Edwidge Danticat writes of is the only inventive space from which the exiled artist can continue creating dangerously, writing her or his "imaginary homeland,"[15] her or his "Haiti of the mind" into being. It is in this way that Dany Laferrière the author negotiates a space of cultural belonging within the text itself—interwoven into the protagonist's narrative of return. Such a strategy posits a diasporic, post-territorial understanding of national identity, one that ties in with Laferrière's own deliberate self-fashioning, interestingly, as an *American* (and not Haitian or Canadian) writer, and that manifests itself in his lifelong project of (re)writing the "American autobiography" (his multinovel series *Une autobiographie américaine*, of which *The Return* is part).[16]

Toward the end of *The Return*, Dany Laferrière poses the following question:

If we return to the point of departure
does that mean
the journey is over? (2011, 182)

Although the novel deceptively ends with an answer in the affirmative when the narrator arrives in Les Abricots, the village where he had been raised by his grandmother, it is the opposite that, I would suggest, holds true. On

January 12, 2010, a 7.0 magnitude earthquake hit Haiti, devastating its capital, Port-au-Prince. An estimated 316,000 people died (this is the official, though disputed, figure released by the Haitian government) and 1 million were made homeless. As Edwidge Danticat writes in *Create Dangerously*, which she dedicated to the victims of the disaster, "after the earthquake, the way we read and the way we write, both inside and outside of Haiti, will never be the same. . . . [P]erhaps we will write with the same fervor and intensity (or even more) as before. Perhaps we will write with the same sense of fearlessness or hope. Perhaps we will continue to create as dangerously as possible, but our muse has been irreparably altered" (2010, 162). Likewise, returning to Montreal after the earthquake, Laferrière expresses how he realized his determination to "correct lazy misconceptions" (Jaggi 2013) about the Haitian nation, its political history, and its people. In this respect, the journeys of Haitian immigrant authors in exile have not yet come to an end. Retaining a "poetics of relation" (Glissant 1997a) with the physical geographies of home, these writers document and reflect/refract the experience of exile and diaspora through, in Rushdie's words, "broken mirrors" (1991, 11). This strategy of writing illustrates how the realities of exile and displacement restructure existing models of national belonging and identification, engendering "new notions of membership, solidarity and alienage" (Holston and Appadurai 1999, 10) and generating new forms of cultural citizenship. In doing so, Edwidge Danticat's memoir and Dany Laferrière's autobiography effectively broaden the scope of "national" literature in order to articulate a form of "post-territorial citizenship"[17] and diasporic belonging that transcends the boundaries of the nation-state.

12

CITIZENSHIP DEFERRED
· · · · · · · · · ·

Cherokee Freedmen versus Cherokee Nation in
Sharon Ewell Foster's *Abraham's Well* and Tiya Miles's
*Ties That Bind: The Story of an Afro-Cherokee Family
in Slavery and Freedom*

*If a tribe cannot decide the question of citizenship, there is little left of its
sovereignty. It's a basic, inherent right to determine our own citizenry. We
paid very dearly for those rights.*

> Chad Smith, former principal chief of the
> Cherokee Nation of Oklahoma, 2009

*I would not take a million dollars to give up my treaty rights and legal rights
to citizenship.*

> Marilyn Vann, president of the Descendants of Freedmen
> of the Five Civilized Tribes Association, 2007

This last chapter turns to the subject of Indigenous or tribal citizenship, in
particular, the dispute surrounding black freedmen and their contested membership in the Cherokee Nation, as encapsulated by the two opposing viewpoints above.[1] Because academic discussions of Indigenous/First Nations

nationalisms have not received as much attention as conventional studies of the national that remain within the paradigm of the modern nation-state, I will begin by examining how Indigenous notions of nationhood, kinship, community, place, and belonging in an American context[2] differ from, challenge, and revise non-Indigenous ideas of U.S. national identity.[3] Using the assertions made by Indigenous scholars that the bestowing of U.S. citizenship on Indigenous peoples was received with ambiguity,[4] and hence that "U.S. citizenship was a gift that native peoples, already citizens of their own nations, neither wanted nor needed" (Saunt 2004, 93) as my starting hypothesis, this chapter will examine how Indigenous understandings of the nation and Indigenous citizenship represent a counter-discourse to dominant non-Indigenous narratives of the American nation.[5] It will explore how Indigenous subjects—who have come to be regarded, and perhaps, to a certain extent, regard themselves, as "ambivalent Americans" because they are "neither fully inside nor fully outside the political, legal, and cultural boundaries of the United States" (Bruyneel 2004, 30)—have struggled to assert their Indigenous sovereignty and self-government from within the boundaries of the U.S. nation; so much so that Indigenous nationality runs the risk of reproducing the same potentially exclusionary/discriminatory logic that characterizes non-Indigenous national(ist) discourses on immigration.

In a twenty-first-century context in which national(ist) formations are increasingly being deconstructed, contested, and revised, what does it mean, therefore, to articulate claims to the nation (whether as a symbolic or geopolitical entity) in an Indigenous context, and to claim that political and cultural sovereignty are derived from the Creator? Accordingly, to what extent are definitions of citizenship and Indigenous nationhood as voiced in Indigenous writing viable ways of understanding community and collectivity? How are the key issues of sovereignty, nationhood, self-government, and decolonization addressed in Indigenous literature and criticism?[6] Finally, and perhaps most importantly for my present purposes, how does the exclusion of black freedmen by the Cherokee Nation, as evinced in the ongoing Cherokee freedmen versus Cherokee Nation controversy, reflect as well as complicate the objectives of Indigenous sovereignty and autonomy? It is these crucial questions that form the basis of my critical interpretations of the novel *Abraham's Well* (2006) by Sharon Ewell Foster, a descendent of Cherokee freedmen, and the historical biography *Ties That Bind: The Story of an Afro-Cherokee Family in Slavery and Freedom* (2005) by Tiya Miles in this final chapter of my study.

"I AM MARRIED TO THAT LAND": PLACE, IDENTITY, AND INDIGENOUS CITIZENSHIP

In *Our Fire Survives the Storm: A Cherokee Literary History*, Cherokee literary critic and activist Daniel Heath Justice contends that Indigenous understandings of cultural and national identity, kinship ties and genealogies, tradition and heritage, of collective living in the Kituwah spirit, must be distinguished from non-Indigenous paradigms of the American nation.

> Nation-state nationalism is often dependent upon the erasure of kinship bonds in favor of a code of patriotism that places loyalty to the state above kinship obligations, and emphasizes the assimilative military history of the nation (generally along a progressivist mythological arc) above the specific geographic, genealogical, and spiritual histories of the people. . . . By contrast, Indigenous nationhood is a concept rooted in community values, histories, and traditions that, at the same time, assert a sense of active sociopolitical agency. . . . Indigenous nationhood . . . challenges the assimilative foundations of state nationalism by its assertion of an inherent distinction based on tradition, culture, language, and relationship to the world and its various peoples. Fundamental to this distinction is the ability of Indigenous nationalism to extend recognition to other sovereignties without that recognition implying a necessary need to consume, displace, or become absorbed by those nations. (2006, 23)

Whether such a clear-cut distinction between Indigenous and non-Indigenous U.S. nationhoods can be drawn is a question that will be considered later on in the course of this chapter. For now, it is significant that Indigenous scholars such as Justice have argued for the "analysis, interpretation, and dissemination of Indigenous literatures" (Justice et al. 2008, 149) according to principles of Indigenous nationhood. This critical opinion motivates Justice's reading of Indigenous literature as an expression of resistance and rebellion again the "assimilationist directive of Eurowestern imperialism" (2006, 8).

The notion of kinship in the quote above is important because it is not only a kinship among the members of an Indigenous tribe but kinship with the land on which they live that distinguishes the model of Indigenous nationhood. In other words, the connection between place and identity is crucial to Indigenous cultures. Citing Craig S. Womack's observation that "land, more than a matter of ownership (which was inimical to a traditional Cherokee worldview), is an identity marker, literally an indicator of Cherokee national citizenship," Daniel Heath Justice points out that the Indigenous belief in the communal "ownership" and right of access of land renders the latter not only a material but also a spiritual and symbolic marker of identity and belonging (2006, 101). The Trail of Tears (*Nunna Daul Isunyi*), or the forced relocation of Indigenous tribes from their homes in the southeastern states to Indian Territory west of the Mississippi River between the years 1831 and 1839 in the wake of the Indian Removal Act of 1830, is thus a central event in Indigenous history: not only was it physically harrowing, it represented a deracination of the five Indigenous tribes (the Cherokee being one of them) from their sacred land. This forced diaspora not only resulted in the death of more than ten thousand Indigenous people, it signified a loss of political and territorial sovereignty, a severance of connection to the land of the ancestors, and a coerced assimilation to Euro-American values and systems of land allotment and individual property ownership. For the Cherokee, this involuntary acculturation was perceived as an assault on their cultural and political distinctiveness and as an infringement of the principles of sovereignty and self-determination of the historical Cherokee Nation.

The significance of the latter came to a head in 1906 when the U.S. government declared the dissolution of the original Cherokee Nation as a precondition of Oklahoma statehood (Justice 2006, 21). Attempts to rebuild the nation took place in the 1930s in conjunction with President Franklin D. Roosevelt's Indian Reorganization Act of 1934, which restored communal tribal land rights and local self-government, leading to issues of Indigenous sovereignty and self-governance emerging at the forefront of the Cherokee Nation's political agenda. This resulted in the establishment of the modern Cherokee Nation, whose constitution was ratified in 1976 and which has its seat in Tahlequah, Oklahoma. Since then, the U.S. Congress and the nation's federal and state courts have upheld the sovereignty of the Cherokee Nation.[7] Yet this principle of self-determination and Indigenous sovereignty continues to be challenged by several issues.

One of these is the heated dispute over the right to Cherokee citizenship for the descendants of black Cherokee freedmen, which remains unresolved.[8] Cherokee freedmen are the descendants of black slaves owned by citizens of the Cherokee Nation before the American Civil War. In 1838–39, many of them walked the Trail of Tears with their Cherokee masters from the southeastern states, crossing the Mississippi River to Indian Territory in the Midwest. Significantly, Indian Territory was never recognized by the U.S. government as an "organized incorporated territory of the United States" (this recognition was a prerequisite to the conferral of statehood). Indian Territory was thus not officially under the jurisdiction of the United States and therefore not subject to the Thirteenth and Fourteenth amendments to the U.S. Constitution in the aftermath of the Civil War that abolished slavery and granted U.S. citizenship to all persons born or naturalized in the United States, including ex-slaves, in 1865 and 1868 respectively. As a result, a separate treaty had to be signed in 1866 that applied to Indian Territory. The problem, however, was the ongoing split in the Cherokee Nation between pro-Union and pro-Confederate supporters that effectively meant a difference of opinion about slavery. This remained unresolved despite the declaration that John Ross, the principal chief of the Cherokee Nation, had already signed decreeing the abolishment of slavery in the Cherokee Nation in February 1863,[9] soon after the U.S. Emancipation Proclamation of 1862.[10]

The split between pro-Union and pro-Confederate Cherokees at the time of the Treaty of 1866 reflected an internal disagreement over issues of Cherokee sovereignty (which, some argued, included the right to decide who had access to membership in the community), Indigenous values, kinship, and cultural continuity. The pro-Union faction, led by Principal Chief John Ross, wanted to adopt freedmen into the Cherokee Nation and assign land to them, while the pro-Confederate party, led by Stand Watie and Elias Cornelius Boudinot, favored separate status for a southern Cherokee Nation and wanted the U.S. government to pay for the relocation of freedmen out of the Cherokee Nation (Sturm 1998, 232). When the leaders of the two factions met with U.S. Commissioner of Indian Affairs Dennis N. Cooley at Fort Smith, Arkansas, their internal disagreements were ignored by the U.S. delegation and the Cherokee were addressed as one entity. The U.S. commission insisted that the Cherokee abolish slavery and grant the black freedmen full Cherokee citizenship, with rights to land and annuities. That specific clause in the treaty reads: "[The Cherokee Nation] further agree that all freedmen who have been liberated by voluntary act of their former owners or by law, as well as all free colored persons who were in the country at the commencement of the rebellion, and are now residents therein, or who may return within six months, and their descendants, shall have all the rights of native Cherokees."[11] In order to dispel any ambiguities about what exactly "the rights of native Cherokees" comprised, an amendment was made to article 4, section 5 of the 1839 Cherokee Nation Constitution that read: "All native born Cherokees, all Indians, and whites legally members of the Nation by adoption, *and all freedmen who have been liberated by voluntary act of their former owners or by law,* . . . and their descendants, who reside within the limits of the Cherokee Nation, *shall be taken and deemed to be, citizens of the Cherokee Nation*" (Cherokee Nation 1998, 31; my emphasis). Thus black freedmen were to be accorded the right of citizenship of the Cherokee Nation.[12]

Despite this formulation, the citizenship of black freedmen has repeatedly been contested by members of the Cherokee Nation who petition to uphold the "Cherokee by blood" rule. Although there are no blood quantum limitations[13] for tribal citizenship in the Cherokee Nation today, this has not always been the case. In 1985, for example, Principal Chief Wilma Mankiller issued an executive order requiring all enrolled citizens of the Cherokee Nation to have a CDIB (certificate of degree of Indian blood) card. Cherokee citizenship was thus granted only to individuals with a direct ancestor on the "Cherokee-by-Blood" Dawes Commission Rolls. As a result, about twenty-five thousand freedmen were excluded from citizenship of the Cherokee Nation and stripped of their right to vote in tribal elections. In the current version of the Constitution of the Cherokee Nation, article 4 on "Citizenship" states that "all citizens of the Cherokee Nation must be original enrollees or descendants of original enrollees listed on the Dawes Commission Rolls."[14] In adoption cases, eligibility for a federal CDIB and Cherokee Nation tribal citizenship must be proven "through the biological parent to the enrolled ancestor."[15] Examples of individual cases of legal claims made by descendants of Cherokee freedmen against the Cherokee Nation include *Rev. Roger N. Nero* (1989), *Riggs v. Ummerteskee* (2001), *Marilyn Vann et al. v. Ken Salazar* (2003), *Allen v. Cherokee Nation Tribal Council* (2004), and *Cherokee Nation v. Raymond Nash et al.* (2009). In all of these cases, the opponents of tribal citizenship for freedmen descendants justified their position as one in line with preserving the sovereignty and self-determination of the Cherokee Nation, which included the freedom to decide who constituted its citizenry.[16]

Paradoxically, therefore, at the same time that the Cherokee Nation asserts its Indigenous sovereignty, which includes an emphasis on a distinctive tradition, culture, language, kinship, and collectivity over the individual, the claim that it has the right, as a nation, to decide its own citizenry effectively replicates the logic of modern nation-state formations, whose discourses and legal processes control and regulate the right to citizenship. This is significant if one considers the fact that, historically, the notion of legal citizenship in an Indigenous Cherokee context arose later than in a U.S. context. As Fay A. Yarbrough points out, in the eighteenth century, the Cherokees defined citizenship less rigidly than in the present day and their "ideas of race and identity were still fluid and negotiable" (2008, 25).[17] Yarbrough summarizes, "[T]he Cherokees subscribed to more performative definitions of citizenship and race while Americans understood race as a biological fact" (68). It was therefore not until in the early nineteenth century that the Cherokees passed laws to organize their nation, drawing up "provisions defining membership in the Nation, outlining voter eligibility, regulating property ownership, establishing criminal behavior and punishment, and standardizing marriage" (15). The most significant of these actions was the drawing up of the Constitution of the Cherokee Nation in 1827. Based on the American Constitution, it established formal structures of governance modeled after U.S. legal and political institutions.[18] According to this Constitution, citizenship could be conferred on a spouse via marriage, but marriage was prohibited between Cherokees and slaves and later with black freedmen. The Cherokee Nation's ability to regulate its marriage laws served on the one hand, therefore, as a demonstration of its sovereignty (12) and on the other as a way of limiting citizenship because the population determined the size of land allocated and the amount of annuity payments (the result of treaty agreements between the U.S. federal government and the Indigenous nations) made to each citizen. The inclusion of new members into the Cherokee Nation through intermarriage and later the adoption of black freedmen would hence put further pressures on already strained resources. When, in the aftermath of the Civil War, the U.S. federal government required the Cherokee Nation to grant its black freedmen tribal citizenship, the nation responded by "legally re-defining Cherokee citizenship and creating new categories of citizens with varying legal rights" (93). As a result, Cherokee freedmen were not afforded all the rights of Cherokee citizens by birth or by blood.

The Fourteenth Amendment to the U.S. Constitution, which conferred citizenship rights upon "all persons born or naturalized in the United States, and subject to the jurisdiction thereof," was thus not only fiercely contested by the Southern states but also regarded as highly problematic by Indigenous nations, which felt that they were sovereign nations not subject to the jurisdiction of the U.S. federal government. Although tribal sovereignty[19] and local self-determination were acknowledged by the federal government,[20] Indigenous nations were, and still are, regarded as "domestic dependent nations." This status differentiates them from "foreign" nations and diminishes their rights of sovereignty and self-government. The exclusion of black Cherokee freedmen, as evinced in the ongoing Cherokee Nation versus Cherokee freedmen controversy, can thus be understood partly as a repercussion of the limitations placed on Cherokee autonomy and self-determination by the U.S. government. On August 21, 2011, the Cherokee Nation Supreme Court upheld a referendum passed in 2007 that rejected the notion that the Treaty of 1866 granted black freedmen citizenship in the Cherokee Nation. As a result, twenty-eight hundred Cherokee freedmen lost their citizenship and food and medical benefits granted by this status. In response to the Cherokee Supreme Court ruling, the U.S. Department of Housing and Urban Development suspended US$33 million in funds to the Cherokee Nation, an act that made the Cherokee Nation "agree" to reinstate the citizenship of black freedmen, including their right to vote in general elections. Despite this ruling, the issue remains largely unresolved, with the descendants of black freedmen continuing to face exclusion, prejudice, and nonrecognition within the Cherokee Nation.

Although the debate remains unsettled, some Indigenous scholars have suggested a way out of the impasse. Circe Sturm, for instance, views the Cherokee freedmen dispute not as an irresolvable conflict between Indigenous sovereignty and racial justice/equality but as a case study that opens up alternative ways of thinking about identity politics within both Indigenous and non-Indigenous frameworks. In seeking to examine how "Cherokee identity is socially and politically constructed around hegemonic notions of blood, color, race, and culture that permeate discourses of social belonging in the United States," Sturm makes the critical observation that "Cherokee Freedmen . . . who choose to identify as both Indian and Black challenge the prevailing racial ideologies that ask us to 'choose one' racial or ethnic identity, often at the expense of another" (2002, 224). Sturm's argument is convincing to the extent that freedmen's identification as both black *and* Cherokee offers a radical alternative to the "either/or" mentality pervading the discourse of Indigenous citizenship that, likewise, remains entrenched in categorical debates around the issues of sovereignty and self-determination. Yet clearly, the continued denial of both legal and substantive Cherokee citizenship and its full rights (including voting and marriage rights) to descendants of black

Cherokee freedmen continues to represent a very real and pressing problem that a transcending of the either/or, mutually exclusive mentality does not "solve" satisfactorily.

Perhaps it would be helpful, therefore, to shift the critical lens and reframe the Cherokee freedmen debate within the broader discourses of citizenship and belonging in a twenty-first-century context in which national formations are increasingly being deconstructed, contested, and revised, especially in a North American framework. Specifically, how does the Cherokee freedmen issue shed light on different perceptions and understandings of the nation (whether as a geopolitical or symbolic entity) in an Indigenous context? Can the exclusion of the descendants of black freedmen and the firm avowals to defend the sovereignty of the Cherokee Nation be read as an attempt to preserve Indigenous ideas of nation, community, and membership against a scenario in which the significance of non-Indigenous nation-states has declined in an age of globalizing processes that have produced transnational and post-national forms of identification and collectivity? Or ought it be understood as a reiteration of the histories of disenfranchisement, exclusion, and colonization that the Indigenous tribes themselves suffered at the hands of the U.S. federal government? What are the limits of Indigenous autonomy, and do the rights of tribal citizenship include the right to deny this citizenship to some? In the following, I will explore how these questions continue to inform and complicate expressions of Indigenous belonging and identity in two literary texts: Sharon Ewell Foster's novel *Abraham's Well* and Tiya Miles's historical biography, *Ties That Bind*.

"EVEN THE MOST PAINFUL PARTS MUST BE TOLD": THE TRAIL OF TEARS AND THE ETHICS OF NARRATION

In Sharon Ewell Foster's *Abraham's Well*, a novel that the author claims is a work of fiction "inspired by true events and accounts" (2006, 330), the protagonist, Armentia, recounts her experiences as a black Cherokee girl along with those of the other members of her Cherokee clan, the Deer tribe. As the daughter of black slaves who work for Mama Emma and Papa, their Cherokee owners, Armentia is initially treated well by them, but "things changed" (17) with the Indian Removal Act in 1830. The tribulations Armentia suffers from then on include forced relocation across the Mississippi River on the Trail of Tears in 1838–39; the experiences of her brother, Abraham, and herself being sold, enduring rape and childbirth, only to have her son taken away from her and also sold; moving with her owners, the McDowells, to Texas, a slave state that joined the Confederacy during the Civil War; and enduring the long journey back to Indian Territory in Oklahoma in the aftermath of the Civil War when slavery is abolished in the United States.

Via Armentia's first-person narration, in which she recalls her life story in retrospect as an old woman, *Abraham's Well* broaches familiar themes and concerns: the relationship between place and identity; the sacredness of the land of the ancestors; the significance of community and collectivity over individuality; the importance of family ties, clan, and kinship; and the determination to uphold the Cherokee Nation's sovereignty and self-determination. In central passages throughout the novel, the Cherokee characters reaffirm their connection to the land that has been bequeathed to them by the Creator. When missionaries come to visit the Cherokees to encourage them to voluntarily move from the southeastern states to land that has been "set aside" for them by the U.S. government west of the Mississippi, Armentia's father, a black Cherokee, firmly repeats that he is "married to that land" (2006, 63) on which he has built his home and is not leaving or giving it up. In a poignant passage, Armentia echoes her father's words when she recalls their journey on the Trail of Tears: "They removed us. That's what they called it. But it was not removal; *we were married to the land. They dragged us kicking and screaming* at gunpoint from the arms of the land, *from the arms of the one we loved.* It was all planned; it was all as sure as the rising of the sun. *We were stripped from the arms of our beloved*, yet they wanted us to sing instead of cry" (84; my emphasis).

As Sharon Ewell Foster is a well-known writer of Christian fiction, and *Abraham's Well* was published by Bethany House, it should come as no surprise that much of the imagery and descriptions in the novel draws on biblical allusions.[21] In the quotation above, for example, the biblical imagery of marriage is used as part of the figural discourse of identity and belonging. With reference to Mark 10:6–9, in which it is written, "[W]hat God has joined together, let man not separate," the significance of being separated from one's ancestral land becomes an unnatural and sinful act committed by the U.S. government.

Indigenous belief in the sacredness of the land of the Principal People, the land that carries the "bones and dust of our fathers" (Foster 2006, 80), is significant because it represents a direct form of counter-discourse to non-Indigenous U.S. exceptionalist narratives that, from the earliest beginnings in John Winthrop's vision of a "City upon a Hill" in 1630,[22] perceived the New World as land given to the Puritans by God in order to start anew, away from the "ills" of the Church of England. Such narratives have, over the centuries, adopted images of the homeland to construct a unified sense of national identity through a process of what Hayden White has termed "emplotment" (1973), which refers to the organization of a series of historical events into a narrative with a plot. Or, as Stuart Hall contends, "Just as individuals and families construct their identities in part by 'storying' the various random incidents and contingent turning points of their lives into a single, coherent, narrative, so nations construct identities by selectively binding their chosen high points and memorable achievements into an unfolding 'national story'" (2002, 74). Such "national stories" or emplotments, however, gloss over the histories and cultures of Indigenous peoples, which predated the arrival of the Puritans in New England on the *Mayflower* in November 1620. They also often gloss over regional, cultural, religious, and ethnic differences in order to present a unique "American" national identity embedded within a larger unified narrative of national progress and sovereignty.[23] By Armentia's reiteration of her firm intention to "tell my story" (Foster 2006, 14), even though it is "a hard story to tell" (81), because "even the most painful parts must be told" (111), the novel's first-person testimonial narrative[24] becomes a form of counter-storytelling and the narrative site of black Indigenous resistance that counters the exclusionary logic of both Indigenous and non-Indigenous U.S. concepts of nationhood and citizenship in the nineteenth century.

In keeping with the literary convention of slave testimonial and witness narratives, such as Frederick Douglass's 1845 autobiography, *Narrative of the Life of Frederick Douglass*, and Harriet Jacobs's 1861 memoir, published under the pen name Linda Brent, *Incidents in the Life of a Slave Girl, Written by Herself*, Armentia promises that she will take on the responsibility of telling her reader nothing but "the *whole* truth, even if it hurt" (2006, 121):

> This is shameful to tell, but it's true. I've been trying not to tell you. No one wants to tell. . . . It is hard to tell this part of the story. So, I beg your pardon for taking so long, for crying. It's been a whole lot of years, but it's still just the same for me.
>
> I would tell the story without it, but it wouldn't be the truth without it. Even the most painful parts must be told. (110–11)

The moral imperative Armentia feels to tell the truth, to tell the story that must be told,[25] to speak fully of the harrowing, shameful moments of despair during her witnessing of the atrocities committed against her father and other members of her clan, recalls the "ethics of narration" (Booth 1990; Nussbaum 2007) previously discussed in this study. In this instance, the ethics of narration becomes part of a larger strategy of black freedmen protest against marginalization and disownership by members of the Cherokee Nation.

This is illustrated in the following passage from the first section of the novel. The white missionary Wilters has come to Armentia and her people to warn them that President Andrew Jackson has signed the Indian Removal Act of 1830 that paves the way for the forced relocation of the Cherokee westward to Indian Territory:

> Golden Bear's father . . . raised an eyebrow. "The Great One gave us this land for all to share alive; land for all, water for all. . . . It is the way of the Principal People. It is not our way . . . to own things that cannot be owned; the sky, the land, or even men. Are White men greater than the Creator?"
>
> Missionary Wilters . . . cleared his throat. "The government of the United States is sovereign. You mustn't just think of yourselves, *you must think of the whole nation.* This is for *the good of the whole nation.*"
>
> Johnnie Freeman's father looked up from where he was whittling on a piece of wood. "We are thinking of the good of *our nation . . . the Cherokee Nation.*" (2006, 63; my emphasis)

The white missionary makes the assumption that Indigenous notions of nationhood and sovereignty should be subsumed or assimilated into non-Indigenous paradigms of the modern nation-state in the interest of "the larger good." Johnnie Freeman's father's reply, however, makes it clear that he identifies not as a citizen of the American nation but as a black citizen of the Cherokee Nation. The episode can thus be read as an episode of black Indigenous "writing back" against narratives of U.S. "internal colonialism" (Marquard 1957; Gonzalez 1965; hooks 1994; Spivak 1996) that sought to homogenize and assimilate Indigenous populations in the nineteenth century. As Eva Mackey argues in her study of nationalist narratives, "Narratives of nationhood are 'discursive devices' that represent difference as unity, and which try to stitch up differences into one identity, an identity that represents everyone as belonging to the 'same great national family'" (1998, 151, citing Hall 1992, 297–99).

In Foster's novel, it is the black Cherokee characters who embody the spirit of resistance and change. Johnnie Freeman's father personifies this force of black freedmen resistance. He firmly aligns himself with his nation, the Cherokee Nation, claiming his heritage, his identity, and his membership as one of the Principal People. When the missionary Wilters tells him that, as a black freedman, he is free to choose between his black or Cherokee identity, and hence whether or not to make the arduous journey to Indian Territory, Johnnie Freeman's father says calmly that he will not give up his Cherokee identity, and that he will walk the Trail of Tears with his clan:

> Johnnie Freeman's father stopped whittling and stared at the man. "Stay here alone, just me and my family? How long you think we'll be free? . . . "Leave my people?" He touched his forearm to Golden Bear's father's arm; black against copper. "Nothing between us different that matters." He raised an eyebrow. "Hear these words I'm speaking? I speak Tsalagi. See my family, my friends? These are my people." He pointed around the circle, then pounded his chest with his fist. "These are my people! Where they go, I go!" (2006, 64)

In this passage, Johnnie Freeman's father's declaration of solidarity and unity with his Indigenous tribe, despite his lack of Cherokee blood and hence direct ancestry as well as his subordinate status as a black freedman, constitutes an alter-national act of citizenship that seeks to reconfigure the concept of nationhood along the lines of shared cultural and linguistic traditions rather than bloodlines. His self-identification as a Cherokee (as well as his emphasis on the importance of the oral tradition and his speaking of the Iroquoian language of Tsalagi) is another example of counter-storytelling in the novel, an act of resistance that speaks out against the experiences of deracination, loss, and internal division that separation from his Cherokee brothers and sisters would cause.

One other example of counter-storytelling in *Abraham's Well* emerges in the form of the practice of quilting. When Armentia is separated from her family and sold into slavery, she turns to the African American tradition of quilting in order to preserve her cultural and personal memories. In a performative act of vocally asserting her black Indigenous identity, she speaks the language of her Cherokee people as she sews so as not forget it: "Every stitch I sewed was a memory" (2006, 142), Armentia recalls. As numerous scholarly studies have demonstrated, African American story-quilts serve as a repository of counter-memories that challenge the erasure of the brutal histories of slavery that have either been suppressed or remain unacknowledged and unredressed. In the period of the American Civil War, quilts were made to raise funds to support the abolitionist cause. Antislavery poems and aphorisms were also often stitched into the quilts to illustrate the plight of black slaves.[26] Armentia's practice of quilting thus serves a double purpose—as a form of Indigenous cultural expression and remembrance and as a means of literally recording the trauma of black slavery in the stiches and the fabric of history. In section 2 of the novel, when Armentia is returned home to her family (though not permanently), she and her mother sew blankets that they then sell at the marketplace for a few pennies in order to save up enough money to buy some land. Although their hopes are dashed when their Cherokee owner, Mama Emma, discovers the jar full of pennies and smashes it to the ground, injuring Armentia's mother fatally with one of its broken shards, the third section of the novel enacts the fulfillment of Armentia's father's promise that one day she will own her own plot of land on which she will build a well.

Foster's novel ends with a fictional depiction of the real-life historical land rush of April 22, 1889, in Oklahoma, where approximately 2 million acres of choice unassigned land in Indian Territory were opened up to (mainly white) settlement.[27] In line with the author's Christian beliefs, hope and faith prevail, and the novel has a happy ending. Armentia is reunited with her descendants, the children and grandchildren of her son, Abraham Proof,[28] who have come back looking for her. Participating in the land run on her behalf, as they are U.S. citizens by paternal lineage, they claim ownership of a plot of good land and symbolically stick a flag into the ground. When they carry Armentia to the land to see it, she gives praise and thanks to the Great Spirit and the Good Lord, recalling Psalm 126, "When the Lord turned again the captivity of Zion, we were like them that dream." At the end of the novel, Armentia affirms her black Cherokee identity:

> I come from people who come from over the seas and I am also Cherokee, one of the Principal People. They may no longer know me, I may be in exile, but I know who I am. And I believe that someday they will call me home.
>
> I walked the Trail of Tears. I lost my mother, my father, my sweet Johnnie Freeman, and The One Who Guards His Family [her older brother Abraham].

I walked a thousand miles. I am still Black. I am still Cherokee.
I have a son named Abraham. (2006, 316)

The novel closes with a description of Armentia and her descendants digging a well on her land, hence fulfilling her father's prophesy, and naming it Abraham's Well. Despite the hardships she has faced, the traumatic experiences, including include slavery, rape, betrayal, disownment, the death of her family, exile, and forced relocation, Armentia lives to tell her tale, to tell it for the others who have not survived to tell their stories. As Sharon Ewell Foster writes in a postscript to the novel, "I began writing to tell . . . the story of African Americans on the Trail, those that were servants to the despised; *to speak in slave narrative format*—more episodic than driven by dates or locations—*so that I could give voice to a story rarely told*" (325; my emphasis).

Interestingly, despite the author's own description of her speaking "in slave narrative format," the novel's reliance on mimetic representation and traditional historiography shares more in common with forms of witness and religious narratives than postmodern slave narratives such as Ishmael Reed's *Flight to Canada* (1976), Octavia Butler's *Kindred* (1979), Samuel Delany's *Stars in My Pocket Like Grains of Sand* (1984), or Toni Morrison's *Beloved* (1987). These postmodern narratives, as A. Timothy Spaulding has contended, set out to counter the nineteenth-century slave narrative's reliance on realism and objectivity by "creating alternative histories based on subjective, fantastic, and non-realistic representations of slavery" (2005, 154). Eschewing narrative linearity and clear distinctions between past and present, these narratives imply that forms of modern-day oppression, neo-imperialism, and racial prejudice still exist. They depict the harrowing, unreal, incoherent, fractured experiences of slavery, the points at which words failed to construe "reality." In comparison, Armentia's (and, by extension, the author's) insistence on telling the truth of what happened in linear fashion presents her story not only as one of struggle and ultimate victory but as a complete, authoritative narrative without any reference to possible gaps in knowledge or the unreliability of memory.

Indeed, the novel's ending on a note of triumph renders it problematic because the narrative enacts the very cultural assimilation and "internal colonialism" that it purportedly resists, hence undermining its project of foregrounding black Indigenous identity as a site of resistance to dominant discourses of both Indigenous and non-Indigenous U.S. nationhood. The end of the novel is particularly awkward because of the way in which Armentia's father's dreams of owning his own plot of land are fulfilled. This is enacted not via a reinstating of land to the black Cherokee, land that had been taken away from them as a result of the Indian Removal Act (and reinforced by their inability, as slaves, to own any possessions, including property), but through an act of domestic imperialism unique to the United States. When Armentia's descendants participate in the land run and claim their own plot of land, driving a flag into the ground to signify ownership, the episode effectively represents the assimilation of Cherokee ways of communal ownership of the land (or, more accurately, bequeathal to the community) to a non-Indigenous U.S. system of land ownership that entails obtaining land deeds and "parcel[ing] out the land, let[ting] each man stake his claim" (2006, 43). Alternatively, a different reading equally problematically suggests that the novel's closing episode reenacts the dispossession of the Cherokee and the acquisition of their land—to the gain of the black Cherokee freedmen, who have now indirectly "chosen" being black over being Indigenous.

The question therefore arises if the form and structure of Foster's novel—the linear progression of Armentia's life story from trauma to, ultimately, fulfillment and reunification with her descendants, and the message of Christian hope and faith that the end of the novel conveys—are compatible with its gesture of acknowledgment and redress, of "tell[ing] the tale," the legacy, of black Cherokee freedmen and their descendants who have been marginalized and excluded on the grounds of their race and skin color. Specifically, the novel's mimetic depiction of the experiences of the black Cherokee ultimately fails to constitute a harsh critique of slavery or its legacy in the ongoing plight of the descendants of Cherokee freedmen who are still being denied their full rights of citizenship in the Cherokee Nation. The novel fails to compel its readers to "confront slavery, not as a distant and containable moment, but as a precursor to the present" (Spaulding 2005, 26–27). Instead, it champions the Christian values of patience, endurance, courage, hope, and faith that lead to an overcoming of the protagonists' desperate circumstances, to a survival of the wrongs and traumas of slavery. The protagonist Armentia's transition from "rags to riches" also awkwardly follows the conventional narrative pattern of the American Dream, which reinforces the national ideology of American exceptionalism.

Additionally, the storyline of *Abraham's Well* closely mimics the archetypal form of the traditional slave narrative in which the slave writes her- or himself into being through the process of self-education and literacy (Spaulding 2005, 30). The novel ends with Armentia declaring in an assuaging tone,

> I've had some sorrow in my life. You know all about my loss, but I've had a lot of gain. . . . In my heart, I still have all my family and even the land that was stolen from us. I don't have Africa, and my Cherokee still claim they don't know who I am.
>
> Still, I got no more more secrets bottled up inside me. . . . And I feel mighty good about that.
>
> And that girl, Emma, she even taught me to read. (2006, 315)

This is awkward because, in this closing passage of the novel, writing becomes a "romantic" act that depicts the humanity of the black slave—who is taught how to read and write by a white, upper-middle-class girl—rather than a mode of critiquing the marginalization of the descendants of black freedmen by the Cherokee Nation. In addition, the reader is encouraged to identify with Armentia through her first-person narrative account of her life story, which places hope, courage, and faith in the goodness of the (Christian) Creator above all other emotions and beliefs. When atrocities are described in the novel, they become episodes of heightened emotional release or its opposite—the reader, like Armentia, too, is variously choked by fear, "los[es] the courage to be angry" (92), and becomes "numb" (112). At only one point in the novel does Armentia overcome her fear, recalling her mother's voice in her ear, "Sometimes even deer must stand and fight" (274)—when she comes face-to-face with a big grizzly bear during her journey with the other slaves and servants of the McDowell family southward toward Texas.[29]

Sharon Ewell Foster's *Abraham's Well* is thus an example of a contemporary neo-slave narrative that tells the tale of a members of a black Cherokee family who walked the Trail of Tears alongside their clansmen and kin. The novel is based on true events and accounts as well as on the author's own archival research into her family ancestry. Foster includes a bibliography of scholarship and sources (mostly online resources) at the end of the book, encouraging her readers to read more about the Cherokee Nation, the Trail of Tears, African and Native American relations, and the Cherokee freedmen controversy. This call to further research and reading, while commendable, nonetheless seems at odds with the preceding long tale of Armentia and her family, which, together with a note from the author about her own ancestry and investment in the freedmen debate, amounts to little more than a personal testimony of the Christian faith rather than a social critique of the double marginalization of black Cherokee subjects by both Indigenous and non-Indigenous concepts of nationhood and citizenship. The didactic tone of the end of the book also reflects a curiously individual rather than collective experience, and hence reveals the work as a fictional exploration of one woman's journey from slavery into freedom against all odds rather than a critical commentary on the complex issues of sovereignty and self-determination, race, ethnicity, kinship, place, and community that factor into contemporary discussions of Indigenous nationhood, citizenship, and belonging.

TIES THAT BIND: BLOOD, RACE, KINSHIP, AND CHEROKEE CITIZENSHIP

In contrast, *Ties That Bind: The Story of an Afro-Cherokee Family in Slavery and Freedom* by Indigenous studies scholar Tiya Miles exemplifies a very different mode of critical narration, one that transcends a mere replication of the structures of inclusion and exclusion that have inscribed the discourse of white settler democracy in the United States faced by Indigenous tribes.[30] By uncovering the complex structures of "internal colonialism" as well as the racialized discourses of social oppression and disenfranchisement that affect *both* Indigenous and black American populations, Miles's biography also offers a "solution" to the conundrum that Indigenous notions of nationhood, sovereignty, and citizenship actually share quite a few similarities with their non-Indigenous American counterparts. In recounting the Cherokees' institution of black slavery within their own internally colonized nation, *Ties That Bind* adopts a resolute stance to the Cherokee freedmen controversy by suggesting that the Cherokee Nation could resolve the issue through a radical act of sovereignty that bestows the status of full citizenship, and its accompanying rights, on the black freedmen. In this respect, Tiya Miles voices the opinion of other Indigenous scholars who contend that

> the inclusion of the Freedmen . . . does not need to be framed as an issue of competition over scarce resources, an attack on [Indigenous] sovereignty, or a reenactment of the removal from traditional homelands that casts Freedmen as intruders threatening the rights and lands of traditional peoples. Rather, it is a unique opportunity for the colonized Southeastern Indian nations to enact the kinship

sovereignties that have for so long been part of [Indigenous] governance structures in order to form the kind of relations that will not only reconcile the violences of the past but move us towards a decolonial future. (Byrd 2011, 50)

In agreement with this critical strategy, I argue that, in contrast to Foster's novel, Miles's biographical study urges moving out of a backward-looking impasse and into a discursive framework in the future where black-Indigenous relations can be addressed without "speaking through and against the material . . . structures of American colonialism" (Miles 2005, xv).[31]

Tiya Miles's book is a biography of the first recorded black-Cherokee lifelong partnership, between a black slave woman, Doll, and her Cherokee owner and "husband," Shoe Boots. Shoe Boots appeals to the Cherokee Nation in 1824 to confer Cherokee citizenship on his five biracial children with Doll. In exploring the "historical development of intimate relations between Cherokees and blacks" and inquiring into "the role of the Cherokee nation-state in defining and regulating race as a category of social, political and economic life" (Miles 2005, 2), the book is a concerted endeavor, in the author's own words, to "writ[e] into the historical silence that often surrounds interactions between black and Native people." It is also an attempt at voicing the "unspeakable" history of slave-owning Indigenous Americans, which "both black and Native people had willed themselves to forget" (xiv). In this respect, Miles's book constitutes a textual site of counter-memory, of "remembering" as a tool/act of political intervention and a narrative device that acknowledges the painful histories of black slavery in an Indigenous context.

The saga of the Afro-Cherokee Shoe Boots family in *Ties That Bind* thus reflects "the complexities of colonialism, slavery, racialization, nationalism and the family as a site of subjugation and resistance" (Miles 2005, 4). More specifically, it encourages a rethinking of the binary of Indigenous sovereignty and self-determination versus racial justice, equality, and citizenship rights for black freedmen, concepts that, as the ongoing Cherokee freedmen controversy demonstrates, are typically framed in opposition to one another. A fundamental question Miles's book addresses is why it is such a central paradox that the liberation and self-determination of two oppressed peoples were/are positioned as mutually exclusive. The author's attempt to address this question results in her decision to tell "two stories," "sketch two histories, enter two worlds, enlist two purposes, and sound two calls for justice—*at once*" (5; my emphasis). This emphasis on the intersectional concurrence and interlacing of both perspectives and "realities" acknowledges the significance of both and does not place one over the other. The first recounts the struggle to maintain Indigenous sovereignty and self-determination from the perspective of the Cherokee in the face of myriad challenges, including forced removal by the U.S. federal government and the dissolution of the original Cherokee Nation in 1906, while the second charts the history of black slavery in Native America, examining the principal values of freedom, kinship, and citizenship from the perspective of black Cherokees.

Significantly, these two story lines do not correspond to the two roughly equal halves of the book—a deliberate decision, perhaps, so as not to replicate the oppositional structure of the contemporary Cherokee Nation versus the Cherokee freedmen controversy. Instead, Miles chooses to organize the book geographically and chronologically into two parts. The first part, chapters 1 to 7, titled "Bone of My Bone: Slavery, Race, and Nation—East," chronicles the story of Shoe Boots from his early years as a Cherokee warrior in the southeastern states before the forced removal of Indigenous peoples, exploring the subjects of intermarriage (between Cherokee men and white women but also Cherokee men and black female slaves), the role of abolitionist Protestant missionaries in the Cherokee Nation, and the articulation of Cherokee sovereignty and citizenship in the 1820s.[32] The second part, consisting of chapters 8 to 10, an epilogue, and a coda, collectively titled "Of Blood and Bone: Freedom, Kinship and Citizenship—West," follows Shoe Boots and his family on the Trail of Tears to Indian Territory in Oklahoma, exploring the precariousness of their situation and the psychological impact of dislocation and deracination on the Cherokee and their black slaves as well as the effects of abolition in the aftermath of the Civil War, and ending with Shoe Boots's youngest son's failed application for Cherokee citizenship. The intertwining of Cherokee and black slave/freedmen perspectives in the book illustrates, I argue, the inseparability of the "two stories," the "two histories," and the "two calls for justice."

In tracing these two narratives, *Ties That Bind* also calls attention to the gaps and ambivalences that permeate historical accounts and chronicles of black slavery in the Cherokee community. As Doll's biographer, Miles does not claim complete knowledge of her protagonist's tale; quite the contrary, in fact: "To write about Doll . . . is to pay tribute to her life, a life that would otherwise be lost to history. But do not be lulled. To write about Doll is also a wholly inadequate exercise. For every scrap about her past that I have scavenged and reconstructed here might just as well have been captured by a chapter of blank, white pages" (2005, 26). By foregrounding, instead of glossing over, the absences and gaps in knowledge of Doll's life, Tiya Miles critically addresses the ways in which other works of scholarship have symbolically committed further violence by "misnaming her, calling her anything from Lucy and Lilcy . . . to 'the dark faced one' and 'the servant woman.'" In contrast, Miles ponders over the intricacies of naming, asking if Doll was the name given her by her maternal relatives, or perhaps "a label that, when uttered, did violence to her by erasing another name that we will never know" (27). Chapter 3, titled "Motherhood," focuses on Doll's (non)status within Shoe Boots's clan. Miles emphasizes her "presence and simultaneous absence in Cherokee life," which placed her in a liminal position, often "standing on the outside looking in" (57). Because Doll is not Cherokee by blood, she is not considered one of AniYun Wiya, the Real People. Miles also points out that although she lived with Shoe Boots in his quarters and not with his other slaves, wore Cherokee jewelry, and became fluent in the Cherokee language, Doll was nevertheless "viewed as an outsider whose presence was open to interrogation" (58). When she becomes pregnant with her and Shoe Boots's first child, Miles surmises, Doll might have "felt her exclusion most at this time of ceremonial and spiritual importance, when the centrality of clan membership rose to the fore" (59). Instead of being celebrated, however, the child, whom Doll and Shoe Boots name Kahuga/Elizabeth, is born, as American slave law dictated, into "the condition of the mother"—that is, into slavery. This has double implications, Miles notes, as Doll gives birth not only to a slave but to someone who reproduces her own clanless status.

In this respect, the book draws attention to the erasure of African customs and cultures by the phenomenon of slavery in Indigenous communities. Nevertheless, to present the other side of the coin to the reader, *Ties That Bind* also details the process of "internal colonialism" by the U.S. government that forced the Cherokees to "re-envision their relationship to the natural world, to reinvent work patterns, and to reshape gender roles" in the name of "a greater degree of civilization" (2005, 35).[33] Miles is thus also highly critical of the influence the U.S. government had on the Cherokee, especially its major disruption of Cherokee customs and subsistence patterns; its masculinizing of Cherokee men, who were regarded as effeminate and, conversely, its feminizing of Cherokee women, who were viewed as too "masculine" in their fieldwork;[34] its introduction of individual property ownership, a market economy,[35] and, ultimately, the practice of slave ownership. Furthermore, the book casts a critical eye on the role of "federally subsidized" Christian missionaries in Native American history, wryly commenting on "the intimate relationship between establishing missions and colonialism" (91). Miles notes the access that black slaves in Cherokee missionary towns had to religious education, in the course of which they also learned how to read and write English. In many instances, these educated black slaves would then act as intermediaries and interpreters for their Cherokee masters in dealings with white U.S. officials. These occasions, Miles observes, represented moments of black slave resistance and a disruption of the status quo. Nevertheless, Miles concedes that these were also "fragmented moments" as "the power that slaves usurped from their masters was transitory, since they were still chattel by social custom, and increasingly, by law" (96). Clearly, from a postcolonial perspective, learning to read and write in English also presented a considerable double bind for black Cherokees, who had to choose between illiteracy and being taught in the colonizer's language, a process that would gradually efface their mother tongue.

Undercutting racial stereotypes and thus problematizing the issues of race and belonging, *Ties That Bind* also details how, ironically, it is through the assistance of the white missionary William Thompson that Shoe Boots petitions in 1824 for his children's freedom from bondage. Miles surmises that it was Shoe Boots's exposure to the missionaries' abolitionist sentiments, coupled with his awareness of a changing political climate in the Cherokee government, that made him file this petition and overcome the taboo of disclosing his longtime sexual relationship with Doll, his slave. In chapter 6, "Nationhood," Miles narrates the difficulties Shoe Boots encountered. Three weeks after receiving his petition, on November 11, 1824, the General Council ruled illegal "intermarriages between negro slaves and Indians, or whites." Any Cherokee male marrying a black slave would be punished with "fifty-nine stripes on the bareback" (Cherokee Nation 1998). Miles recounts that the Cherokee General Council passed another act on the same day banishing freedmen from the Cherokee Nation. Shoe Boots's children, Elizabeth, Polly, John, William, and Lewis, were exempted from this ruling because of Shoe Boots's status in his clan. In an unprecedented decision, they were granted Cherokee citizenship through the recognition of their patrilineal, not matrilineal, descent. As Miles argues, the children thus "claimed a right to Cherokee belonging at the crossroads of cultural change. This dialectic of race and kinship would continue to influence the family's future, even as it reflected a broader pattern of transformation and contestation within the Cherokee populace, as women and men, . . . red and black, recalled and re-envisioned what it meant to be Cherokee" (2005, 128).

Nevertheless, the path to Indigenous citizenship for Afro-Cherokee was abruptly curtailed by the Indian Removal Act of 1830 and the forced relocation of the Cherokee between 1838 to 1839 from the southeastern states to Indian Territory in present-day Oklahoma. Chapter 8 of the book, "Removal," recounts the significance of the homeland, as a physical and psychological repository of Indigenous ways and beliefs, in Native constructions of identity, culture, and values. As Miles encapsulates, "Indian Removal disrupted the relationship between Cherokees, their homeland, and the stories that lived there. As a result, the cultural values embedded in those stories could no longer be reinforced through the visible markers of place" (2005, 159). In other words, Miles records how forced relocation resulted in the erasure of an Indigenous inscription of kinship, communal identities, epistemologies, value systems, and cultural heritage onto the landscape. The narrative chronicles how the Shoe Boots were forced to make this journey of no return: Doll went first by flatboat and steamship in 1837 ahead of her daughters Elizabeth and Polly, who walked the Trail of Tears with their own young children and relatives. Chapter 9, "Capture," records how this journey worsened tensions between blacks and Cherokees. When, for instance, Elizabeth and Polly Shoe Boots arrived in Indian Territory in the winter of 1839, they were caught in bitter factionalism between the Western and Eastern Cherokee nations and had to face not only emotional upheaval and deracination but also material poverty because payments promised by the U.S. government were slow in arriving (163).

The penultimate chapter of Miles's biography of the Shoe Boots family offers a critical commentary on the Civil War and its particular significance for the Cherokee Nation, which was split into pro-Confederate and pro-Union camps. The former, under the leadership of Stand Watie of the Treaty Party, proclaimed allegiance to the South in a mass meeting in Tahlequah organized by the National Council. The latter, which formed the Keetoowah Society, insisted on a return to traditional Cherokee values which, they stressed, "preceded and rejected the ownership of Black slaves" (2005, 186). Miles quotes historian Daniel Littlefield Jr.'s summarizing of the situation for the Cherokee at the end of the Civil War: "When the war ended, the Cherokee Nation was in ruin. Crossed and re-crossed by both Union and Confederate military units ... the Cherokee country suffered more destruction than did any of the other Indian nations" (188, citing Littlefield 1978, 15). In an attempt to protect its sovereignty in the face of increasing pressure, the Cherokee Nation began to argue in favor of its own right to decide who had access to Cherokee citizenship, a proposition that countered the Treaty of 1866 signed with the U.S. government, which bestowed Cherokee citizenship upon all freedmen who returned to Indian Territory within six months after the treaty.

The issue of Indigenous citizenship for black freedmen is the central concern of the final pages of Miles's book. The epilogue, titled "Citizenship," recounts William Shoe Boots's (Doll and Shoe Boots's last surviving child) application in 1887 to the Cherokee Commission on Citizenship for "full rights in the community and nation of his birth" (2005, 196). Interestingly, Miles points out, in his application, William Shoe Boots did not mention the fact that his mother, was a slave, only that she was black. He did, however, repeatedly mention that his father was a "full-blooded Cherokee." The conundrum in William Shoe Boots's appeal was that he could not trace his lineage to Cherokee rolls beginning in 1835, as his father had died in 1829. William Shoe Boots died in 1894, his Cherokee citizenship application still pending. Subsequently, William's own children, Rufus and Lizzie Shoe Boots, made a posthumous appeal for his citizenship application to be reconsidered, as the decision would affect their own entitlements to citizenship in the Cherokee Nation. Their petition was turned down by the Dawes Commission, which firmly stated that their father, William Shoe Boots, "is not now and has not been a citizen of the Cherokee Nation" (201). Although the Cherokee National Council largely rejected the authority of the Dawes Commission, it ruled that because William Shoe Boots was a freedman at the time of his birth, he was technically not eligible for citizenship under the terms of the Treaty of 1866, which granted Cherokee citizenship to *ex-slaves* who had been freed under the Thirteenth Amendment to the U.S. Constitution.

In Tiya Miles's *Ties That Bind*, therefore, the story of Doll Shoe Boots and her descendants' struggle for acceptance within their Indigenous community and to attain the full rights of Cherokee citizenship is situated within a broader critical discourse of notions of kinship, cultural identity, and belonging that complicate nation-based models of citizenship in both Indigenous and non-Indigenous U.S. contexts. Miles's biographical documentation of the Shoe Boots family saga and Sharon Ewell Foster's novel *Abraham's Well* thus represent two different narrative modes of representing the Cherokee freedmen controversy in writing. In my opinion, Miles's work constitutes a more critically perceptive and sophisticated rendering of the complex issues surrounding the controversy than Foster's novel, which ends up being little more than a formulaic Christian tale of endurance, survival, and strength in the face of adversity rather than a narrative of social critique, political redress, and hence a textual/literary site of black Indigenous resistance. *Abraham's Well* evocatively and unflinchingly depicts the physical and mental sufferings borne by the black Cherokee slave girl Armentia and her family, but its mimetic mode of narration circumvents a more critical examination of established understandings of the nation/nationhood, community, race, kinship, sovereignty and, by extension, conventional notions of national identity, citizenship, and belonging in both a nineteenth-century and a contemporary twenty-first-century framework.

In comparison, *Ties That Bind* "marks the places where 'Cherokeeness' and Blackness overlap" (Miles 2005, 6). It draws the reader's attention to the gaps, ambiguities, and controversies in the triangulation of white-black-Indigenous relations. In its deconstruction of the concepts of race, kinship, nation, identity, and history, Miles's text, part historical biography, part literary criticism, is not being afraid of "telling it slant" (5). The text places itself in conversation with the tradition of nineteenth-century slave narratives such as Harriet Jacobs's seminal *Incidents in the Life of a Slave Girl*. Yet its rejection of traditional historiography and its attempt to tell both black freedmen and Native Cherokee sides of the story represent a more discerning critical approach, sensitive to the complexities, paradoxes, and ambivalences that are part of the history of slavery in the Cherokee Nation. In comparison, Foster's adoption of a singular—and ultimately highly personal—perspective, from which her "authoritative" account of historical events ("the *whole* truth" [2006, 121]) stems, suggests a more uncomplicated attempt to smooth over the differences between Indigenous and non-Indigenous notions of nationhood and citizenship. In negotiating, through the story of the Shoe Boots family, the experience of being racialized as black in an Indigenous community, Miles's biographical study thoroughly examines the ties (of kinship, community, nation, blood, and bone) that bind. It also records the double bind that black Cherokee subjects faced in being twice marginalized:

in neither the Indigenous nor non-Indigenous nations were they regarded as citizens. Miles's text thus interrogates the various moments throughout Cherokee and American history in which established definitions of nationality and citizenship were contested, challenged, and renegotiated, either by force or necessity, and the repercussions of these acts of redress, these acts of citizenship. In this fashion, I argue, Miles's book opens up alternative ways of thinking about identity politics within—and also beyond—both Indigenous and non-Indigenous concepts of the nation, while also critically intervening in discourses of citizenship in the United States that still remain entrenched in socially and politically constructed categories of race, blood, and color.

CONCLUSION

· · · · · · · · · ·

Reconfiguring Citizenship: Nationhood and Post-national
Imaginaries in North America

Coming full circle to the introduction of my book, in which I considered Jin-me Yoon's *Group of Sixty-Seven* as an illustrative example of how citizenship is contested and renegotiated in visual narratives, I want to conclude with a different reflection on how citizenship might be visually constructed: not in the genres of painting or photography but in cartography. In this respect, it seems fitting to bring this study to a close with a striking visual commentary on the state of the nation and nation-based models of citizenship in a North American context. Figure 6 (see color insert) by historian and journalist Colin Woodard is taken from his recent book, *American Nations: A History of the Eleven Rival Regional Cultures of North America* (2012). The visual demonstrates the simple, yet often glossed-over, maxim that "[t]here isn't and never has been one America, but rather several Americas." In his version of "America," Woodard regroups the United States and parts of Canada and Mexico into eleven regions demarcated by their historical and cultural fault lines, recharting the "fractured continent" (2) along the contours of regional affiliations delineated by political, ethnic, and cultural affinities. In so doing, Woodard bids his readers to "banish the meaningless 'regions' of 'the North-east,' 'the West,' 'the Midwest,' or 'the South,'" whose "boundaries are marked by those of their constituent states in complete disregard for the continent's actual settlement history and sectional rivalries" (xi)—a polemical proposition, indeed, especially for area studies scholars.

The claim that the American nation exists in the plural, that national and state borders are arbitrary and have become increasingly obsolete, is certainly not new, as indicated by the resurgence over the last three decades of scholarship on cultural regionalism and, conversely, transnational and global American studies as well as a move toward global citizenship studies. Other studies that make arguments very similar to Woodard's include Joel Garreau's *The Nine Nations of North America* (1982) and Dante Chinni and James Gimpel's *Our Patchwork Nation: The Surprising Truth about the "Real" America* (2010). Indeed, the former, with its "Nine Nations map," has become a seminal text on the regionalization of North America, and the latter proposes a remapping of the United States into "twelve community types," each sharing a set of social, political, and cultural perspectives and economic "realities." Where Woodard's map and his study of the eleven regional cultures depart from these works, however, is in their concerted attempt to adopt a hemispheric approach that, in line with the recent "turn" to hemispheric methodologies of analysis and inquiry in the field of American studies and other disciplines in the humanities and social sciences, charts the "interconnections among nations, peoples, institutions, and intellectual and political movements in the larger [historical] context of the American hemisphere" (Levander and Levine 2007, 2).

Accordingly, Woodard's map and his analysis aim to demonstrate, first, how naming and mapping the nation(s) is a contested practice that stretches back to the earliest periods of American colonial history and, second, how it is important to take into consideration the position of the United States in relation to its neighboring nations, Mexico and Canada, which themselves are nonhomogenous entities.[1] In emphasizing the historical dimensions of processes of national identity formation and collective identification, therefore, Woodard's map does more than suggest a contemporary revival of regional identity politics over national/federal identity—it underscores that nationhood and nation-based notions of citizenship are, from the outset, concepts that are open to debate and dispute.

While Colin Woodard's map of eleven nations might put forward an alternative hemispheric model of nationhood, regional affiliation, and collective identification that transcends the idea of nation-state and geopolitical borders as well as national notions of citizenship and belonging, I propose that it is nevertheless flawed on two counts. First, it leaves out the thirteen sovereign states and seventeen dependent territories in the Caribbean entirely, hence reproducing the discourses of exclusion and marginalization that arose out of histories of colonization, institutionalized slavery, and indentured labor in the region.[2] Second, even though Woodard's remapping of North America implicitly makes reference to the clash of perspectives and vested interests between cultural and national minorities and the dominant racial and ethnic groups,[3] it does not reflect how the tensions and ruptures, territorial disputes, and forced migrations that ensued as a result of these conflicts have contributed to the growth of alternative nationalisms that exemplify trans- and post-national paradigms of identification and belonging. As my study has demonstrated, such alternative nationalisms in the form of "willful"/"insurgent," precarious, queer, diasporic, and Indigenous subjectivities are significant because they denote the limitations of nation-based models of liberal and civic republican citizenship and indicate the coexistence of non–nation-centric models of citizenship. Indeed, these alternative modes of configuring and construing citizenship represent forms of "counter cartographies"[4] or strategies of counter-hegemonic mapping that incorporate the interests of previously marginalized groups, communities that have been excluded on the grounds of their "radical alterity" (Baudrillard and Guillaume 2008).

Accordingly, those intrigued by, and yet seeking to expand, Colin Woodard's "hemispheric" model of eleven nations may find Gayatri Spivak's concept of "planetarity" (2003) and Paul Gilroy's notion of a "planetary humanism" (2000, 2004) useful, as they are attentive to the marginalization of non-normative subjectivities or those who fall outside the parameters of national models of citizenship. In *Death of a Discipline* (2003), Spivak's introduces a concept of *planetarity* as a substitute for the ubiquitous term *globalization* which, for her, denotes neo-imperialist systems of capitalist exploitation. According to Spivak, a politics of planetarity involves a critical practice, driven by the desire for a new para-national imaginary, that cultivates an ethics of resistance to normative structures of control and governance. In its aspiration to a new world order where marginalized and subaltern populations are not assimilated or homogenized by a governing global uniformity, Spivak's notion of planetarity is significant as it calls for a re-formation of models of collectivity that do not adopt the nation-state as their core. Likewise, Paul Gilroy's version of planetarity, which he defines as a form of "anti-racist solidarity" (2000, 290) that would enable a critical reorientation of the moral and political dimensions of living as citizens on the planet, is also important for its far-reaching, if contentious, proposal of a postracial politics.[5] Gilroy's and Spivak's concepts of planetarity are therefore useful in a reevaluation of the relationship between models of collective identification, membership, and participation that transcend paradigms of the nation-state.

In this respect, it might also be worthwhile considering Wai Chee Dimock's "planetary" approach to literature that she advanced in her well-known, yet not unproblematic, essay "Literature for the Planet."[6] In this essay, Dimock critiques what she terms the "almost automatic equation between the literary and the territorial [in] the study of national literatures." Challenging the established centrality of the nation-state in ideas of national literature, Dimock argues for "a conception of literature" that will unsettle "territorial sovereignty" (2001, 175) and uncouple the synchronicities of place-based identities within the framework of the nation. As her prime example, Dimock refers to how Osip Mandelstam's poems were written in conversation with Dante's *Divine Comedy*—an undertaking that, according to her, establishes a "continuum extended from fourteenth-century Italy to twentieth-century Russia." Mandelstam's reading of Dante, Dimock asserts, not only "put the two poets side by side, in defiance of chronology," it also "denationalized each of them, making each Italian and not Italian, Russian and not Russian." She goes on to argue that literature in such a "foreign tongue" suggests "a counterpoint to the entity called the nation, showing up its limits, its failure to dictate an exact match between the linguistic and the territorial" (176). Ultimately, Dimock posits, "[r]eading ushers in a continuum that mocks the form of any finite entity. It mocks the borders of the nation. . . . As a global process of extension, elaboration, and randomization, reading turns literature into the collective life of the planet" (178).

Although I agree with the general thrust of Dimock's argument, her analysis remains disappointingly on the level of the abstract. In fact, it quickly becomes an exercise in reading-back, in tracing "texts [that] hav[e] a prolonged life and a global following" (Dimock 2001, 175), one that is akin to the reductive claim, for instance, that Shakespeare is a planetary playwright because his works can be universally adapted across the centuries and adopted in different geopolitical and cultural settings. Dimock's "planetary" approach to literature also makes short shrift of the hegemonic structures that keep marginalized/subaltern groups excluded from dominant society. Unlike Spivak, she does not critique the homogenizing structures of national formations or their assimilation (or not, as the case may be) of radical alterity. In my opinion, therefore, Dimock's analysis does not come across as a nuanced or attuned way of comprehending our positions (as writers, readers, scholars, and critics in the humanities) as planetary subjects who have the potential to—if not a collective responsibility to—espouse an "ethics of narration" (Booth 1990; Nussbaum 2007) that is attuned to the human conditions of precariousness, injurability, and vulnerability.[7] As the previous chapters demonstrate, one of the larger objectives of this book project has been to explore how such an "ethics of narration" can be adopted in literary texts that challenge and reinscribe nation-centric understandings of citizenship and propose alternative forms of membership, participation, and belonging.

A second reason why Dimock's essay "Literature for the Planet" remains unconvincing is that she sets up a binary of "planetary"[8] versus national, in which she curiously adopts a rather conventional understanding of the nation as "a territorial regime" with "finite" or "static borders" (2001, 177).[9] In this study, I have demonstrated that the situation is far more complex, namely, in the way the nation itself has always been, even at the point of its inception/birth, an arbitrary and contested concept. In addition, I have indicated how various issues factor into the discussion: for instance, how Indigenous, migrant, expatriate, queer, "dissident" communities and "willful" individuals challenge, "infringe" upon, critique, widen, and reconfigure the "hard" and "soft" borders of the nation-state; how urban citizens occupy and negotiate the contested spaces in which they live; and how diaspora, exile, and hybridity contest notions of geopolitical national boundaries and nation-based ideas of citizenship and belonging.

My study thus offers a reframing of dominant understandings of the nation and citizenship in a way that aspires to Spivak's theory of planetarity: in particular, its attentiveness to alter-national- and post-national-centric models of political collectivity, economic participation, and social membership. Nevertheless, I want to differentiate my work from academic discussions of global or planetary citizenship that have become ubiquitous since the turn of the new millennium. I have not adopted, and do not subscribe to, a global or planetary approach to citizenship, as some other studies in the field have done.[10] Rather, my aim in this project has been to lay the groundwork for a different trajectory of citizenship studies that seeks to reexamine and remap the contours of the nation-state. Despite the flourishing of studies on global and planetary citizenship in the last few decades, national citizenship still continues to be *the* dominant model of citizenship. Consequently, it is necessary to examine how alternative nonnational models of citizenship, as considered in this study, are located first and foremost *within* the nation and its imaginaries. Only subsequently do/can they surpass the boundaries of the nation and extend into forms of post-national belonging and identity. Put differently, my close readings of the various novels, prose texts, and literary essays in this study pose the question of how nonnational forms of citizenship and belonging can be conceived not necessarily *beyond* the scope of the nation but already *from within* its imaginative and geopolitical boundaries. In this respect, my project is an extension and a re-sounding of Winfried Fluck's contention that "transnational American studies should not do away with the nation-state but should contribute to the effort of theorizing American culture with the goal of gaining a more adequate understanding thereof" (quoted in Bieger, Saldívar, and Voelz 2013, ix).

In its consideration of the limits (yet the persistence) of the concept of national citizenship, this book offers a genealogy of alternative forms of subjectivity, membership, participation, belonging, and collective identification within a North American context, tracing how the prevalent attributes of citizenship and national belonging are reinscribed in a selection of prose writings that themselves become textual and affective sites of political contestation, racial struggle, social resistance and, ultimately, transformation and change. Engaging with previous scholarly work that puts forward the premise that America is "an assumed relation" (Berlant 1991, 4) and noting "the palimpsestic cultural geographies . . . out of which the nation takes shape as an alternately assumed, imagined, and [yet] enduringly important category" (Levander and Levine 2007, 9), my study situates citizenship and national identity within a broader interpretive framework, one attentive to different forms of political, social, economic, cultural, and sexual belonging that are enacted in and through the literary text. In so doing, it charts citizenship in transit(ion) from established nation-based models of membership, participation, and community to alternative paradigms of alter- and post-national subjectivities that challenge the homogenizing and assimilative logic of the nation-state. A rethinking of citizenship along these lines has been long overdue.

NOTES

INTRODUCTION

1. The Group of Seven originally comprised the seven painters Frederick Varley (1881–1969), A. Y. Jackson (1882–1972), Arthur Lismer (1885–1969), Lawren Harris (1885–1970), Franklin Carmichael (1890–1945), Frank Johnston (1888–1949), and J. E. H. MacDonald (1873–1932). The ethos of the group was that a distinctly Canadian art could emerge from direct contact with nature/the wilderness. The paintings of the Group of Seven constituted the first major Canadian national art movement, and they were succeeded by the Canadian Group of Painters, a collective of twenty-eight artists, in 1933. For a more detailed account of the work of the Group of Seven, see the catalogue to the exhibition of the same name, *Painting Canada: Tom Thomson and the Group of Seven* (Concannon 2011).

2. Jasper Park is the largest national park in the Canadian Rockies.

3. The name "Canada" originates from the Huron-Iroquoian word *kanata* ("settlement" or "village"), and the names of many Canadian cities, such as Toronto, have First Nations origins. See "Canada," in *The Canadian Encyclopedia*, www.thecanadianencyclopedia.com/articles/canada.

4. I use this term in the sense of an "alternative" (to conventional definitions of the nation) but also in the sense of "altering" (the established structures of the nation).

5. I am referring, in particular, to Frantz Fanon's *The Wretched of the Earth* (2004) and Stuart Hall's essay "Cultural Identity and Diaspora" (1994).

6. Interestingly, the term *post-national* has proven to be less popular in scholarly literature than *transnational*. "Post-national" has principally been associated

with the writings of Yasemin Soysal (1994), Jürgen Habermas (2001), and Saskia Sassen (2002).

7. I will not expand on the term *imaginary* in my study, as this has already been done adroitly by other scholarly work in the field. For a comprehensive conceptual overview of the term as it has been used in literary and cultural studies, particularly in the discipline of American studies, see Bieger, Saldívar, and Voelz 2013.

8. A notable exception is the collection edited by Donald Pease, *National Identities and Post-Americanist Narratives* (1994). In his introduction, Pease astutely argues that post-national forces emerge from "an internal [or what he calls 'intranational'] divide . . . whereby the structures underwriting the stability of that national narrative can undergo transformations" (5). According to Pease, the post-national moment occurs when the "revision in the genealogy of national identity rediscovers its source in social movements rather than national narratives" (6). Pease's arguments are situated within the larger "New Americanist" critical debate he had with Frederick Crews on the restructuring of the American studies as a discipline. Pease's edited collection also includes an essay by Lauren Berlant and Elizabeth Freeman, "Queer Nationality."

9. I am referring to the concept of "intersectionality," a term coined by Kimberlé Crenshaw and commonly used in critical race theory, that acknowledges the intersections between multiple forms of discrimination on the grounds of gender, class, ethnicity, and sexual orientation. For more critical reading on intersectionality, see Crenshaw 1991.

10. Canadian writer Margaret Atwood's collection of short stories *Wilderness Tips* (1989), for example, extends a variety of different representations of the trope of the Canadian wilderness. The story "Death by Landscape" from the collection is also a satiric commentary on the paintings of the Group of Seven that constructed Canadian identity as intricately linked to this "natural" landscape.

11. Lauren Berlant defines the "National Symbolic" as "the order of discursive practices whose reign within a national space produces . . . the 'law' in which the accident of birth within a geographic political boundary transforms individuals into subjects of a collectively-held history" (1991, 20).

12. Or, as Richard Cavell puts it, paraphrasing Marshall McLuhan's theoretical reflections on Canada's colonial history, "[W]hile the United States . . . emerged from its cultural colonization by Britain, Canada . . . [was] hampered in this regard by its political loyalty to Britain" (2002, 200).

13. MacLulich asserts that Canadians "habitually define their country's identity by contrasting it with the United States" (1988, 13). MacLulich's argument alludes to Marshall McLuhan's critical discussions of the "flexibility" of Canada's national identity, which he attributes to its "multiple borderlines, psychic, social and geographic" (1977, 244).

14. Stephen Leacock's humorous satire of small-town provincial Canadian life in *Sunshine Sketches of a Little Town* (1912) is a good example.

15. See Frye 1971; Atwood 1972; McLuhan 1977; and Cohen 2007.

16. Government of Canada, "Canadian Charter of Rights and Freedoms," www.pch.gc.ca/eng/1355931562580/1355931640787#a27.

17. Including Kamboureli 2000; Miki 2011; Moss 2003; Sugars 2004; Kim, McCall, and Singer 2012; and last but certainly not least, Godard 2008.

18. In 1951, the Royal Commission on National Development in the Arts, Letters, and Sciences issued a report cautioning that Canadian culture had been "invaded" by U.S. film, radio, and printed media. Chaired by Vincent Massey, the commission recommended the federal funding of cultural activities in Canada, which resulted in the establishment of the National Library of Canada, the Canada Council for the Arts, and the conservation of national historic sites. The Massey Report is widely regarded as a central move by the Canadian government to preserve, encourage, and foster Canadian culture in the 1950s.

19. The era known as the "American Renaissance" in literature is commonly understood to be the period from 1830 roughly up until the beginning of the Civil War in 1861. This was a period where, in the wake of the romantic movement, the expression of a national spirit came of age. In his seminal study, *American Renaissance* (1941), F. O. Matthiessen more narrowly refers to the five-year period of 1850–55 as the "American Renaissance" in his literary analysis of the works of Emerson, Thoreau, Hawthorne, Melville, and of Whitman's early writings. See also Michaels and Pease 1989.

20. This led to the adoption of the Fourteenth Amendment to the U.S. Constitution on July 9, 1868, which states that "all persons born or naturalized in the United States, and subject to the jurisdiction thereof, are citizens of the United States and of the State wherein they reside." This conferred, for the first time, U.S. citizenship on African American males and extended liberties and rights to former slaves. The Fifteenth Amendment, ratified on February 3, 1870, granted African American men the right to vote. Despite the ratification of these amendments, African Americans were still effectively disenfranchised in the Southern states (for example, through the use of poll taxes and literacy tests as well as restrictive/arbitrary registration practices and electoral fraud).

21. These include William Kirby's *The Golden Dog* (1877), a historical romance set in Quebec in 1748 during the rule of Louis XV; Sara Jeannette Duncan's *The Imperialist* (1904), set in a town in Ontario modeled on her hometown of Brantford that explores Canadian attitudes toward Britain, the United States, and itself; L. M. Montgomery's *Anne of Green Gables* (1908), set on an idyllic, pastoral Prince Edward Island; and Stephen Leacock's *Sunshine Sketches of a Little Town* (1912), a satiric depiction of a fictional small, parochial Ontario community.

22. Although, or perhaps because, Atwood's book was written for a popular readership rather than an academic one, her critique of the Canadian literary scene (or its lack thereof) struck home. Even though critic Russell Brown remarks that both Atwood's and Northrop Frye's (1971) thematic criticism of Canadian literature were "completely out of fashion" within a decade of their publication (1978, 657), they nevertheless had a considerable impact when they were first published.

23. Citing Arthur Lower's *Colony to Nation* (1944) and Donald Creighton's *Dominion of the North* (1944) as prime examples, Canadian historians have noted the emergence, as late as in the post–World War II period, of "new [nonfictional] interpretations of Canadian history . . . that sought to understand Canada as a nation, rather than as an economic or constitutional offshoot of Great Britain or the United States" (Hamel 2009, 26).

24. The phallic nature of the painting also demonstrates, perhaps, the androcentrism of the Group of Seven painters, who were all white male Canadians. Emily Carr, who is commonly associated with members of the group, did not meet them until 1927.

25. In *Survival: A Thematic Guide to Canadian Literature* (1972), Margaret Atwood defines survival as the central motif of Canadian literature, one comparable to the frontier myth in American literature and popular culture. The theme of survival is closely associated with another archetypal characteristic of Canadian literature that influential critic Northrop Frye termed the "garrison mentality"—the phenomenon of "small and isolated communities surrounded with a physical or psychological 'frontier,' separated from one another and from their American and British cultural sources . . . confronted with a huge, unthinking, menacing, and formidable physical setting" (1971, 227).

26. Cole's "Essay on American Scenery," which was published in the same year as Ralph Waldo Emerson's essay "Nature," reflects a transcendental appreciation of nature as a system of belief.

27. I emphasize the phrase "to the nation as a whole" because the foundation myths and beliefs of the Indigenous First Nations in Canada and Native American tribes in the United States are clearly deeply rooted systems of cultural practice and ancestral heritage. Nevertheless, these foundation myths and narratives have been marginalized by dominant non-Indigenous cultures and societies in North America.

28. I use the term *national imaginary* to denote the social imaginary in a specific nation, the "social imaginary" being, according to Charles Taylor in *Modern Social Imaginaries* (2004), who adopted the term from Cornelius Castoriadis's *The Imaginary Institution of Society* (1975), "the ways people imagine their social existence, how they fit together with others, how things go on between them and their fellows, the expectations that are normally met, and the deeper normative notions and images that underlie these notions" (23). The national imaginary thus encompasses a set of values and a system of beliefs that govern social structures within a national framework.

29. Notable exceptions include Crane 2002; Knadle 2004; Thomas 2007; Francis 2010; Schlund-Vials 2011; Lehnen 2013; and Keith 2012. Keith's study interestingly argues that writers considered "un-American" during the Cold War (left-wing intellectuals and black radicals alike) employed alternative literary forms such as the memoir and travel narrative to challenge dominant notions of race, nation, and citizenship reflected in the genre of the novel (which was regarded as the exemplary literary genre of the nation) during the height of American exceptionalism in the 1940s to 1960s.

30. One of the underlying premises of my study is that, contrary to its conventional definition as "a legally recognized subject or national of a state or commonwealth, either native or naturalized" (*New Oxford American Dictionary*, 3rd ed.), the term *citizenship* has always been inherently unstable and hence contested, even in its very moment(s) of conferment or manifestation.

31. Notable publications include Isin and Wood 1999; Isin 2002; Isin and Nielsen 2008; Turner 1993; and Tilly 1996.

32. Carr was closely associated with the Group of Seven painters, whom she first met in 1927. Lawren Harris, who became a significant and lasting influence on Carr's work, even purportedly remarked that she was "one of them."

33. Carr especially liked painting totem poles set in deep forests or the sites of abandoned Indigenous villages such as Kispiox and Kitwanga.

34. *The Canadian Encyclopedia* calls Emily Carr a "Canadian icon," declaring her "one of the preeminent, and perhaps most original, Canadian painters of

the first half of the twentieth century." www.thecanadianencyclopedia.com/ articles/emily-carr.

CHAPTER 1

1. The Revolutionary War (1775–83) and the adoption of the Declaration of Independence (1776) by the thirteen American colonies outlined the basic tenets of American citizenship (as encapsulated in the unalienable rights of "Life, Liberty, and the Pursuit of Happiness"). When Abraham Lincoln drew centrally upon the Declaration in his Gettysburg Address of 1863, he was only voicing an appeal to the American nation to stand together as one but also reassuring residents of both the Northern and Southern U.S. states of their equal rights as American citizens during a period of national crisis.

2. See Roche 1949; and Kettner 1978.

3. These include the national figures of Columbia, America's response to Britannia, and her twin, the Goddess of Liberty. For further reading on the relationship between literature and national formation in the period of the American Renaissance, see Michaels and Pease 1989; Clark 1985; Tompkins 1986; Reynolds 1988; and Grossman 1993.

4. As Kenneth Stampp (1981) acknowledges, however, the divergent economic situations in the Northern and Southern states are now no longer commonly viewed by historians and scholars as a central issue that led to the Civil War.

5. By this, I mean the resurgence and proliferation of national images, emblems, and symbols during and after of the War of 1812 against Great Britain. These include the depiction of the national arms and great seal on U.S. coins such as the double eagle, a $20 gold coin piece minted in 1849, with the addition of the (then unofficial) motto "In God We Trust" in 1866. Another example is Francis Scott Key's writing of the poem "Defense of Fort McHenry," inspired by America's successful defense of that fort against British warships in September 1814. Key's poem, set to a well-known British tune, "The Anacreontic Song," became the lyrics of "The Star-Spangled Banner," the American national anthem (adopted much later, in 1930).

6. I am borrowing this term from Edward Said's notion of "critical nationalism" (although he does not explicitly use this term) in *Culture and Imperialism*. For Said, all postcolonial nationalist movements are sites of violence unless they are "critical." Said writes, "[Fanon's notion was that] unless national consciousness at its moment of success was somehow changed into a social consciousness, the future would not hold liberation but an extension of imperialism" (1993, 267).

7. There was a concerted attempt to restrict the establishment of slavery in the new territories/states acquired by westward expansion as it became common opinion that the only way to stop slavery was to stop its expansion into the new states. This was also to counteract the influence of the states that had entered the Union in the decades up until the 1850s—Louisiana (1812), Missouri (1821), Arkansas (1836), Florida (1845), and Texas (1845) as well as the southern portions of Alabama and Mississippi were all slave states.

8. Hawthorne, a Democrat, was sacked from his job after the election of General Zachary Taylor, a Whig, as president of the United States in 1849.

9. Hawthorne worked as a Custom-House officer in Boston in 1839–41 and was appointed surveyor for the District of Salem and Beverly and inspector of the revenue for the Port of Salem in 1846.

10. Hawthorne's description of the Custom-House officers anticipates Whitman's broader criticism of public office and the judiciary in *Democratic Vistas*: "The official services of America, national, state, and municipal, in all their branches and departments, except the judiciary, are saturated in corruption, bribery, falsehood, mal-administration; and the judiciary is tainted. The great cities reek with respectable as much as non-respectable robbery and scoundrelism. In fashionable life, flippancy, tepid amours, weak infidelism, small aims, or no aims at all, only to kill time. In business, (this all-devouring modern word, business,) the one sole object is, by any means, pecuniary gain" (2010, 12).

11. Hawthorne is referring to his great-great-great-grandfather, Major William Hathorne (Nathaniel Hawthorne added the "w" to the spelling of his surname as a gesture of distancing himself from his paternal ancestry), a merchant and magistrate of the Massachusetts Bay Colony. William Hathorne's son, John Hathorne, was one of the most notorious judges involved in the Salem witch trials.

12. In this respect, the narrator of "The Custom-House" utters a different proclamation than the fictional character Lieutenant Philip Nolan (based on the real-life Clement Vallandigham, leader of the Copperhead antiwar Democrats) of Edward Hale's patriotic cautionary tale "The Man without a Country" (1863), even though both experience a similar falling out of favor due to patronage politics. In Hale's story, Nolan renounces his country during a trial in which he is accused of treason, declaring, "I wish I may never hear of the United States again!" True to his request, Nolan is cast away to spend his remaining days at sea on vessels stripped of all icons and symbols of the United States, and not allowed to hear any news of America ever again. When Nolan dies at the end of the story, his deathbed is a miniature shrine

to the United States, with the American flag draped around a picture of George Washington and a painted mural of the bald eagle over his bed. Nolan even writes his own epitaph: "In memory of Philip Nolan, Lieutenant in the army of the United States. He loved his country as no other man has loved her; but no man deserved less at her hands." Although Hale set the story in the early nineteenth century, it was clearly published to garner support for the Union cause during the Civil War. In comparison, although the narrator of Hawthorne's "The Custom-House" declares himself to be, like Nolan, a "politically dead man" and "a citizen of somewhere else," he does not explicitly renounce his citizenship.

13. While Berlant sees in Hawthorne's writing "an attempt to break the frame of national hegemony itself" (1991, 9), other Hawthorne scholars such as Sacvan Bercovitch have claimed him as a nationalist reformer. See Bercovitch 1988a and 1988b. I am, personally, not swayed by Bercovitch's interpretation.

14. I will expand on this concept of abstract, prescriptive American citizenship in chapter 3 in the context of Philip Roth's American trilogy.

15. Apparently, Hawthorne's mother, Elizabeth Clarke Manning, to whom he was very attached, was also rejected by her in-laws, the Hathornes. After her husband's death, she and her children, including the young Hawthorne, moved in with maternal relatives, the Mannings, in Salem. Hawthorne's mother's sudden death in 1849 has also been cited as a dominant reason for the centrality of "the figure of the mother and child united against the world" (Baym 1983, 23) in *The Scarlet Letter*.

16. The headless horseman is a mythical character from older European folktales and has several incarnations, such as the Irish "dulachán" and the German "der kopflose Reiter."

17. This is a reference, perhaps, to the various land acquisitions of the United States in the early to mid-nineteenth century, from the Louisiana Purchase in 1803 to the annexation of Texas in 1845 and Oregon in 1846 as well as the Alaska Purchase in 1867. Later on in the essay, Whitman refers to these land purchases directly: "In vain have we annex'd Texas, California, Alaska, and reach north for Canada and south for Cuba. It is as if we were somehow being endow'd with a vast and more and more thoroughly-appointed body, and then left with little or no soul" (2010, 12).

CHAPTER 2

1. Etienne Balibar (1991), for instance, delineates the emergence of the "citizen-subject" in the aftermath of the French Revolution in 1789. In the

"Declaration of the Rights of Man and of the Citizen" the citizen-subject is defined as a sovereign, autonomous individual.

2. The criticism directed against the latter being that they are not attuned to more complex pluralist situations as is the case, for example, in Quebec, where not only gender but language, culture, and class play a central role in the formation of cultural and political identity.

3. To complicate matters somewhat, Gail Scott has also, however, referred to the narrator of *Heroine* as her own "heroine." See Scott's essay "Paragraphs Blowing on a Line" in *Spaces Like Stairs* (1989).

4. The October Crisis in 1970 was the culmination of a series of attacks by the Front de libération du Québec (FLQ, or Quebec Liberation Front). It was triggered by the kidnapping of British trade commissioner James Cross and Labour minister Pierre Laporte (who was murdered) in Montreal. The October Crisis led to the only peacetime use of the War Measures Act and the suspension of habeas corpus (entitlement to a trial before the court and the right of release from unlawful detention). In the aftermath of the October Crisis, there was widespread consensus supporting nonviolent tactics in the efforts for Quebec sovereignty and autonomy.

5. For the sake of clarity, the protagonist of Gail Scott's *Heroine* will be referred to henceforth as "G.S."

6. The phrase "Play it again, Sam" is itself a misquotation of the phrase "Play it, Sam" from the 1942 film *Casablanca*, with whose star, Humphrey Bogart, the character played by Woody Allen in *Play It Again, Sam*, identifies.

7. "Male" melancholia, also known as the Elizabethan malady, was common in the early seventeenth century, which witnessed the publication of Robert Burton's "medical textbook" and scholastic treatise on the subject, *The Anatomy of Melancholy* (1621) as well as the post-Elizabethan "Cult of Melancholia" associated with composer John Dowland. Depictions of the melancholy man, or "malcontent," loomed large in literature; a prime example being Shakespeare's Hamlet.

8. Whereas male melancholy was "a malady associated with creativity, interiority and intellect," female melancholy was, as was the case with hysteria, regarded as a disorder of the womb. See chapter 3 of Dawson 2008.

9. Kristeva takes up these concerns in *Black Sun: Depression and Melancholia* (1992).

10. Interestingly, Kristeva also makes the observation that "melancholy is not French," relating it to "Protestantism's rigour or Christian Orthodoxy's matriarchal weight" rather than French Catholicism, which regards "sadness

as a sin" (1987, 5). This is an additional marker of difference with respect to the narrator of Gail Scott's *Heroine*, who is an Anglo-Protestant Canadian.

11. "New Woman" is used in Scott's novel as the counterpart of the "New Man" in Marxist and Communist ideologies, which itself was an appropriation of the feminist ideal that emerged in the late nineteenth century and was popularized in the writings of Henry James.

12. Nevertheless, the Equal Rights Act was not adopted as it did not receive the requisite number of ratifications in 1982.

13. See Wenman 2003.

14. Although in Scott's *Heroine*, the "tickle" or orgasm that the narrator feels toward the close of the novel actually leaves her desiring more. Due to the circular structure of the text, G.S.'s orgasm can be situated in a continuum of other orgasms she has experienced in her bathtub on other days of the year.

15. The concept of "sexual citizenship," coined by David Evans (1993), refers to the political and cultural dimensions of sexual intimacy and expression. This will be discussed in greater depth in chapter 7.

16. See Laura Briggs's "The Race of Hysteria: 'Overcivilization' and the 'Savage' Woman in Late Nineteenth-Century Obstetrics and Gynecology," *American Quarterly* 52 (2) (2000): 246–73, for an overview of the history of female hysteria.

17. See Rachel P. Maines's *The Technology of Orgasm: "Hysteria," the Vibrator, and Women's Sexual Satisfaction* (Baltimore: Johns Hopkins University Press, 1999).

18. Originally coined (as "fiction théorique") by Nicole Brossard (1977), the term "fiction theory" has been popularized in literary criticism by Barbara Godard et al. as "a narrative, usually self-mirroring, which exposes defamiliarizes and/ or subverts the fiction and gender codes determining the re-presentation of women in literature and in this way contributes to feminist theory" (1986, 60).

19. Scott's use of the dash here recalls to my mind Emily Dickinson's "famous" use of the dash or hyphen in her poems.

20. See Bakhtin 1941.

21. Scott explicates that the form of the novel, for her, is the "fiction form that most forces the writer to rub against the 'real.' By 'real' I mean the 'universal' represented by society's institutions: the practice of politics, of systems of law, education, etc." (1989, 78).

22. As Cixous maintains in "The Laugh of the Medusa," "She must write her self, because this is the invention of a new insurgent writing which, when the

moment of her liberation has come, will allow her to carry out the indispensable ruptures and transformations in her history" (1976, 880).

23. This is expressed by the character of Marie in the novel, who "experiment[s] in new ways of expressing women's voices" (1987, 58) and tells the narrator, "[a]s for feminist, our responsibility is writing" (113).

24. In her seminal essay, "The Laugh of the Medusa," Cixous defines "écriture feminine" as a style of writing that would articulate the following necessity: "Woman must write her self: must write about women and bring women to writing. . . . Woman must put herself into the text—as into the world and into history—by her own movement" (1976, 875).

25. In "A Feminist at the Carnival," the last essay in *Spaces Like Stairs*, Scott recalls an incident in which an undisclosed feminist writer from English Canada said to her that her work "isn't positive enough to be feminist" because it "doesn't show an upbeat enough image of solidarity." Scott replied that she wants to explore, like Virginia Woolf, "the relationship between thinking and feeling," "the struggle between [a] feminist consciousness—in both its greatness and its limitations—and social constructs, memory, dreams, nightmares" (1989, 131).

26. Here, Scott comments on the literal translation of the French word *incontournable*—"unskirtable" in English—which aptly marks its gendered inflection.

27. My use of the term *contact spaces* is a modification of Mary Louise Pratt's *contact zone*, which she defines in her book *Imperial Eyes* as "the space of colonial encounters, the space in which peoples geographically and historically separated come into contact with each other and establish ongoing relations, usually involving conditions of coercion, radical inequality, and intractable conflict" (1992, 6–7).

CHAPTER 3

1. The Weathermen, or Weather Underground, was a radical left-wing student organization founded in 1969. The Weathermen fought for black power and violently opposed the Vietnam War.

2. The term *Middle American*, which gained popular usage in the 1960s, colloquially refers to the cultural attitudes of the United States that broadly encompass its rural or suburban areas. It is used in contradistinction to the more "big-city" mindset in metropolitan areas of the country. "Middle American" also refers to the average middle-class (and also politically conservative) American, as opposed to the extremely poor or rich. See the article

"The Middle Americans," *Time*, January 5, 1970, chnm.gmu.edu/hardhats/time.middleamericans.html.

3. In February 1999, Clinton was acquitted of the two charges—perjury and the obstruction of justice—for which he was impeached.

4. The antagonism between reason and emotion is an age-old construct and can be traced back to Plato and Aristotle. The division between the "head" and the "heart" has played a central role in U.S. politics. James Madison, the "Father of the U.S. Constitution," declared in the *Federalist Papers* (1787–88) that emotions play a central role in politics but that passions drive citizens to seek self-advantage rather than an advancement of the good of all. Madison thus appealed to reason over passion for the sake of clear judgment and rational, nonpartisan political rule he termed "rational liberty" (Paper 53, February 12, 1788).

5. Some other civic textbooks and conduct manuals on how to be good American citizens in this period were *Good Citizen: The Rights and Duties of an American* (1948), *Elementary Community Civics*, by R. O. Hughes (1932), *You and Your Community*, by L. J. O'Rourke (1941), *Visualized Civics*, by Charles E. Perry and William E. Buckley (1962), and the *"Good American" Citizenship Posters*, by William J. Hutchins. Some of these are reproduced in McKnight-Trontz 2001.

6. The sixth and seventh editions of the *Boy Scout Handbooks*, written by William "Green Bar Bill" Hillcourt, had a print run of thirteen years altogether (1959–72), during which a total of 8.2 million copies were released.

7. Fittingly, all but two of the Boy Scouts calendars from 1924 to 1974, and many of the *Boys' Life* (the Boy Scouts' magazine) covers, were painted by Norman Rockwell, best known perhaps for his painting *Four Freedoms* (1943), based on President Franklin Roosevelt's 1941 State of the Union Address. Rockwell's Boy Scouts visuals depicted the "American" values of patriotism, bravery, loyalty, liberty, virtue, and the Christian faith. Brownie, Junior, Cadette, and Senior handbooks for Girl Scouts from the 1950s and early 1960s, too, stressed the importance of good conduct, patriotism, and service to one's country. Perhaps unsurprisingly, due to the gender roles of the time, they also included sections on "homemaking," "feeling good about yourself," and "puppets, dolls and plays."

8. In this respect, I am in agreement with Anne-Marie Fortier's argument (2010) that emotions have long played a central part in constructions of citizenship, not merely in the late twentieth century.

9. These critics deem affective citizenship as a model that extends the promise of an embodied political subjectivity, envisaging and even cultivating a

politics of empathy. The latter, to quote Carol Johnson, "develops a citizen identity that is more compassionate and socially connected than extreme neoliberal forms of the abstract, self-reliant citizen" (2010, 504).

10. See Marcus 2002; Mookherjee 2005; Brydon 2007; Wahl-Jorgensen 2008; and Johnson 2010.

11. As Clare Sigrist-Sutton points out, Zuckerman seems to be echoing the close of Todd Gitlin's *The Sixties: Years of Hope, Days of Rage*, wherein he writes, "Any finality I can imagine for this book seems false, for I write not just about history but imprisoned within it, enclosed within the aftermath of the Sixties, trying to peer over the walls" (quoted in Sigrist-Sutton 2010, 47).

12. This is a variation of Linda Hutcheon's term *historiographic metafiction*, which she defines as "fiction that is at once metafictional and historical in its echoes of the texts and contexts of the past" (1989, 3). Hutcheon first defined metafiction as a situation wherein "the reader or the act of reading itself often become thematized parts of the narrative situation" (1980, 37). Patricia Waugh defines metafiction as fiction that "self- consciously reflects upon its own structure as language" (1984, 14). See also Fludernik 1994. For a delineation of the difference between metafiction and metanarration, see Nünning 2004.

13. It would be interesting, within the framework of a longer study, to do a comparative reading of Roth's trilogy with Don DeLillo's novels, especially *Libra* (1988), a speculative account of the life of Lee Harvey Oswald prior to the assassination of John F. Kennedy, and *Underworld* (1997), DeLillo's fictional epic on the Cold War.

14. Ironically, of course, Swede Levov is not a WASP male, and his wife, Dawn, is of Irish ancestry. At one point in the novel, his brother Jerry Levov accuses him of "playing at being Wasps, a little Mick girl from the Elizabeth docks and a Jewboy from Weequahic High" (1997, 280).

15. These are the core values stated in the American Security Council Foundation (ASCF)'s memorandum on American values in the twenty-first century, available at www.ascfusa.org/content_pages/view/american_values.

16. See "Desire: Sweetness/Plant: The Apple" in Michael Pollan's *The Botany of Desire: A Plant's-Eye View of the World* (New York: Random House, 2001), 1–58, wherein he traces the story of Johnny Appleseed.

17. One cannot help but compare Roth's fictional depiction of the Newark riots with social media and newspaper reports of recent events surrounding police violence against black youth including Ferguson, Trayvon Martin, and numerous others.

18. See Mumford 2007.

19. See Parrish 2000; and Stanley 2005.

20. Section 3 of Adrienne Rich's poem "Cartographies of Silence" (1978) contains the following lines: "Silence can be a plan / rigorously executed // the blueprint to a life // It is a presence / it has a history a form // Do not confuse it / with any kind of absence" (Rich, *The Fact of a Doorframe: Poems, 1950–2001* [New York: Norton, 2002], 138–42). For more critical reading on this topic of silence as empowerment, see Glenn 2004. This trope of silence as resistance, which has its biblical roots in the silence of Jonah (Jonah 4:1–11), has been reinscribed in the form of feminine silence (in particular, on the part of daughters) in literary works as diverse as Shakespeare's *King Lear* (when Cordelia, Lear's youngest daughter, refuses to speak) and Sarah Orne Jewett's "A While Heron" (nine-year-old Sylvia's silence).

21. The full version of Norman Corwin's speech can heard on NPR: www.npr.org/templates/story/story.php?storyId=4668028.

22. Corwin's rhetoric also recalls the earlier passage I cited from *American Pastoral*, wherein the narrator Zuckerman speaks admiringly of the fact that the Swede manages to personify his "Americanness" in the most unremarkable, "ordinary way, the natural way, the regular American-guy way" (1997, 89).

23. Interestingly, in 1946, HUAC decided against opening investigations into the Ku Klux Klan because, according to committee member John E. Rankin, "[a]fter all, the KKK is an old American institution" (cited in Michael Newton, *The Ku Klux Klan in Mississippi: A History* [Jefferson, NC: McFarland, 2010], 102). The focus on investigating and eradicating specifically "un-*American*" activities foregrounds the height of American nationalism and the significance of the "National Symbolic" in the run-up to and the decades following World War II, especially during the McCarthy era and the Cold War.

24. This is a direct reference to Marxist historian and member of the Communist Party USA James Allen's 1946 pamphlet *Who Owns America?*

25. A popular best-seller on the level of Communist "infiltration" in the United States was Herbert Philbrick's *I Led Three Lives: Citizen, "Communist," Counterspy* (1952), which later was turned into a popular TV series that was based loosely on the experiences of Philbrick, a Boston advertising executive who infiltrated the U.S. Communist Party on behalf of the FBI. The book and the series helped to fuel the Red Scare, or the culture of fear and uncertainty as to who (friends, family, neighbors) might be involved in the Communist Party.

26. The frontier tradition is a nineteenth-century literary phenomenon in settler colonies that depicted brave men who embarked on adventures in the

untamed wilderness, emboldened by the "American spirit" to push existing frontiers back. Davy Crockett (1786–1836) is a famous example of an American frontiersman and folk hero, and Frederick Jackson Turner's *The Significance of the Frontier in American History* (1893; see Turner 2011) remains one of the most seminal essays on theories of the frontier in an American context.

27. I use the term *self-fashioning* here to denote a process of constructing one's identity and public persona according to a set of socially acceptable standards. See Stephen Greenblatt's seminal study on the topic, *Renaissance Self-Fashioning* (1980).

CHAPTER 4

1. One might recall George W. Bush's post-9/11 address in which he condemned the attacks on the World Trade Center as "evil, despicable acts of terror" and promised he would "find those responsible and bring them to justice" (*New York Times*, September 12, 2001, http://www.nytimes.com/2001/09/12/us/a-day-of-terror-bush-s-remarks-to-the-nation-on-the-terrorist-attacks.html).

2. The English term *precarious* stems from the Latin *precarius*, which denotes "obtained by entreaty, begging or prayer, hence depending on the goodwill or favor of another" (*Oxford English Dictionary*, 2nd ed.). Precariousness is commonly understood, in accordance with Isabell Lorey's (2010) definition of the term, as "both the condition and the effect of domination and security. . . . In the broadest sense, it can be described as insecurity and vulnerability, as uncertainty and endangerment." See also Lorey 2011.

3. Butler's ideas are an extension of Hannah Arendt's critical writings on universal human rights in *The Origins of Totalitarianism* (1951), which I will explore in greater detail in the next chapter.

4. I am referring to Jonathan Culler's notion of "naturalization," or the rendering familiar of the strange, in which readers, "faced with initially inconsistent or incomprehensible texts, attempt to find a frame that can naturalize the inconsistencies or oddities in a meaningful way" (2002, 33).

5. See also Nussbaum 2007; and Newton 1995.

6. These measures include the Enhanced Border Security and Visa Entry Reform Act and the Homeland Security Act, both of 2002. For a full list of legislations passed in the aftermath of 9/11, see the Library of Congress website: thomas.loc.gov/home/terrorleg.htm. The highly controversial Arizona Senate Bill 1070, passed in April 2010, is the harshest of these recent law enforcement measures. The act makes it a state misdemeanor for an alien (any noncitizen over the age of fourteen in the United States for more than

thirty days) to be in Arizona without carrying required documentation and allows police to determine a person's immigration status (via detention and arrest without a warrant) if there is reasonable suspicion that the person is an undocumented alien.

7. "Identity management" refers to the management, authorization, and authentication of identities with the aim of increasing security and enhancing as well as standardizing processes of identification. See Muller 2004.

8. Biometrics is defined as "[t]he use of unique physical characteristics (fingerprints, iris pattern, etc.) to identify individuals, typically for the purposes of security" (*Oxford English Dictionary*, 2nd ed.).

9. In her interview with Richard Kearney, Nussbaum gives some examples of the different types of "ethical" narratives: first, "narratives that show the dangers and defects of narrowly partisan loyalties." which include "tragedies of civil war, stories of ethnic conflict and genocide, stories of nationalism run amok"; second, "stories of lives in other places, through which we expand our imaginations to take in the predicaments of people different from ourselves," which include "narratives of racial difference"; and third, "tragedies of the human predicament" that depict vulnerability, pain, and disability (2007, 49–50). According to Nussbaum's categorizations, Etel Adnan's writings constitute "ethical" narratives, or narratives that engage in an "ethics of narration," on all three counts.

10. If we read *In the Heart of the Heart of Another Country* as a work of autofiction, or fictionalized autobiography, then the year of the speaker's return to Beirut would be in 1966, seventeen years after she left the city when she was twenty-four.

11. The Lebanese Civil War, which lasted from 1975 to 1990, and in which an estimated 7 percent of the population of Lebanon was killed, divided the country along the lines of religion, ethnicity, and class. Issues at the forefront of Middle Eastern politics in the 1950s and 1960s, including the Palestine-Israel conflict, the Cold War, and pan-Arab nationalism, led to the war's outbreak. Rightwing, Westernized, Maronite Christians (who dominate the government) and left-wing, pan-Arab, Muslim Lebanese (and Palestinian refugees) clashed in a complex and drawn-out war that included the Israeli invasion of Lebanon and the siege of Beirut in 1982.

12. In similar vein, the speaker's house is not a structure that affords her protection and shelter but a "cage," a "mausoleum," a "worried object" that "makes [her] feel insecure" (13). Instead of residing in her own house, the speaker spends her days in various cafés in Beirut and Paris, which are her "real homes" (22).

13. This piece was first published in the literary magazine *Penumbra* in 1999.

14. For the full text of George W. Bush's speech on Iraq in March 2008, see the Council for Foreign Relations' website: www.cfr.org/iraq/bushs-speech -iraq-march-2008/p15778.

15. This recalls the text's kaleidoscopic perspective on the subject-in-process in Gail Scott's *Heroine* that was explored in the previous chapter.

16. Proust's work was written between 1908 and 1920, and published between 1913 and 1927.

17. The Green Line in Beirut was a line of demarcation during the Lebanese Civil War. It divided the mainly Muslim factions, including a large population of Palestinian refugees, in West Beirut from the Christian Maronites in East Beirut. For more information, including a detailed interactive map of the Green Line, see almashriq.hiof.no/lebanon/900/910/919/beirut/green-line/index.html.

18. Indeed, although the civil war ended in 1990, Syrian occupation of Lebanon was to continue until 2005 and Israeli troops did not withdraw from southern Lebanon until 2001, only to be employed again in the 2006 Israel-Hezbollah War.

19. For the latest statistics on international recognition of the state of Palestine, see the documents on the United Nations website, including the recent General Assembly draft resolution, "The Right of the Palestinian People to Self-Determination," unispal.un.org/unispal.nsf/udc.htm.

20. Born in Geneva of German nationality in 1925, Jean Mohr recounts how, in 1936, "the word 'exile' ceases to be an abstract idea" (quoted in Said 1986, 8) for him when his family applied for Swiss naturalization. His fifty-year retrospective of photographic work on Palestinian refugees, *Côte à côte ou face à face* (*Side by Side or Face to Face*) (2003) offers a comprehensive overview of his work on the Palestinian issue.

21. Augé defines the term as "a space which cannot be defined as relational, or historical, or concerned with identity" (77–78).

22. As Said writes, "To most people Palestinians are visible principally as fighters, terrorists pariahs. Say the word 'terror' and a man wearing a *kaffiyah* and mask and carrying a *kalachnikov* immediately leaps before one's eyes. To a degree, the image of a helpless, miserable-looking refugee has been replaced by this menacing one as the veritable icon of 'Palestinian'" (1986, 4).

CHAPTER 5

1. The term *Atlantic Canada* was coined by Joey Smallwood, the first premier of Newfoundland, upon Newfoundland and Labrador's entry into the Canadian

Confederation in 1949. I use "Atlantic Canada" with some caution because, as Herb Wyile writes, "the very notion of 'Atlantic Canada' is a novel and contested one, especially because of the difference in the histories of the Maritimes and Newfoundland" (2011, 7) and, as Margaret Conrad and James Hiller note, many actually "have trouble imagining such a community" (2001, 1).

2. License reduction programs, higher overhead costs, and federal budget cuts in the fishing industry in the 1990s made it difficult for fishermen and smaller fisheries in Atlantic Canada to make a living. See L. S. Parsons and W. H. Lear, eds., *Perspectives on Canadian Marine Fisheries Management* Canadian Bulletin of Fisheries and Aquatic Science No. 226 (Ottawa: National Research Council of Canada and Department of Fisheries and Oceans, 1993); and Joseph Gough's "Fisheries History," *The Canadian Encyclopedia*, www.thecanadianencyclopedia.com/articles/fisheries-history.

3. For a comprehensive critical account of regionalism in Atlantic Canada, see Slumkoski 2011. I adopt Slumkoski's definition of regionalism which, as he writes, "implies a political stance, a consciousness of shared outlook that can be summoned up when all other structures—familial, communal, provincial, national, global—fail" (10, quoting Conrad and Hiller 2001, 6). Slumkoski notes that this "shared outlook" is often more imagined (recalling Benedict Anderson's "imagined communities") than "real." A drawback of regionalism lies (especially in the phenomenon of cultural tourism) in its proliferation of stereotypes—imagined cultural images associated with specific regions that bear little resemblance to the "reality" of Canada's geographies (11).

4. One might recall, for example, the regionalist condemnation in 2002 of the comments of Stephen Harper, then leader of the Canadian Alliance, on what he deemed a "culture of defeatism" in Atlantic Canada.

5. As Slumkoski summarizes, "On the surface, the union [between Newfoundland and the Maritimes] seemed like an unprecedented opportunity to resurrect the regional spirit of the Maritime Rights movement of the 1920s, which advocated a cooperative approach to addressing regional underdevelopment. However, Newfoundland's arrival did little at first to bring about a comprehensive Atlantic Canadian regionalism" (2011, back cover).

6. It is important that one distinguish this from the ethno-regionalism of the New Right. For a definition of the latter, see Spektorowski 2003.

7. "Local-color writing" refers to a popular form of writing that flourished in the late nineteenth century in the southern states. These works, written predominantly by white writers—a few exceptions being Charles Chesnutt (1858–1932), Paul Laurence Dunbar (1872–1906), and Alice Dunbar-Nelson

(1875–1935)—were mostly humorous short stories "devoted to capturing the unique customs, manners, speech, folklore, and other qualities of a particular regional community" (*Oxford Dictionary of Literary Terms*, 3rd ed.) and tended to idealize life in the antebellum South. Local-color writers included Mark Twain, George W. Cable, Kate Chopin, and Sarah Orne Jewett. Regional writing, on the other hand, refers to a broader recognition of differences between life in specific areas of the country. In this respect, I would argue that the works that depict Africville are regional writings rather than contemporary works of local color. For a comparison of regionalism and local color, see Sundquist 1988; and Greeson 2006.

8. These include George Boyd's play *Consecrated Ground* (1998), Dorothy Perkyns's novel *Last Days in Africville* (2006), Neil Donaldson's film *Stolen from Africville* (2008), activist and folk singer Faith Nolan's album *Africville* (1986), jazz pianist Joe Sealy's album *Africville Suite* (1996), and Angel Gannon's paintings and sculptures featured in the exhibit Africville Memories: Paintings and Carvings (2012).

9. Foucault uses the term *counter-memory* to refer to the archive of popular memory, narratives, and accounts that are in contradistinction to official versions of history and its political formations. See Foucault 1977, 2003.

10. Due to the constraints of scope, I will not consider the work of white regionalist Atlantic Canadian writers such as Alistair MacLeod, Wayne Johnston, L. M. Montgomery, and Bernice Morgan, although some of their works are commentaries on the omission of regional cultural heritage in "official" national narratives. Bernice Morgan's *Cloud of Bone* (2007), for example, seeks to redress the elimination of the Beothuk native inhabitants of Newfoundland, and Wayne Johnston's *The Colony of Unrequited Dreams* (1998) is a fictional depiction of Joey Smallwood's contentious battle to lead Newfoundland into Canadian Confederation in 1949.

11. These Jamaican Maroons were deported by the British to Sierra Leone in 1800.

12. According to an 1812 official document by William Sabatier, one-sixth of the population of Halifax was black. "African Nova Scotians: In the Age of Slavery and Abolition," *The Nova Scotian Archives*, www.gov.ns.ca/nsarm/virtual/africanns/.

13. See Clairmont and Magill 1971, especially chapter 7, "Mechanics of the Relocation."

14. For a detailed firsthand account of the relocation, see *The Spirit of Africville*, a work of remembrance and documentation published by the African Genealogy Society (1992).

15. In order to provide a point of comparative analysis, I will examine the status of black freedmen and their claims to citizenship in a U.S. context (their exclusion from political membership of the Cherokee Nation of Oklahoma), in chapter 12.

16. The name Arcadia was initially bestowed by sixteenth-century Italian explorer Giovanni da Verrazzano on the entire North American Atlantic coast north of Virginia. In the seventeenth century, Samuel de Champlain, navigator, cartographer, and "Father of New France" omitted the "r," thus giving birth to Acadia.

17. For a more detailed explanation and a comparison of the various models of relocation, see Clairmont and Magill 1999, 5–10.

18. This was the most common model of relocation in North America. A prime example of this type of relocation was the forced removal of Cree Indians in northern Manitoba in the 1970s to make way for the construction of large hydropower generators.

19. An example from the documentary is an ex-resident recalling how she would come home from school and think to herself how the houses, all painted in different colors like a rainbow, were so "pretty" (3:20).

20. Indeed, the novel was subsequently turned into a play in 1999.

21. Clarke's use of "variegate composition" recalls the hybrid, creolized, multiple-rooted, and relational or "rhizomatic" identity of which Édouard Glissant, borrowing from Deleuze and Guattari's *Rhizome* (1976), writes in *Traité du tout-monde* (1997b).

22. The title of Foucault's lectures has often been misquoted as *Society Must Be Defended*. The correct title actually contains the phrase in quotation marks: *"Society Must Be Defended."*

23. Interestingly, these are African American not black Canadian artists. Clarke's "importing" of these black voices from the United States might thus be read as a result of his criticism that black Canadian identities are more heterogeneous than African American identities, which are more "coherent."

24. The concept of "writing back," which has now become a mainstay of postcolonial theory, was first proposed by Bill Ashcroft, Gareth Griffiths, and Helen Tiffin in *The Empire Writes Back* (1989), which takes its title from Salman Rushdie's polemic essay "The Empire Strikes Back with a Vengeance" (1981). The expression *writing back* denotes the developing of national literatures in colonized communities after political independence that challenge the traditional literary canon, as well as dominant ideas of literature and culture, of the colonizer.

25. Critical race theory (CRT), which originated in the mid-1970s in the discipline of law, can broadly be defined as an interdisciplinary attempt by activists

and scholars to explore, through theory and practice, the relationships between race, racism, and power structures. Interestingly, although it originated in the 1970s, CRT has only more recently begun to be acknowledged within an academic context, as reflected in several symposiums, such as the "Frontiers in Social Justice Lawyering: Critical Race Revisited" (2009) and "Critical Race Theory: From the Academy to the Community" (2013), conferences held at Yale University, as well as the annual conventions held by the Critical Race Studies in Education Association (CRSEA), www.crseassoc.org/.

26. In their explorations and depictions of the complex history of "Africadian" identity and culture, *Whylah Falls* and George Elliott Clarke's other writings represent "acts of self-definition and resistance against a city and a legal system that do not want to hear voices . . . that deviate from the dominant white Loyalist heritage . . . of the Maritimes" (Andrews 2008, 125).

27. Homi Bhabha uses the term *mimicry* to describe the imitation of the colonial language, social codes, dress, and cultural traditions by the colonized. In his essay "Of Mimicry and Man" (1991), Bhabha also suggests the potentially subversive nature of mimicry because it exposes the artificiality of symbolic and discursive modes of power. As Ashcroft, Griffiths, and Tiffin encapsulate, "[M]imicry is never far from mockery, since it can appear to parody whatever it mimics" (1989, 139).

28. The class struggle of Maritime fish-plant workers who provide "tough labour for one cent per pound of gutted fish" ("Class Struggle," Clarke 2000, 81).

29. The Cotton Belt denotes the former agricultural region of the United States where cotton was grown and harvested as the major cash crop from the late eighteenth to the twentieth centuries. The Cotton Belt includes the states of North Carolina, South Carolina, Georgia, Alabama, Mississippi, and Louisiana as well as parts of Tennessee, Arkansas, Texas, Oklahoma, Missouri, Kentucky, Florida, and Virginia. See Burton 1984.

30. For more on the trope of flight in African American folktales and folksongs, such as the popular "Myth of the Flying Africans" associated with Igbo Landing in Georgia, see Snyder 2010; and Wamba 1999.

31. Heritage tourism, widespread in this region, purports to offer a retreat from the hectic pace of life, from the "anxiety occasioned by the mobility, deracination, and sense of placelessness [/homelessness] that characterize our highly technological, our globalized consumer society" (Wyile 2011, 233). Nevertheless, the commoditization and marketing of nostalgic, sepia-toned versions of the past and its folklore tend to obscure the power structures that "displaced, subjected

and exploited subaltern subjects" (234), be they the Indigenous Mi'kmaq, freed slaves, or socioeconomically disadvantaged black communities.

CHAPTER 6

1. The main difference between refugee and asylum status is as follows: in the United States, a refugee denotes a person who applies for refugee protection status from *outside* the United States. Once *physically present in the country*, a refugee (and her or his spouse and children) may be eligible for asylum. See www.uscis.gov/humanitarian/refugees-asylum. In Canada, the distinction is slightly more complex as there are two "classes" of "resettlement *from outside Canada*"—the "convention refugee abroad class" and "country of asylum class." The first denotes people currently outside of their home country who "*cannot return there* due to a well-founded fear of persecution based on race, religion, political opinion, nationality, or membership in a particular social group, such as women or people with a particular sexual orientation." The second denotes people who are "outside of their home country or the country where they normally live and have been, *and continue to be*, seriously and personally affected by civil war or armed conflict, or have suffered massive violations of human rights." The applications for refugee protection by people who are already *physically within* Canada are also classified as asylum claims. See www.cic.gc.ca/english/refugees/inside/index.asp.

2. The figure stands at 51.2 million and comprises 16.7 million refugees, 33.3 million internally displaced persons, and 1.2 million asylum seekers. If these 51.2 million people were to come together to form a nation, it would be the twenty-sixth largest in the world. See "UNHCR Global Trends," unhcr.org.au/unhcr/images/Global%20Trends%202013.pdf.

3. Agamben's comment recalls Salman Rushdie's contention in *Imaginary Homelands* that "the migrant is, perhaps, the central or defining figure of the twentieth century" (1991, 277). I will discuss Rushdie's comment later.

4. The twentieth century, according to Agamben, witnessed "the inexorable decline of the nation-state and the general corrosion of traditional legal-political categories" (1995, 114).

5. In *Soft Borders: Rethinking Sovereignty and Democracy*, Julie Mostov argues that the soft border approach "explicitly rejects the hard border approach of ethno-nationalism and is suspicious of nationalist arguments for hardening borders in the name of domestic and social solidarity [and] it does not deny the importance of associative obligations or special relationships and commitments among members of particular groups" (2008, 5). Mostov continues

that the "soft border argument envisions that rights and responsibilities of citizenship ought to be enjoyed by all people wherever they live and work on equal terms with others within (multilevel) political associations. Under these conditions, movement across borders would be unconstrained by nationality of ethnicity" (6).

6. The H-1B visa is a nonimmigrant visa that allows U.S. employers to temporarily employ foreign workers in specialty professions. H-1B visa holders must possess at least a bachelor's degree or its equivalent. They can apply for and obtain permanent residency (a green card) while still holders of the visa and are allowed to bring immediate family members (spouse and children under twenty-one) to the United States with them. When H-1B workers travel outside of the United States, they have to get a visa stamped in their passport for reentry unless they have already done so.

7. The statue's full name was originally Liberty Enlightening the World or, in the French, "La Liberté éclairant le monde."

8. These enhanced security measures included the introduction of the Patriot Act (Uniting and Strengthening America by Providing Appropriate Tools Required to Intercept and Obstruct Terrorism) of 2001, the Homeland Security Act of 2002, the Real ID Act of 2005, and increased detentions, deportations, heightened screening, and controls by Border Patrol along the U.S.-Mexican border. Anne McNevin provides food for thought when she observes in *Contesting Citizenship*, "According to the Department of Homeland Security, the number of immigrants living in the United States without authorization increased by 27 percent between 2000 and 2009, bringing the total number of irregular migrants close to eleven million. This increase occurred despite the dramatic upscaling of border-patrol agencies, budgets, operations, and technologies during the 1990s" (2011, 119). McNevin argues that the effect of increased border policing is not so much to counter the trend of migration flows across the border from Mexico to the United States but "to change the status of migrant workers to 'illegal immigrants' and to intensify the surveillance to which they are subject" (123).

9. One of them includes an ironic rendition of the common experience Indian migrants face while humorously making fun of the (presumably white) American's ignorance. Kumar writes, "When you turn to me in the bus or the plane and talk to me—*if* you talk to me—you might comment, trying to be kind, 'Your English is very good.' If I am feeling relaxed, and the burden of the permanent chip on my shoulder seems light, I will smile and say, 'Thank you' (I never add, 'So is yours'). Perhaps I will say, 'Unfortunately, the

credit goes to imperialism. The British, you know . . .' (Once a fellow traveler widened her eyes and asked, 'The British still rule over *India*?'") (2000, 23).

10. The accompanying stage direction for reading these lines aloud are "with thick Mexican accent, pointing at specific audience members." See Gómez-Peña 1991, 52.

11. This was initiated later by the Enhanced Border Security and Visa Entry Reform Act of 2002.

12. Kumar's argument calls to mind Alice Edwards and Carla Ferstman's concise observation in "Humanizing Non-citizens: The Convergence of Human Rights and Human Security" that in security paradigms where "notions of sovereignty, border control and citizenship are of primary importance, . . . the non-citizen is usually the first to be excluded, neglected or treated with suspicion as threats to the security of the state surface" (2010, 4).

13. See the U.S. Department of State's online guidelines for passport photographs, travel.state.gov/passport/pptphotoreq/pptphotoreq_5333.html.

14. This is a direct quote from John Berger's influential essay "Uses of Photography" (1978) in *About Looking* (1980, 63).

15. I will elaborate on the depiction of this topic in Shani Mootoo's novel *Valmiki's Daughter* in chapter 8.

16. The term NRI is also jokingly interpreted as "Neo Rich Indian," "Newly Respected Indian," and "Never Return to India." According to the Foreign Exchange Management Act (FEMA) of India, an NRI is defined as "a person resident outside India who is either a citizen of India or is a person of Indian origin (PIO)." PIOs are persons of Indian ancestry who may or may not be Indian citizens. See the Reserve Bank of India's Notification No. 5/2000-RB (dealing with various kinds of bank accounts) for the full definition of NRI and PIO: rbi.org.in/scripts/BS_FemaNotifications.aspx?Id=159.

17. For an empirical analysis of the impact of the Overseas Citizen of India scheme on applications for naturalization in the United States by persons of Indian origin, see Naujoks 2012. Naujoks argues that the introduction of the OCI scheme has led to higher naturalization rates (and hence acquisition of American citizenship) among Indian immigrants to the United States.

18. One common critique is that the OCI card is not a substitute for an Indian passport. Because of this grievance, many holders of the OCI card have complained that this document does not effectively confer "dual citizenship" despite the use of the term *citizen* in its designation.

19. The film depicts a lesbian relationship between Radha and Sita that outraged Hindu fundamentalists in India who attacked some of the movie theaters on

its opening day. The movie was banned in India and Pakistan on the grounds of religious insensitivity and the depiction of lesbian desire.

20. Sociologist William Petersen coined the term *model minority* in a *New York Times Magazine* article in 1966 to describe Asian Americans as ethnic minorities who, despite marginalization, had achieved considerable personal and financial success in the United States. Petersen's description of Japanese Americans' strong work ethics and family values is akin to the qualities commonly ascribed to the Indian "model minority." As Kumar notes, Shashi Tharoor has also described these qualities in his book *India: From Midnight to Millennium* as characteristic of dominant perceptions in the West of the nonresident Indian.

21. Kumar cites, for example, the Bhagat Singh Thind case: in 1923, an Indian World War I veteran's appeal for U.S. citizenship was turned down by the Supreme Court, which ruled that Indians were not "Caucasian" and hence not eligible for citizenship (2000, 197).

22. The exclusion of and denial of citizenship to Asian migrants in the United States stretches back to the Immigration Acts of 1882, 1917, 1924, and 1934, which excluded immigrants from Asia. The Immigration Act of 1917 even designated an "Asiatic Barred Zone," which was not abolished until the McCarran-Walter Act of 1952. Asian migrant quotas were not lifted in the United States until the implementation of the Immigration and Nationality Act of 1965. A year later, as noted in the introduction of this study, Canada followed suit.

23. news.nationalpost.com/2011/12/12/niqabs-burkas-must-be-removed-during-citizenship-ceremonies-jason-kenney/.

24. Kumar's analysis of the headscarf debate can be read in conjunction with Seyla Benhabib's commentary on the "scarf affair" in France and Germany in the last chapter of her study "Democratic Iterations: The Local, the National, and the Global" in *The Rights of Others* (2004).

25. Benhabib proposes an alternative form of democratic, "disaggregated citizenship" whereby "individuals can develop and sustain multiple allegiances and networks across nation-state boundaries, in inter- as well as transnational contexts" (174–75).

CHAPTER 7

1. Feminist modernist scholar Jane Marcus lauds *Nightwood* for its "linguistic richness," its "abundance of puns and plays on words, its fierce allusiveness to medieval and Jacobean high and low art, and the extraordinary range of its learned reach across the history of Western culture" (1991, 163).

2. In her article "Expatriate Sapphic Modernism," Benstock defines two types of Sapphic modernism as represented by "those women of the London and Paris communities whose writings followed traditional models of form and style, but whose subject matter was Sapphism (Radclyffe Hall's *The Well of Loneliness* . . .), and those writers who filtered the lesbian content of their writing through the screen of presumably heterosexual subject matter or behind experimental styles (Virginia Woolf, H.D.)" (1994, 99). Although, clearly, the bigger picture is more complex, Benstock's two categories are useful points of departure. Barnes's *Nightwood* clearly surpasses both categories in its experimental form and its depiction of a sexual love triangle between three women.

3. Nevertheless, Carolyn Allen has a point when she states that "*Nightwood*'s lesbian erotics position subjects who are white, middle-class, and U.S. Americans and who divide their time between the United States and Europe. As is often true of Anglo-American novels of the period, the race and class positions of the characters are marked by the absence of explicit markings as if their privileged status made it unnecessary to describe their whiteness" (1993, 181).

4. Examples include Sashi Nair's recent study, *Secrecy and Sapphic Modernism* (2012); and modernist scholar Phillip Herring's "Djuna Barnes and the Narrative of Violation" (1990).

5. Elisabeth Bronfen, too, cautions against "focusing on the biographical details of [Barnes's] life and her situation as a female writer," as such an approach "would ignore the fact that Barnes addresses the question of gender and writing not only by writing as a woman but more importantly by showing how femininity as a cultural construct, as an image, functions to support and sustain the process by which meaning in narratives is produced" (1988, 169).

6. Clearly, as the experiences of American expatriate artists and writers such Josephine Baker and James Baldwin illustrate, living in Europe was exceedingly preferable to living in the United States in the early and mid-twentieth century due to restrictive American laws pertaining to issues of sexuality and race. Especially in Baldwin's case, his involvement in the cultural radicalism and bohemianism of the Parisian Left Bank was less a straightforward expression of anti-Americanism than a desire for himself and his writing to be considered beyond an African American context—in Baldwin's own words, he wanted to be read as not "merely a Negro; or, even, merely a Negro writer" (1961, 3).

7. I will elaborate this point later in the section on Robin's bestiality and animalism.

8. Scholars affiliated with the "new western history" movement have called for a rethinking of frontier theory along the lines of race, class, and gender. For example, Ward and Maveety (1995) have commented on the almost complete absence of women of all ethnicities in Turner's frontier thesis. See also Limerick 1987; and Limerick, Milner, and Rankin 1991.

9. Shari Benstock argues that the character of Nora Flood signifies what she has termed a "Sapphic modernism" (1994, 97), one that not only "announces itself as a rupture, a break with the past, and marks a cultural-historical shift" (like the "serious" works of "high" and "avant-garde modernism") but that also articulates a poetics of "playfulness" and transgression that centers on the "excluded Other" (100).

10. Although modernist circles included both male and female American expatriates, contemporary critical reception largely applauded the works of male writers like T. S. Eliot and Ezra Pound, over their female counterparts such as Djuna Barnes, H.D., and Gertrude Stein, whose work was deemed "difficult" or "opaque."

11. Lyotard's term *grand narrative* is akin to "master narrative" or "metanarrative." In this respect, Stephens and McCallum's definition of a "metanarrative" as "a global or totalizing cultural narrative schema which orders and explains knowledge and experience" (1998, 6) is useful.

12. I am clearly referring to the 1935 American western film starring John Wayne, and not to two British works of the same name—the 1607 Jacobean satire by Thomas Dekker and John Webster, and the 1855 historical novel by Charles Kingsley.

13. Victoria L. Smith argues that *Nightwood* is written in a "language of loss," the narrative "shap[ing] itself around a blank space, an absence, that outlines a loss of access to history, to language, and to representation in general for those consigned to the margins of culture because of their gender, sexuality, religion, or color" (1999, 194–95).

14. *Nightwood* was first published in 1936 in London by Faber and Faber, and then in 1937 by Harcourt, Brace in the United States, after Barnes had struggled to find a publisher for the novel for several years. Another modernist masterpiece, James Joyce's *Ulysses*, was banned from publication in the United States in 1921 on charges of pornography. It was not allowed into the country until a court case overruled this decision in 1933.

15. *New Oxford American Dictionary*, 3rd ed.

16. *Oxford English Dictionary*, 2nd ed.

17. Robin Vote's bestiality, which challenges the Darwinist theory that humankind is the "highest" form of animal, can also be interpreted as a critique of social Darwinism, a theory that motivated theories of fascism and Nazism that were witnessing their height in the 1930s in the years just before *Nightwood* was published.

18. See also Knapp 1986–87 for a comprehensive analytical overview of scholarly work and research on primitivism and modernism.

19. Barnes also directly references Rousseau's jungle paintings in this scene: Robin "seem[s] to lie in a jungle trapped in a drawing room (in the apprehension of which the walls have made their escape), thrown in among the carnivorous flowers as their ration" (38).

20. The primitivist paintings of Gauguin, Rousseau, and Klee, among others, clearly draw upon the romanticizing of nature and the wilderness that was common in nineteenth-century painting.

21. Modern biological classifications are based on the studies of Carl Linnaeus, an eighteenth-century Swedish botanist and zoologist, and Darwinism in the nineteenth century. For further reading, see Goodman, Heat, and Linde 2003.

22. For further critical reading on the trope of excess in modernist writing, see Rasula 2002. Rasula argues that hyperbole, extravagance, dissonance, and rupture are characteristic of modernist writing's poetics of excess.

23. Unemployment in the United States peaked at 25 percent in 1933. See Swanson and Williamson 1972.

24. As Aldous Huxley writes in *Along the Road: Notes And Essays of a Tourist* (1925), "We read and travel, not that we may broaden and enrich our minds, but that we may pleasantly forget they exist" (18).

25. Catherine Whitley describes her in the "jungle" scene as "rotting vegetation or, alternatively, a decomposing corpse" (2000, 91).

26. The "self-made man" is perhaps one of the foremost of American tropes, embodied as early as during the American Revolutionary War by Benjamin Franklin's personal rags-to-riches experience. The term *self-made men* was first used by Frederick Douglass in a speech delivered in 1859, wherein he spoke of "men who owe little or nothing to birth, relationship, friendly surroundings; to wealth inherited or to early approved means of education; who are what they are, without the aid of any of the favoring conditions by which other men usually rise in the world and achieve great results" (1992, 549–50).

27. Notably, Felix does not mention Robin by name; instead, she is simply reduced to her nationality.

28. For instance, Sandra Gilbert and Susan Gubar have interpreted this final scene in affirmative terms, perceiving Robin as "the invert who recaptures

the physical, the bestial, that has been debased by culture" (1989, 361), whereas Diane Warren is of a different opinion, pointing out the dog's terrified reaction to Robin's turning animal (2008, 137).

29. The phrase "national life" was common in U.S. political discourse at the time. It was used, for instance, by both Herbert Hoover and Franklin D. Roosevelt. Hoover used it in his "Rugged Individualism" speech of 1928, which supported free private enterprise over government intervention into commercial business. He proclaimed, "The principles to which [the Republican Party] adheres are rooted deeply in the foundations of our national life." For the full text of Hoover's speech, see http://millercenter.org/president/speeches/speech-6000. In comparison, Roosevelt used the phrase in his 1933 inaugural address, stressing that economic recovery could be brought about only with new policies and a new national attitude. Roosevelt's memorable words were, "This great Nation will endure as it has endured. . . . In every dark hour of our national life a leadership of frankness and vigor has met with that understanding and support of the people themselves which is essential to victory." Michael Nelson, ed., *Guide to the Presidency and the Executive Branch*, 5th ed. (Thousand Oaks, CA: CQ Press / Sage, 2013), 1871.

30. See, for example, T. S. Eliot's unreserved praise of this section in his introduction to the novel (2006, xvii–xxiii).

31. Angela Carter performs a similar rewriting of "Little Red Riding Hood" in her short story "The Company of Wolves" in the collection *The Bloody Chamber* (2000). In Carter's story, the roles of the wolf and Little Red Riding Hood are reversed; she seduces him, and the story ends with the lines, "See! Sweet and sound she sleeps in granny's bed, between the paws of the tender wolf" (139).

32. This also reflects a feminist response to Charles Perrault's moral of "Don't talk to strangers" at the end of his story "Le petit chaperon rouge," the earliest known printed version of the fable: "Children, especially attractive, well bred young ladies, should never talk to strangers, for if they should do so, they may well provide dinner for a wolf. I say 'wolf,' but there are various kinds of wolves. There are also those who are charming, quiet, polite, unassuming, complacent, and sweet, who pursue young women at home and in the streets. And unfortunately, it is these gentle wolves who are the most dangerous ones of all" (Lang 1965, 53)

33. This is a reference to the stock figure of the bearded lady common in circus freak shows of the nineteenth and early twentieth centuries. As a gesture of subversion, Matthew O'Connor identifies himself as a freak (as opposed to being labeled a freak by others). He also indulges in camp and exaggeration, two performative modes of willful resistance.

34. Ahmed Nimeiri reads O'Connor as "the degenerated and vulgarized form" of Herman Melville's confidence man (the protagonist of his 1857 eponymous novel), although "he [O'Connor] plays his own tricks on himself" and "lacks the control and mastery over experience . . . and the sense of purpose that distinguishes [Melville's] original character" (109).

35. As the diametrical opposite of the "tragic trickster" figure, Smith-Rosenberg cites Shakespeare's character of Rosalind in *As You Like It*, who carries out her "gender trick" with wit and intelligence, as a prime example of the "triumphant trickster" (293).

36. The New Woman—a feminist ideal of the late nineteenth century—was active in the suffragette movement, "challeng[ing] existing gender relations and the distribution of power" (Smith-Rosenberg 1985, 245) and threatening the legitimacy and "naturalness" of the bourgeois order. The New Woman "adopted male language to [her] own symbolic and political intent," "invested male images with female political intent," and "sought to use male myths to repudiate male power" (246). Ruth Bordin argues that Henry James, who popularized the figure of the New Woman in his writings, intended her "to characterize American expatriates living in Europe: women of affluence and sensitivity, who despite or perhaps because of their wealth exhibited an independent spirit and were accustomed to acting on their own" (1993, 2). The emergence in the early 1920s of the decadent, reckless, and excessive flapper who flouted social and sexual conventions is now commonly perceived as marking the end of the era of the New Woman.

37. For example, T. S. Eliot had to censor some passages in the manuscript of *Nightwood* before Faber and Faber would agree to publish it.

38. Barnes's other works, such as *The Book of Repulsive Women* (1915) and *Ladies Almanack* (1928), better serve this purpose of satirizing social and cultural attitudes toward women.

39. See Julia Kristeva's *Powers of Horror: An Essay on Abjection* (1982), in particular the last chapter, where she states, "[L]iterature may also involve not an ultimate resistance to but an unveiling of the abject" (208).

CHAPTER 8

1. Queer migration scholarship has flourished in the last two decades and it would be impossible to list all the book-length studies in this field. Nevertheless, two excellent edited collections deserve special mention here: Patton and Sánchez-Eppler 2000; and Luibhéid and Cantú 2005.

2. See Luibhéid 2004; and Manalansan 2006.

3. One common perception, for instance, is that the heterosexual migrant is favorable to the homosexual one because the former can be incorporated more easily into hegemonic national(ist) identities and projects as well as contribute to the future generations of the nation. In contrast, the queer migrant is an "undesirable" body because, as it is commonly assumed, it is a nonreproductive one.

4. See Luibhèid 2008, 170. See also the introduction to Manalansan 2003 as well as the chapter "'Out There': The Topography of Race and Desire in the Global City."

5. As M. Jacqui Alexander notes, "[N]ot just (any) body can be a citizen any more, for some bodies have been marked by the state as non-procreative, in pursuit of sex only for pleasure, a sex that is non-productive of babies and of no economic gain. Having refused the heterosexual imperative of citizenship, these bodies, according to the state, pose a profound threat to the very survival of the nation. Thus, . . . as the state moves to reconfigure the nation it simultaneously resuscitates the nation as heterosexual" (1994, 6).

6. Affect theory is a flourishing field of interdisciplinary studies. It would be impossible to outline its main arguments here in their entirety, but Ruth Leys's essay "The Turn to Affect: A Critique" (2011) gives a useful critical overview of the field and discusses the seminal works of its main proponents: Silvan Tomkins (1963); Brian Massumi (2002); and Eve Kosofsky Sedgwick (2003), among others.

7. This reminds me of Jeannette Winterson's response to Dylan Thomas's similar praise of Djuna Barnes's *Nightwood* as "one of the three great prose books ever written by a woman." Winterson writes in her preface to the New Directions edition of *Nightwood*, "[A]ccept the compliment to DB, ignore the insult directed elsewhere" (2006, ix). I read Brathwaite's compliment in similar fashion.

8. This line, taken from Derek Walcott's *Midsummer*, is also the title of Brand's collection of poems from 1990.

9. Brand's appointment as Toronto's poet laureate, or the city's "ambassador of poetry," exemplifies this.

10. I will come back to this point in chapter 10 in my reading of Dionne Brand's *What We All Long For*.

11. It is also significant that, although Brand emigrated to Canada in the late 1970s and her work has been published by presses based in Toronto since then, her fictional writings from the 1980s and 1990s continue to be predominantly set in the Caribbean.

12. Omise'eke Natasha Tinsley makes this salient point in her essay "Black Atlantic, Queer Atlantic: Queer Imaginings of the Middle Passage." She writes, "[T]he black Atlantic has always been the queer Atlantic. What Paul Gilroy never told us is how queer relationships were forged on merchant and pirate ships, where Europeans and Africans slept with fellow—and I mean same-sex—sailors. [These relationships] resisted the commodification of their bought and sold bodies by feeling and feeling for their co-occupants on these ships" (2008, 191–92).

13. The character of Verlia is especially associated with water, the element to which she returns in her moment of death, plunging off the cliff into the sea.

14. See the work of another Trinidad and Tobago–born Torontian writer, M. NourbeSe Philip's *Zong!* (2008), a complex, multivoiced, linguistically and formally experimental textual soundscape that pays tribute to the case of the slave ship *Zong*. In November 1781, Captain Luke Collingwood, on account of a navigational error that prolonged the journey from Africa to the New World by two months, ordered that some 150 Africans be murdered by drowning so that the ship's owners could collect insurance money for the "cargo" they had lost. Relying on the only existing legal document that records the massacre of these African slaves, the case of *Gregson v. Gilbert*, *Zong!* is M. NourbeSe Philip's attempt to "(not) tell the story that must be told" (189), an endeavor to depict the fragmentation and violent disfigurement central to the experience and memory of the Middle Passage via a poetics of "not-telling," of antinarrative, that breaks the boundaries of poetic form.

15. Repeating this refusal to name on a metafictional level, the setting of Brand's novel is also an unnamed Caribbean island that, however, strongly resembles Grenada.

16. The title *A Map to the Door of No Return* refers to both a real and metaphorical place, its physical location being on Gorée Island, Senegal, in the history of the transatlantic slave trade.

17. The concept of "rememory" was coined by Toni Morrison in her novel *Beloved* to denote a shared, intersubjective, collective act of memory as well as a tangible object that can be bumped into, inhabited, occupied. Rememories symbolically recall colonial legacies of dispossession and cultural erasure; narratives of the black Atlantic, for example, form collective "rememories" of the experience of slavery.

18. For this reason, Césaire is often regarded as one of the founders of the négritude movement in francophone literature.

19. Brand writes, "Black experience in any modern city or town in America is a haunting. One enters a room and history follows; one enters a room and history precedes. History is already seated in the chair in the empty room when one arrives. . . . Where one can be observed is relative to that history. . . . How do I know this? Only by self-observation, only by looking. Only by feeling. Only by being a part, sitting in the room with history (2002, 25).

20. This illustrates the viewpoint that citizenship is a practice as, being marginalized by society and having no one to practice it on/with, these migrants are not regarded as citizens.

21. I will expand on Brand's critique of Canadian multiculturalism in chapter 10.

22. Mae Ngai, for example, argues convincingly in *Impossible Subjects: Illegal Aliens and the Making of Modern America* that "illegal alienage is not a natural or fixed condition, but the product of . . . law; it is contingent and at times unstable. . . . [T]he line between legal and illegal status can be crossed in both directions" (2004, 6).

23. The Immigration and Refugee Protection Act of Canada, established in 2003, gives officers of the Canada Border Service Agency (CBSA) the authority to detain permanent residents and foreign nationals if they have violated the rulings of the act. Interestingly, on February 20, 2013, the city council of Toronto voted in favor of Motion CD 18.5 with regard to undocumented workers in Toronto, which "re-affirm[ed] its commitment to ensuring access to services without fear to immigrants without full status or without full status documents." This makes Toronto the first city in Canada with a formal policy allowing undocumented migrants access to services such as food banks and homeless shelters. app.toronto.ca/tmmis/viewAgendaItemHistory. do?item=2013.CD18.5.

24. The United Nations General Assembly Resolution 38/7 records that the U.S. invasion of Grenada "constitutes a flagrant violation of international law and of the independence, sovereignty and territorial integrity of that State" (www.un.org/depts/dhl/resguide/r38.htm), although in the United States the invasion was described by *Time* magazine as having "broad popular support." "Getting Back to Normal: As Grenada Begins to Rebuild, Support Solidifies for the Invasion" *Time*, November 21, 1983, 16–17.

25. See Castronovo 2001, which traces the intimate relationship between death and citizenship in American politics and social ideology.

26. Carib's Leap is a forty-meter-tall cliff in the town of Sauters (French for "jumpers") on the north coast of Grenada.

27. These include revolts in St. John (in 1733), Jamaica (Tacky's Rebellion in 1760), Guyana (the Berbice slave revolt in 1763 and the Demerara Rebellion of 1795), Haiti (the Haitian Revolution, 1790), Jamaica (the Second Maroon War, 1795–96), and Grenada (Fédon's Rebellion, 1795–96) as well as numerous uprisings in Cuba (from 1795 to 1844) and other parts of the Caribbean.

28. The Marxist-Leninist New Jewel Movement (1974–1983) and the People's Revolutionary Government of Grenada under the presidency of Maurice Bishop firmly established ideological ties with Cuba and the USSR. Male homosexuality remains illegal in Grenada. Female homosexuality in Grenada is discriminated against but not legally punishable, as, according to the criminal law concerning same-sex intimacy, "the offence [unnatural carnal knowledge] cannot be committed by two females." www2.ohchr.org/english/bodies/hrc/docs/ngos/LGBTShadow_Grenada_annex.pdf.

29. *L. Camara* is the botanical name of the common lantana plant. It is considered an invasive toxic species in many tropical and subtropical areas and is poisonous to animals. Mootoo's use of this name for the setting of her debut novel is thus darkly ironic, and far from paradisal.

30. These would, by contrast, include the likes of V. S. Naipaul, Neil Bissoondath, Samuel Salvon, David Dabydeen, and his cousin, Cyril Dabydeen (the last two writers hailing from Guyana and not Trinidad and Tobago).

31. Indo-Trinidadians are largely descendants of the indentured workers brought from India to replace freed African slaves who stopped working on the island's sugar plantations after the British Parliament passed the Slavery Abolition Act of 1833. Trinidad and Tobago was a British colony from 1802 to 1962.

32. See Baronov and Yelvington 2009.

33. For example, the steel pan or steel drum, which is the country's national instrument, had its origins in African percussion music. During colonial times, African slaves who were not allowed to take part in Carnival formed their own alternative celebration called Canboulay. The steel pan is the descendant of percussion instruments banned in the aftermath of the Canboulay riots in 1880s, wherein the descendants of black freedmen protested attempts by the British authorities to crack down on Canboulay. See Stuempfle 1996.

34. Interestingly, Trinidad and Tobago's national anthem contains the line "Here every creed and race find an equal place," repeated twice for emphasis.

35. Ralph Singh, the narrator of Naipaul's *The Mimic Men*, a forty-year-old colonial minister living in London, tries to overcome his sense of displacement and dislocation by writing his memoirs. The island of his birth, Isabella (a fictional island closely resembling post-independence Trinidad) is a place he

associates with disorder, and the act of writing becomes one way of putting his life into order. When he fails as a politician in Isabella's post-independence nationalist and transitional government, another means of achieving self-definition and order, he feels a sense of defeat, loss, and shame.

36. In his seminal essay "The Precession of Simulacra" from *Simulacra and Simulation*, Jean Baudrillard defines the term as follows: "Simulation is no longer that of a territory, a referential being, or a substance. It is the generation by models of a real without origin or reality: a hyperreal. . . . It is no longer a question of imitation, nor duplication, nor even parody. It is a question of substituting the signs of the real for the real. . . . Never again will the real have a chance to produce itself" (1994, 1–2).

37. Glissant terms "creolization" *métissage* as "the meeting, interference, shock, harmonies and disharmonies between the cultures of the world" that takes place in the Caribbean, which becomes the site of cultural (mis)encounter, negotiation, struggle, and translation. Glissant stresses that there is no one claim to "absolute legitimacy"; rather, creolization, because it "has no presupposed scale of values," produces "unforeseeable and unanticipated results" (cited in Mignolo 2000, 41).

38. Robert Young observes, in his essay "The Postcolonial Condition" that the phrase is "usually invoked with respect to the particular state, as well as the common circumstances, of the many colonies that were freed from colonial rule during the second half of the twentieth century and are now living on the legacy of colonialism" (2012, 600).

39. Ralph Singh's attitude illustrates Albert Memmi's controversial description in *The Colonizer and the Colonized* of the psychological effects of colonialism wherein the colonized subject experiences a "love of the colonizer . . . subtended by a complex of feelings ranging from shame to self-hate" (1965, 121). I would argue that *Valmiki's Daughter*, as well as Mootoo's other writings, challenge and oppose Memmi's rather oversimplified and thus slightly distorted, if well-meaning, analysis/indictment of colonialism by positing that the post-independence, postcolonial "condition" is a much more complex, diverse, and dissimilar experience for people of different gender, race, class, religion, and sexual orientation, not to mention the fact that the experience even varies in different former colonies within the Caribbean itself.

40. Indeed, Naipaul has been accused of misogynist attitudes for his remarks on the "inferiority" of female authors, including Jane Austen, whom he does not deem his equals. In an interview with the Royal Geographic Society, for instance, he notoriously commented, "I read a piece of writing and within a paragraph or two I know whether it is by a woman or not. I think [it

is] unequal to me." *Guardian*, February 26, 2011, www.theguardian.com/books/2011/jun/02/vs-naipaul-jane-austen-women-writers.

41. Aliyah Khan has argued that Viveka's "mannishness" poses a particular threat to "the postcolonial national project" (2012, 279) because it disrupts the legitimacy of the heterosexual family as a moral institution of national beliefs.

CHAPTER 9

1. For a selection of posters that were effectively visual narratives of the AIDS epidemic and depictions of people with AIDS, see NIH Library of Medicine's "Visual Culture and Public Posters" online exhibit, www.nlm.nih.gov/exhibition/visualculture/hivaids.html.

2. For a more comprehensive analysis of American media representations of AIDS in the 1980s, see Cook and Colby 1992. While Cook and Colby's analysis is, for the most part, insightful, I disagree with their negative depiction of ACT UP as a "confrontational organization" whose members have a "penchant for disrupting speeches, conducting sit-ins (or 'die-ins'), and getting arrested" (114).

3. I am using Althusser's notion of interpellation, namely, the process by which individuals are made to recognize themselves as subjects through ideology. As Althusser declared in his seminal essay "Ideology and Ideological State Apparatuses (Notes towards an Investigation)," "[I]deology has always-already interpellated individuals as subjects, which amounts to making it clear that individuals are always-already interpellated by ideology as subjects" (1971, 176).

4. Critics have written widely about the problematic media depiction of AIDS as a gay male disease in the early 1980s. See, for example, Gross 1994; and Hart 2003.

5. Private correspondence with Sarah Schulman, December 7, 2013.

6. In fact, Sarah Schulman has commented elsewhere that, in *People of Trouble*, she wanted to "express a precise political idea—namely, how personal homophobia becomes societal neglect" (1994, 195).

7. Although the novels *People in Trouble* and *Rat Bohemia* were published in 1990 and 1995 respectively, Schulman's observations and her critique of gentrification continue to be relevant. The latter are formulated in more essayistic form in her most recent volume of nonfiction, *The Gentrification of the Mind* (2012a).

8. As the character of Peter, Kate's husband, thinks to himself, "We New Yorkers always have something else to fear. . . . First it was herpes, this year it's crossfire" (1990, 4).

9. As Schulman comments, "[It is] easy to blame AIDS on the infected, and much more difficult to take in all of the social, economic, epidemiological, sexual, emotional, and political questions" (2012a, 36).

10. Foremost among these misrepresentations was the common regard of AIDS as a gay male disease. In its early history, AIDS was known as GRID (Gay-Related Immune Deficiency) or, more colloquially, as the "gay plague." For an early newspaper report that uses this term, see Lawrence Altman, "New Homosexual Disorder Worries Health Officials," *New York Times*, May 11, 1982, www.nytimes.com/1982/05/11/science/new-homosexual-disorder-worries-health-officials.html.

11. Schulman herself was a member of the real-life queer activist group ACT UP, whose logo was the gay pink triangle and the words "Silence = Death" against a black background. The logo drew clear parallels between the Nazi period and the AIDS health crisis, declaring that "silence about the oppression and annihilation of gay people, then and now, must be broken as a matter of our survival" (Crimp and Rolston 1990, 14). Other parallel slogans included "Action = Life" and "Ignorance = Fear."

12. Schulman writes, "[D]uring the epicenter of the mass death experience, we wished for 'citizenship' which was a metaphor for not being brutalized. . . . What I, at least, didn't understand was that 'we' would be divided by citizenship itself into the people who can access the punitive arm of the state (citizens, families, the HIV negative) and the new abject objects (non-citizens, queers without families, the HIV positive). . . . So the meaning of citizen, when one is not one, is different than when one is" (private correspondence, December 7, 2013).

13. Ironically, Peter has "once had a gay affair," but he dismisses it as an "experiment" (31).

14. This is perhaps an allusion to the sense of nostalgia for a pre-HIV/AIDS world that was evoked in visual advertising such as an AIDS Action Committee poster that featured a Norman Rockwell American family values painting in which a father is explaining a passage from a schoolbook to his red-faced son. The caption at the bottom of the poster read, "Don't Forget the Chapter on AIDS."

15. This is a direct reference to the symbol of the inverted pink triangle that ACT UP adopted in 1987 along with the slogan "Silence = Death."

16. My exploration in chapter 10 of the spaces of "insurgent citizenship" (Holston 1999b) in the city, or the contested spaces where claims to the city are articulated by marginalized and dispossessed groups, is in part an attempt to think

through and respond to Schulman's critical observations on the far-reaching effects and implications of gentrification in urban spaces.

17. Kate has titled this art installation, a collage of images of suffering and resistance collected from magazines, "People in Trouble."

18. The DREAM Act (Development, Relief and Education for Alien Minors) is a legislative proposal originally introduced in the Senate in 2001 that would allow undocumented immigrants to obtain legal U.S. residency via higher education or military participation and give them the opportunity to apply for legal permanent resident status. The policy is aimed at the children of undocumented migrants who arrived in the United States as minors and have graduated from high school but fail to obtain admission to college because of their "illegal" status. At the time of writing, the U.S. Congress has yet to pass the DREAM Act as it continues to debate immigrant reform.

19. See Howard Rheingold's *Smart Mobs: The Next Social Revolution* (2002), in which he defines the term as a mass of people who come together for reasons of social activism and demonstration, and "who are able to act in concert even if they don't know each other" and "cooperate in ways never before possible because they carry devices that possess both communication and computing capabilities" (xii). Schulman's *People in Trouble*, written in the years before this technological boom, nevertheless anticipates the smart mob phenomenon in the activities of the Justice resistance movement.

20. Examples of this include ACT UP's provocative "Kissing Doesn't Kill: Greed and Indifference Do" poster; their Wall Street demonstrations; their shutting down of the Food and Drug Administration for a day; and their disruption of a mass in St. Patrick's Cathedral in protest against the Catholic Church's hypocrisy (later reported by some media as "Catholic bashing"). ACT UP suffered from some internal disagreements that led to the offshoot group Treatment Activist Group, or TAG, formed by Mark Harrington after an internal split in the ranks.

21. ACT UP did enact a Stop the Church demonstration at St. Patrick's on December 10, 1989, but Sarah Schulman has commented that she had actually already written about the fictional incident before it happened in real life on a much larger scale (1994, 194).

22. In turn, Molly's objection to Kate's description of Peter as a "passive," helpless, weak "girl" and her annoyed dismissal of Kate's stereotypical depiction of girlhood with the offhand comment, "[T]hat's not a girl. That sounds exactly like a man to me" (23) effectively invert gender roles by playing off one gender stereotype against another.

23. I read Kate's progress throughout the novel as an example of what Sonya Andermahr, drawing upon the theories of Gayatri Gopinath and Jasbir Puar, has detected as a mode of "queer diaspora" that takes the form of a "historically specific response to the AIDS crisis and a rejection of the so-called 'homonormative' discourse that came to dominate lesbian and gay politics of the 1970s and 1980s" (2011, 714–15). Accordingly, I read Kate's cross-dressing/drag as part of her development as a dynamic character who acknowledges the "diversity, fragmentation, and the constantly changing patterns of sexual identities that necessitate different forms of resistance to oppression" (715).

24. The skit anticipates the form that Schulman would use in her subsequent novel, *Empathy*, which is much more formally experimental in its use of multiple genres: poem, commercial, term paper, play, screenplay, short story, recipe, and personal advertisement.

25. This contrasts sharply with James's final instructions to the Justice activists, delivered with great deliberation, before they charge the platform to interrupt the Taj McHorne inauguration event: "If you instigate chaos, make sure it is to your advantage or that you have no other choice" (221).

26. When the scandal broke in November 1986, it was revealed that the Reagan administration had secretly facilitated arms to Iran, which was under an arms embargo at the time, in exchange for the freedom of American hostages held in Lebanon. A portion of the money from weapon sales was diverted to Nicaragua in late 1985 to fund anti-Sandinista rebels, or Contras, an anti-Communist militant group that had committed serious human rights violations including the rape, torture, and execution of civilians as well as the targeting of health care facilities.

27. In a provocative statement, Schulman compares the 81,542 deaths from AIDS in New York City (as of August 16, 2008) to the 2,752 deaths on 9/11. She critiques the "ritualized and institutionalized mourning of the acceptable dead" (the victims of 9/11) that overshadowed the "disallowed grief of twenty years of AIDS deaths," a move that effectively constituted, in her words, "the replacement of deaths that don't matter with deaths that do" (2012a, 46). I fully agree with Schulman.

28. To recall briefly here, Berlant defines the "National Symbolic" as a "tangled cluster" of official texts, narratives, affects, symbols, icons, and totalized images that mediate a "seamless" national identity (1991, 5, 51).

29. On May 25, 1986, for instance, 5 million people formed a human chain across the country in the Hands across America campaign against hunger and homelessness. Another event that overshadowed the domestic AIDS crisis

and replaced it with the "goodwill" of Americans who wanted to help alleviate hunger and starvation in Africa was Live Aid, a 1985 charity concert held simultaneously in London and Philadelphia to raise funds for the Ethiopian famine under the aegis of Bob Geldof and Midge Ure. Live Aid raised UK£150 million in total; in comparison, in 1982, US$5 million was allocated to the U.S. Centers for Disease Control and Prevention for surveillance and US$10 million to the National Institutes of Health for AIDS research, and US$20 million was granted by the U.S. Health Resources and Services Administration for HIV care and treatment in 1989.

30. It was only on May 31, 1987, that President Reagan made his first public speech about AIDS and established a Presidential Commission on HIV. This was not, however, the start of a concerted attempt to acknowledge AIDS and to increase awareness of HIV prevention. In July of that same year, the U.S. Congress adopted the Helms Amendment, which banned the use of federal tax dollars to fund AIDS education materials that "promote[d] or encourage[d], directly or indirectly, homosexual activities" (Rimmerman 2002, 133).

31. On December 6, 1983, a congressional subcommittee released "The Federal Response to AIDS," a report criticizing the U.S. government for failing to invest sufficient funding in AIDS research. AIDS Timeline,aids.gov/hiv-aids-basics/hiv-aids-101/aids-timeline/.

32. The gender equality motto "Different but equal" is another instance of a conundrum that denotes an awkward espousing, and hence reinforcing, of gender inequality. The phrase also uncomfortably recalls the "Separate but equal" legal doctrine during racial segregation in the United States.

33. Together with other internal conflicts about whether the group should focus on issues of racism or sexism, these contradictions ultimately led to the dissolution of Queer Nation in 1992, although regional "chapters" still continued their activities. Queer Nation witnessed a revival in 2013 after Russia passed a law prohibiting gay "propaganda" from being displayed publicly. Queer Nation protested against the implications of the law on the forthcoming Winter Olympics Games in Sochi, Russia, in 2014, demanding, for example, that Coca-Cola withdraw its sponsorship of the Winter Olympics.

34. I am referring here to Halberstam's critical attempt in *The Queer Art of Failure* (2011) to find alternatives to prevalent understandings of success in a heteronormative, neocapitalist Western society.

35. The full manifesto is available here: www.historyisaweapon.com/defcon1/queernation.html.

36. The term *queer nationalism* is adopted by advocates who support the campaign for the creation of a queer nation-state or gay "homeland," such as those initiated by the groups Gay Homeland Foundation, Unified Gay Tribe, or Gay and Lesbian Commonwealth Kingdom. Examples of campaigns for such micronations (entities that claim the status of independent nations or states but that are not recognized by world governments) include Australian activists' declaration of the Cato Islands as the Gay and Lesbian Kingdom of the Coral Sea in 2004.

37. One example is the morning ritual of reciting the U.S. Pledge of Allegiance that takes place in schools in most states: pupils "stan[d] at attention facing the American flag with the right hand over the heart" (U.S. Flag Code).

38. The civil rights movement of the 1960s led by Martin Luther King Jr. also drew heavily upon Thoreau's essay.

39. In her article, Brown draws on Walter Benjamin's notion from his 1931 essay "Left-wing Melancholy." See Benjamin 1999.

40. See Edelman 2004; and Bersani 1996.

41. Schulman's satirical depiction of the Meals on Wheels delivery service as "God's Love—We Deliver" is also a comment on the close affinity of Christianity/Catholicism with the affect of shame.

42. This tripartite configuration adds another dimension to the Schulman quote with which I began this section, on AIDS as "equally *the* and equally *not* [the]" (2012a, 69) American experience.

43. See Puar 2007, which examines how neoliberal politics incorporate some queer subjects into the nation-state while marginalizing and excluding others. See also Kulick 2009. Kulick defines "homonationalism" as "an understanding and enactment of homosexual acts, identities, and relationships that incorporates them as not only compatible with but even exemplary of neoliberal democratic ethics and citizenship" (28).

CHAPTER 10

1. Swedish political scientist Tomas Hammar (1990) first used the term *denizen* to denote a yet-to-be naturalized permanent resident in the host country. Today, "denizen" is a broad umbrella term used to denote foreign nationals, nonresident aliens (guest workers, visiting students), and permanent residents. Kees Groenendijk defines "denizenship" as "a status granted to nonnationals giving them permanent right of residence, most citizenship rights that nationals benefit from, and limited protection against expulsion from the country of residence" (2005).

2. As Bosniak writes, "[C]itizenship has been, can be, and arguably should sometimes be enacted not merely within national borders but beyond and across them, as well" (5).

3. I have put this term in quotation marks because clearly there is nothing "natural" about the process of naturalization, which is characterized by formal oaths/pledges, rituals, and administrative bureaucracy.

4. I am referring here in particular to Judith Butler's recent book based on conversations with social anthropologist Athena Athanasiou, *Dispossession: The Performative in the Political* (2013), in which she seeks to "formulate a theory of political performativity" that takes into account two versions of dispossession—the form of resistance that occurs "when a sovereign and unitary subject is challenged," and the "form of suffering for those displaced and colonized" (ix). Other studies exploring how new forms of urban segregation, social exclusion, and economic disenfranchisement impact citizenship and democracy while simultaneously regarding the precarious subject as a calculable opposition to neoliberalism include Caldeira 1999; and Kawash 1998.

5. I am speaking of the "'new' metropolis" in contradistinction to the "old(er)" metropolises of London, Paris, and New York as well as the ancient metropolises of Constantinople (Istanbul), Athens, and Rome.

6. Holston argues that the palimpsestic nature of cities' layered surfaces "tell time and stories." Yet their narratives are "never wholly legible, because each foray into the palimpsest of city surfaces reveals only traces of these relations" (1999b, 155).

7. Saskia Sassen notes, for instance, that there is "a new geography of centrality and marginality" (1999, 182) emerging in global cities. Sassen perceives of the city as the site of an "unmooring of identities" from "traditional sources of identity, such as the nation or the village." Such an unmooring, she claims, "engenders new notions of community, of membership, and of entitlement" (191).

8. See Soja 2010. In this book, as in most of his previous work, Soja argues that geography is an inherent and essential constituent of justice—a point illustrated, for example, in the "rights to the city" theory espoused by David Harvey, Henri Lefebvre, and others. For a comparative reading, see Fainstein 2010, in which the author offers a theory of justice for assessing urban policy.

9. These include basic rights such as access to adequate health care, education, employment, and affordable housing as well as the ethical dimensions of membership such as equal opportunity, justice, dignity, and well-being.

10. As Linda Bosniak remarks, "[T]he global is not merely situated 'out there' but is also located, increasingly, within national borders" (2006, 7).

11. One of them is political scientist Michael Janoschka's research project "NEO-LIBERAL_CITI: Re-framing Urban Neoliberalism and Neo-liberal Citizenship: Conceptualising Emancipatory Struggles as Acts of Citizenship" (see michael-janoschka.de/pdfs/NEOLIBERAL_CITI_Info_Flyer.pdf).

12. These include (and this is by no means an exhaustive list) Mary Louise Pratt's influential notion of "contact spaces" (1992); Homi Bhabha's concept of "Third Space" (1991) and Edward Soja's corresponding "thirdspace," wherein he posits a "trialectics" of being consisting of "spatiality, historicality and sociality" (1996, 71); Michel Foucault's notion of "heterotopias" or other spaces (1997); Henri Lefebvre's seminal work (originally published in 1974) on the social production of space (1991) as well as his championing of the "right to the city" in *Le droit à la ville* (1968); Martina Löw's "relational" model of space (2008, 11); and postcolonial theories of space by critics such as Doreen Massey (1999).

13. Purcell (2003) regards the right to the city as a fundamental constituent of urban citizenship.

14. I have borrowed the concept of "diffuse urbanism" from Sandten 2011. Sandten, in turn, is drawing on Sieverts's concept of the "Zwischenstadt" ("in-between city") (2003).

15. According to the 2006 census of the city of Toronto, visible minority groups accounted for 46.9 percent of the population. www12.statcan.gc.ca/census-recensement/2006/as-sa/97-557/p24-eng.cfm.

16. As Wenche Ommundsen et al. write, cultural citizenship aims to "destabilize boundaries between culture and state, self and other, sameness and difference . . . bring[ing] out tensions between individuals and group rights, between human and cultural rights, between principles of universalism and respect for cultural difference" (2010, 2).

17. Indeed, when Brand's novel was published, "it was widely hailed in the popular press as a comment on 'hyphenated-Canadianness,' an expression of the urban, multicultural, and cosmopolitan 'new' realities of Canadian society and space" (Buma 2009, 12).

18. Rather willfully, the unnamed white narrator of the first chapter of the novel does not mention the fact that the Ojibway actually displaced the Iroquois from Ontario in the seventeenth century—Brand's authorial comment, perhaps, on the marginalization of certain strands of Indigenous history despite Canada's official policy of multiculturalism since 1971. Toronto's transition from an Iroquoian to an Ojibway/Mississauga settlement denotes another prior palimpsestic layer of the history of the city. The unnamed narrator is

presumably white because she or he misrecognizes one of the protagonists, Carla, as "Italian, southern" (3). Later on in the novel, we learn that Carla is the biracial daughter of a white mother and black father.

19. Officially, Canada is a federal state comprising ten provinces and three territories ruled collectively as a parliamentary democracy and by the British sovereign Queen Elizabeth II as its head of state.

20. The 2006 census of the city of Toronto records that Indigenous people comprised 0.5 percent of the total population (0.4 percent First Nations and 0.1 percent Métis). www12.statcan.gc.ca/census-recensement/2006/as-sa/97-557/p24-eng.cfm.

21. These include "much" or "many" in the Huron language; "timber in the water" in the Iroquois word "Thoron-to-hen"; and "where there are trees standing in the water" from the Mohawk term "Tkaronto." See Heather A. Howard and A. Rodney Bobiwash, "Toronto's Native History," *First Nations House Magazine*, www.fnhmagazine.com/issue1/nativehistory.html.

22. See Cairns 2000; and Blackburn 2009.

23. Kymlica's concept of "multicultural citizenship" aims to sketch out a new liberal theory of minority rights that differentiates between the entitlements of "national minorities" (distinct national groups with a language, culture, and territory) in "multination" states and ethnic groups (having a distinct culture and language but without a defined territory) in "polyethnic" states. See chapter 2, "A Politics of Multiculturalism," of his *Multicultural Citizenship* (1995). Iris Young takes the concept of "multicultural citizenship" one step further, proposing what she terms a theory of "differentiated citizenship" (1989).

24. As Joppke summarizes, "The Québécois have always fiercely rejected Canada's multiculturalist policies, because Canada's binational founding structure is insufficiently visible in them" (2011, 248).

25. The First Nations in Canada also protested that the charter did not respect their native cultures and traditional ways of autonomy. Internal divisions within the First Nation tribes themselves ensued, for example, between the French-speaking minority in English-speaking territories and the English-speaking minority in French-speaking parts of Quebec.

26. As Donna Bailey Nurse asserts, "[B]eing Canadian means being two things (at least) at once" (2012).

27. Stuart Hall, too, uses the concept of "vernacular cosmopolitanism," although his definition of the term differs slightly from Bhabha's. Hall speaks of "cosmopolitanism from below" as the experience of asylum seekers, refugees, and clandestine migrants who are uprooted, displaced, and "driven across borders"

(2008, 346)—an ugly underside of the glamorous cosmopolitan lifestyles of the elite. Hall's usage of the term is akin, as one critic has noted, to Julia Kristeva's "cosmopolitanism of those who have been flayed" (Gonzalez-Ruibal 2009, 119, citing Kristeva). Accordingly, Nick Stevenson writes of a "dual cosmopolitanism built out of wealth and poverty"—the juxtaposition of "spaces for global cosmopolitan elites to live and consume a diverse array of goods and services," or "zones of exclusion," and spaces with socioeconomically disadvantaged, "poorly housed migrant populations," or "zones of poverty." It is this "dual cosmopolitanism," Stevenson claims, that has "come to shape globally oriented subjectivities and citizenships" (2003, 58). For a discussion of "vernacular cosmopolitanism" within a postcolonial context, see Werbner 2008.

28. See Härting and Kamboureli 2009.

29. In this respect, Brand echoes the opinion expressed in critical scholarship. Christian Joppke observes a "gap between the theory and the practice of multicultural citizenship"—between a "mechanism to accommodate ethnic, national, and other minorities in theory" and "a variant of nation-building in a few new settler societies without independent founding myths" (2011, 245), which, he criticizes, is the result of official multicultural policies embraced by, for example, the Canadian and Australian governments since the 1970s. Numerous others have also openly criticized Canada's official policy of multiculturalism since 1971. Minelle Mahtani, for example, is skeptical of the contentious "official, legislative response in Canada to ethnic plurality," criticizing this as Pierre Trudeau's flawed "design to fit minority cultural differences into a workable national framework" (2006, 164).

30. Tuyen's long-lost brother Quy's first-person narrative accounts, which are interspersed throughout the novel, tell of his experiences as a Vietnamese refugee in the Pulau Bidong camp in Malaysia in the late 1970s. He is reunited with his parents at the end of the novel.

31. These are the defining characteristics of Canadian literature that Margaret Atwood cites in her seminal study of the genre, *Survival: A Thematic Guide to Canadian Literature* (1972).

32. Interestingly, Dionne Brand was made a Fellow of the Royal Society of Canada in 2006 and appointed Toronto's third poet laureate in 2009. The latter role as the city's literary ambassador implies the official sanction of her work by the government. I read Brand's novel as exhibiting a somewhat more defiant poetics.

33. One recalls Sarah Schulman's description of gentrification as "the removal of communities of diverse classes, ethnicities, races, sexualities, languages and

points of view from the central neighborhoods of cities, and their replacement by more homogenized [white, middle-class] groups" (2012a, 14).

34. Zygmunt Bauman's theories of urban spectatorship also come to mind here. Bauman argues that in the modern world, Benjamin's original flâneur becomes its "mirror image, its imitation, the product of . . . forced adjustment and mimicry" (1994, 139). See also Mazlish 1994.

35. Teju Cole's *Open City* (2011) is another recent novel whose protagonist walks the urban grid (in this case Manhattan) in flâneur fashion.

36. articles.washingtonpost.com/2011-03-24/local/35208419_1_black-middle-class-black-population-income-and-education.

37. The quotation is Khaled Hosseini's, taken from a blurb on the back cover of Mengestu's novel.

38. See Linda Kulman's review of the novel (2008).

39. For that matter, it also refuses to be read as a semiautobiographic account, as some reviewers make it out to be by tracing the parallels in the lives of Mengestu and his fictional protagonist. See, for example, Kulman 2008.

40. This is a reference to Emperor Haile Selassie (1892–1975) of Ethiopia, who was deposed by the Derg (Coordinating Committee of the Armed Forces, Police, and Territorial Army) in 1974 and imprisoned until his death.

CHAPTER 11

1. Michael Sprinkler's comment on the process of "writing the self" in autobiographical writings is relevant here—"No autobiography," he holds, "can take place except within the boundaries of a writing where concepts of subject, self, and author collapse into the act of producing a text" (1980, 327).

2. I am aware of Salman Rushdie's claim, in his oft-cited essay "Imaginary Homelands," that description *itself* is a political act, or, rather, it is the act of "re-description," which is a "necessary first step toward changing 'a world'" (1991, 13). Nevertheless, Rushdie's usage of the term *description* differs from the commonly held definition of the word.

3. The highly controversial United Nations Stabilization Mission in Haiti (MINUSTAH) has been stationed in the country since 2004.

4. Said points out that this is perhaps another way of voicing Adorno's reflections, in *Minima Moralia: Reflexionen aus dem beschädigten Leben* (his autobiography written in exile), that in the context of World War II the only home available, however precarious and fragile, is in writing, although the very idea of home is a contingent and provisional one that demands viewing with an exile's detachment (146).

5. See Sara Ahmed's recent book *Willful Subjects* (2014) on how the notions of will and willfulness are embedded in political and cultural landscapes and thus socially mediated.

6. I am, of course, referring to the MINUSTAH.

7. Salman Rushdie, too, speaks of the real risks that a writer takes in her or his writing in terms of "pushing the work to the limits of what is possible, in the attempt to increase the sum of what it is possible to think." "Books become good," Rushdie writes, "when they go to this edge and risk falling over it—when they endanger the artist by reason of what he has, and has not, artistically dared" (1991, 15).

8. For Uncle Joseph, this is not only metaphorically but also literally the case, as he loses his voice completely due to throat cancer and has to speak through an artificial voice box.

9. A process that Georges Gusdorf describes as "reassembl[ing] the scattered elements of an individual life and regrouping them in a comprehensive sketch" (1980, 35).

10. I am reminded of Rushdie's assertion in his essay "Imaginary Homelands" that "when the State takes reality into its own hands, and sets about distorting it, . . . then the making of the alternative realities of art, including the novel of memory, becomes politicized." Indeed, Rushdie contends that the novel "is one way of denying the official, politicians' version of truth" (1991, 14).

11. Such an intimate sense of continuity in the family that remains unbroken is expressed in the opening sentence of *Brother, I'm Dying*: "I found out I was pregnant the same day that my father's rapid weight loss and chronic shortness of breath were positively diagnosed as end-stage pulmonary fibrosis" (2007, 3).

12. Edward Said coined the term *imaginative geography* to critique the ways in which Western narratives have represented "other" places, cultures, and peoples, ways that reflect the power relations between these authors and the imperial subjects of their "imaginings" (1979, 55). I am borrowing Said's term and adapting it from its original context.

13. In Gail Scott's words, "Standing on the outside—the better, perhaps, to create" (1989, 41).

14. Édouard Glissant, a writer and literary critic from Martinique who has spent much of his life in the United States, speaks of a "poetics of relation" as an aesthetic and political mode wherein identity is not constructed in isolation or out of one's past but in rhizomic fashion where one exists in relation to the diverse cultural, linguistic, and sociological forces (Glissant's context is specifically the Caribbean) that surround it in the present. In Glissant's words, "Rhizomic thought is the principle behind what I call the Poetics of

Relation, in which each and every identity is extended through a relationship with the Other" (1997a, 11).

15. In "Imaginary Homelands," Rushdie writes of his relationship with Bombay (Mumbai), the city of his birth, "It may be that writers in my position, exiles or emigrants or expatriates, are haunted by some sense of loss, some urge to reclaim, to look back. . . . But if we do look back, we must also do so in the knowledge . . . that our physical alienation from India almost inevitably means that we will not be capable of reclaiming precisely the thing that was lost; that we will, in short, create fictions, not actual cities or villages, but invisible ones, imaginary homelands, Indias of the mind" (1991, 10).

16. Born in Haiti in 1953 and exiled to Montreal in 1976, Laferrière lived in Miami's Little Haiti from 1990 to 2002, whereupon he returned to Montreal.

17. Francesco Ragazzi defines "post-territorial citizenship" as an abandonment of "the territorial referent as the main criterion for inclusion and exclusion from citizenship, focusing instead on ethnocultural markers of identity, irrespective of the place of residence" (2014, 492).

CHAPTER 12

1. The Seminole, Creek, Choctaw, and Chickasaw nations have all experienced similar debates. For a comprehensive study of the status of freedmen within the Seminole Nation, see Littlefield 1977; and W. Porter 1996. For an examination of the status of freedmen within the Chickasaw Nation, see Littlefield 1980.

2. The situation in Canada is different. Since the adoption of the Indian Act in 1876, a Native person has had to choose between Indigenous citizenship and Canadian citizenship. As Claude Denis summarizes, "[A] person could not, in other words, at once be 'Indian' and a Canadian citizen" (2002, 113).

3. This being strongly influenced by, for example, Benedict Anderson's definition of the modern nation-state as a socially constructed and mediated "imagined political community that is imagined as both inherently limited and sovereign" (1983, 7).

4. As Kevin Bruyneel comments with regard to the Indian Citizenship Act of June 2, 1924, which made all Indigenous people living in the United States citizens of the country, "[U]sually, people who have been excluded from American political life see the codification of their citizenship status as an unambiguously positive political development. In the case of Indigenous people and U.S. citizenship, however, one cannot find such clear and certain

statements. All Indigenous people certainly did not look at U.S. citizenship in the same light; in fact, very few saw it as unambiguously positive" (2004, 30).

5. Critical viewpoints in a Canadian context are similar. Lynn Chabot, for instance, writing from a First Nations context, contends that "self-identification and the open, kinship- and community-based methods of recognizing tribal membership" were "superseded by externally imposed, culturally incompatible methods of acknowledging citizenship" (cited in Alfred 2009, 3). See also Blackburn 2009.

6. How do they, in other words, broach the topic of "the community's capacity (social, political, and legal) to grant or deny citizenship," "the issue of what right a community has to constitute itself . . . and exercise the authority to designate citizens" (Denis 2002, 115)?

7. Albeit as a "domestic dependent nation." This term, which was coined by Supreme Court Chief Justice John Marshall in the *Cherokee Nation v. Georgia* (1831) case, refers to the status of Indigenous tribes in U.S. federal law that accords them an inherent, though limited, sovereignty.

8. The dispute remains unresolved at the present time of writing. A landmark hearing on May 5, 2014, in the DC Federal District Court in front of U.S. District Judge Thomas F. Hogan may lead to the issue of the future of Cherokee freedmen as citizens of the tribe being decided upon ahead of the Cherokee Nation's general elections in June 2015.

9. For the full text of the Cherokee Emancipation Proclamation, see "Cherokee Emancipation Proclamation," Archives Division, Oklahoma Historical Society, Cherokee vol. 248 (February 18–19, 1863), faculty.washington.edu/qtaylor/documents_us/cherokee_emancipation_proclamation.htm.

10. The U.S. Emancipation Proclamation was an executive order signed by Abraham Lincoln in 1862 declaring that "all persons held as slaves" within the rebellious states "are, and henceforward shall be free." For a facsimile of the Emancipation Proclamation, see the National Archives website,www.archives.gov/exhibits/featured_documents/emancipation_proclamation/.

11. *Indian Affairs, Laws and Treaties*, vol. 2, *Treaties*, ed. Charles J. Kappler (Washington, DC: Government Printing Office, 1904),digital.library.okstate.edu/Kappler/Vol2/treaties/che0942.htm#mn18.

12. Nevertheless, it was also stipulated that black freedmen had to "reside within the limits of the Cherokee Nation" or return there within six months of the Treaty of 1866 in order to attain Cherokee citizenship. In most cases, this meant that they had to embark on a journey back to Indian Territory after having traveled south to Texas and other Confederate states because their

NOTES TO CHAPTER 12

owners had supported the Confederacy. I will discuss this treaty in greater detail later in this chapter. In the most comprehensive book-length analysis of the Cherokee freedmen controversy to date, *The Cherokee Freedmen: From Emancipation to American Citizenship*, Daniel F. Littlefield Jr. details the historical cases of a group of "too late" freedmen and their appeal to the secretary of the interior regarding their treatment by the Cherokee Nation (1978, 81).

13. This refers to the degree of ancestry: for example, the incumbent principal chief of the Cherokee Nation, Bill John Baker, who is of mixed ethnicity, is $^1/_{32}$ Cherokee by blood.

14. www.cherokee.org/Portals/0/Documents/2011/4/308011999-2003-CN-CONSTITUTION.pdf. The Dawes Rolls, or the Final Rolls of Citizens and Freedmen of the Five Civilized Tribes, was part of the General Allotment Act (or Dawes Act) of 1887, wherein the U.S. government divided up Indian Territory into allotments for each member of the Five Tribes. Between 1899 and 1906, the names of 41,798 citizens of the Cherokee Nation and 4,924 freedmen were recorded. The Dawes Act was adopted as part of the U.S. government's attempt to assimilate Indians into mainstream U.S. society. One of the steps deemed necessary was the individual, and not communal, ownership of land. For the full text of the Dawes Act, see digital. library.okstate.edu/kappler/vol1/ html_files/ses0033.html. The Dawes Rolls can be accessed, viewed, and searched here: www.archives.gov/research/native-americans/dawes/.

15. See the official Cherokee Nation website, www.cherokee.org/Services/TribalCitizenship/Citizenship.aspx.

16. See, for example, former principal chief Chad Smith's comments at the beginning of this chapter.

17. Taylor Keen, a former member of the Cherokee Nation Tribal Council, observes, "[H]istorically, citizenship in the Cherokee Nation has been an inclusive process; it was only at the time of the Dawes Commission that there was a racial definition of what Cherokee meant" (quoted in Daffron 2007).

18. The U.S. Constitution had already come into effect almost four decades earlier, in 1789.

19. According to the Leadership Conference on Civil and Human Rights, a U.S. civil and human rights coalition, tribal sovereignty refers to "tribes' right to govern themselves, define their own membership, manage tribal property, and regulate tribal business and domestic relations; it further recognizes the existence of a government-to-government relationship between

such tribes and the federal government." www.civilrights.org/Indigenous/tribal-sovereignty/.

20. This was established by the Marshall Trilogy, *Johnson v. M'Intosh* (1823), *Cherokee Nation v. Georgia* (1831), and *Worcester v. Georgia* (1832), which provided the foundations for determining federal-Indigenous relations and steered the course of future Native American treaties.

21. The title of Foster's novel itself is also a biblical allusion, to the book of Genesis, where it is told that when Abraham arrived in Be'er Sheva, he dug a well and planted a tamarisk tree. Abraham, possessing the knowledge of well digging, chose that spot even though it was in the midst of the Negev Desert because he knew that underneath the riverbed there was a constant flow of water.

22. This phrase, from John Winthrop's famous "A Model of Christian Charity" speech (1630), contains the proclamation that "the Lord our God may bless us in the land whither we go to possess it."

23. One of the premises of the theory of American exceptionalism, as expressed in the writings of Alexis de Tocqueville in the 1830s (culminating in the publication of his two-volume opus, *Democracy in America*, in 1835 and 1840) was such an eliding of differences to form a united national front.

24. Nevertheless, for reasons I elaborate upon later in this chapter, Foster's *Abraham's Well* is problematic partly because of the comparisons to earlier slave narratives that the novel invites.

25. See M. NourbeSe Philip's attempt to "(not) tell the story that must be told" in *Zong!* (2008).

26. For a more extensive analysis of quilting in African American history, see Eva Ungar Grudin, *Stitching Memories: African-American Story Quilts* (Williamstown: Williams College Museum of Art, 19900; Patricia Turner, *Crafted Lives: Stories and Studies of African American Quilters* (Jackson: University Press of Mississippi, 2009); Maude Southwell Wahlman's visually arresting *Signs and Symbols: African Images in African American Quilts* (Atlanta: Tinwood Books, 2001); and Kyra Hick's comprehensive *Black Threads: An African American Quilting Sourcebook* (Jefferson, NC: McFarland 2003).

27. At noon on April 22, 1889, a mixture of tradesmen, professionals, common laborers, politicians, and other prospective settlers who had gathered at the Texas or Arkansas borders were allowed to enter the territory by train, horseback, wagon, or foot to seek out a parcel of unclaimed land and file a claim of ownership. About fifty thousand people participated in the land rush, among them, about 2 percent of them black. The only people prevented from participating in the land run were Native Americans, as they were not considered

U.S. citizens at that time (this was granted by the Indian Citizenship Act of 1924).

28. The son of Armentia and her white master, Jacob McDowell, Abraham Proof is described in the novel as "a light-skinned piece of possibility" (231) with fair complexion and blue eyes.

29. The bear symbolizes wisdom, power, courage, freedom, protection, and healing in Indigenous cultures. Foster uses the episode to metaphorically signify the end of slavery on June 2, 1865, when Confederate general Edmund Kirby Smith, commander of Confederate forces west of the Mississippi, signed the surrender terms offered by Union delegates.

30. Jodi A. Byrd describes this catch-22 as "a competition between racist ideologies of exclusion that deny Southeastern Freedmen within the 'Five Civilized Tribes' and colonialist hegemonies of inclusion to the U.S. that seek to deny utterly those nations' inherent rights to sovereignty and land" (2011, 37).

31. From a legal perspective, the framing of the Cherokee freedmen affair in a discourse of Indigenous over federal sovereignty has resulted in a gridlock, or "an ongoing struggle to define the appropriate role for the federal government in Indian matters—one that preserves the tribes' rights to self-determination, while also protecting individual tribal members from violations of their fundamental rights" (Mousakhani 2013, 938).

32. Tiya Miles writes that the Cherokee Constitution of 1827 was not only a charter that defined the sovereignty of the Cherokee Nation but also a legal document that "defined 'Blackness' as a racial category and excluded and controlled Black and mixed-race Afro-Cherokee people. Cherokee lawmakers, like U.S. statesmen, were defining a nation with particular and exclusionary racial parameters" (2005, 108).

33. In a letter to the Cherokees in 1796, for instance, President George Washington instructed that the Cherokee men should become herdsmen and cultivators instead of hunters, and the women should occupy themselves with spinning and weaving.

34. Miles also makes the interesting point that Cherokee conceptions of womanhood greatly differed from Euro-American conceptions of white femininity (vessels of purity) and its opposite, black womanhood (embodiments of deviant sexuality). Cherokee women were, for the most part, understood to be keepers of their own sexuality (52–53).

35. Miles writes, "[T]he notion of a market economy in which surplus goods were sold for profit did not figure into Cherokee understandings or systems

of exchange. . . . Ultimately, Cherokees valued the well-being of people in the community over the ownership of things" (69–70).

CONCLUSION

1. This is evinced by the different cultural heritages and claims to a distinct national identity voiced by, for example, the francophone Quebecois population as well as the First Nations, the Inuit, and Métis communities in Nunavut and the Northwest Territories.

2. On this note, one might also take issue with Woodard's rather flippant, even if ironic, generalizations of "Yankee efforts to liberate African slaves" in "Yankeedom" (2012, 7) (the region he demarcates as stretching from Nova Scotia through New England to the eastern boundaries of North and South Dakota) and his caricatured depiction of "The Deep South" as a region "founded by Barbados slave lords as a West Indies–style slave society, a system so cruel and despotic that it shocked even its seventeenth century English contemporaries" (10).

3. This is illustrated, for example, in the juxtaposition on the map of "El Norte" (literally translated as "the North," the term is used commonly in Mexican slang to refer to the United States) and the "Deep South."

4. I have adapted this term from Nancy Peluso's notion of "counter-mapping" (1995). Peluso originally used the term in relation to the implementation of two oppositional forest-mapping strategies in Kalimantan, Indonesia, whereby two sets of maps were produced: one drawn up by forest managers and the global financial institutions (including the World Bank) that supported them and the other by Indonesian nongovernmental organizations in favor of the Indigenous Dayak population who claimed rights to forest use.

5. Gilroy's notion of "planetary humanism" has been criticized (by proponents of critical race theory, for example) for its postracial politics—that is, an insistence that race is an anachronistic category and that "we" should strive for "a world that is undivided by the petty differences we retain and inflate by calling them racial" (2000, 356). As Diana Brydon (2013) has insightfully commented, Gilroy's concept of planetarity unfortunately "downplays radical alterity" by suggesting that race is a category that can/should be transcended in the pursuit of more universal "planetary humanism."

6. This is an essay that Dimock and Lawrence Buell later developed into the seminal book-length edited collection, *Shades of the Planet: American Literature as World Literature* (2007).

7. See also Butler 2004.

8. It is questionable to what extent the term *planetary* is in itself a misnomer for the type of analytical interpretation that Dimock conceives, as there can clearly be no truly "global" or purely "objective" reading of a literary text. Perhaps the phrase "non–U.S.-centric paradigm" or a "deterritorialization of American literature" (Giles 2007) might have been more appropriate in the context of Dimock's arguments.

9. Interestingly, Dimock espouses a slightly different view when in her introduction to *Shades of the Planet* she writes of the nation as an "epiphenomenon," a "superficial construct," "a set of erasable lines on the face of the earth" (Dimock and Buell 2007, 1).

10. These include Dower and William 2002; Schattle 2007; de Oliveira Andreotti and de Souza 2012; Cabrera 2010; and global activists Hazel Henderson and Daisaku Ikeda's *Planetary Citizenship* (2004) with its in-depth analysis of economic justice, Indigenous rights, and sustainability.

REFERENCES

Adnan, Etel. 1977. *Sitt Marie Rose: A Novel*. Sausalito: Post-Apollo.

———. 2005. *In the Heart of the Heart of Another Country*. San Francisco: City Lights Books.

African Genealogy Society. 1992. *The Spirit of Africville*. Halifax: Formac.

Agamben, Giorgio. 1995. "We Refugees." Translated by Michael Rocke. *Symposium* 49 (2): 114–19.

Ahmed, Sara. 2014. *Willful Subjects*. Durham: Duke University Press.

Alexander, M. Jacqui. 1994. "Not Just (Any) Body Can Be a Citizen: The Politics of Law." In "The New Politics of Sex and the State," special issue, *Feminist Review* 48 (Autumn): 5–23.

Alfred, Taiaiake. 2009. *First Nation Perspectives on Political Identity*. Ottawa: Assembly of First Nations.

Allen, Carolyn. 1993. "The Erotics of Nora's Narrative in Djuna Barnes's *Nightwood*." *Signs* 19 (1): 177–200.

Althusser, Louis. 1971. "Ideology and Ideological State Apparatuses (Notes towards an Investigation)." In *Lenin and Philosophy and Other Essays*, translated by Ben Brewster. New York: Monthly Review. www.marxists. org/reference/archive/althusser/1970/ideology.htm.

Andermahr, Sonya. 2011. "Sarah Schulman's Queer Diasporas: *People in Trouble* and Empathy." *Textual Practice* 25 (4): 711–29.

Anderson, Benedict. 1983. *Imagined Communities: Reflections on the Origin and Spread of Nationalism*. London: Verso.

Andrews, Jennifer. 2008. "Re-visioning Fredericton: Reading George Elliott Clarke's *Execution Poems*." *Studies in Canadian Literature / Études en littérature canadienne* 33 (2).journals.hil.unb.ca/index.php/SCL/article/view/11232/11990.

Appiah, Anthony, and Amy Gutmann. 1996. *Color Conscious: The Political Morality of Race*. Princeton: Princeton University Press.

Arendt, Hannah. 1973. *The Origins of Totalitarianism*. New York: Harcourt, Brace. First published 1951.

Ashcroft, Bill, Gareth Griffiths, and Helen Tiffin. 1989. *The Empire Writes Back: Theory and Practice in Post-colonial Literatures*. London: Routledge.

Atwood, Margaret. 1972. *Survival: A Thematic Guide to Canadian Literature*. Toronto: House of Anansi.

Augé, Marc. 1995. *Non-places: Introduction to an Anthropology of Supermodernity*. Translated by John Howe. New York: Verso.

Bakhtin, Mikhail. 1941. *Rabelais and His World*. Bloomington: Indiana University Press.

Baldwin, James. 1961. *Nobody Knows My Name*. New York: Random House.

Balibar, Etienne. 1991. "Citizen Subject." In *Who Comes After the Subject?* edited by E. Cavada, P. Connor, and J. L. Nancy. New York: Routledge.

Barbour, John D. 2007. "Edward Said and the Space of Exile." *Literature & Theology* 21 (3): 293–301.

Barnes, Djuna. 2006. *Nightwood*. New York: New Directions. First published 1936.

Baronov, David, and Kevin A. Yelvington. 2009. "Ethnicity, Race, Class, and Nationality." In *Understanding the Contemporary Caribbean*, 2nd ed., edited by Richard S. Hillman and Thomas J. D'Agostino, 225–56. Boulder: Lynne Rienner.

Barth, John. 1984. "The Literature of Exhaustion." In *The Friday Book: Essays and Other Non-fiction*. Baltimore: Johns Hopkins University Press.

Barthes, Roland. 1975. *The Pleasure of the Text*. New York: Farrar, Straus and Giroux.

Bauböck, Rainer. 2003. "Reinventing Urban Citizenship." *Citizenship Studies* 7 (2): 139–60.

Baudrillard, Jean. 1994. *Simulacra and Simulation*. Translated by Sheila Faria Glaser. Ann Arbor: University of Michigan Press.

Baudrillard, Jean, and Marc Guillaume. 2008. *Radical Alterity*. Cambridge, MA: MIT Press.

Bauman, Zygmunt. 1994. "Desert Spectacular." In Tester 1994, 138–57.

Baym, Nina. 1983. Introduction to *The Scarlet Letter*, by Nathaniel Haw-thorne, 1–24. New York: Penguin Books.

Bell, David. 1995. "Pleasure and Danger: The Paradoxical Spaces of Sexual Citizenship." *Political Geography* 14 (2): 139–53.

Bell, David, and Jon Binnie. 2000. *The Sexual Citizen: Queer Politics and Beyond*. Cambridge: Polity.

Benhabib, Seyla. 2004. *The Rights of Others: Aliens, Residents, and Citizens*. Cambridge: Cambridge University Press.

Benjamin, Walter. 1992. "Thesis on the Philosophy of History." In *Illuminations: Essays and Reflections*, edited by Hannah Arendt, translated by Harry Zohn, 253–64. New York: Harcourt, Brace and World. First published 1940.

———. 1999. "Left-wing Melancholy." In *Selected Writings*, vol. 2, part 2, 423–27. Cambridge, MA: Belknap. First published 1931.

Benstock, Shari. 1986. *Women of the Left Bank: Paris, 1900–1940*. Austin: University of Texas Press.

———. 1994. "Expatriate Sapphic Modernism: Entering Literary History." In *Rereading Modernism: New Directions in Feminist Criticism*, edited by Lisa Rado, 97–122. New York: Routledge.

Bercovitch, Sacvan. 1988a. "The A-politics of Ambiguity in *The Scarlet Letter*." *New Literary History* 19 (3): 629–54.

———. 1988b. "Hawthorne's A-morality of Compromise." *Representations* 24 (Fall): 1–27.

Berger, John. 1980. "Uses of Photography." In *About Looking*, 52–69. Vintage: Random House.

Berlant, Lauren. 1991. *The Anatomy of National Fantasy: Hawthorne, Utopia, and Everyday Life*. Chicago: University of Chicago Press.

———. 1997. *The Queen of America Goes to Washington City: Essays on Sex and Citizenship*. Durham: Duke University Press.

———. 2008. *The Female Complaint: The Unfinished Business of Sentimentality in American Culture*. Durham: Duke University Press.

Bersani, Leo. 1996. *Homos*. Cambridge, MA: Harvard University Press.

Bertacco, Simona. 2009. "Imagining Bodies in the Work of Dionne Brand." *Saggi/Ensayos/Essais/Essays*, no. 1 (March 2009): 9–17.

Bhabha, Homi, ed. 1990. *Nation and Narration*. London: Routledge.

———. 1991. *The Location of Culture*. New York: Routledge.

————. 2000. "The Vernacular Cosmopolitan." In *Voices of the Crossing: The Impact of Britain on Writers from Asia, the Caribbean and Africa*, edited by Ferdinand Dennis and Naseen Khan, 133–42. London: Serpent's Tail.

Bieger, Laura, Ramón Saldívar, and Johannes Voelz. 2013. "The Imaginary and Its Worlds: An Introduction." In *The Imaginary and Its Worlds: American Studies After the Transnational Turn*, edited by Laura Bieger, Ramón Saldívar, and Johannes Voelz, vii–xx. Hanover: Dartmouth College Press.

Blackburn, Carole. 2009. "Differentiating Indigenous Citizenship: Seeking Multiplicity in Rights, Identity, and Sovereignty in Canada." *American Ethnologist* 36 (1): 66–78.

Blight, David. 2007. *A Slave No More: Two Men Who Escaped to Freedom, Including Their Own Narratives of Emancipation*. Boston: Houghton Mifflin Harcourt.

Booth, Wayne C. 1990. *The Company We Keep: An Ethics of Fiction*. Berkeley: University of California Press.

Bordin, Ruth. 1993. *Alice Freeman Palmer: The Evolution of a New Woman*. Ann Arbor: University of Michigan Press.

Bosniak, Linda. 2006. *The Citizen and the Alien: Dilemmas of Contemporary Membership*. Princeton: Princeton University Press.

Brand, Dionne. 1990. *No Language Is Neutral*. Toronto: Coach House.

————. 1996. *In Another Place, Not Here*. Toronto: Knopf.

————. 2001. *A Map to the Door of No Return: Notes on Belonging*. Toronto: Vintage Canada.

————. 2005. *What We All Long For*. New York: St. Martin's.

Brathwaite, Edward Kamau. 1985. "Dionne Brand's Winter Epigrams." *Canadian Literature* 105:18–30.

Bronfen, Elisabeth. 1988. "Wandering in Mind or Body: Death, Narration and Gender in Djuna Barnes's novel *Nightwood*." *Amerkastudien / American Studies* 33 (1): 167–77.

Brossard, Nicole. 1977. *L'amer; ou, Le chapitre effrite*. Quebec: Nouvelles Messageries Internationales du Livre.

Brown, Russell. 1978. "Critic, Culture, Text: Beyond Thematics." *Essays on Canadian Writing* 11:151–83.

Brown, Wendy. 2003. "Resisting Left Melancholy." In *Loss: The Politics of Mourning*, edited by David Eng and David Kazanjian, 458–66. Berkeley: University of California Press.

Bruyneel, Kevin. 2004. "Challenging American Boundaries: Indigenous People and the 'Gift' of U.S. Citizenship." *Studies in American Political Development* 18 (1): 30–43.

Brydon, Diana. 2007. "Dionne Brand's Global Intimacies: Practising Affective Citizenship." *University of Toronto Quarterly* 76 (3): 990–1006.

———. 2013. "Autonomy, Transnational Literacies, and Planetarity: Emergent Cultural Imaginaries of Research Engagement." dianabrydon.com/page/2/.

Buma, Michael. 2009. "Soccer and the City: The Unwieldy National in Dionne Brand's *What We All Long For.*" *Canadian Literature* 202 (Autumn): 12–27.

Burton, Anthony. 1984. *The Rise and Fall of King Cotton*. London: Andre Deutsch.

Butler, Judith. 2004. *Precarious Life: The Powers of Mourning and Violence.* New York: Verso.

———. 2009. *Frames of War: When Is Life Grievable?* New York: Verso.

Butler, Judith, and Athena Athanasiou. 2013. *Dispossession: The Performative in the Political.* Cambridge: Polity.

Byrd, Jodi A. 2011. "'Been to the Nation, Lord, but I Couldn't Stay There': American Indian Sovereignty, Cherokee Freedmen and the Incommensurability of the Internal." *Interventions* 13 (1): 31–52.

Cabrera, Luis. 2010. *The Practice of Global Citizenship.* Cambridge: Cambridge University Press.

Cairns, Alan A. 2000. *Citizens Plus: Aboriginal Peoples and the Canadian State.* Vancouver: University of British Columbia Press.

Caldeiria, Teresa P. R. 1999. "Fortified Enclaves: The New Urban Segregation." In Holston 1999a, 114–38.

Canclini, Nestor Garcia. 2001. *Consumers and Citizens: Globalization and Multicultural Conflicts.* Translated by George Yudice. Minneapolis: University of Minnesota Press.

Carlston, Erin G. 1998. *Thinking Fascism: Sapphic Modernism and Fascist Modernity.* Redwood City, CA: Stanford University Press.

Carter, Angela. 2000. *The Bloody Chamber.* London: Vintage. First published 1979.

Castronovo, Russ. 2001. *Necro Citizenship: Death, Eroticism, and the Public Sphere in the Nineteenth-Century United States.* Durham: Duke University Press.

Cavell, Richard. 2002. *McLuhan in Space: A Cultural Geography.* Toronto: University of Toronto Press.

Chamberlain, J. Edward. 1993. *Come Back to Me, My Language: Poetry and the West Indies.* Champaign: University of Illinois Press.

Cherokee Nation. 1998. *Compiled Laws of the Cherokee Nation.* Union, NJ: Lawbook Exchange.

Chidester, David. 2002. *Global Citizenship, Cultural Citizenship and World Religions in Religious Education.* Cape Town: Human Sciences Research Council.

Chinni, Dante, and James Gimpel. 2010. *Our Patchwork Nation: The Surprising Truth about the "Real" America.* New York: Gotham Books (Penguin).

Cho, Lily. 2007. "Diasporic Citizenship: Inhabiting Contradictions and Challenging Exclusions." In *Trans.Can.Lit: Resituating the Study of Canadian Literature,* edited by Smaro Kamboureli and Roy Miki, 93–110. Waterloo: Wilfrid Laurier University Press.

———. 2009. "Citizenship, Diaspora and the Bonds of Affect: The Passport Photograph." *Photography and Culture* 2 (3): 275–87.

Christiansen, Adrienne E., and Jeremy J. Hanson. 1996. "Comedy as Cure for Tragedy: ACT UP and the Rhetoric of AIDS." *Quarterly Journal of Speech* 82 (2): 157–70.

Cixous, Hélène. 1976. "The Laugh of the Medusa." Translated by Keith Cohen and Paula Cohen. *Signs: Journal of Women in Culture and Society* 1 (4): 875–93.

Clairmont, Donald H., and Dennis William Magill. 1971. *Africville Relocation Report.* Halifax, Nova Scotia: Institute of Public Affairs.

———. 1999. *Africville: The Life and Death of a Canadian Black Community.* Toronto: McClelland and Stewart. First published 1974.

Clark, Robert. 1985. *History and Myth in American Fiction, 1823–1852.* New York: St. Martin's.

Clarke, George Elliott, ed. 1997. *Eyeing the North Star: Directions in African-Canadian Literature.* Toronto: McClelland and Stewart.

———. 2000. *Whylah Falls.* 10th anniversary ed. Toronto: Polestar Books. First published 1990.

Clough, Patricia, and Jean Halley, eds. 2007. *The Affective Turn: Theorizing the Social.* Durham: Duke University Press.

Coffman, Christine. 2006. *Insane Passions: Lesbianism and Psychosis in Literature and Film.* Middletown: Wesleyan University Press.

Cohen, Andrew. 2007. *The Unfinished Canadian: The People We Are.* Toronto: McClelland and Stewart.

Cole, Merrill. 2006. "Backwards Ventriloquy: The Historical Uncanny in Barnes's *Nightwood.*" *Twentieth-Century Literature* 52 (4): 391–412.

Cole, Thomas. 1836. "Essay on American Scenery." *American Monthly Magazine* I (January): 1–12.

Concannon, Amy, ed. 2011. *Painting Canada: Tom Thomson and the Group of Seven.* London: Philip Wilson.

Conrad, Margaret, and James Hiller. 2001. *Atlantic Canada: A Region in the Making.* Toronto: Oxford University Press.

Cook, Timothy E., and David C. Colby. 1992. "The Mass-Mediated Epidemic: The Politics of AIDS on the Nightly Network News." In *AIDS: The Making of a Chronic Disease*, edited by Elizabeth Fee and Daniel M. Fox, 84–114. Berkeley: University of California Press.

Crane, Gregg. 2002. *Race, Citizenship, and Law in American Literature.* Cambridge: Cambridge University Press.

Crenshaw, Kimberlé. 1991. "Mapping the Margins: Intersectionality, Identity Politics, and Violence against Women of Color." *Stanford Law Review* 43 (6): 1241–99.

Crimp, Douglas, and Adam Rolston. 1990. *AIDS Demographics.* Seattle: Bay.

Culler, Jonathan. 2002. *Structuralist Poetics: Structuralism, Linguistics and the Study of Literature.* London: Routledge.

Cunningham, Frank. 2011. "The Virtues of Urban Citizenship." *City, Culture and Society* 2:35–44.

Daffron, Brian. 2007. "Freedmen Descendants Struggle to Maintain Their Cherokee Identity." *Indian Country Today*, March 30. indiancountrytodaymedianetwork.com/2007/03/30/freedmen-descendants-struggle-maintain-their-cherokee-identity-90552.

Danticat, Edwidge. 2007. *Brother, I'm Dying.* New York: Knopf.

———. 2010. *Create Dangerously: The Immigrant Artist at Work.* Princeton: Princeton University Press.

Dawson, Lesel. 2008. *Lovesickness and Gender in Early Modern English Literature.* Oxford: Oxford University Press.

Delanty, Gerard. 2002. "Two Conceptions of Cultural Citizenship: A Review of Recent Literature on Culture and Citizenship." *Global Review of Ethnopolitics* I (3): 60–66.

Delgado-Moreira, Juan M. 1997. "Cultural Citizenship and the Creation of European Identity." *Electronic Journal of Sociology*. http://www.sociology. org/content/vol002.003/delgado.html.

Denis, Claude. 2002. "Indigenous Citizenship and History in Canada: Between Denial and Imposition." In *Contesting Canadian Citizenship: Historical Readings*, edited by R. Adamoski, D. Chunn and R. Menzies, 113–26. Peterborough: Broadview.

de Oliveira Andreotti, Vanessa, and Lynn Mario T. M. de Souza, eds. 2012. *Postcolonial Perspectives on Global Citizenship Education*. New York: Routledge.

Dickinson, Peter. 1998. "*In Another Place, Not Here*: Dionne Brand's Politics of (Dis)Location." In *Painting the Maple: Essays on Race, Gender, and the Construction of Canada*, edited by Peter Dickinson, Veronica Strong-Boag, et al., 113–29. Vancouver: University of British Columbia Press.

Dimock, Wai Chee. 2001. "Literature for the Planet." In "Globalizing Literary Studies," special issue, *PMLA* 116 (1): 173–88.

Dimock, Wai Chee, and Lawrence Buell, eds. 2007. *Shades of the Planet: American Literature as World Literature*. Princeton: Princeton University Press.

Dobson, Kit. 2006. "'Struggle Work': Global and Urban Citizenship in Dionne Brand's *What We All Long For*." *Studies in Canadian Literature* 31 (2): 88–104.

Douglass, Frederick. 1992. "Self-Made Men." In *The Frederick Douglass Papers*, edited by John Blassingame and John McKivigan, series 1, vol. 4, 545–75. New Haven: Yale University Press.

Dower, Nigel, and John William, eds. 2002. *Global Citizenship: A Critical Introduction*. New York: Routledge.

Duchanaud, Elizabeth. 2011. "Finding Inspiration in Chaos." *SX Salon*, April 30. smallaxe.net/wordpress3/discussions/2011/04/30/ finding-inspiration-in-chaos/.

Dumper, Michael. 2006. *Palestinian Refugee Repatriation: Global Perspectives*. New York: Routledge, 2006.

DuPlessis, Rachel. 1985. *Writing beyond the Ending: Narrative Strategies of Twentieth-Century Women Writers*. Bloomington: Indiana University Press.

Edelman, Lee. 2004. *No Future: Queer Theory and the Death Drive*. Durham: Duke University Press.

Edwards, Alice, and Carla Ferstman. 2010. "Humanizing Non-citizens: The Convergence of Human Rights and Human Security." In *Human*

Security and Non-citizens: Law, Policy and International Affairs, edited by Alice Edwards and Carla Ferstman, 3–46. Cambridge: Cambridge University Press.

Eliot, T. S. 2006. Introduction to *Nightwood*, by Djuna Barnes, xvii–xxiii. New York: New Directions. First published 1936.

Epstein, Julia. 1992. "AIDS, Stigma, and Narratives of Containment." *American Imago* 49:293–310.

Escoffier, Jeffrey. 1998. *American Homo: Community and Perversity*. Oakland: University of California Press.

Evans, David. 1993. *Sexual Citizenship: The Material Construction of Sexualities*. New York: Routledge.

Fainstein, Susan S. 2010. *The Just City*. Ithaca: Cornell University Press.

Fanon, Frantz. 2004. *The Wretched of the Earth*. Translated by Richard Philcox. New York: Grove. First published 1961.

Fludernik, Monika. 1994. "History and Metafiction: Experientiality, Causality, and Myth." In *Historiographic Metafiction in Modern American and Canadian Literature*, edited by Bernd Engler, 81–101. Paderborn: Schöningh.

Folsom, Ed. 2010. Introduction to *Democratic Vistas: The Original Edition in Facsimile*, by Walt Whitman. Edited by Ed Folsom. Iowa City: University of Iowa Press.

Fortier, Anne-Marie. 2010. "Proximity by Design? Affective Citizenship and the Management of Unease." *Citizenship Studies* 14 (1): 17–30.

Foster, Sharon Ewell. 2006. *Abraham's Well: A Novel*. Bloomington: Bethany House.

Foucault, Michel. 1977. *Language, Counter-Memory, Practice: Selected Essays and Interviews*. Edited and translated by Donald F. Bouchard. Ithaca: Cornell University Press.

————. 1990. "Right of Death and Power over Life." In *The History of Sexuality*, vol.1, *An Introduction*, translated by Robert Hurley, 135–59. New York: Vintage Books, First published 1978.

————. 1997. "Of Other Spaces: Utopias and Heterotopias." In *Rethinking Architecture: A Reader in Cultural Theory*, edited by Neil Leach, 330–36. New York: Routledge. First published 1967.

————. 2003. *"Society Must Be Defended": Lectures at the Collège de France, 1975–1976*. Edited by Mauro Bertani and Alessandro Fontana. Translated by David Macey. New York: Picador.

Francis, Donette. 2010. *Fictions of Feminine Citizenship: Sexuality and the Nation in Contemporary Caribbean Literature*. New York: Palgrave Macmillan.

Freiwald, Bina Toledo. 2002. "Nation and Self-Narration: A View from Québec/Quebec." *Canadian Literature* 172 (Spring): 17–40.

Froula, Christina. 2005. *Virginia Woolf and the Bloomsbury Avant-garde: War, Civilization, Modernity*. New York: Columbia University Press.

Frye, Northrop. 1971. *The Bush Garden: Essays on the Canadian Imagination*. Toronto: Anansi.

Garreau, Joel. 1982. *The Nine Nations of North America*. New York: Avon Books.

Gass, William H. 1968. *In the Heart of the Heart of the Country, and Other Stories*. New York: Harper Collins.

Gibbon, John. 1938. *Canadian Mosaic: The Making of a Northern Nation*. Toronto: McClelland and Stewart.

Gilbert, Emily. 2010. "Eye to Eye: Biometrics, the Observer, the Observed and the Body Politic." In *Observant States: Geopolitics and Visual Culture*, edited by Fraser Macdonald, Rachel Hughes, and Klaus Dodds, 225–46. London: I. B. Taurus.

Gilbert, Sandra M., and Susan Gubar. 1989. *Sexchanges*, vol. 2 of *No Man's Land: The Place of the Woman Writer in the Twentieth Century*. New Haven: Yale University Press.

Giles, Paul. 2007. "The Deterritorialization of American Literature." In *Shades of the Planet: American Literature as World Literature*, edited by Wai Chee Dimock and Lawrence Buell, 39–61. Princeton: Princeton University Press.

Gilroy, Paul. 1993. *The Black Atlantic: Modernity and Double Consciousness*. Cambridge, MA: Harvard University Press.

———. 2000. *Against Race: Imagining Political Culture beyond the Color Line*. Cambridge, MA: Harvard University Press.

———. 2004. *After Empire: Multiculture or Postcolonial Melancholia*. London: Routledge.

Glenn, Cheryl. 2004. *Unspoken: A Rhetoric of Silence*. Carbondale: Southern Illinois University Press.

Glissant, Édouard. 1997a. *Poetics of Relation*. Translated by Betsy Wing. Ann Arbor: University of Michigan Press.

———. 1997b. *Traité du tout-monde* [Treatise on the Whole World]. Paris: Gallimard.

Godard, Barbara. 1994. "From Vision of the Other to Theory of Difference: The Canadian Literatures." In *Visions of the Other*, Proceedings of the XIIIth Congress of the International Comparative Literature Association, vol. 2, edited by Earl Miner, Haga Toru, Kawamoto Koji, and Ohsawa Yoshihiro, 646–57. Tokyo: University of Tokyo Press.

———. 2008. *Canadian Literature at the Crossroads of Language and Culture.* Edited by Smaro Kamboureli. Edmonton: Newest.

Godard, Barbara et al. 1986. "Theorizing Fiction Theory." *Canadian Fiction Magazine* 57:6–12.

Gómez-Peña, Guillermo. 1991. "Border Brujo: A Performance Poem." *Drama Review* 35 (3): 48–66.

Gonzalez, Pablo Casanova. 1965. "Internal Colonialism and National Development." *Studies in Comparative International Development* 1 (4): 27–37.

Gonzalez-Ruibal, Alfredo. 2009. "Vernacular Cosmopolitanism: An Archaeological Critique of Universalistic Reason." In *Cosmopolitan Archaeologies*, edited by Lynn Meskell, 113–39. Durham: Duke University Press.

Goodman, Alan H., Deborah Heat, and Susan M. Linde. 2003. *Genetic Nature/Culture: Anthropology and Science beyond the Two-Culture Divide.* Berkeley: University of California Press.

Gopinath, Gayatri. 2005. *Impossible Desires: Queer Diasporas and South Asian Public Cultures.* Durham: Duke University Press.

Graham, Stephen, and Simon Marvin. 2001. *Splintering Urbanism: Networked Infrastructures, Technological Mobilities and the Urban Condition.* London: Routledge.

Greenblatt, Stephen. 1980. *Renaissance Self-Fashioning: From More to Shakespeare.* Chicago: University of Chicago Press.

———. 1990. *Learning to Curse: Essays in Early Modern Culture.* New York: Routledge.

Greeson, Jennifer. 2006. "Expropriating the Great South and Exporting 'Local Color': Global and Hemispheric Imaginaries of the First Reconstruction." *American Literary History* 18 (3): 496–520.

Groenendijk, Kees. 2005. "Questions concerning Special Statuses of 'Denizenship' or 'Civic Citizenship.'" www.imiscoe.org/natac/documents/questions_concerning_special_statuses_of_denizenship.pdf.

Gross, Larry. 1994. "What Is Wrong with This Picture? Lesbian Women and Gay Men on Television." In *Queer Words, Queer Images:*

Communication and the Construction of Homosexuality, edited by Jeffrey R. Ringer, 143–57. New York: New York University Press.

Grossman, Jay. 1993. *Reconstituting the American Renaissance: Emerson, Whitman and the Politics of Representation*. Durham: Duke University Press.

Gusdorf, Georges. 1980. "Conditions and Limits of Autobiography." In *Autobiography: Essays Theoretical and Critical*, edited by James Olney, 15–33. Princeton: Princeton University Press.

Habermas, Jürgen. 2001. *The Postnational Constellation*. Cambridge, MA: MIT Press.

Halberstam, Judith. 2011. *The Queer Art of Failure*. Durham: Duke University Press.

Hale, Edward Everett. 1971. *The Man without a Country and Other Tales*. Freeport, NY: Books for Libraries Press.

Hall, Stuart. 1992. "The Question of Cultural Identity." In *Modernity and Its Futures*, edited by Stuart Hall, David Held, and Anthony McGrew, 274–316. Cambridge: Polity.

———. 1994. "Cultural Identity and Diaspora." In *Colonial Discourse & Postcolonial Theory: A Reader*, edited by Patrick Williams and Laura Chrisman, 392–403. New York: Columbia University Press.

———. 2002. "Whose Heritage? Un-settling 'The Heritage,' Re-imagining the Post-nation." In *The Third Text Reader: On Art, Culture, and Theory*, edited by Rasheed Araeen, Sean Cubitt, and Ziauddin Sardar, 72–84. New York: Continuum. First published 1999–2000.

———. 2008. "Cosmopolitanism, Globalization and Diaspora: Stuart Hall in Conversation with Pnina Werbner." In *Anthropology and the New Cosmopolitanism: Rooted, Feminist and Vernacular Perspectives*, edited by Pnina Werbner, 345–60. Oxford: Berg.

Hamel, Jennifer. 2009. "A Brief History of the Writing (and Re-writing) of Canadian National History." PhD diss., University of Saskatchewan.

Hammar, Tomas. 1990. *Democracy and the Nation-State: Aliens, Denizens and Citizens in a World of International Migration*. Aldershot, UK: Avebury.

Hart, Kylo-Patrick R. 2003. "Representing Gay Men on American Television." In *Gender, Race, and Class in Media: A Text-Reader*, edited by Gail Dines and Jean M. Humez, 597–607. Thousand Oaks, CA: Sage.

Härting, Heike, and Smaro Kamboureli. 2009. Introduction to "Discourses of Security, Peacekeeping Narratives, and the Cultural Imagination in Canada," special issue, *University of Toronto Quarterly* 78 (2): 659–86.

Hawthorne, Nathaniel. 1983. *The Scarlet Letter*. New York: Penguin Books. First published 1850.

Henderson, Hazel, and Daisaku Ikeda. 2004. *Planetary* Citizenship. Santa Monica: Middleway.

Henstra, Sarah. 2000. "Looking the Part: Performative Narration in Djuna Barnes's *Nightwood* and Katherine Mansfield's 'Je Ne Parle Pas Français.'" *Twentieth Century Literature* 46 (2): 125–49.

Herring, Phillip. 1990. "Djuna Barnes and the Narrative of Violation." In *Modes of Narrative: Approaches to American, Canadian, and British Fiction*, edited by Reingard Nischik and Barbara Korte, 100–109. Wurzburg: Konigshausen and Neumann.

Holston, James. 1998. "Spaces of Insurgent Citizenship." In *Making the Invisible Visible: A Multicultural Planning History*, edited by Leonie Sandercock, 37–56. Oakland: University of California Press.

———, ed. 1999a. *Cities and Citizenship*. Durham: Duke University Press.

———. 1999b. "Spaces of Insurgent Citizenship." In Holston 1999a, 155–76.

Holston, James, and Arjun Appadurai. 1999. Introduction to Holston 1999a, 1–20.

hooks, bell. 1994. *Outlaw Culture: Resisting Representations*. London: Routledge.

Hutcheon, Linda. 1980. *Narcissistic Narrative: The Metafictional Paradox*. New York: Methuen.

———. 1989. "Historiographic Metafiction Parody and the Intertextuality of History." In *Intertextuality and Contemporary American Fiction*, edited by Patrick O'Donnell and Robert Con Davis, 3–32. Baltimore: Johns Hopkins University Press.

———. 2007. "The Canadian Mosaic: A Melting Pot on Ice? The Ironies of Ethnicity and Race." In *(De)Constructing Canadianness: Myth of the Nation and Its Discontents*, edited by Eugenia Sojka, 230–49. Katowice, Poland: Slask.

Huxley, Aldous. 1925. *Along the Road: Notes and Essays of a Tourist*. London: Chatto and Windus.

Irigaray, Luce. 1985. *This Sex Which Is Not One*. Ithaca: Cornell University Press.

Isin, Engin. 1999 "Citizenship, Class and the Global City." *Citizenship Studies* 3 (2): 267–83.

———, ed. 2000. *Democracy, Citizenship, and the Global City*. London: Routledge.

———. 2002. *Being Political: Genealogies of Citizenship*. Minneapolis: University of Minnesota Press.

Isin, Engin, and Greg Nielsen, eds. 2008. *Acts of Citizenship*. London: Zed Books.

Isin, Engin, and Patricia Wood. 1999. *Citizenship and Identity*. London: Sage.

Jaggi, Maya. 2013. "Dany Laferrière: A Life in Books." *Guardian*, February 1. www.theguardian.com/books/2013/feb/01/dany-laferriere-life-in-books.

Jervis, John. 2008. "Uncanny Presences." In *Uncanny Modernity: Cultural Theories, Modern Anxieties*, edited by Jo Collins and John Jervis, 10–50. Basingstoke, UK: Palgrave.

Johnson, Carol. 2010. "Affective Citizenship and National Identity: From Blair to Obama." *Citizenship Studies* 14 (5): 495–509.

Joppke, Christian. 2011. "Multicultural Citizenship." In *Handbook of Citizenship Studies*, edited by Engin Isin and Bryan S. Turner, 245–358. London: Sage.

Justice, Daniel Heath. 2006. *Our Fire Survives the Storm: A Cherokee Literary History*. Minneapolis: University of Minnesota Press.

Justice, Daniel Heath et al., eds. 2008. *Reasoning Together: The Native Critics Collective*. Norman: University of Oklahoma Press.

Kamboureli, Smaro. 2000. *Scandalous Bodies: Diasporic Literature in English Canada*. Waterloo: Wilfrid Laurier University Press.

Kawash, Samira. 1998. "The Homeless Body." *Public Culture* 10 (2): 319–39.

Keith, Joseph. 2012. *Unbecoming Americans: Writing Race and Nation from the Shadows of Citizenship, 1945–1960*. New Brunswick: Rutgers University Press.

Kerber, Linda K. 2009. "The Stateless as the Citizen's Other: A View from the United States." In *Migrations and Mobilities: Citizenship, Borders, and Gender*, edited by Seyla Benhabib and Judith Resnik, 76–126. New York: New York University Press.

Kettner, James H. 1978. *The Development of American Citizenship, 1608–1870*. Chapel Hill: University of North Carolina Press.

Khan, Aliyah. 2012. "'Calling the Magician': The Metamorphic Indo-Caribbean." PhD diss., University of California Santa Cruz.

Khan, Yasmin. 2007. *The Great Partition: The Making of India and Pakistan*. New Haven: Yale University Press.

Kim, Christine, Sophie McCall, and Melina Baum Singer, eds. 2012. *Cultural Grammars of Nation, Diaspora and Indigeneity in Canada*. Waterloo: Wilfrid Laurier University Press.

Knadle, Stephen. 2004. *Remapping Citizenship and the Nation in African-American Literature*. New York: Routledge.

Knapp, James F. 1986–87. "Primitivism and the Modern." *boundary 2* 15 (1–2): 365–79.

Kristeva, Julia. 1982. *Powers of Horror: An Essay on Abjection*. Translated by Leon S. Roudiez. New York: Columbia University Press.

———. 1987. "On the Melancholic Imaginary." *New Formations*, no. 3: 5–18.

———. 1992. *Black Sun: Depression and Melancholia*. New York: Columbia University Press.

Kruger, Steven F. 1996. *AIDS Narratives: Gender and Sexuality, Fiction and Science*. New York: Garland.

Kulick, Don. 2009. "Can There Be an Anthropology of Homophobia?" In *Homophobias: Lust and Loathing across Time and Space*, edited by David A. Murray, 19–33. Durham: Duke University Press.

Kulman, Linda. 2008. "Dinaw Mengestu Caputres Immigrant Life," NPR, February 19. www.npr.org/2008/02/19/18932579/dinaw-mengestu-captures-immigrant-life.

Kumar, Amitava. 2000. *Passport Photos*. Berkeley: University of California Press.

Kymlica, Will. 1995. *Multicultural Citizenship: A Liberal Theory of Minority Rights*. Oxford: Oxford University Press.

Lacan, Jacques. 1992. *The Ethics of Psychoanalysis*. Translated by Dennis Porter. New York: Norton. First published 1986.

Laferrière, Dany. 2011. *The Return: A Novel*. Translated by David Homel. Vancouver: Douglas and McIntyre. First published 2009.

Lang, Andrew, ed. 1965. *The Blue Fairy Book*. New York: Dover. First published 1889.

Lefebvre, Henri. 1968. *Le droit à la ville* Collection Société et Urbanisme. Paris: Anthropos.

———. 1991. *The Production of Space*. Translated by Donald Nicholson-Smith. Oxford: Blackwell. First published 1974.

Lehnen, Leila. 2013. *Citizenship and Crisis in Contemporary Brazilian Literature*. New York: Palgrave Macmillan.

Levander, Caroline F., and Robert S. Levine, eds. 2007. *Hemispheric American Studies*. New Brunswick: Rutgers University Press.

Levenstein, Harvey. 2010. *We'll Always Have Paris: American Tourists in France since 1930*. Chicago: Chicago University Press.

Leys, Ruth. 2011. "The Turn to Affect: A Critique." *Critical Inquiry* 37 (Spring): 434–72.

Limerick, Patricia Nelson. 1987. *The Legacy of Conquest: The Unbroken Past of the American West*. New York: Norton.

Limerick, Patricia Nelson, Clyde Milner II, and Charles E. Rankin, eds. 1991. *Trails: Toward a New Western History*. Lawrence: University Press of Kansas.

Linklater, Andrew. 1998. "Cosmopolitan Citizenship." *Citizenship Studies* 2 (1): 23–41.

Littlefield, Daniel Jr. 1977. *Africans and Seminoles: From Removal to Emancipation*. Westport, CT: Greenwood.

———. 1978. *The Cherokee Freedmen: From Emancipation to American Citizenship*. Westport, CT: Praeger.

———. 1980. *The Chickasaw Freedmen: A People without a Country*. Westport, CT: Greenwood.

Lorey, Isabell. 2010. "Becoming Common: Precarization as Political Constituting." Translated by Aileen Derieg. *e-flux* 17. www.e-flux.com/journal/view/148.

———. 2011. "Governmental Precarization." Translated by Aileen Derieg. eipcp.net/transversal/0811/lorey/en.

Love, Heather. 2007. *Feeling Backward: Loss and the Politics of Queer History*. Cambridge, MA: Harvard University Press.

Löw, Martina. 2008. "The Constitution of Space: The Structuration of Spaces through the Simultaneity of Effects and Perception." *European Journal of Social Theory* 1:11.

Luibhéid, Eithne. 2004. "Heteronormativity and Immigration Scholarship: A Call for Change." *GLQ: A Journal of Lesbian and Gay Studies* 10:227–35.

———. 2008. "Queer/Migration: An Unruly Body of Scholarship." *GLQ: A Journal of Lesbian and Gay Studies* 14:169–90.

Luibhéid, Eithne, and Lionel Cantú, eds. 2005. *Queer Migrations: Sexuality, U.S. Citizenship, and Border Crossings*. Minneapolis: University of Minnesota Press.

Lyotard, Jean-François. 1984. *The Postmodern Condition: A Report on Knowledge*. Translated by Geoff Bennington and Brian Massumi. Minneapolis: University of Minnesota Press.

Mackey, Eva. 1998. "Becoming Indigenous: Land, Belonging, and the Appropriation of Aboriginality in Canadian Nationalist Narratives." *Social Analysis* 42 (2): 149–78.

MacLulich, T. D. 1988. *Between Europe and America: The Canadian Tradition in Fiction*. Toronto: ECW.

Mahtani, Minelle. 2006. "Interrogating the Hyphen-Nation: Canadian Multicultural Policy and 'Mixed Race' Identities." In *Identity and Belonging: Rethinking Race and Ethnicity in Canadian Society*, edited by Sean P. Hier and B. Singh Bolaria, 163–77. Toronto: Canadian Scholars' Press.

Manalansan, Martin F., IV. 2003. *Global Divas: Filipino Gay Men in the Diaspora*. Durham: Duke University Press.

———. 2006. "Queer Intersections: Sexuality and Gender in Migration Studies." *International Migration Review* 40 (1): 224–49.

Marcus, George E. 2002. *The Sentimental Citizen: Emotion in Democratic Politics*. University Park: Pennsylvania State University Press.

Marcus, Jane. 1991. "Laughing at Leviticus: *Nightwood* as Woman's Circus Epic." In *Silence and Power: A Reevaluation of Djuna Barnes*, edited by Mary Lynn Broe, 221–51. Carbondale: Southern Illinois University Press. First published 1989.

Markotic, Nicole. 2002. "Freedom's Just Another Word / For Nothin' Left to Close / Desire Constructing Desire Constructing in Gail Scott's *Heroine*." In Moyes 2002, 37–51.

Marquard, Leo. 1957. *South Africa's Colonial Policy*. Johannesburg: Institute of Race Relations.

Maslan, Mark. 2005. "The Faking of the Americans: Passing, Trauma, and National Identity in Philip Roth's *Human Stain*." *Modern Language Quarterly* 66 (3): 365–89.

Massey, Doreen. 1999. "Spaces of Politics." In *Human Geography Today*, edited by Doreen Massey, John Allen, and Philip Sarre, 279–94. Cambridge: Polity.

Massumi, Brian. 2002. *Parables for the Virtual: Movement, Affect, Sensation*. Durham: Duke University Press.

Matthiessen, F. O. 1941. *American Renaissance: Art and Expression in the Age of Emerson and Whitman*. Oxford: Oxford University Press.

Mazlish, Bruce. 1994. "The Flâneur: From Spectator to Representation." In Tester 1994, 43–60.

Mbembe, Achille. 2003. "Necropolitics." *Public Culture* 15 (1): 11–40.

McKnight-Trontz, Jennifer. 2001. *The Good Citizen's Handbook: A Guide to Proper Behavior*. San Francisco: Chronicle Books.

McLuhan, Marshall. 1977. "Canada: The Borderline Case." In *The Canadian Imagination: Dimensions of a Literary Culture*, edited by David Staines, 226–48. Cambridge, MA: Harvard University Press.

McNevin, Anne. 2011. *Contesting Citizenship: Irregular Migrants and New Frontiers of the Political*. New York: Columbia University Press.

Medina, José. 2011. "Toward a Foucaultian Epistemology of Resistance: Counter-Memory, Epistemic Friction, and Guerrilla Pluralism." *Foucault Studies* 12 (October): 9–35.

Memmi, Albert. 1965. *The Colonizer and the Colonized*. New York: Orion.

Mengestu, Dinaw. 2007. *The Beautiful Things That Heaven Bears*. New York: Riverhead Books.

Michaels, Walter Benn, and Donald Pease, eds. 1989. *The American Renaissance Reconsidered*. Baltimore: Johns Hopkins University Press.

Mignolo, Walter. 2000. *Local Histories / Global Designs: Coloniality, Subaltern Knowledges and Border Thinking*. Princeton: Princeton University Press.

Miki, Roy. 2011. *In Flux: Transnational Shifts in Asian Canadian Writing*. Edmonton: Newest.

Miles, Tiya. 2005. *Ties That Bind: The Story of an Afro-Cherokee Family in Slavery and Freedom*. Berkeley: University of California Press.

Minh-ha, Trinh T. 1988. "Not You/Like You: Post-colonial Women and the Interlocking Questions of Identity and Difference." In "Feminism and the Critique of Colonial Discourse," special issue, *Inscriptions* 3–4. culturalstudies.ucsc.edu/PUBS/Inscriptions/vol_3-4/minh-ha.html.

Mohr, Jean. 2003. *Côte à côte ou face à face (Side by Side or Face to Face)*. Paris: Labor et Fides.

Monahan, Peter Friedrich. 2008. "The American Wild Man: The Science and Theatricality of Nondescription in the Works of Edgar Allan Poe, Jack London, and Djuna Barnes." PhD diss., Washington University.

Monmonier, Mark. 1991. *How to Lie with Maps*. Chicago: University of Chicago Press.

Moodie, Susanna. 2007. *Roughing It in the Bush*. New York: Norton. First published 1852.

Mookherjee, Monica. 2005. "Affective Citizenship: Feminism, Postcolonialism and the Politics of Recognition. *Critical Review of International Social and Political Philosophy* 8 (1): 31–50.

Mootoo, Shani. 2008. *Valmiki's Daughter*. Toronto: House of Anansi.

Morrison, Toni. 1987. *Beloved*. New York: Knopf.

Moss, Laura, ed. 2003. *Is Canada Postcolonial? Unsettling Canadian Literature*. Waterloo: Wilfrid Laurier University Press.

Mostov, Julie. 2008. *Soft Borders: Rethinking Sovereignty and Democracy*. London: Palgrave Macmillan.

Mousakhani, Sepideh. 2013. "Seeking to Emerge from Slavery's Long Shadow: The Interplay of Tribal Sovereignty and Federal Oversight in the Context of the Recent Disenrollment of the Cherokee Freedmen." *Santa Clara Law Review* 53:937–62.

Moyes, Lianne, ed. 2002. *Gail Scott: Essays on Her Works*. Toronto: Guernica.

Mulder, Arjen. 2002. *TransUrbanism*. Amsterdam: NAI.

Muller, Benjamin. 2004. "(Dis)qualified bodies: Securitization, Citizenship and 'Identity Management.'" *Citizenship Studies* 8 (3): 279–94.

Mumford, Kevin. 2007. *Newark: A History of Race, Rights, and Riots in America*. New York: New York University Press.

Mustov, Julie. 2008. *Soft Borders: Rethinking Sovereignty and Democracy*. London: Palgrave Macmillan.

Nabholz, Ann-Catherine. 2007. "The Crisis of Modernity: Culture, Nature and the Modernist Yearning for Authenticity." PhD diss., University of Basel.

Naipaul, V. S. 1967. *The Mimic Men*. Harmondsworth, UK: Penguin.

Nair, Sashi. 2012. *Secrecy and Sapphic Modernism: Reading Romans à Clef between the Wars*. New York: Palgrave.

Naujoks, Daniel. 2012. *Does Dual Citizenship Increase Naturalization? Evidence from Indian Immigrants in the U.S.* Hamburg: Hamburg Institute of International Economics.

Newton, Adam Zachary. 1995. *Narrative Ethics*. Cambridge, MA: Harvard University Press.

Ngai, Mae. 2004. *Impossible Subjects: Illegal Aliens and the Making of Modern America*. Princeton: Princeton University Press.

Nimeiri, Ahmed. 1993. "Djuna Barnes's *Nightwood* and 'the Experience of America.'" *Critique: Studies in Contemporary Fiction* 34 (2): 100–112.

Nixon, Rob. 1992. *London Calling: V. S. Naipaul and the License of Exile*. New York: Oxford University Press.

Norton, Camille. 2002. "After Reading Gail Scott's *Spaces Like Stairs*." In Moyes 2002, 19–36. First published 1989.

Nünning, Ansgar. 2004. "Towards a Definition, a Typology and an Outline of the Functions of Metanarrative Commentary." In *The Dynamics of*

Narrative Form: Studies in Anglo-American Narratology, edited by J. Pier, 11–57. Berlin: de Gruyter.

Nurse, Donna Bailey. 2012. "The New Black." *National Post*, February 13. arts.nationalpost.com/2012/02/03/the-new-black/.

Nussbaum, Martha. 2007. "Ethics of Narration." In *Traversing the Imaginary: Richard Kearney and the Postmodern Challenge*, edited by Peter Gratton and John Panteleimon Manoussakis. Evanston: Northwestern University Press.

Nyers, Peter. 2003. "Abject Cosmopolitanism: The Politics of Protection in the Anti-deportation Movement." *Third World Quarterly* 24 (6): 1069–93.

Olney, James. 1980. "Some Versions of Memory / Some Versions of Bios: The Ontology of Autobiography." In *Autobiography: Essays Theoretical and Critical*, edited by James Olney, 236–67. Princeton: Princeton University Press.

Ommundsen, Wenche et al. 2010. *Cultural Citizenship and the Challenges of Globalization*. New York: Hampton.

Ong, Aihwa. 1999. *Flexible Citizenship: The Cultural Logics of Transnationality*. Durham: Duke University Press.

Parrish, Timothy. 2000. "The End of Identity: Philip Roth's *American Pastoral*." *Shofar: An Interdisciplinary Journal of Jewish Studies* 19 (1): 84 –99.

Parry, Benita. 1991. "The Contradictions of Cultural Studies." *Transition* 53:37–45.

Patton, Cindy, and Benigno Sanchez-Eppler, eds. 2000. *Queer Diasporas*. Durham: Duke University Press.

Pease, Donald. 1992. "National Identities, Postmodern Artifacts, and Postnational Narratives." In "New Americanists 2: National Identities and Postnational Narratives," special issue, *boundary 2* 19 (1): 1–13.

———, ed. 1994. *National Identities and Post-Americanist Narratives*. Durham: Duke University Press.

Peluso, Nancy. 1995. "Whose Forests Are These? Counter-Mapping Forest Territories in Kalimantan, Indonesia." *Antipode* 27 (4): 383–406.

Petersen, William. 1966. "Success Story, Japanese-American Style." *New York Times Magazine*, January 9, 20–43.

Philip, M. NourbeSe. 2008. *Zong!* Middletown: Wesleyan University Press.

Porter, Kenneth W. 1996. *The Black Seminoles: History of a Freedom-Seeking People*. Gainesville: University Press of Florida.

Pratt, Mary Louise. 1992. *Imperial Eyes: Travel and Transculturation*. London: Routledge.

Probyn, Elspeth. 2005. *Blush: Faces of Shame*. Minneapolis: University of Minnesota Press.

Puar, Jasbir. 2007. *Terrorist Assemblages: Homonationalism in Queer Times*. Durham: Duke University Press.

Purcell, Mark. 2003. "Citizenship and the Right to the Global City: Reimagining the Capitalist World Order." *International Journal of Urban and Regional Research* 27 (3): 564–90.

Quartermain, Meredith. 2012. "How Fiction Works: Gail Scott's *Heroine* and *The Obituary*." *Open Letter* 14 (9): 112–27.

Ragazzi, Francesco. 2014. "Post-territorial Citizenship in Post-Communist Europe." In *Routledge Handbook of Global Citizenship Studies*, edited by Engin Isin and Peter Nyers, 489–97. London: Routledge.

Ramos, Julio. 2001. *Divergent Modernities: Culture and Politics in Nineteenth-Century Latin America*. Translated by John D. Blanco. Durham: Duke University Press.

Rasula, Jed. 2002. "The Pathic Receptacles of Modernism." epc.buffalo.edu/authors/bernstein/syllabi/readings/Rasula.htm.

Remember Africville. 1991. Dir. Shelagh Mackenzie. National Film Board.

Reynolds, David. 1988. *Beneath the American Renaissance: The Subversive Imagination in the Age of Emerson and Melville*. New York: Knopf.

Rheingold, Howard. 2002. *Smart Mobs: The Next Social Revolution*. New York: Basic Books.

Rich, Adrienne. 2003. "Compulsory Heterosexuality and the Lesbian Experience." *Journal of Women's History* 15:9–48. First published 1980.

Richardson, Diane. 2000. "Constructing Sexual Citizenship: Theorizing Sexual Rights." *Critical Social Policy* 20 (1): 105–35.

Richardson, Niall. 2010. *Transgressive Bodies: Representations in Film and Popular Culture*. Burlington, VT: Ashgate.

Rimmerman, Craig. 2002. *From Identity to Politics: The Lesbian and Gay Movements in the United States*. Philadelphia: Temple University Press.

Roche, John P. 1949. *The Early Development of United States Citizenship*. Ithaca: Cornell University Press.

Rosaldo, Renato. 1994. "Cultural Citizenship and Educational Democracy." *Cultural Anthropology* 9 (3): 402–11.

Rosenthal, Caroline. 2008. "English-Canadian Literary Theory and Literary Criticism." In *History of Literature in Canada: English-Canadian and French-Canadian*, edited by Reinhard Nischik, 291–309. Suffolk: Camden House.

Roth, Philip. 1997. *American Pastoral*. London: Vintage.

———. 1998. *I Married a Communist*. London: Vintage.

———. 2000. *The Human Stain*. London: Vintage.

Royal, Derek Parker. 2007. "Roth, Literary Influence, and Postmodernism." In *The Cambridge Companion to Philip Roth*, edited by Timothy Parrish, 22–34. Cambridge: Cambridge University Press.

Rubin, Gayle. 1993. "Thinking Sex: Notes for a Radical Theory of the Politics of Sexuality." In *Pleasure and Danger: Exploring Female Sexuality*, edited by Carole S. Vance, 143–78. Kitchener: Pandora.

Rubin, William. 1984. "Primitive Modernism." In *Primitivism and Twentieth-Century Art: A Documentary History*, edited by Jack Flam and Miriam Deutch, 315–34. Berkeley: University of California Press.

Rudnick, Paul. 1993. "Laughing at AIDS." *New York Times*, January 23. www.nytimes.com/1993/01/23/opinion/laughing-at-aids.html.

Rudy, Kathy. 2001. "Radical Feminism, Lesbian Separatism and Queer Theory." *Feminist Studies* 27:191–222.

Rushdie, Salman. 1991. *Imaginary Homelands: Essays & Criticism, 1981 to 1991*. London: Penguin.

Said, Edward. 1979. *Orientalism*. London: Vintage.

———. 1986. *After the Last Sky*. With photographs by Jean Mohr. London: Faber and Faber.

———. 1993. *Culture and Imperialism*. New York: Knopf.

———. 2001. *Reflections on Exile and Other Essays*. Cambridge, MA: Harvard University Press.

Saldívar, Ramón. 2006. *The Borderlands of Culture: Américo Paredes and the Transnational Imaginary*. Durham: Duke University Press.

Sanders, Leslie. 1989. "'I Am Stateless Anyway': The Poetry of Dionne Brand." *Zora Neale Hurston Forum* 3 (2): 19–29.

Sandten, Cecile. 2011. "Metroglorification and Diffuse Urbanism: Literarische und Mediale Repräsentation des Postkolonialen im Palimpsestraum der neuen Metropolen." *Anglia: Journal of English Philology* 130 (3): 344–63.

Sassen, Saskia. 1999. "Whose City Is It? Globalization and the Formation of New Claims." In Holston 1999a, 177–94.

———. 2002. "Towards Post-national and De-nationalized Citizenship." In *Handbook of Citizenship Studies,* edited by Engin Isin and Bryan S. Turner, 277–92. London: Sage.

Saunt, Claudio. 2004. "The Paradox of Freedom: Tribal Sovereignty and Emancipation during the Reconstruction of Indian Territory." *Journal of Southern History* 70 (1): 63–94.

Schattle, Hans. 2007. *The Practices of Global Citizenship.* Lanham, MD: Rowman and Littlefield.

Schlund-Vials, Cathy J. 2006. "Pledging Transnational Allegiances: Nationhood, Selfhood, and Belonging in Jewish American and Asian American Immigrant Narratives." In *Electronic Doctoral Dissertations for UMass Amherst.*

———. 2011. *Modeling Citizenship: Jewish and Asian American Writing.* Philadelphia: Temple University Press.

Schulman, Sarah. 1990. *People in Trouble.* London: Sheba Feminist.

———. 1994. *My American History: Lesbian and Gay Life during the Reagan/ Bush Years.* New York: Routledge.

———. 1995. *Rat Bohemia.* London: Penguin.

———. 1998. *Stagestruck: Theater, AIDS, and the Marketing of Gay America.* Durham: Duke University Press.

———. 2012a. *The Gentrification of the Mind: Witness to a Lost Imagination.* Berkeley: University of California Press.

———. 2012b. *Israel/Palestine and the Queer International.* Durham: Duke University Press.

———. 2013. "Queers Who Punish and the Challenge of Feminism." Keynote address, Santa Catarina, Brazil, September 20.

Scott, Gail. 1987. *Heroine.* Toronto: Coach House Books.

———. 1989. *Spaces Like Stairs.* Toronto: Women's Press of Canada.

Sears, Alan. 1992. "After Queer Nation Which Way Forward for Lesbian and Gay Liberation?" In *Queer Resources Directory.* www.qrd.org/qrd/ orgs/QN/which.way.queer.nation-10.92.

Sedgwick, Eve Kosofsky. 2003. "Paranoid Reading and Reparative Reading; or, You're So Paranoid, You Probably Think This Essay Is about You." In *Touching Feeling: Affect, Pedagogy, Performativity,* 123–51. Durham: Duke University Press.

Sieverts, Thomas. 2003. *Cities without Cities: An Interpretation of the Zwischenstadt.* Oxford: Taylor and Francis.

Sigrist-Sutton, Clare. 2010. "Mistaking Merry: Tearing off the Veil in *American Pastoral.*" *Philip Roth Studies* 6 (1): 47–68.

Singer, Alan. 1984. "The Horse Who Knew Too Much: Metaphor and the Narrative of Discontinuity in *Nightwood*." *Contemporary Literature* 25 (1): 66–87.

Slumkoski, Corey. 2011. *Inventing Atlantic Canada: Regionalism and the Maritime Reaction to Newfoundland's Entry into Canadian Confederation.* Toronto: University of Toronto Press.

Smith, A. J. M. 1978. "The Lonely Land: Group of Seven." In *The Classic Shade: Selected Poems*, 38–39. Toronto: McClelland and Stewart.

Smith, Victoria L. 1999. "A Story Beside(s) Itself: The Language of Loss in Djuna Barnes's *Nightwood*." *PMLA* 114 (2): 194–206.

Smith-Rosenberg, Carroll. 1985. *Disorderly Conduct: Visions of Gender in Victorian America.* Oxford: Oxford University Press.

Snyder, Terri. 2010. "Suicide, Slavery, and Memory in North America." *Journal of American History* 97 (1): 39–62.

Soja, Edward. 1992. "Inside Exopolis: Scenes from Orange County." In *Variations on a Theme Park: The New American City and the End of Public Space*, edited by Michael Sorkin, 94–122. New York: Hill and Wang.

———. 1996. *Thirdspace: Journeys to Los Angeles and Other Real-and-Imagined Places.* Oxford: Blackwell.

———. 2010. *Seeking Spatial Justice.* Minneapolis: University of Minnesota Press.

Somers, Margaret R. 2008. *Genealogies of Citizenship: Markets, Statelessness, and the Right to Have Rights.* Cambridge: Cambridge University Press.

Soysal, Yasemin. 1994. *Limits of Citizenship: Migrants and Postnational Membership in Europe.* Chicago: University of Chicago Press.

Spaulding, A. Timothy. 2005. *Re-forming the Past: History, the Fantastic, and the Postmodern Slave Narrative.* Columbus: Ohio State University Press.

Spektorowski, Alberto. 2003. "The New Right: Ethno-regionalism, Ethnopluralism and the Emergence of a Neo-fascist 'Third Way.'" *Journal of Political Ideologies* 8 (1): 111–30.

Spivak, Gayatri Chakravorty. 1996. "Bonding in Difference: Interview with Alfred Arteaga." In *The Spivak Reader*, edited by Donna Landry and Gerald Maclean, 15–28. London: Routledge.

———. 2003. "Planetarity." In *Death of a Discipline*, 71–102. New York: Columbia University Press.

Sprinkler, Michael. 1980. "Fictions of the Self: The End of Autobiography." In *Autobiography: Essays Theoretical and Critical*, edited by James Olney, 321–42. Princeton: Princeton University Press.

Stampp, Kenneth. 1981. *The Imperiled Union: Essays on the Background of the Civil War*. Oxford: Oxford University Press.

Stanley, Sandra. 2005. "Mourning the 'Greatest Generation': Myth and History in Philip Roth's *American Pastoral*." *Twentieth Century Literature* 51 (1): 124.

Stephens, John, and Robyn McCallum, eds. 1998. *Retelling Stories, Framing Culture: Traditional Story and Metanarratives in Children's Literature*. New York: Garland.

Stevenson, Nick. 2003. *Cultural Citizenship: Cosmopolitan Questions*. Maidenhead, UK: Open University Press.

Stuempfle, Stephen. 1996. *The Steelband Movement: The Forging of a National Art in Trinidad and Tobago*. Philadelphia: University of Pennsylvania Press.

Sturgess, Charlotte. 2003. *Redefining the Subject: Sites of Play in Canadian Women's Writing*. Amsterdam: Rodopi.

Sturm, Circe. 1998. "Blood Politics, Racial Classification, and Cherokee National Identity." *American Indian Quarterly* 22 (1–2): 230–58.

——. 2002. *Blood Politics: Race, Culture, and Identity in the Cherokee Nation of Oklahoma*. Berkeley: University of California Press.

Sturm, Jules. 2007. "Reading for Monsters: Transgressive Corporeality in Djuna Barnes's *Nightwood*." In *Sexual Politics of Desire and Belonging*, edited by Nick Rumens and Alejandro Cervantes-Carson, 249–70. Amsterdam: Rodopi.

Sugars, Cynthia, ed. 2004. *Unhomely States: Theorizing English-Canadian Postcolonialism*. Peterborough: Broadview.

Sundquist, Eric. 1988. "Realism and Regionalism." In the *Columbia Literary History of the United States*, edited by Emory Elliott, 501–24. New York: Columbia University Press.

Swanson, Joseph, and Samuel Williamson. 1972. "Estimates of National Product and Income for the United States Economy, 1919–1941." *Explorations in Economic History* 10:53–73.

Tanenbaum, Laura. 2004. "Reading Roth's Sixties." In "Philip Roth's America: The Later Novels," special issue, *Studies in American Jewish Literature* 23:41–54.

Taylor, Charles. 2004. *Modern Social Imaginaries*. Durham: Duke University Press.

Tester, Keith, ed. 1994. *The Flâneur*. London: Routledge.

Thomas, Brook. 2007. *Civic Myths: A Law-and-Literature Approach to Citizenship*. Chapel Hill: University of North Carolina Press.

Thoreau, Henry David. 2013. *On the Duty of Civil Disobedience*. New York: Harper Collins. First published 1849.

Tilly, Charles, ed. 1996. *Citizenship, Identity and Social History*. Cambridge: Cambridge University Press.

Tinsley, Omise'eke Natasha. 2008. "Black Atlantic, Queer Atlantic: Queer Imaginings of the Middle Passage." *GLQ: A Journal of Lesbian and Gay Studies* 14 (2–3): 191–215.

Tomkins, Silvan. 1963. *Affect, Imagery, Consciousness*. New York: Springer.

Tompkins, Jane. 1986. *Sensational Designs: The Cultural Work of American Fiction, 1790–1860*. Oxford: Oxford University Press.

Tully, James. 1995. *Strange Multiplicity: Constitutionalism in an Age of Diversity*. Cambridge: Cambridge University Press.

Turner, Bryan S. 1993. *Citizenship and Social Theory*. New York: Sage.

———. 2001. "Outline of a General Theory of Cultural Citizenship." In *Culture and Citizenship*, edited by Nick Stevenson, 11–32. London: Sage.

Turner, Frederick Jackson. 2011. *The Significance of the Frontier in American History*. New York: Penguin. First published 1893.

Van Toorn, Roemer. 1999. "The And-Space in the Third Millennium." *IO_dencies*. http://www.ferzkopp.net/MediaAndArt/IO_dencies/Roemer_van_Toorn_on_IOdencies.pdf.

Varsanyi, Monica W. 2006. "Interrogating 'Urban Citizenship' vis-à-vis Undocumented Migration." *Citizenship Studies* 10:229–49.

Volpp, Leti. 2005. "Impossible Subjects: Illegal Aliens and Alien Citizens." *Michigan Law Review* 103 (6): 1595–1630.

Wahl-Jorgensen, Karin. 2008. *Mediated Citizenships*. London: Routledge.

Wamba, Philippe. 1999. *Kinship: A Family's Journey in Africa and America*. New York: Penguin.

Ward, Jean M., and Elaine A. Maveety. 1995. *Pacific Northwest Women: 1815–1925*. Corvallis: Oregon State University Press.

Warren, Diane. 2008. *Djuna Barnes's Consuming Fictions*. Burlington, VT: Ashgate.

Watson, Thomas J., Jr. 1965. *Boy Scout Handbook*. 7th ed. Irving, TX: Boy Scouts of America.

Waugh, Patricia. 1984. *Metafiction: The Theory and Practice of Self-Conscious Fiction*. London: Methuen.

Wenman, Mark Anthony. 2003. "What Is Politics? The Approach of Radical Pluralism." *Politics* 23:57–65.

Werbner, Pnina. 2008. "Towards a New Cosmopolitan Anthropology." In *Anthropology and the New Cosmopolitanism*, edited by Pnina Werbner, 47–68. New York: Berg.

White, Hayden. 1973. *Metahistory: The Historical Imagination in Nineteenth-Century Europe*. Baltimore: Johns Hopkins University Press.

Whitley, Catherine. 2000. "Nations and the Night: Excremental History in James Joyce's *Finnegans Wake* and Djuna Barnes's *Nightwood*." *Journal of Modern Literature* 24 (1): 81–98.

Whitman, Walt. 2010. *Democratic Vistas: The Original Edition in Facsimile*. Edited by Ed Folsom. Iowa City: University of Iowa Press. First published 1871.

Wilson, Rob, and Wimal Dissanayake, eds. 1996. *Global/Local: Cultural Production and the Transnational Imaginary*, Durham: Duke University Press.

Wimsatt, W. K., Jr., and Monroe C. Beardsley. 1954. "The Intentional Fallacy." In *The Verbal Icon: Studies in the Meaning of Poetry*, by W. K. Wimsatt Jr., 3–20. Lexington: University of Kentucky Press. First published 1945.

Winterson, Jeannette. 2006. Preface to *Nightwood*, by Djuna Barnes. New York: New Directions.

Woodard, Colin. 2012. *American Nations: A History of the Eleven Rival Regional Cultures of North America*. Rev ed. London: Penguin.

Woolf, Virginia. 1953. *A Writer's Diary: Being Extracts from the Diary of Virginia Woolf*. San Diego: Harcourt.

Wunker, Erin. 2007. "Timing 'I': An Investigation of the Autofictional 'I' in Gail Scott's *Heroine*." *English Studies in Canada* 33 (1–2): 147–64.

Wyile, Herb. 2011. *Anne of Tim Hortons: Globalization and the Reshaping of Atlantic-Canadian Literature*. Waterloo: Wilfrid Laurier University Press.

Yarbrough, Fay A. 2008. *Race and the Cherokee Nation: Sovereignty in the Nineteenth Century*. Philadelphia: University of Pennsylvania Press.

Young, Iris. 1989. "Residential Segregation and Differentiated Citizenship." *Citizenship Studies* 3 (2): 237–52.

Young, Robert. 2012. "The Postcolonial Condition." In *The Oxford Handbook of Postwar European History*, edited by Dan Stone, 600–612. Oxford: Oxford University Press.

Zangwill, Israel. 1909. *The Melting Pot*. Baltimore: Lord Baltimore Press.

337

INDEX

liberal-welfare model of, 95, 96–97;
media depictions of, 97
Africville Relocation Report (Clairmont and Magill), 99, 100
Afro-Trinidadians, 147–57; of San
Fernando, 160; segregation of, 162
After the Last Sky (Said and Mohr),
87–92, 124; "After Jerusalem, 1979.
The Photographer Photographed"
91; gaze in, 91, 92; Palestinian
identity in, 76–77, 88; Palestinian
nationalism in, 90; Palestinian
wedding party in, 89; Palestinian
women in, 90–91; precariousness
in, 88–98; refugees in, 88
Agamben, Giorgio, 278nn3–4; on citizenship, 195; "We Refugees," 108–9
Ahmed, Sara: *Willful Subjects*, 303n5
AIDS: blame for, 293n9; fear of, 173;
US federal inaction on, 182, 191,
296nn29–31; funding for research,
184; as gay male disease, 292n4,
293n10; Helms Amendment on,
296n30; in laissez-faire economy, 176;
media depictions of, 170, 173, 181–84,
292nn1–2,4; narratives of containment, 170–71; narratives of proximity,
171; public discourse on, 189–90; as
un-American experience, 183–92
AIDS Action Committee, posters of,
293n14
AIDS activism, 190; in *People in
Trouble*, 173, 174, 175–78, 180, 183,
295n25; narratives of, 170. *See also*
ACT UP; Queer Nation
AIDS crisis: denial in, 172, 182, 188;
discourse of victimization, 183;
dominant discourse on, 182; "feeling

backward" in, 189; media representation of, 171; modes of resistance
in, 172; narratives of, 15, 172; in New
York, 178, 187, 295n27; nostalgia
in, 174, 293n24; overshadowing of,
295n29; politics of, 173; queer citizenship in, 293n11; queer politics of, 181;
silence about, 293n11; social neglect
in, 192; visual narratives of, 292n1
AIDS patients: citizenship and, 173,
183, 184, 187, 191; closet cases, 172;
laughter of, 178–79; marginalization
of, 177, 182, 187; proximity to, 171;
right to medical care, 172; shame
of, 188–89; stereotypes of, 173, 191;
as transgressive citizens, 184
Allen, Woody, 40, 180, 265n6
Althusser, Louis, 292n3
Americanness: contested notions of,
56; crises in, 54; in Roth's American Trilogy, 13. *See also* national
identity, U.S.
American Renaissance: cultural
climate of, 36; end of, 22; literary nationalism in, 13; national
formation during, 262n3; national
symbols of, 22, 262n3; political climate of, 36; time frame of, 259n19;
writers of, 6–7, 22
American studies, hemispheric methodologies of, 252; the term "imaginary" in, 258n7; restructuring of as
a discipline in "New Americanist"
debate, 258n8
Anderson, Benedict: imagined community of, 16, 274n3, 304n3
antebellum era, U.S.: citizenship
during, 21, 27–28, 36; crisis of, 24,

border control, U.S., 110

borders, literary: crossing of, 148

borders, national: hard/soft, 109, 111, 123, 255, 278n5; queer migrant bodies at, 146; transgressive, 100

Bosniak, Linda, 196, 298n2; on the global, 298n10

Boy Scout calendars, 268n7

Boy Scout Handbooks, 268n6; abstract citizenship in, 56, 57

Brand, Dionne: on Afro-Caribbean traditions, 169; on black American experience, 289n19; on Canadian multiculturalism, 289n21; on Caribbean imaginary, 148; critical reception of, 148; emigration to Canada, 287n11; during Grenada invasion, 155–56; Royal Society of Canada fellowship, 301n32; Toronto poet laureateship of, 287n9, 301n32

—*At the Full and Change of the Moon*, 150–51

—*The Beautiful Things That Heaven Bears*, contested spaces of, 214

—*In Another Place, Not Here*, 15, 145, 169; affective citizenship in, 147; ancestry in, 152; black liberation in, 155; "Elizete, Beckoned," 149; exclusion in, 157; female protagonists of, 149; lesbian subjectivity in, 150; Middle Passage in, 150, 151–52, 153; necro citizenship in, 156–57; nonassimilation in, 154–55; "Nowhere," 150; queer affect in, 148; queer migrant bodies in, 146–47, 156–57; same-sex desire in, 149, 150; setting of, 288n15; sexual violence in, 149; spaces of possibility in, 149; survival strategy of, 152; Toronto in,

153–55; transgression in, 156; undesirable subject in, 154; undocumented migrants in, 153–55; unforgetting/ unremembering in, 152; "Verlia, Flying," 149; water motif in, 150, 288n13

—*A Map to the Door of No Return*, 151, 288n16; deracination in, 152

—*No Language Is Neutral*, 148, 149

—*What We All Long For*, 16, 208–14, 287n10; becoming in, 204–5; belonging in, 204, 207; citizenship in, 204; contested space in, 207, 214, 215; cosmopolitanism in, 204; cultural citizenship in, 201; cultural stereotypes in, 204, 206; denizenship in, 207; entanglement metaphors of, 206; exclusion in, 206, 215; First Nations in, 202; linguistic difference in, 205; multiculturalism in, 207; narrator of, 299n18; national identity in, 207; protagonists of, 201, 203, 207; publication of, 299n17; reinvention in, 204; resistance in, 203–4; sites of struggle in, 200–201; Toronto in, 201, 202–7; transnational subjectivity in, 207; urban citizenship in, 203; urban spatial relations in, 203

Brathwaite, Kamau, 148, 287n7

Bronfen, Elisabeth, 133, 282n5

Brooklyn (New York), 190–91

Brossard, Nicole, 46, 266n18

Brown, Wendy, 189, 297n39

burqa, Western perceptions of, 121–22

Bush, George W.: Iraq rhetoric of, 81, 273n14; post-9/11 address of, 271n1

Butler, Judith: *Dispossession*, 298n4; on human vulnerability, 91, 109; *Precarious Life*, 73–74, 199

in, 68, 69, 70; white citizenship in,
68; willful citizen-subject of, 68
—*I Married a Communist*, 63–67; antimetabole in, 64; decontamination
metaphors in, 67; McCarthy era in,
65–66; as metafiction, 67; national
character in, 64, 66; Communism
in, 65–66; protagonist of, 65–66; soul
in, 64; wayward citizenship in, 66
Rousseau, Henri: *The Dream*, 134, 135;
jungle paintings of, 134–35, 284n19
Rubin, Gayle, 42; "Thinking Sex," 44
Rushdie, Salman, 303n7; "Imaginary
Homelands," 221, 302n2, 303n10,
304n15; on migrants, 278n3

Said, Edward: on contrapuntal awareness, 222; on critical nationalism,
23, 262n6; on exile, 216, 217, 221, 222,
302n4; on imaginative geography,
303n12; on Palestinians, 90, 273n22;
"Reflections on Exile," 16. See also
After the Last Sky
Salem (Mass.), Hawthorn on, 26–27
San Fernando (Trinidad), 158–60;
Afro-Trinidadians of, 160; Indo-
Trinidadians of, 159–60; travel
guides to, 159
Sassen, Saskia, 3, 298n7
Schulman, Sarah: AIDS activism
of, 190; on AIDS crisis, 15, 183; on
gentrification, 301n33; membership
in ACT UP, 293n11
—*Empathy*, 295n24
—*The Gentrification of the Mind*, 173,
174, 292n7
—*People in Trouble*, 15; AIDS activism
in, 173, 174, 175–78, 180, 183, 295n25;

AIDS crisis in, 173–83; anger in,
179; collective resistance in, 176;
consumerism in, 177; cross-dressing
in, 179–80, 295n23; denial in, 183;
disenfranchisement in, 190; ethics of narration in, 173; funerals
in, 172–74; gender stereotypes in,
294n22; homophobia in, 191–92,
292n6; masculinity in, 180–81; media
in, 181–82; narrative modes of, 171,
178, 182; narrative of proximity, 173,
177–78; narratives of containment,
178, 182, 192; neoliberal capitalism
in, 175; nostalgia in, 174; publication
of, 292n7; queer characters of, 172,
174–75, 180; queer citizenship in, 177,
183; satiric exaggeration in, 171–72,
177, 182; subversive gay laughter in,
178–79; title of, 182; unequal citizenship in, 171–83; as witness fiction, 173
—*Rat Bohemia*, 15, 171, 186–92; AIDs
crisis in, 186; Brooklyn in, 190–91;
concept of nation in, 186; homonationalism in, 190; homophobia
in, 191–92; narratives of containment, 192; national symbolic in,
187; poetry in, 187; protagonists
of, 187–88; publication of, 292n7;
Queer Nation in, 186–87; resistance
in, 189; shame in, 189
Scott, Gail, 303n13; Anglo-Protestant
background of, 49–50, 51
—"A Feminist at the Carnival," 267n25
—*Heroine*, 13, 37; the abject in, 45;
approach to nation, 52; becoming in, 48, 50; belonging in, 52;
circular narrative of, 39, 40–41, 46,
49, 52; composition of, 47; female